DUMBARTON OAKS
MEDIEVAL LIBRARY

Jan M. Ziolkowski, *General Editor*

TRIA SUNT:

AN ART OF POETRY

AND PROSE

DOML 53

Tria sunt:
An Art of Poetry
and Prose

Edited and Translated by

MARTIN CAMARGO

DUMBARTON OAKS
MEDIEVAL LIBRARY

HARVARD UNIVERSITY PRESS
CAMBRIDGE, MASSACHUSETTS
LONDON, ENGLAND
2019

Library of Congress Cataloging-in-Publication Data

Names: Camargo, Martin, editor, translator.

Title: Tria sunt : an art of poetry and prose / edited and translated by Martin Camargo.

Other titles: Container of (expression): Tria sunt. | Container of (expression): Tria sunt. English | Dumbarton Oaks medieval library ; 53.

Description: Cambridge, Massachusetts : Harvard University Press, 2019. |
    Series: Dumbarton Oaks medieval library ; 53 | This is a facing-page volume. Latin on the versos; English translation on the rectos. |
    Includes bibliographical references and index.

Identifiers: LCCN 2018012322 | ISBN 9780674987531 (alk. paper)

Subjects: LCSH: Didactic literature, Latin (Medieval and modern) | Latin poetry, Medieval and modern. | Rhetoric, Medieval.

Classification: LCC PA8057 .T75 2018 | DDC 808/.0471—dc23 LC record available at https://lccn.loc.gov/2018012322

Contents

Introduction

The *Tria sunt* (named for the first two words of the text, also known as the *incipit*) is the most ambitious and apparently the most widely used of the treatises composed in association with a late fourteenth-century renaissance in the study of rhetoric at Oxford. The identity of its author is not known, but he probably was a Benedictine monk who taught rhetorical composition as part of a course that prepared younger monks for more advanced studies at the university.[1] More a compiler than an author in the modern sense, he sought to gather the most useful precepts from the twelfth- and thirteenth-century arts of poetry and prose, supplement them with additional doctrine and illustrative examples from other works of the same period, and combine all of these materials into a new synthesis tailored to the pedagogical needs of his own time and place. Because so much of the *Tria sunt* is quoted or paraphrased from other sources, its language and style provide few clues that would help to identify other works that might have been produced by the same anonymous author-compiler.[2]

The *Tria sunt* must have been completed by around 1400, since the earliest of the surviving manuscript copies date from the turn of the fifteenth century. Only one of the many sources that are quoted verbatim is later than the mid-

thirteenth century: a poem composed at Krakow during the first half of the fourteenth century, before 1346 (see chap. 7.34). Unless, and until other, still later sources can be identified, any attempt to specify the *Tria sunt*'s date of composition must be conjectural. It may be significant that there is no sign of the *Tria sunt*'s influence in the *Formula moderni et usitati dictaminis* ("A Rule for Modern and Familiar Prose Composition"), a treatise on letter writing composed at Oxford around 1390 by the Benedictine monk Thomas Merke.[3] If the *Tria sunt* is also the work of an Oxford Benedictine, it could not have escaped Merke's notice had it been available when he composed his own textbook on rhetoric. While this negative evidence suggests that the *Tria sunt* might have been completed during the 1390s, its composition can be dated with certainty only to the second half of the fourteenth century.

The *Tria sunt* belongs to the genre frequently called "arts of poetry" but more accurately designated "arts of poetry and prose." These are comprehensive guides to composing well-wrought Latin texts. The two most popular works in the genre, the early thirteenth-century *Poetria nova* ("New Poetics") by the Englishman Geoffrey of Vinsauf and the *Laborintus* ("The Labyrinth"; before 1280) by Eberhard the German, are written in verse; the remaining examples, like the *Tria sunt,* are in prose. Yet the instruction that each offers can be applied to any kind of text. This feature distinguishes this type of rhetorical manual (i.e., "arts of poetry and prose") from the medieval "arts of letter writing" *(artes dictandi)* and "arts of preaching" *(artes praedicandi)* that provide specific instruction in composing letters and sermons, respectively.[4]

In England, the late fourteenth century saw a marked revival of interest in the twelfth- and thirteenth-century arts of poetry and prose. After a lapse of nearly a century, new copies of the treatises were made, and new textbooks were composed using materials borrowed from them.[5] The *Tria sunt* may have been composed specifically to serve as a companion to Geoffrey of Vinsauf's *Poetria nova* (1200–1202; revised up to around 1215), the best known of the arts of poetry and prose. A majority of the teachers who used the *Tria sunt* certainly treated it as complementary to the *Poetria nova.* More than half of the surviving copies of the *Tria sunt* are bound together with a copy of the *Poetria nova.*[6] In one of those manuscripts, the scribe goes as far as to call the *Tria sunt* a "commentary" *(exposicio)* on the earlier treatise.[7] The author-compiler of the *Tria sunt* quotes frequently from the *Poetria nova,* which he always calls the "Book of Verses" *(Liber versuum),* and owes much of his doctrine to Geoffrey of Vinsauf; but there are important differences between the two texts. The structure of his prose treatise differs from that of Geoffrey's verse treatise, and its contents encompass many points of doctrine that are mentioned only in passing or omitted entirely from the *Poetria nova.*

The principal source for the *Tria sunt* and the chief model for its structure is another art of poetry and prose by Geoffrey of Vinsauf: the *Documentum de modo et arte dictandi et versificandi* ("Instruction in the Method and Art of Composing in Prose and in Verse"), a textbook in prose that Geoffrey completed near the end of the twelfth century and may have revised at the beginning of the thirteenth.[8] While the *Poetria nova* is organized around the five parts of rhetoric, beginning with invention and ending with delivery, the *Doc-*

umentum, like the *Tria sunt,* bases its design on what it identifies as the three parts of any artful composition: the beginning, the middle, and the end. Both the *Documentum* and the *Tria sunt* open by describing and illustrating the various ways to begin a composition and close with the various ways to end one. In the much lengthier instructions concerning the "middle" of a composition, the *Tria sunt* treats all of the topics covered by the *Documentum* and in the same order. The most immediately apparent differences between the two textbooks are the *Tria sunt*'s division into clearly demarcated chapters and its coverage of some topics that are not treated in the *Documentum.*

The resemblance between the *Tria sunt* and the *Documentum* is more than structural. In the opening and closing chapters, as in many of the other chapters, the *Tria sunt* either quotes the *Documentum* verbatim or paraphrases it closely. For this reason, until recently, the *Tria sunt* was thought to be a longer version of the *Documentum* that Geoffrey of Vinsauf created either before or after a shorter version (printed in 1924 by Edmond Faral).[9] However, the *Tria sunt* also derives much of its content from sources other than the *Documentum* and the *Poetria nova,* including several that were composed too late to have been available to Geoffrey of Vinsauf. Chief among these other sources are two arts of poetry and prose, Matthew of Vendôme's *Ars versificatoria* (before 1175; the earliest surviving example of the genre) and Gervase of Melkley's *De arte versificatoria et modo dictandi* (1215–16), and two literary works by Alan of Lille that taught the same art by modeling its precepts, the allegorical poem *Anticlaudianus* and the prosimetrum *De planctu Naturae* (late twelfth century). The author-compiler of the *Tria sunt* may have used a

third art of poetry and prose, John of Garland's *Parisiana poetria* (around 1220, revised 1231–1235), though it also is possible that both the anonymous author-compiler and John of Garland independently drew on the same source for the material they share. The author-compiler also quotes extensively from Horace's *Ars poetica* (and a commentary on it) and from the *Rhetorica ad Herennium,* a work he and all his contemporaries believed to be by Cicero. Many other works, both ancient and medieval, sacred and secular, scholastic and literary, are quoted on a more limited basis, whether to supply a point of rhetorical doctrine or, more frequently, to illustrate a particular stylistic technique.

While directly indebted to earlier texts for much of its content, the *Tria sunt* is an original work in other respects. Its author-compiler may well have composed the passages for which no other source has yet been found; but even if all of the components turn out to have been borrowed, they have been reconstituted as a new treatise not only through the process of *compilatio* but also through its complement, *ordinatio*.[10] Even as he augmented and modified Geoffrey of Vinsauf's *Documentum* with rhetorical doctrine and illustrative examples drawn from the most relevant sources available to him, the author-compiler of the *Tria sunt* imposed a new order on his compendium by dividing it into sixteen chapters, each with a descriptive heading for easy reference. The chapters vary greatly in length, from a mere two pages to more than thirty, and are arranged in four groups of related topics, three of them fairly well-defined and one of them considerably less so.

Among the most obvious groups is the discontinuous one that frames the entire treatise. The opening two chapters

deal with techniques for beginning a composition (chap. 1) and for managing the transition from the beginning to the body of a composition (2), and the final chapter deals with techniques for ending a composition (16). Many of the chapters in between can be said to concern the techniques for creating and elaborating the more variable "middle" of a composition. Among the most important of these are the methods of amplifying (3) and abbreviating a text (4), since imitation, interpretation, and manipulation of existing texts were practices fundamental to the rhetorical instruction that the arts of poetry and prose were designed to support. The placement of these paired chapters near the beginning of the treatise underscores the importance of their content. Perhaps the same logic motivates the more unusual placement of a short handbook on letter writing at the end of the chapter on amplification. Letters were the most widely taught variety of prose in the rhetorical curriculum and also are treated in the arts of poetry and prose by Gervase of Melkley and John of Garland. By attaching an appendix on letter writing to the chapter on amplification, the author-compiler of the *Tria sunt* suggests that prose composition is essentially a process of expanding upon a concise core message.

Already at the end of chapter 4 the focus shifts from the more basic strategies of textual expansion and contraction to the techniques that add variety and elegance to verbal expression. A series of five chapters, including two of the three longest chapters in the *Tria sunt*, are devoted to stylistic ornamentation. At the beginning of chapter 5, two large categories of figurative language are distinguished: difficult and easy ornamentation. Difficult ornamentation is produced

by ten figures of speech that are known as "tropes" (from the Greek *trepo,* "I turn"), because they "turn" language away from its proper signification or syntax. These are defined and illustrated at great length in chapter 5. Chapter 6 not only serves as a transition from difficult to easy ornamentation but also reflects a brief shift from Geoffrey of Vinsauf to Matthew of Vendôme as the source of the doctrine being expounded. Chapter 7, which brings together material from Geoffrey of Vinsauf and the *Rhetorica ad Herennium,* is explicitly dedicated to the three varieties of easy ornamentation: "determination" (that is, refining the meaning of a keyword by adding words that modify it), the thirty-six nonmetaphorical figures of speech, and the nineteen figures of thought. This very long chapter is followed by the very short chapter 8, which compares and reconciles the different sets of terms used by grammarians and rhetoricians to denote the stylistic techniques described in chapters 5 and 7. The section of the *Tria sunt* that deals with ornamentation and stylistic variation then concludes with a copiously illustrated chapter on one of the most popular methods of stylistic variation taught by medieval rhetoricians, often called "conversion" *(conversio),* but here called "permutation" *(permutatio).* This kind of variation is accomplished by replacing individual words or entire phrases with synonymous words or phrases or else by changing the grammatical form of a keyword in a phrase (9).

The group constituted by the following six chapters is more heterogeneous than the other three. This is partly due to a greater eclecticism in the selection of sources. If there is anything that unites these chapters in terms of subject matter, it is a much stronger and more exclusive focus on rhe-

torical theory, by contrast with the overwhelming emphasis
on pragmatic strategies for text production in all but one of
the chapters described above. The first two chapters in the
group form another complementary pair, on the strategies
for treating original subject matter (10) and for treating familiar subject matter (11). Next comes a longer and highly
eclectic chapter on a major category of topical invention:
argument from the attributes of persons and actions. The
same topic was treated more briefly in the section on letters at the end of chapter 3 (3.52–59), suggesting that this
type of rhetorical argumentation was a major component of
the teaching offered by the *Tria sunt*'s author-compiler. The
remaining three chapters are closely related to parts of John
of Garland's *Parisiana poetria*. These concern the three levels
and the four "modern" varieties of style (13), the six faults to
be avoided in any type of composition (14), and the modes
of discourse and the genres of prose and poetry (15). Either
the anonymous compiler abridged and excerpted what he
found on these topics in the *Parisiana poetria*, or he and John
of Garland made different use of a common source, such as
a revised version of the *Documentum* that has not survived
independently.

The process of *compilatio* and *ordinatio* that transformed
Geoffrey of Vinsauf's late twelfth-century *Documentum* into
the *Tria sunt* must have required considerable time and effort. Many of the sources quoted were not widely available in late fourteenth-century England, and the labor of
hunting them down would have been followed by that of
sifting for relevant content, excerpting or paraphrasing se-
lect passages, sorting the collected materials into coherent
categories, and modifying the textbook's existing design to

accommodate its broadened scope. Presumably the new textbook was created to meet needs that were not served adequately by the one on which it was modeled (the *Documentum*) or the one that it was understood to complement (the *Poetria nova*), and it is worth asking what those needs might have been.

Since many of the compiler's additions treat topics that are covered in some arts of poetry and prose but not in those by Geoffrey of Vinsauf, clearly one of his chief intentions was to produce a textbook more comprehensive than any other single art of poetry and prose. There are limits to this comprehensiveness, however. The *Tria sunt* omits topics such as memory and delivery that are treated in the *Poetria nova*, and its treatment of any given topic usually is abridged by comparison with the source(s) from which it has been taken. Added breadth does not always come with loss of depth, however, as seen especially in the *Tria sunt*'s chapters on the figures. The *Poetria nova* treats the full set of figures from the fourth book of the *Rhetorica ad Herennium*, but it neither defines the individual figures of speech nor illustrates any of the figures in a form other than hexameter verse; and the *Documentum* lacks a separate section dedicated to the figures, though it treats many of them in a less systematic way, under headings such as amplification. By contrast, the *Tria sunt* supplies at least one definition for each figure and usually offers examples both in prose and in verse. Its comprehensive and systematic discussion of the figures must have been a major source of the *Tria sunt*'s appeal, given the central place of stylistic variation and elaboration in medieval writing instruction.

The *Tria sunt* also stands out from the other textbooks in

its genre by virtue of its focus on rhetorical argumentation. All of chapter 12 and parts of 3 are devoted to the attributes of persons and actions as sources of argument. Brief references to what is "advantageous to the case" are also scattered throughout the other chapters. Among the arts of poetry and prose, only Matthew of Vendôme's *Ars versificatoria* matches the *Tria sunt*'s investment in topical argumentation; but while Matthew's textbook is a major source for the *Tria sunt*'s treatment of the attributes, its range of citation is much narrower. Argumentation based on the particular circumstances of a case is the defining feature of rhetoric according to the only text on the subject that was required for the Master of Arts at Oxford: Book 4 of Boethius's *De topicis differentiis*.[11] The anonymous author-compiler of the *Tria sunt* cites this text by name at the end of chapter 12 (12.36), where he shows how the attributes of persons and actions correspond to the circumstances enumerated by Boethius. The *Tria sunt*'s distinctive emphasis on rhetorical argumentation and its alignment with a curricular text are consistent with other evidence that suggests it was composed at Oxford for use by teachers and students affiliated with the university.

The *Tria sunt*'s specialized treatment of letter writing in chapter 3.48–67 is also consistent with instruction in Latin composition at a more advanced level than was offered by a typical grammar school in medieval England. Already in the thirteenth century, Oxford had become the preeminent English center for training in the rhetorical art of letter writing *(ars dictaminis)*, and during the second half of the fourteenth century many of the teachers who operated at the margins of the university began to produce new textbooks on the subject *(artes dictandi)*. By representing letter

writing as a particular form of amplification and comparing
the structure of a letter to that of a syllogistic argument
whose major premise is based on the attributes of persons
and actions, the *Tria sunt*'s author-compiler made his textbook especially useful to those who prepared students for
the university's Arts course or for clerical careers beyond
Oxford. Such teachers were required to assign their students exercises in composing poems and prose letters on
the same topic, in each case by starting with a proverb or
an exemplum and building a complete text from this nu-
cleus.[12] The first three chapters of the *Tria sunt* perfectly em-
body this pedagogical method, and evidence in some of
the manuscript copies may indicate a special interest in
those chapters on the part of students and teachers who
used the treatise.[13]

Ownership marks in some of the surviving manuscript
copies not only confirm the *Tria sunt*'s special connection to
Oxford but also indicate a wider transmission both within
and to a lesser extent beyond England. At least three manuscripts belonged to monks who studied at one of the three
Benedictine colleges in Oxford during the first half of the
fifteenth century: William Babyngton, a monk and later abbot of Bury St Edmunds who studied at Gloucester College
(F); Richard Bell, William Seton, and William Law, monks
of Durham who studied at Durham College *(Cs);* and Henry
Cranebroke, a monk of Canterbury who studied at Canterbury College *(Os).*[14] John Maunshull, a fellow of Oriel College, probably made or acquired his copy of the *Tria sunt*
(Ol) while at Oxford and brought the manuscript with him
in 1447 when he became a fellow of the recently founded
Eton College, where he continued to use it in teaching rhetorical composition. Still farther afield, a copy of the *Tria*

sunt belonged to the Collegiate Church of Ottery St. Mary, in Devon *(B)*. The original owner may have been a certain John Exceter, M.A., who was canon and prebendary of that church from 1436 and bequeathed his books in a 1445 will. Other copies are more difficult to localize, but nearly all of them are written in English hands dating from the first half of the fifteenth century. The single exception is a copy that was made in the mid-fifteenth century in Italy *(A)*. One of the English monastic copies *(F)* also found its way to Rome, where it was sold to an Italian buyer in 1455. Aside from what appears to be limited circulation in Italy, the *Tria sunt*'s influence was greatest in England, chiefly in the grammar schools at Oxford, during the first half of the fifteenth century. The *Tria sunt* is mentioned by name as an authority on the "colors of rhetoric" in *The Court of Sapience* (l. 1914), a poem composed during the third quarter of the fifteenth century. No surviving manuscript copies of the *Tria sunt* are later than this date, which suggests that the treatise's authority already had begun to wane as the New Learning imported from the Continent promoted other sources of rhetorical doctrine and different models of eloquence.

A few features of the English translation deserve brief comment. Much of the *Tria sunt* is quoted verbatim or nearly verbatim from other sources, and the translator must decide whether and how to represent the multiplicity of these voices. Whenever feasible, this has been done by quoting an existing translation, particularly one published in the Loeb Classical Library or the Dumbarton Oaks Medieval Library

series. For the *Ars versificatoria* by Matthew of Vendôme, the translation by Galyon has been used, and for Geoffrey of Vinsauf's *Poetria nova,* the translation by Nims.[15] Quotations from the masterpieces of rhetorical literature by Alan of Lille, Bernard Silvestris, and John of Hauville are rendered in the translations by Winthrop Wetherbee. In cases where the text of the *Tria sunt* differs from the edition on which the quoted translation is based, the quoted translation does not follow the sense of the original as closely as desired, or the language of the quoted translation is needlessly obscure or archaic, the facing translation has been modified accordingly.

Alongside and contrasting with this diversity of citation is a frequent uniformity of expression that is a characteristic feature of the textbook genre. Phrases and even entire sentences are repeated verbatim as each permutation of a given compositional technique is enumerated and illustrated. No attempt has been made to disguise this fact by introducing variety in the translation where none exists in the original Latin. Similarly, in those passages where the Latin is deliberately obscure, the translation may duplicate some of this obscurity in order to capture the intended effect or replicate the stylistic technique being illustrated. Where necessary, brief clarification is provided in a note.

Over the long duration of this project I have accumulated more debts than it is possible to acknowledge. The earliest phase of the work was supported by generous fellowships from the American Council of Learned Societies (1996–97)

and the National Endowment for the Humanities (2000), which were supplemented by research leaves from the University of Missouri. After delays associated with heading three different departments at two different universities, a sabbatical leave from the University of Illinois allowed me to regain lost momentum. Jan Ziolkowski's offer to publish the commentary as a separate volume further hastened the completion and publication of this edition and translation. Gregory Hays read the submitted manuscript with extraordinary care and offered many suggestions that helped make it much better. I am deeply grateful to the many other friends and colleagues who shared their expertise and encouragement, granted me access to manuscript collections, responded to my requests for information, and suggested improvements as the completed text approached its final, published form. My greatest thanks go to my wife Sandy, a collaborator at every step of the way. Without her constant love and support, the journey would have been still longer and its ending less happy.

Notes

1 See, for example, chapter 9.8, where the author-compiler of the *Tria sunt* has modified his source by alluding to monastic reading practices and changing the verbs from third to first person. On the contributions of the Benedictines to the revival of rhetorical studies at Oxford, see also Camargo, "Rhetoricians in Black."

2 More detailed information about the sources of the *Tria sunt*, as well as its manuscript tradition and the context of its creation and reception, will be provided in a volume of commentary that is currently in preparation.

3 Edition and commentary by Camargo, in *Medieval Rhetorics of Prose Composition*, 105–47.

4 The best guide to this genre is Kelly, *Arts of Poetry and Prose*.

5 Camargo, "Late Fourteenth-Century Renaissance" and "Chaucer and the Oxford Renaissance."

6 These are manuscripts *B, Ct, D, L, Ob, Ol, Os,* and *W.*

7 *B,* fol. iiir (flyleaf).

8 Camargo, "In Search of Geoffrey's of Vinsauf's Lost 'Long *Documentum.*'" Geoffrey of Vinsauf employed a similar structure in his earlier *Summa de coloribus rhetoricis,* a work from which the compiler of the *Tria sunt* also borrowed.

9 *Les arts poétiques,* 265–320. Faral lists four manuscript copies of the *Tria sunt (Cs, Ct, Ob, Ol)* together with three copies of the *Documentum,* apparently unaware of the significant differences between the texts (pp. 22–23). His edition of the *Documentum* is based on a single witness (Glasgow, Hunterian Library, MS Hunterian V.8.14 [formerly 511]), and so it is possible that he did not consult the others. Ten years later, Noel Denholm-Young was the first to recognize the existence of a "better and fuller version" ("*Cursus* in England," 75n3). He adds six manuscripts to Faral's list, four of them containing the *Tria sunt (L, Od, Os, W)* and the other two containing the *Documentum* (p. 93).

10 On these two concepts, see especially Parkes, "The Influence of the Concepts of *Ordinatio* and *Compilatio,*" a seminal essay that has been reprinted several times.

11 *Statuta antiqua,* edited by Gibson, 33.

12 The use of proverbs and exempla in this type of exercise is spelled out in the fourteenth-century statutes of St. Albans School (edited and translated by Leach, *Educational Charters,* 244–45). The Oxford University statutes are less explicit about this component in prescribing what is probably the same exercise (*Statuta antiqua,* edited by Gibson, 21–22, 171).

13 In the copy of the *Tria sunt* that belonged to John Maunshull *(Ol),* most of the glosses are concentrated in chapter 3. Another copy of the *Tria sunt (Od)* breaks off near the end of chapter 3, as does a summary of the treatise that probably was made by a student of rhetoric at Oxford (Cambridge, St. John's College F.18, fols. 93r–96v).

14 David Howlett has argued that *Os* originally belonged to Abbot John Whethamstede, who had it made for use by the monks of St. Albans, including those who studied at Gloucester College, Oxford, as he had done.

15 For the passages borrowed from the *De arte versificatoria et modo dic-tandi* by Gervase of Melkley and the passages shared with John of Garland's *Parisiana poetria*, the translations of these works by Giles and by Lawler have been consulted but have not been quoted verbatim: the former because it remains unpublished, the latter because it is uncertain whether John of Garland's treatise was the *Tria sunt*'s source or whether both texts drew upon a common source.

TRIA SUNT

Capitulum 1

Tria sunt circa que cuiuslibet operis versatur artificium: principium, scilicet, progressus et consummacio. Set quoniam principium prima obvoluit difficultas, ab ipso principio sumamus inicium. Principium aliud naturale, aliud artificiale. Principium naturale est quando sermo inde incipit unde res geri incepit. Et hoc genus principii potest dici agreste vel vulgare, quia cuilibet e vulgo et eciam agresti sic datum est incipere.

2 Set quoniam facilis est exemplaris doctrina, difficultatis offendiculum eliminent exempla. Procedant igitur in medium Minos, Androcheus, Nisus et Scilla, de quibus hec tractatur fabula: Minos rex Cretensis erat, cuius unicus filius Androcheus litteralibus instruendus artibus Athenas transmissus et Niso regi Athenarum commissus, propter virtutis sue precellenciam neci traditur suorum invidia sociorum. In cuius ulcionem ira pariter et armis pater excanduit Nisumque regem Athenarum, tamquam illius facinoris auctorem, in manu valida pertinaciter est aggressus. Set cum tota vis Nisi de crine penderet purpureo, pociore potitus concilio, pocius artem quam arma consuluit et dolus, non gladius prelium terminavit. Scilla namque Nisi filia, promissum a Minoe sperans coniugium, crinem purpureum de capite

Chapter 1

The crafting of any work is concerned with three things: namely, the beginning, the development, and the end. Because our first challenge involves the beginning, let us take our start from the beginning itself. One kind of beginning is natural, another is artificial. A natural beginning is when the discourse begins at the point where the action commenced. This kind of beginning can be called uncultivated or common because any common person, or even a rustic is permitted to begin in this way.

Because teaching by example is easy, let examples remove the stumbling block of difficulty. Therefore, let us bring onstage those whom the following tale concerns: Minos, Androgeos, Nisus, and Scylla. Minos was a king of Crete. His only son Androgeos, who had been sent to Athens in order to receive instruction in the arts of literacy and had been entrusted to Nisus the king of Athens, was treacherously killed by his companions, who were jealous of his outstanding virtue. His father blazed with anger and arms alike to avenge him and with his strong hand obstinately attacked Nisus king of Athens, as if he were the perpetrator of the crime. However, since all the strength of Nisus depended on a purple hair, after receiving better advice Minos resorted to art rather than arms, so that guile rather than the sword determined the outcome of the battle. For Scylla, the daughter of Nisus, expecting the marriage that Minos had promised her,

patris abrupit. Unde Minos Nisum devicit vidensque Scillam, quod patrem proprium tradiderat, solam et desolatam dereliquit. Inde pietas deorum Scillam in alaudam et Nisum patrem suum in nisum mutavit. Unde Ovidius:

Et preter nomen sua perdidit omnia Nisus.

3   In hac materia sumitur naturale principium quando predicto modo sumitur, scilicet a Minoe, qui filium suum misit Athenas, ubi ex invidia interfectus est. Sumitur eciam principium naturale quando materiam iniciamur a laude Minois et immoramur circa laudem eius. Set iste modus tractantis est et non narrantis. Narracio namque, iuxta doctrinam Tullii in *Rethorica,* brevis debet esse, probabilis et dilucida.

4   A laude Minois cum inicium naturale sumatur, prosaicum exemplum sit istud: "Minoem Cretensibus imperantem Natura suis insignivit donariis: faciem signavit privilegio pulcritudinis, infudit lingue torrentem eloquencie, corpus armavit viribus et animum prefecit maturum omnibus, cuius concilio nichil fieret temerate." Metricum exemplum sit istud:

Ad titulum faciunt Minois gracia forme,
   virtus mentis, apex sanguinis, omen opum.

Vel sic:

plucked the purple hair from her father's head. By this means Minos overcame Nisus, but when he saw Scylla he left her alone and forsaken because she had betrayed her own father. Thereupon the gods' pity transformed Scylla into a lark and her father Nisus into a sparrow hawk. For this reason Ovid says:

And except for his name, Nisus lost everything.

The beginning of this subject matter is natural when it takes its starting point in the manner outlined above, namely from Minos, who sent his son to Athens, where he was killed through envy. A natural beginning is also employed when we begin the story with praise of Minos and dwell on his praise. However, this is a mode of treatment and not one of narration; for, according to Cicero's teaching in the *Rhetoric,* narration should be brief, plausible, and clear.

Here is an example of a natural beginning that is derived from praise of Minos, in prose: "While Minos ruled over the Cretans, Nature adorned him with her gifts: she stamped his face with the distinction of beauty, she infused his tongue with a torrent of eloquence, she equipped his body with strength, and over all these she placed a thoughtful intellect, so that by virtue of its deliberation nothing might be done rashly." Here is an example in verse:

Minos was distinguished by the beauty of his appearance, the excellence of his mind, the eminence of his blood, the prodigy of his riches.

Or thus:

> Stirpe nitens, opibus fluitans, ad cetera Minos
> felix, excepto funere prolis, erat.

5   Principium artificiale est quando sermo non inde incipit unde res geri incepit. Sumitur autem octo modis: tum a medio materie, tum a fine, tum a proverbio tripliciter, tum ab exemplo tripliciter.

6   A medio materie sumitur artificiale principium in eadem materia quando sumitur ab Androcheo, quem interfecit Atheniensium invidia. Prosaicum exemplum sit istud: "Androcheum, liberalibus nutritum artibus, illiberale consorcium veneno respersum invidie stilorum invasit aculeis et quoniam in ipso sciencie preeminenciam obstupuit, vite spiraculum obstruxit. Sicque quod in virtute defuit vicio supplevit." Metricum exemplum sit istud:

> Androchei titulus et amicus et hostis eidem.
> In preceps corpus, nomen in astra tulit.

Vel sic:

> Consociis iram sibi fata suisque dolorem
> Minoide virtus invidiosa parit.

7   A fine sumitur principium artificiale in eadem materia cum inde sumitur ubi Minos Scillam reppulit quia patrem proprium seduxit. Prosaicum exemplum sit istud: "Scilla Minois sauciata pulcritudine, regnum patris fraudulenter

Brilliant in lineage, swimming in riches, in all else Minos was fortunate, save in the death of his child.

A beginning is artificial when the discourse does not begin at the point where the action commenced. An artificial beginning is fashioned in eight ways: sometimes from the middle of the subject matter; sometimes from the end; sometimes from a proverb, in three different ways; and sometimes from an exemplum, in three different ways.

An artificial beginning takes its starting point from the middle of this same story when we begin with Androgeos, whom the envy of the Athenians killed. Here is an example in prose: "An ignoble fellowship, dripping with the poison of envy, used the sharp points of their writing implements to attack Androgeos, who was nourished by the liberal arts, and because they were astounded by his preeminent knowledge, they stifled his life's breath. And thus what they lacked in virtue they made up in vice." Here is an example in verse:

The fame of Androgeos was both friend and foe to him: it bore his body over a cliff but his name to the stars.

Or thus:

The invidious virtue of Minos's son begets wrath for his companions, death for himself, and grief for his family.

An artificial beginning takes its starting point from the end of this same story when it begins at the point when Minos rejected Scylla because she had deceived her own father. Here is an example in prose: "Scylla, wounded by the beauty

convertit in ipsius dominium et hac fraude coniugium impetrare credidit. Set a proprio repercussa iaculo: quoniam illum prodidit, istum perdidit et ex eo quod fecit a proposito defecit." Metricum exemplum:

Scille sedicio Scillam seduxit: eodem
  quo lesit patrem vulnere lesa fuit.

Vel sic:

In Scillam rediit fraus propria; lex dedit equa
  auctorem fraudis fraude perire sua.

8   A proverbio sumitur principium artificiale in eadem materia, set refert utrum sumatur proverbium iuxta principium, iuxta medium vel iuxta finem. Proverbium, ut ait Matheus Vindosinensis, est "generalis sentencia, cui consuetudo fidem attribuit, opinio communis assensum accomodat et incorrupte veritatis integritas adquiescit."

9   Si proverbium sumatur iuxta principium materie, sic sumitur. Prosaicum exemplum sit istud: "Hec est Fortune condicio, quod prosperitatis moram non patitur set que sunt animo dulciora celeriorem fugam pollicentur." Metricum exemplum sit istud:

Quod magis optatur magis effluit, omnia lapsum
  spondent et cicius fata serena ruunt.

10   Si proverbium sumatur iuxta medium, sic sumitur. Prosaicum exemplum sit istud: "Ad letos aliorum successus

of Minos, deceitfully turned her father's kingdom over to his control and thought by this deceit to procure marriage. But she was struck by her own dart: because she double-crossed the one, she lost the other, and by what she did she undid her plan." Here is an example in verse:

Scylla's sedition seduced Scylla: she was hurt by the same wound with which she hurt her father.

Or thus:

Scylla's own deceit turned back against her; a just law caused the author of deceit to perish through her own deceit.

An artificial beginning for this same story can take its 8 starting point from a proverb, but it depends upon whether the proverb is employed with reference to the beginning, the middle, or the end of the story. A proverb, as Matthew of Vendôme says, is "a universal sentiment, which custom deems trustworthy, on which common opinion agrees, and to which the purity of unalloyed truth acquiesces."

If a proverb is employed with reference to the beginning 9 of the story, it is employed as follows. Here is an example in prose: "This is the nature of Fortune, that she does not allow prosperity to linger, but the dearer things are to the heart the more swiftly we can expect them to flee." Here is an example in verse:

What is desired more flows away more; all things promise to fall and joyous destinies fall more quickly.

If a proverb is employed with reference to the middle of 10 the story, it is employed as follows. Here is an example in

suspirat invidia, cuius malicia machinatur in illum pocius quem miratur pociorem." Metricum exemplum sit istud:

> Hii sunt invidie mores: ad gaudia luget
> et contra fata dulcia virus habet.

Vel sic:

> Cum viciis iniit fedus, virtutibus hostis
> Livor et anticipat omnia livor edax.

11   Si proverbium sumatur iuxta finem materie, sic sumitur. Prosaicum exemplum sit istud: "Malignantis perfidia, cum alterius mollitur perniciem, aculeus perfidie proprium refurcatur in auctorem." Metricum exemplum sit istud:

> Fraudis in auctorem fraus sepe retorquet habenas
> et repetit per quas venerat ante vias.

Vel sic:

> Quos nimis impronat sceleri natura vel usus
> vix reperit virtus deseruisse scelus.

12   Ab exemplo sumitur principium artificiale, set refert utrum sumatur iuxta principium vel iuxta medium vel iuxta finem. Est autem exemplum specialis sentencia a rebus finitis vel specificis inventa et per similitudinem materie comparata.

13   Si exemplum sumatur iuxta principium, sic sumitur. Prosaicum exemplum sit istud: "Post tranquillum festinat aer in

prose: "Envy sighs at the happy achievements of others: its malice conspires more against whomever it admires more." Here is an example in verse:

These are the habits of Envy: she weeps at joys and prepares venom against sweet destinies.

Or thus:

Envy, the enemy of virtues, enters into a league with the vices and devouring Envy surpasses them all.

If a proverb is employed with reference to the end of the 11 subject matter, it is employed as follows. Here is an example in prose: "When the treachery of one who plots evil attempts another's destruction, the barb of treachery skewers its own author in turn." Here is an example in verse:

Deceit often reins in the author of deceit and returns along the road by which it came.

Or thus:

Virtue seldom finds that they have abandoned sin whom nature or habit strongly inclines to sin.

An artificial beginning can take its starting point from an 12 exemplum, but it depends upon whether it is employed with reference to the beginning or the middle or the end of the story. And note that an exemplum is a particular sentiment discovered from limited or specific events and compared through likeness of subject matter.

If an exemplum is employed with reference to the begin- 13 ning of the story, it is employed as follows. Here is an example in prose: "After a period of calm the air rushes into a

turbinem et est volubilior in tenebras quam in lucem." Metricum exemplum sit istud:

> Si Phebus blanditur humo, caligo repente
> irruit et claudit noctis ymago diem.

14   Exempli sumpti a medio materie prosaicum exemplum sit istud: "Invidia zizannie granum subruit et herbe sterilis malicia fructiferam occidit." Metricum exemplum sit istud:

> Falce sua semen iactum zizannia falcat
> et magis acceptam nequior herba necat.

Vel sic:

> Invidia fruticum languescunt semina frugum
> et torpet sterili stipite lesa seges.

15   Exempli sumpti iuxta finem prosaicum exemplum sit istud: "Accidit sepe sagitta ferientem eadem esse repercussum et venenum propinantem simile bibiturum." Metricum exemplum sit istud:

> Sepe venenator alii quod porrigit haurit
> inque sagittantem missa sagitta redit.

16   Hec dicta sunt de principio.

whirlwind and is more apt to change into darkness than into light." Here is an example in verse:

Even as Phoebus caresses the earth, darkness suddenly rushes in and the likeness of night blocks out the day.

Here is an example in prose of an exemplum employed 14 with reference to the middle of the subject matter: "The envy of the cockle destroys the good seed and the malice of the barren plant kills the fruitful one." Here is an example in verse:

With its scythe the cockle mows down the sown seed and the worthless plant kills the more welcome one.

Or thus:

Through the shrub's envy the seeds of the corn grow weak and the crop damaged by the barren stock languishes.

Here is an example in prose of an exemplum employed 15 with reference to the end of the subject matter: "It often happens that the striker is struck in turn by the same arrow, and that the one proffering poison will drink its like." Here is an example in verse:

Often the poisoner of another drinks what he proffered, and the arrow, once shot, rebounds on the one who shot it.

These things have been said concerning the beginning of 16 a composition.

Capitulum 2

De prosecucione materie

In ipsa prosecucione, primum est continuare. Set facilis est continuacio ubi naturalis observatur ordo, quia res ipsa se ipsam continuat et iuxta naturalem seriem progrediendum. Qui ordo, si fuerit artificialis, eget deliberacione qualiter continuanda sit materia, quia iuxta diversitatem principiorum est diversimode continuandum. Si namque recessum fuerit a naturali principio per principium artificiale sumptum a medio vel a fine, suo modo continuandum est; si materiam inchoemus a proverbio, alio modo; si ab exemplo, tercio modo.

2   Si principium artificiale sumptum fuerit a medio vel a fine materie, continuandum est per relativa, scilicet talia: qui, que, quod. Talibus enim retorquetur stilus ad priora et quantumlibet distancia. Supponamus exempla.

3   Principium artificiale prosaicum sumptum a medio tale

Chapter 2

On the development of the subject matter

In the development, the first concern is to continue. Now continuation is easy when natural order is maintained, because the very action continues itself and one must progress in accordance with the natural sequence of events. But if the order is artificial, it will require thought as to how the subject matter ought to be continued, because in keeping with the diversity of beginnings, one ought to continue in diverse ways. So if one has departed from the natural beginning by means of an artificial beginning that takes its starting point from the middle or the end of the story, one should continue in the appropriate way; if we begin the subject matter from a proverb, in a different way; if from an exemplum, in a third way.

If an artificial beginning has taken its starting point from 2
the middle or the end of the subject matter, one should continue by means of relative pronouns, namely, words such as these: "who," "which." For with such words the pen is turned back toward what comes earlier, no matter how far off. Let us provide some examples.

An artificial beginning that has taken its starting point 3

est: "Androcheum etc." Iuxta premissam doctrinam sic continuandum est: "Quem, iam pululantibus annis et studium poscentibus, pater eius Minos Attice transmisit discipline, ubi puerilis animus, tamquam in cunis positus, ad ubera prelactens arcium, per breve temporis compendium in virilis roboris evasit incrementum." Metricum exemplum tale est: "Androchei titulus etc." Iuxta premissam doctrinam sic continuandum est:

Cuius eo missi, cum forte studeret Athenis,
corpus erat pueri, pectus ymago senis.
Misit eum Minos: eius de germine flos
hic prodiit et sub quo Creta superba fuit.

4   Principium artificiale sumptum a fine prosaicum tale est: "Scilla, Minois etc." Iuxta premissam doctrinam sic continuandum est: "Quem Cretensibus imperantem in regem Nisum dolor armavit filii, cuius mortem licet machinatus fuerat dolus Atheniensium, delictum tamen membrorum in capite voluit ulcisci." Metricum exemplum sit istud: "Scille sedicio etc." Iuxta premissam doctrinam sic continuandum est:

Cuius amor vehemens Minos; hoc fomite flamme
arsit et hec hami machina cepit eam.

from the middle of the story, in prose, is of this sort: "Androgeos etc." In accordance with the precept stated above, it should be continued thus: "Whom, having already reached the age when growth is rapid and study is required, his father Minos sent off for instruction at Athens, where his boyish mind, as if placed in a cradle, nursing eagerly at the breasts of the arts, within a short span of time came to develop manly strength." An example in verse is of this sort: "The fame of Androgeos etc." In accordance with the precept stated above, it should be continued thus:

> Whose body, when he was sent to Athens in his student days, was that of a boy, his mind the likeness of an old man. Minos sent him: from his seed he was the flower and he blossomed as one under whom Crete was proud.

An artificial beginning that has taken its starting point 4 from the end of the story, in prose, is of this sort: "Scylla, wounded by the beauty of Minos etc." In accordance with the precept stated above, it should be continued thus: "Whom, while he ruled over the Cretans, sorrow for his son caused to take up arms against king Nisus; although it was the guile of the Athenians that had contrived his son's death, nonetheless he wanted to avenge upon the head the crime of the limbs." Here is an example in verse: "Scylla's sedition etc." In accordance with the precept stated above, it should be continued thus:

> Whose passionate love was Minos; from this flame's kindling she burned up, and this artifice caught her on its hook.

Vel sic:

> Cui spes coniugii suasit scelus et tibi Minos,
> a patre, fraudis ope, patris abegit opes.

5   Si principium artificiale sumptum fuerit a proverbio, continuandum est per hec verba: "fatetur," "attestatur," "loquitur," "docet," "indicat," "exprimit," "arguit" vel per equipollentes sentencias. Et hac racione: proverbium est generalis sentencia et illud quod dicitur per generalem sentenciam docetur, probatur per aliquod speciale. Quod liquido patebit in omni genere proverbii, sive sumatur iuxta principium, medium vel finem. De singulis ponantur exempla.

6   Proverbium sumptum iuxta principium prosaicum tale est: "Hec est fortune etc." Iuxta premissam doctrinam sic continuandum est: "Huius rei habemus argumentum Minoem regem Crethensium, cuius fortune tranquillitas declinavit in turbinem, serenitas in caliginem, iocunditas in merorem." Metricum exemplum tale est: "Quod magis optatur etc." Iuxta premissam doctrinam sic continuandum est:

> Regna penes Crete sors mesta, subambula lete,
> principis extincta prole, fatetur idem.

7   Proverbium sumptum iuxta medium prosaicum tale est: "Ad letos etc." Iuxta premissam doctrinam sic continuan-

Or thus:

> Whom the hope of marriage urged to crime and who
> for you, Minos, from her father, by means of deceit,
> stole her father's means.

If the artificial beginning has taken its starting point 5
from a proverb, it should be continued by means of these
words: "it admits," "it attests," "it says," "it teaches," "it indicates," "it expresses," "it asserts" or equivalent expressions.
And for this reason: a proverb is a universal sentiment, and
that which is said is taught by a universal sentiment and
proven by something particular. This will be clearly evident
in every kind of proverb, whether it is employed with reference to the beginning, the middle, or the end of the story.
Let us give some examples of each.

A proverb in prose, employed with reference to the be- 6
ginning, is of this sort: "This is the nature of Fortune etc." In
accordance with the precept stated above, it should be continued thus: "As evidence of this fact we have Minos king of
the Cretans, the tranquility of whose fortune turned into
confusion, its brightness into gloom, its delight into grief."
An example in verse is of this sort: "What is desired more
etc." In accordance with the precept stated above, it should
be continued thus:

> In the realms of Crete, a sad fate that is successor to a
> happy one, after the sovereign's child has been killed,
> admits as much.

A proverb in prose, employed with reference to the mid- 7
dle, is of this sort: "Envy sighs at the happy etc." In accordance with the precept stated above, it should be continued

dum est: "Attestatur huic veritati lacrimabilis exitus Androchei, cuius sciencia preeminens et invidiosa sociorum (set
non sociales) manus irritavit ad maleficium et proprie ruine
maturavit adventum." Metricum exemplum sit istud: "Hii
sunt invidie etc." Iuxta premissam doctrinam sic continuandum est:

> Quod puer Androcheus sensit, quem gracia forme
>   extulit, unde necis eius origo fuit.

Vel sic:

> Livoris stimulante stilo, virtute probati
>   Minoide virtus obruta clamat idem.

8   Proverbium sumptum iuxta finem prosaicum est hoc:
"Malignantis etc." Iuxta premissam doctrinam sic continuandum est: "Quod evidentissimum est in Scilla regis
Athenarum filia, cuius in caput patris machinabatur perfidia, set hoc ipso suspendii sui laqueum contexuit et incidit
in foveam quam fecit." Metricum exemplum sit istud: "Fraudis etc." Iuxta premissam doctrinam sic continuandum est:

> Quod liquet in Scilla, que fraude nociva parenti,
>   fraudis idem iaculum sensit obesse sibi.

Vel sic:

thus: "To this truth attests the lamentable death of Androgeos, whose preeminent and enviable knowledge provoked his comrades' noncomradely hands to an evil deed and hastened the arrival of his own destruction." Here is an example in verse: "These are the habits of Envy etc." In accordance with the precept stated above, it should be continued thus:

Which the boy Androgeos experienced, whom a beautiful appearance exalted, which was the origin of his murder.

Or thus:

Overthrown by the goading prod of envy, the virtue of Minos's son, who was proven in virtue, declares as much.

This is a proverb in prose, employed with reference to 8 the end: "When the treachery of one who plots evil etc." In accordance with the precept stated above, it should be continued thus: "Which is most apparent in Scylla the daughter of the king of Athens, whose treachery plotted against the head of her father; but in this very act she wove the noose of her own hanging and fell into the pit she dug." Here is an example in verse: "Deceit etc." In accordance with the precept stated above, it should be continued thus:

Which is clear in Scylla, who, hurtful to her parent through deceit, felt the same dart of deceit come against her.

Or thus:

In patrem molita dolum mentisque venenum
effundens, docet hec Scilla magistra doli.

9   Si principium artificiale sumptum fuerit ab exemplo,
aliter continuandum est quam in premissis. Cum enim
exemplum, que est specialis sentencia, inducatur quasi
quoddam simile, continuandum est per huiusmodi: "sic,"
"eque," "pariter," "similiter," "a simili" vel per equipollentes
sentencias. Set ut elegancior fiat continuacio, considerandum est cuiusmodi res notetur in proposito exemplo, utrum
scilicet levitas vel vicium vel consuetudo vel aliud simile. Et
in continuacione dicatur "simili" vel "pari" vel "eadem levitate," "simili" vel "pari" vel "eodem vicio," "simili" vel "pari"
vel "eadem consuetudine." Ponamus exempla.

10   Exemplum sumptum iuxta principium prosaicum tale
est: "Post tranquillum etc." Ecce in hoc exemplo notatur levitas vel inconstancia per mutacionem sereni aeris in turbu-
lentum. Ideo iuxta predictam doctrinam sic continuandum
est: "Eiusdem inconstancie sunt dona fortune, cuius vultus
celeriter obfuscatur serenitas et blandicie sepe convertuntur in minas." Metricum exemplum est hoc: "Si Phebus etc."
Iuxta predictam doctrinam sic continuandum est:

Having worked her wiles against her father and pour-
ing forth the poison of her mind, Scylla mistress of
fraud teaches these things.

If the artificial beginning has taken its starting point 9
from an exemplum, it should be continued in a manner different from that of the previous examples. For when an exemplum, which is a particular sentiment, is introduced as a
kind of simile, it should be continued with words such as
these: "thus," "equally," "likewise," "similarly," "in like manner" or equivalent expressions. But so that the continuation
may be more elegant, one should pay attention to the sort of
topic that is highlighted in the exemplum that has been set
forth, namely, whether it is fickleness or vice or tendency or
something else of the same sort. And in the continuation
one should say "with a similar" or "with an equal" or "with
the same fickleness," "with a similar" or "with an equal" or
"with the same vice," "with a similar" or "with an equal" or
"with the same tendency." Let us give some examples.

An exemplum in prose, employed with reference to the 10
beginning, is of this sort: "After a period of calm etc." Notice
that in this exemplum fickleness or changeability is designated through the change of clear air into stormy air. Therefore, in accordance with the precept stated above, it should
be continued thus: "Of the same changeability are the gifts
of Fortune, the brightness of whose face is quickly darkened
and whose flatteries are often transformed into threats."
This is an example in verse: "Even as Phoebus etc." In accordance with the precept stated above, it should be continued
thus:

Rerum prosperitas levitate vagatur eadem
et meliora solent deteriora sequi.

11   Exemplum sumptum iuxta medium prosaicum tale est:
"Invidia zizannie etc." Ecce in hoc exemplo notatur vicium:
per vicium enim zizannie granum subruitur. Ideo iuxta predictam doctrinam sic continuandum est: "Eiusdem vicii
sunt mores invidie, que rerum unica pernicies, totis viribus
persequitur meliores." Metricum exemplum est hoc: "Falce
sua etc." Iuxta predictam doctrinam sic continuandum est:

Labe pari livor, solis melioribus hostis
nequior, invehitur in meliora prior.

Vel sic:

Labe pari virtutis opus livoris oberrat
virus et abradit optima peste sua.

12   Exemplum sumptum iuxta finem prosaicum tale est:
"Accidit sepe etc." Ecce in hoc exemplo notatur consuetudo
per hoc adverbium "sepe," quia quod sepe fit ex quadam
consuetudine fit. Ideo iuxta predictam doctrinam sic continuandum est: "Idem mos est in operibus perfidie, que proprium retorquetur in dominum, cum alterius machinatur

Prosperity in material things wavers with the same fickleness, and what is worse typically follows what is better.

An exemplum in prose, employed with reference to the [11] middle, is of this sort: "The envy of the cockle etc." Notice that in this exemplum a vice is designated: for through the vice of the cockle the good seed is destroyed. Therefore, in accordance with the precept stated above, it should be continued thus: "Of the same vice are the practices of Envy, who, the singular ruin of all things, persecutes with all her powers those who are better." This is an example in verse: "With its scythe etc." In accordance with the precept stated above, it should be continued thus:

With an equal defect, Envy, vilest enemy only to those who are better, is the first to speak against what is better.

Or thus:

With an equal defect, the poison of Envy infests the work of virtue and wipes out all the best things with its pestilence.

An exemplum in prose, employed with reference to the [12] end, is of this sort: "It often happens etc." Notice that in this exemplum a tendency is designated through the adverb "often," because what happens often happens through a certain tendency. Therefore, in accordance with the precept stated above, it should be continued thus: "The same tendency exists in the deeds of treachery, which turns back against its own master when it plots the harm of another."

detrimentum." Metricum exemplum est istud: "Sepe venenator etc." Iuxta premissam doctrinam sic continuandum est:

> More suo pariter fraus ipsa revertitur unde
> venit et in domini dampna retorquet iter.

Vel sic:

> More pari scelerum labes, licet in muliere
> dormiat, in sceleris sepius exit opus.

13 Hoc autem diligenter est notandum, quod ubi principium artificiale non sumitur a corpore materie, id est nec a medio nec a fine, anteponendum est tale proverbium vel exemplum in quo sequens materia videatur prelibari, id est ante tangi, ut quod in precedenti proverbio vel exemplo involutum est vel implicitum, in prosecucione materie possit facilius et evidencius explicari, per cuius evidenciam principalis materie veritas elucescat. Dividitur enim predicta materia, sicut quelibet alia, in tres partes, cuius prima pars est prosperitas Minois, qui filium suum misit Athenas. Secunda pars est invidia Atheniensium contra precellenciam virtutis Androchei; tercia, confusio Scille et eius subversio. Ideo iuxta diversitatem istarum parcium, diversimode inveniri debet principium. Verbi gracia, in prima parte continetur repentina fortune mutacio per Minoem, qui de gaudio cecidit in

This is an example in verse: "Often the poisoner etc." In accordance with the precept stated above, it should be continued thus:

In its usual fashion, likewise, deceit returns whence it came and retraces its steps to harm its master.

Or thus:

By a similar tendency, the vice of sins, though it may rest dormant in a woman, very often bursts forth in a sinful deed.

However, it should be noted carefully that when an artificial beginning does not take its starting point from the main body of the narrative subject matter, that is, neither from the middle nor from the end, one should place at the beginning the sort of proverb or exemplum in which the subject matter to follow seems to be anticipated, that is, touched on in advance, so that what is wrapped up or enfolded in the preceding proverb or exemplum, may be unfolded more easily and clearly in the development of the subject matter, so that through its clarity the truth of the primary subject matter may shine forth. For the previously mentioned subject matter is divided, like any other, into three parts, of which the first part is the prosperity of Minos, who sent his son to Athens. The second part is the envy of the Athenians at the excellence of Androgeos's virtue; the third, the confounding of Scylla and her overthrow. Therefore, in keeping with the diversity of these parts, the beginning should be conceived in diverse ways. For example, in the first part, the sudden alteration of fortune is exemplified in Minos, who fell from

13

27

merorem per filii sui mortem. Et ideo invenitur per hanc primam partem tam proverbium quam exemplum in quo talis mutacio fortune continetur cum dicitur "Hec est fortune etc." pro proverbio et "Post tranquillum etc." pro exemplo. Et consimiliter negociandum est in proverbio et exemplo iuxta medium et finem materie sumptis.

14   Set ut in continuacione sciamus que sentencia materie quo ordine prosequatur, notandum quod ubi principium artificiale sumitur iuxta medium materie vel a proverbio vel exemplo sumptis iuxta medium, statim post sentenciam medie materie, antequam veniatur ad finem, tangendum est sentenciam prime partis et ultimo finis, ut patuit in premissis. Ubi vero a fine vel a proverbio vel exemplo sumptis iuxta finem, statim post principium debet tangi sentencia prime partis et ultimo media pars eiusdem. Si vero a proverbio vel exemplo sumptis iuxta principium, tunc in prosecucione debet prima pars primo, secunda secundo, tercia tercio situari.

15   Ita dictum sit de prima parte prosecucionis, scilicet de continuacione vel conchatenacione principii ad ea que sequuntur. Priusquam procedamus in prosecucione, notandum

joy into grief through the death of his son. And thus, with regard to this first part, one devises both a proverb and an exemplum in which such an alteration of fortune is encompassed, when one says "This is the nature of Fortune etc." by way of a proverb and "After a period of calm etc." by way of an exemplum. And one should deal in similar fashion with a proverb or an exemplum employed with reference to the middle and the end.

But so that in the continuation we may know which theme of the subject matter should be pursued in which order, you should note that when an artificial beginning takes its starting point from the middle of the subject matter or from a proverb or an exemplum employed with reference to the middle, immediately after the theme of the middle part of the subject matter—and before you come to the end— you should touch on the theme of the first part and then finally that of the end, as was evident in the foregoing examples. But when an artificial beginning takes its starting point from the end or from a proverb or exemplum employed with reference to the end, then immediately after the beginning you should touch on the theme of the first part and then finally the middle part of the same subject matter. But if the artificial beginning takes its starting point from a proverb or exemplum employed with reference to the beginning, then the first part should be placed first in the development, the second second, and the third third.

And so we have discussed the first part of the development, namely, concerning the continuation or the joining of the beginning to what follows. Before we proceed further with the development, it should be noted that here instruc-

est quod hic docetur de artificio tractandi diffuse, id est prolixe. Sunt enim artificia duo, quorum alterum est dilatandi, reliquum breviandi materiam. Utrumque, Deo cooperante, sufficienter expedietur. Set quod premissum est, in primis ostendetur, scilicet tractare diffuse.

tion is being given in the craft of treating a subject copiously, that is, at length. For there are two crafts, of which one is that of extending, the other that of shortening the subject matter. Each of these, with God's help, will be explained sufficiently. But what already has been set forth will be shown first, namely, how to treat a subject copiously.

Capitulum 3

De octo modis prolongandi
materiam

Octo sunt que ampliant materiam, scilicet interpretacio, circumlocucio, comparacio vel collacio, apostrophacio, prosopopeia, digressio, descripcio, locus oppositorum. Unde versus:

> In, circum, col, apo, pro, di, des, locus oppositorum:
> materiam curtam prolonga viribus horum.

2   Interpretacio diffusiorem reddit materiam et verborum inducit opulenciam. Est enim interpretacio sub diversis verbis eadem sentencia sepius repetita. Per interpretacionem eandem sentenciam quasi per diversas clausulas interpretamur, sic:

> Allicit hec facies oculos, hoc rethe puellas
> implicat, hic Veneris hamus inescat eas.

Quod nichil aliud est dicere quam hoc: "Pulcher provocat ad libidinem." Item in "Libro versuum" dicitur:

Chapter 3

On the eight ways of extending the subject matter

There are eight devices that expand the subject matter, namely, interpretation, circumlocution, comparison or juxtaposition, apostrophe, prosopopoeia, digression, description, and collocation of opposites. From these comes the mnemonic verse:

> In, circum, com, apo, pro, di, des, collocation of opposites: with their aid make brief subject matter prolix.

Interpretation yields a more copious subject matter and 2 introduces a wealth of words. For interpretation is the frequent repetition of the same meaning by means of diverse words. Through interpretation we interpret, as it were, the same meaning through diverse clauses, thus:

> This face attracts eyes, this net entangles girls, this hook of Venus entices them.

All of which is to say nothing but this: "A beautiful person arouses desire." Likewise, in the "Book of Verses" it is said:

> Sentencia cum sit
> unica, non uno veniat contenta paratu,
> set variet vestes et mutatoria sumat.

Item Alanus, *De planctu Nature:*

> In lacrimas risus, in luctus gaudia verto,
> in planctum plausus, in lacrimosa iocos.

Id est, "Ego doleo." Et notandum quod cum unam tantum habeamus racionem ad aliquod persuadendum, tunc ad commodum nostre cause rethoricum est ita illam racionem variare et per voces synonomas, id est idem significantes, frequenter eandem resumere sentenciam, ut per multitudinem appareat copia racionum. Verbi gracia, Piramus et Tisbe, in persuasione sua ut paries ipsis cederet, dixerunt parieti:

> Iunge relativa quos nodat gracia, fedus
> copulat alternum, mutuus unit amor.

Id est, "Iunge nos quos iungit amor."

3   Circumlocucio est quando aliquam sentenciam dicturi, eam non directe dicimus set quasi in circuitu ambulamus et per quasdam circumstancias verborum sub ampliori serie ipsam insinuamus, sicut Virgilius, in primo *Eneidis,* pro Enea ponit circumlocucionem Enee, sic:

> Arma virumque cano, Troie qui primus ab oris
> Italiam fato profugus Lavinaque venit
> littora etc.

Although the meaning is one, let it not come content with only one set of apparel, but let it vary its robes and assume different raiment.

Likewise, Alan of Lille, in *The Plaint of Nature:*

My laughter turns to weeping, my joy to sorrow, rejoicing becomes lamentation, jests give way to tears.

That is, "I lament." And you should note that when we have only one argument with which to make a persuasive case for something, then it benefits our cause rhetorically to vary that argument in this way and through words that are synonymous—that is, that signify the same thing—to restate the same idea frequently, so that through this multitude there will appear to be an abundance of arguments. For example, Pyramus and Thisbe, in their attempts to persuade the wall to give way to them, said to the wall:

Join those whom a reciprocal affection knots, an interchangeable covenant binds, a mutual love unites.

That is, "Join us whom love joins."

Circumlocution is when we have some thought to relate and we do not relate it straightforwardly but, so to speak, walk in a roundabout way and through certain peripheral details insert it into a broader course of words, as when Virgil, in the first book of the *Aeneid,* replaces the name Aeneas with a circumlocution for Aeneas, thus:

Arms I sing and the man who first from the coasts of Troy, exiled by fate, came to Italy and Lavinian shores etc.

Quod nichil aliud est dicere quam "Cano Eneam."

4   Et notandum quod tria circumloquimur: quandoque sentenciam nominis, quandoque verbi, quandoque oracionis.
Sentenciam nominis, ut Virgilius in premisso exemplo pro
Enea ponit circumlocucionem Enee, sic: "Cano virum qui
primus profugus ab oris fato venit in Italiam et in littora La-
vina." Similiter pro Iove ponit "divum pater atque hominum
rex." Item Alanus, *De planctu Nature,* optimam ponit circumlocucionem Nature, sic:

O dei proles genetrixque rerum,
vinculum mundi stabilisque nexus,
gemma terrenis, speculum caducis,
            lucifer orbis.
Que tuis mundum moderans habenis,
cuncta concordi stabilita nodo
nectis et pacis glutino maritas
            celica terris.
Pax, amor, virtus, regimen, potestas,
ordo, lex, finis, via, lux, origo,
vita, laus, splendor, species, figura,
            regula mundi.
Que, Nois puras recolens ydeas,
singulas rerum species monetas,
rem togans forma clamidemque forme
            pollice formas.
Cui favet celum, famulatur aer,
quam colit tellus, veneratur unda,
cui, velut mundi domine, tributum
            singula solvunt.

All of which is to say nothing but "I sing Aeneas."

And you should note that we can circumlocute three 4 things: sometimes the meaning of a noun, sometimes that of a verb, and sometimes that of an entire sentence. The meaning of a noun, as when Virgil in the previous example replaces the name Aeneas with a circumlocution for Aeneas, thus: "I sing the man who first from the coasts, exiled by fate, came to Italy and to Lavinian shores." Similarly, in place of Jove he puts "father of gods and king of men." Likewise, Alan of Lille, in *The Plaint of Nature*, supplies an excellent circumlocution of Nature, thus:

> O child of god and mother of creation, linkage and firm bond of the universe, bright gem for earthly life, mirror for mortal creatures, daystar for the world.
>
> You who, guiding the world with your reins, impose stability on all things in binding agreement, and unite heavenly to earthly in the closeness of peace.
>
> Peace, love, strength, rule, power, order, law, end, path, light, source, life, praise, splendor, beauty, form, universal law.
>
> You who, contemplating the pure ideas of Noys, coin the several kinds of creatures, clothing matter with form and with your hand shaping the mantle of form;
>
> Whom heaven loves, whom the air serves, whom earth worships and water reveres, to whom, as to the mistress of the universe, all things pay tribute;

Que, diem nocti vicibus cathenans,
cereum solis tribuis diei,
lucido lune speculo soporas
                 nubila noctis.
Que polum stellis variis inauras,
etheris nostri solium serenas
siderum gemmis varioque celum
                 milite comples.
Que novis celi faciem figuris
Protheans mutas aviumque vulgus
aeris nostri regione donas
                 legeque stringis.
Cuius ad nutum iuvenescit orbis,
silva crispatur folii capillo
et sua florum tunicata veste
                 terra superbit.
Que minas ponti sepelis et auges,
sincopas cursum pelagi furoris,
ne soli vultum tumulare possit
                 equoris estus.

Et hoc totum nichil aliud est dicere quam hoc: "O Natura."

5   Sentenciam verbi circumloquimur, ut quando ponimus pro hoc verbo "Mortuus est" circumlocucionem eius, sic: "Naturali sorte assumptus est," "Fati munus implevit," "Consummavit cursum vite," "Debitum nature persolvit," "Latro hominum furatus est eum," "Viam universe carnis ingressus est," "Sublatus est e medio," "Decessit in fata." Similiter Alanus, *De planctu,* pro "lucet" ponit "proscribit umbram brume"; unde ubi diceret "sol lucet," dicit:

Proscribit brume solaris cereus umbram.

Who, linking day to night in alternation, assign the candle of the sun to day, and make the clouds of night drowsy with the glowing mirror of the moon;

Who gild the vault with an array of stars, illumining our ethereal domain, and fill heaven with starry gems and a varied soldiery;

Who in Protean fashion change the face of the sky with new shapes, granting to the throngs of birds the regions of the air and confining them there by your law;

At whose nod the world grows young, the woods bristle with curling foliage, and the earth waxes proud, clad in its garment of flowers.

Who lay the threatening seas to rest and cause them to swell, curbing the flow of the raging ocean lest its seething tides bury the face of the land.

And all of this is to say nothing but "O Nature."

We can circumlocute the meaning of a verb, as when we $_5$ put in place of the verb "He died" its circumlocution, thus: "He has been taken by nature's lot," "He fulfilled the duty of fate," "He completed the course of life," "He paid the debt to nature," "The thief of men has stolen him," "He has gone the way of all flesh," "He has been taken away from our midst," "He has gone off to the Fates." Similarly, Alan of Lille, in the *Plaint,* puts "banishes the shadows of winter" in place of "shines"; and so where he could have said "the sun shines," he says:

The sun's candle banishes the shadows of winter.

6   Sentenciam oracionis circumloquimur quando tam nomen quam verbum circumloquimur, ut cum dicendum sit
"Inimici regis suspensi sunt," hac utendum est circumlocu-
cione: "Dampnati sunt suspendio quorum presumpcio se
rebelles opposuit regie maiestati." Nam cum dicitur "Dampnati sunt suspendio," est sentencia verbi circumloquuta,
scilicet huius verbi "suspensi sunt," et cum dicitur "quorum
presumpcio se rebelles opposuit regie maiestati," ponitur
circumlocucio huius nominis "regis inimici." Item Alanus,
cum diceret "Sub brevitate respondi," dicit "Sub castigate
vocis moderamine, responsionis reddidi talionem."

7   Comparacio vel collacio est rerum similium ad aliquod
persuadendum congeries introducta. Et notandum quod
non omnis comparacio prolongat materiam set quandoque
valde abbreviat, ut quando comparamus aliquem vel aliquam
uni rei propter multas illius proprietates inclusas. Verbi gracia, dicturi de aliquo quod mitis est et innocens et expers
fraudis, dicimus "agnus est," nam esse mitem, innocentem
et fraudis expertem sunt proprietates agni. Hac comparacione brevitatis quidam utitur, dicens:

Nos aper auditu, linx visu, simia gustu,
vultur odoratu, set vincit aranea tactu.

8   Comparacio prolongans materiam fit dupliciter: manifeste scilicet et occulte. Manifeste quando similitudo

We circumlocute the meaning of an entire sentence when 6
we circumlocute the noun as much as the verb, so that when
you wish to say "The king's enemies have been hanged," you
could use this circumlocution: "Those whose audacity set
them up as rebels against the royal majesty have been condemned to hanging." For when one says "They have been
condemned to hanging," the meaning of the verb, namely,
"they have been hanged," has been circumlocuted, and when
one says "those whose audacity set them up as rebels against
the royal majesty," one presents a circumlocution of the
noun "the king's enemies." Likewise Alan of Lille, when he
would say "I responded in brief," says "in a voice chastened
and subdued, I gave a fitting reply."

Comparison or juxtaposition is an accumulation of simi- 7
lar things introduced for the purpose of making a persuasive
case for something. And you should note that not every
comparison extends the subject matter but sometimes can
actually shorten it, as when we compare someone with a single thing because of many qualities that are encapsulated in
that thing. For example, when we intend to say that someone is mild and harmless and free of deceit, we say "He's a
lamb," because to be mild, harmless, and free of deceit are
qualities of a lamb. A certain writer uses this sort of comparison for the sake of brevity, saying:

> The wild boar surpasses us in hearing, the lynx in vi-
> sion, the ape in tasting, the vulture in smelling, but the
> spider in touch.

Comparison that extends the subject matter is done in 8
two ways: openly and covertly. Openly, when the similarity is

introducitur per aliquod signum. Tria sunt signa quibus inducitur comparacio manifesta, scilicet magis, minus, eque.

9   Per "magis" introducitur comparacio quando alterum comparatorum maiori inequalitatis porcione superat reliquum. Quando per "magis" introducitur, diversa serviunt ad induccionem comparacionis et maxime nomina et adverbia comparativi gradus, sic:

Nummus habet plures quam celum sidera fures.

Similiter: "Instabilior est mundi prosperitas maris fluctibus et procellis." Similiter Alanus, *De planctu Nature,* ait: "Expolita menti planicies, cristallina luce conspeccior, argenteum induebat fulgorem."

10   Per "minus" introducitur comparacio quando alterum comparatorum minori inequalitatis porcione superat reliquum. Et tunc similiter introducitur similitudo per nomina et adverbia comparativi gradus, sic: "Rarius viget in muliere castitas quam fidelitas in latrone."

11   Per "eque" fit comparacio quando utrumque comparatorum vel quodlibet quadam equalitatis porcione sibi invicem comparatur. Et fit per hec signa et similia: sic, sicut, ut, quasi, taliter, pariter, adeo, tamquam, non aliter. Verbi gracia: "Sicut aviditati iudicis respondet litis controversia, sic respondet voto medici copia languidorum."

12   Occulte fit comparacio quando similitudo sumpta non

made explicit by some sign. There are three signs by which an open comparison is introduced, namely, "more," "less," and "equally."

A comparison is introduced by "more" when one of the 9 things compared surpasses the other because it has the greater share of unequal quantities. When the comparison is introduced by "more," various types of words serve to represent it, and especially nouns and adverbs of the comparative degree, thus:

Money has more thieves than the sky has stars.

Similarly: "The prosperity of this world is more unstable than the waves and storms of the sea." Similarly, Alan of Lille, in *The Plaint of Nature,* says: "The smooth surface of her chin, more striking than the brilliance of crystal, wore a silvery glow."

A comparison is introduced by "less" when one of the 10 things compared surpasses the other because it has the lesser share of unequal quantities. And then the similarity is similarly introduced by means of nouns and adverbs of the comparative degree, thus: "More rarely does chastity thrive in a woman than faithfulness in a thief."

A comparison is made by "equally" when any or each of 11 the things compared is compared to the other by virtue of a certain share of an equal quantity. And this kind of comparison is made by means of these signs and ones like them: "thus," "just as," "as," "as if," "in this way," "in like fashion," "so much," "as much as," "not otherwise." For example: "Just as a judge eagerly desires controversy in a lawsuit, so does a doctor long for an abundance of invalids."

A comparison is made covertly when the similarity on 12

inducitur per aliquod signum set latenter ingreditur quasi quiddam de corpore materie. Et hoc genus comparacionis specialis prerogative gaudet privilegio. Huius comparacionis elegans exemplum habemus in principio *Architrenii,* ubi auctor, dicturus "Omnia vincit labor et ingenium," multas latenter inducit comparaciones, sic incipiens librum:

Velificatur Athos, dubio mare ponte ligatur,
remus arat colles, pedibus substernitur unda,
puppe meatur humus, pelagi Thetis exuit usum,
Salmoneus fulmen iaculatur, Dedalus alas
induit: ingenii furor instat et invia preceps
rumpit et artifici cedit natura labori.

Consimiliter quidam volens hortari episcopum Norwycensem curas parumper suspendere et precibus condescendere minorum tales inducit comparaciones occultas:

Magnus Alexander bellorum sepe procellas
immixtis fregit studiis Socratesque, studendi
continuum solitus interrupisse laborem,
Treicias tremulo numeravit pollice cordas.
Cessit Athlas oneri, civili scriptor ab ense
Iulius abstinuit, invictus sepe quievit
Alcides, rigidum mollis lira flexit Achillem.
Tu quoque lugenti patrie graviterque diuque
expectate parens, sibi quem viduata maritum
iam pastoralis Norwici regia poscit etc.

which it is based is not introduced by means of any sign but enters in a concealed manner, as if it were something inherent in the body of the subject matter. And this kind of comparison enjoys the privilege of a special prerogative. We have an elegant example of this kind of comparison at the beginning of the *Architrenius,* where the author, intending to say "Effort and ingenuity conquer all," secretly brings in many comparisons, beginning the book thus:

> Ships sail over Athos, the ocean is spanned by a shaky bridge, oars furrow the hillsides, the waves are subjected to walking feet, dry land is surveyed from the stern, Thetis has forsaken the deep. Salmoneus hurls his thunderbolt, Daedalus dons his wings, a frenzy of ingenuity is upon us, bursting headlong into regions uncharted, and nature yields to the onslaught of art.

Similarly, someone who wants to urge the bishop of Norwich to suspend his pastoral cares for a little while and comply with the entreaties of his inferiors brings in hidden comparisons such as these:

> Alexander the Great often abated the storms of war with intermingled studies, and Socrates, accustomed to interrupt the continuous effort of studying, strummed with quivering thumb the Thracian strings. Atlas gave up his burden, as a writer Julius abstained from civil war, unconquered Alcides often rested, the tender lyre relaxed inflexible Achilles. You also, long and grievously awaited father to a weeping country, whom the widowed episcopal see of Norwich now demands for herself as husband etc.

Et notandum quod in materiis inchoandis aptissima est occulta comparacio.

13   Copiam comparacionum habemus quasi per totum librum moralis doctrine qui sic incipit: "A Phebo Phebe etc." Comparacio, sicud tradit Petrus Blesensis, in libello suo de dictamine qui sic incipit: "Licet magistri Bernardi etc.," fit quinque modis. A simili ad simile affirmative, sic: "Sicut cervus desiderat ad fontes aquarum, ita animus meus ad scienciam scripturarum." A simili ad simile negative, sic: "Sicut nemo est qui divine disposicioni valeat obviare, ita ipsius mandatis nulli conveniens est contraire." A contrario ad contrarium, sic: "Sicut iniuste petentibus nullus tribuendus est assensus, ita iuste petentibus hillariter concedendum." Ab uno ad plura, sic: "Nimirum licet bonus inter malos corrumpatur, nam et urtica sue veneno malicie rosarum fragranciam inficit et pix preciosis coniuncta panniculis eorum decorem et precium dehonestat." A pluribus ad unum, sic: sicut in predictis versibus ad episcopum Norwicensem.

14   Apostrophacio est quando preter materiam principaliter intentam convertimus sermonem vel ad nos ipsos vel ad aliam rem. Fit autem quattuor modis: primo modo errores reprobando, secundo infortunium plangendo, tercio contra facinus insurgendo, quarto ridiculosos deridendo, ut habetur in "Libro versuum" ad Neustriam et ad Angliam. In apostrophacione quattuor incidunt exornaciones, scilicet exclamacio, conduplicacio, subieccio, dubitacio.

And you should note that a covert comparison is especially appropriate at the beginning of new subject matter.

We have an abundance of comparisons more or less 13 throughout the book of moral teaching that begins thus: "From Phoebus Phoebe etc." As Peter of Blois teaches us in his little book on composition that begins thus: "Although Master Bernard's etc.," comparison is done in five ways. By affirmation, from like to like, thus: "Just as the stag longs for the springs of waters, so does my mind for knowledge of the scriptures." By negation, from like to like, thus: "Just as there is no one who can resist Divine Providence, so it befits no one to oppose its commands." From opposite to opposite, thus: "Just as no assent should be given to those who beseech unjustly, so one should yield cheerfully to those who beseech justly." From one to many, thus: "It is not strange if the good be corrupted among the evil, for so the nettle spoils the fragrance of roses with the poison of its evil, and pitch brought into contact with precious clothes dishonors their beauty and value." From many to one, thus: as in the previously quoted verses addressed to the bishop of Norwich.

Apostrophe is when we go beyond the subject matter 14 that has been our principal concern by shifting the speech either to ourselves or to some other thing. Apostrophe is done in four ways: in the first way by reproving errors, in the second by bewailing misfortune, in the third by rising up against crime, in the fourth by laughing at the laughable, as is done in the "Book of Verses" with regard to Normandy and England. Four kinds of embellishment fall under apostrophe, namely, exclamation, reduplication, hypophora, and indecision.

47

15   Exclamacio est quando apostrophando ex aliqua causa exclamamus, ut hic:

> O Asie flos, Troia potens! O gloria que nunc
> in cinerem collapsa iaces! Ubi regia proles
> ex Ecuba Priami veniens a semine divum? etc.

Et in "Libro versuum":

> O dolor! O plus quam dolor! O mors! O truculenta
> mors! Utinam etc.

16   Conduplicacio est quando idem verbum, motu doloris, amoris, ire, indignacionis vel alicuius anxietatis, principium iteramus. Motu doloris, ut in Virgilio:

> Anna soror, que me suspensam insompnia terrent!
> Anna soror etc.

Bernardus Silvestris, in *Paricidali:*

> Filius ille tuus, cuius racionis acumen,
>   actus mirari, verba probare soles;
> filius ille tuus, de quo quoque livor et hostis,
>   de quo mentiri fama vel ipsa timet;
> filius ille tuus, quem predicat orbis et omnis
>   que sub septeno climate terra iacet.

Motu amoris, ut in Ovidio, *Methamorphoseos:*

> Nimpha, precor, Peneia, mane! Non insequor hostis.
> Nimpha, mane! etc.

Et sic de aliis.

Exclamation is when something causes us to cry out in 15 the course of apostrophizing, as here:

O flower of Asia, mighty Troy! O glory who now lie fallen into ashes! Where is the royal race that through Priam's Hecuba descends from the seed of the gods? etc.

And in the "Book of Verses":

O sorrow! O greater than sorrow! O death! O truculent death! Would that etc.

Reduplication is when we repeat the same word at the 16 beginning, impelled by sorrow, love, anger, indignation, or some sort of anxiety. Impelled by sorrow, as in Virgil:

Anna, my sister, what dreams thrill me with fears? Anna, my sister etc.

Bernard Silvestris, in *The Parricide:*

That son of yours, whose keen reasoning, whose deeds you are accustomed to admire, whose words you are accustomed to approve; that son of yours, about whom even envy and his enemy, about whom even rumor itself fears to lie; that son of yours, whom the world commends and every land that lies beneath the sevenfold heavens.

Impelled by love, as in Ovid's *Metamorphoses:*

O nymph, O Peneus's daughter, stay! I who pursue thee am no enemy. Oh nymph, stay! etc.

And so with the others.

17   Subieccio est quando questionem facimus set anticipa-
mus nos ipsi respondentem. Huius habemus exemplum in
Yponasticon Laurencii Dunelmensis, de Adam quando pecca-
vit, sub hiis versibus:

> O pater! O quid agis? Deus est quem spernis et ipsum
>   qualiter evades, terra cinisque, Deum?
> An fugies? Set ubique manet. Fallesne? Set idem
>   quod fuit, est et erit cognicione tenet.
> An vinces? Set cuncta potest. Ipsumne latebis?
>   Set quod ubique latet vel patet ipse videt.
> Mors igitur vetiti te pena miserima ligni
>   deprimet, in natis ius habitura tuis.

18   Dubitacio est quando, dubia proferendo, procedimus sic:

> Tu michi te confers, homo . . . quo te nomine dicam?
> Nescio. Si dicam "spurcissime," non erit equum.
> Si "scelus" appellem, minus est. Deformior an sis
> nequior ignoro. Non hoc michi nec placet illud.

Similiter, in "Libro versuum":

> Quid ages? Volucrum rimaberis aure
> murmura? Vel motus etc.

19   Prosopopeia est conformacio nove persone, quando scilicet res non loquens introducitur tamquam loquens. Fit autem dupliciter. Uno modo seriose, scilicet in materia seriosa

Hypophora is when we pose a question but we ourselves 17 anticipate the response. We have an example of this in Lawrence of Durham's *Hypognosticon,* in these verses concerning Adam when he sinned:

O father! O what are you doing? It is God whom you scorn, and how will you, dust and ashes, escape God himself? Will you flee? But he is everywhere. Will you deceive him? But whatever was, is, and will be he holds in his knowledge. Will you conquer him in battle? But he can do everything. Will you hide from him? But he sees whatever is hidden or exposed anywhere. Death, therefore, the most wretched punishment of the forbidden tree, will lay you low and will hold dominion over your children.

Indecision is when, revealing doubts, we proceed thus: 18

You show yourself to me, o man . . . by what name shall I call you? I do not know. If I say "most impure," it will be inadequate. If I call you "an atrocity," it is less than you are. I know not whether you are more deformed or more vile. Neither this nor that satisfies me.

Similarly, in the "Book of Verses":

What will you do? Will your ear interpret the singing of birds—or their movements etc.

Prosopopoeia is the creation of a new persona, namely, 19 when a nonspeaking thing is introduced as if it could speak. This is done in two ways. On the one hand seriously, that is, within a serious or fruitful subject matter, as in the "Book of

vel fructuosa, ut in "Libro versuum," ubi crux introducitur
alloquens Christianos, sic:

> Crux ego rapta queror, ego crux, ego crux Crucifixi,
> crux ego sancta, salus populi, reparacio mundi etc.

Alio modo iocose, scilicet in materia iocosa, ut similiter in
"Libro versuum," ubi introducitur mappa valedicens mense,
sic:

> Solebam
> esse decus mense dum primula floruit etas,
> dum faciem gessi sine crimine etc.

Similiter per prosopopeiam terra introducitur loqui in Ovidio, *Methamorphoseos,* ubi queritur Iovi de incendio Pheton-
tis, sic:

> Si placet hoc meruique, quid o tua fulmina cessant,
> summe deum? Liceat periture viribus ignis
> igne perire tuo etc.

Similiter Roma in Lucano, Affrica in Claudiano.

20 Digressio est a principali materia ad aliquod extra materiam quod faciat ad commodum cause recessio moderata. Et
nota quod omnis digressio fit aut per descripcionem aut per
comparacionem aut per poeticum figmentum. Fit autem
duobus modis: uno modo quando digredimur in materia ad

Verses," when the cross is introduced as if it were speaking to Christians, thus:

> I, the ravished cross, make my complaint, I the cross, I the cross of the Crucified, I the holy cross, the salvation of the people, the renewal of the world etc.

On the other hand humorously, that is, in a humorous subject matter, as likewise in the "Book of Verses," when a napkin is introduced as if it were bidding farewell to a table, thus:

> I was once the pride of the table, while my youth was in its first flower and my face knew no blemish etc.

Similarly, by means of prosopopoeia the earth is introduced as if it were to speak in Ovid's *Metamorphoses,* when it complains to Jove about Phaeton's arson, thus:

> If this is your will, and I have deserved all this, why, O king of all the gods, are your lightnings idle? If I must die by fire, oh, let it be your fire by which I perish etc.

Similarly, Rome in Lucan, Africa in Claudian.

Digression is a moderate departure from the principal ₂₀ subject matter to something extraneous to that subject matter that might be advantageous to the case. And note that every digression is made either by means of a description or by means of a comparison or by means of a poetic fiction. Moreover, it is done in two ways: on the one hand, when we digress within the subject matter to another part of the same subject matter; on the other hand, when we digress

aliam partem materie, alio modo quando digredimur a materia ad aliud extra materiam et hec propriissima nominatur.

21   Digredimur in materia ad aliam partem materie quando omittimus illam partem materie que prima est et aliam que sequitur prius assumimus. Verbi gracia, cum dicendum sit "Acteon fessus erat venatu et ideo venit respirare iuxta fontem delectabilem," postquam dictum est eum fuisse fessum, antequam dicamus quod venit ad fontem, digrediendum est ad fontem, ut eius amenitas ad cause commodum describatur, et postea dicendum est quod venit ad fontem causa respirandi. Ad huius doctrine evidenciam supponantur hii versus:

> Sarcina venanti duplex, venatus et estus:
>   languida persuadent membra quiete frui.
> Est locus in cuius sudans Natura decorem,
>   cum fecisset opus, noluit artis opem.
> Libera planicies signatur ymagine spere:
>   murmurat in medio vox salientis aque.
> Circulus arboreus faciem cortinat aquarum.
>   Frondea suppositas umbra sigillat aquas.
> Ludit in arboreis avium lascivia ramis.
>   Vernus aromatico fragrat odore locus.
> Fertilitas inpregnat humum; duo serta coronant,
>   prodiga commoditas, picta figura, locum.
> Gustus et olfactus, oculi pascuntur et aures:
>   omnis ibi sensus est saciata fames.
> Invitant fessum tam mira decencia rerum,
>   deliciosa loci phisica curat eum.

from the subject matter to something extraneous to that subject matter, and this second type is the one that is most properly called digression.

We digress within the subject matter to another part of 21 the same subject matter when we pass over a part of the subject matter that comes at the beginning and take up another part that follows it first. For example, when we wish to say "Actaeon was tired from hunting and therefore came to rest himself beside a delightful spring," after we say that he was tired but before we say that he came to the spring we might digress to the spring, so that its pleasantness can be described to the advantage of the case, and afterward we could say that he came to the spring for the purpose of resting. These verses can be added in support of this precept:

> A double burden is on the hunter, the hunting and the heat: his tired limbs urge him to delight in rest. There is a place for whose embellishment Nature exerted herself, and as she did her work she rejected the power of art. The open plain is marked with the shape of a sphere: in its midst murmurs the sound of spring water. A circle of trees curtains the face of the waters. Leafy shade imprints its image on the waters below. The wantonness of birds plays in the tree branches. The springtime place gives forth a fragrant smell. Fertility impregnates the ground. Two garlands crown the place: lavish ease and embellished form. Taste and smell, eyes and ears are feasted: there the hunger of each sense has been satiated. The wondrous beauties of these things attract the tired man, the delightful medicine of the place restores him.

Et ecce in premisso exemplo non sine racione describitur fontis amenitas, quia multum facit ad commodum cause, ut scilicet per hoc evidens et quasi coniecturale argumentum sit auditori Acteonem fessum in loco tante amenitatis respirasse.

22   Similiter, cum dicendum sit "Amantes recesserunt ab invicem in tempore veris," primo describendum est tempus veris, deinde dicendum est quod amici recesserunt, sic:

Unicus astringit duo pectora nodus amoris,
corpora disiungit nova causa etc.,

sicut habetur in "Libro versuum." Facit enim hec descripcio ad commodum cause: ostendit enim causam et evidenciam vehemencie doloris amicorum recedencium, quia in tempore veris maior est dileccio, causata ex qualitate aeris, et ubi maior est dileccio, magis dolorosa est recessio.

23   Degredimur eciam a materia ad aliud extra materiam, quando scilicet inducimus comparaciones, ut eas materie adaptemus, sicut hic, in hiis versibus:

Predecessoris lugerent cuncta, Iohannes,
fata tui, lacrimasque viro nec dura negarent
Gargara, set gemitus patrie fecundior aufert
gloria; pensat enim trutam balena, camelus
castora, fons ciatum, sol lampada, linea punctum.

And notice that in the above example it is not without reason that the pleasantness of the spring is described, because it works very much to the advantage of the case, namely, that through this description it becomes evident to the reader, as if demonstrated by conjectural argument, that Actaeon, being tired, would have rested in a place of such pleasantness.

Similarly, when you wish to say "The lovers parted from 22 each other in the season of spring," first you would describe the season of spring, then you would say that the friends parted, thus:

A single bond of love bound together two hearts; a new cause divided them one from the other etc.,

as is found in the "Book of Verses." This description works to the advantage of the case, for it shows the cause and the proof of the intense sorrow of the parting friends, because in the season of spring love is all the greater, due to the quality of the air, and when love is greater, parting is more sorrowful.

We also can digress from the subject matter to something 23 else outside the subject matter, namely, when we bring in comparisons, so that we might adapt them to the subject matter, as here, in these verses:

All things, John, would have mourned the calamities of your predecessor, and not even harsh Gargara would have denied the man its tears, but a richer glory banishes the groans of the fatherland: for a whale makes up for a trout, a camel for a beaver, a fountain for a ladle, the sun for a lamp, and a line for a point.

Similitudinarie posita sunt exempla, et ubi dici debuit "ve-
luti penset," dixit simpliciter "pensat." Ecce aliud exemplum
Oracii, in suis *Epistolis:*

> Ut nox longa quibus mentitur amica, diesque
> longa videtur opus debentibus, ut piger annus
> pupillis quos dira premit custodia matrum,
> sic michi tarda fluunt ingrataque tempora, que spem
> conciliumque morantur agendi gnaviter etc.

Quorum versuum ita collige sentenciam: "Quemadmodum
nox videtur longa amatoribus expectantibus amicam mendaciter tardantem et quemadmodum dies videtur longa ope-
rariis pre labore sudantibus et quemadmodum annus videtur longus pupillis quos gravat dira novercarum custodia, sic
michi videtur longum et tardum depromere que compono."
Talibus comparacionibus parcius est utendum. Unde dicit
Gervasius de Saltu Lacteo, qui perfectissime hanc artem
tradidit, quod "Fama nobilissime *Thebaidos* ob comparacionum frequenciam vix permansit illesa."

24   Amplius, fit digressio per poeticum figmentum, sicut habetur in Stacio, *Thebaidos,* ubi Stacius fingit Iovem coa-
dunare deos et disponere bellum Thebanum, ubi et Iovem
introducit dicentem:

> Dire senex! meruere tue, meruere tenebre
> ultorem sperare Iovem. Nova sontibus arma
> iniciam regnis,

Set digressio incipit ad istum versum:

These examples have been put figuratively, and where he should have said "as if it were to make up for," he simply says "it makes up for." Consider another example, by Horace, in his *Epistles:*

> As the night seems long for one whose mistress proves false, and the day long for those who work for hire; as the year lags for wards held in check by their mother's strict guardianship: so slow and thankless flow for me the hours which defer my hope and purpose of setting myself vigorously etc.

Put together the meaning of these verses thus: "Just as the night seems long to lovers awaiting a mistress who delays under false pretenses, and just as the day seems long to workers sweating from their labor, and just as the year seems long to wards whom the strict guardianship of their stepmothers oppresses, so it seems long and slow to me to bring forth what I am composing." You should use such comparisons sparingly. For this reason, Gervase of Melkley, who treated this art most completely, says that "Due to the frequency of its comparisons, the reputation of the most celebrated *Thebaid* scarcely endures unscathed."

Digression also is accomplished by means of a poetic fic- 24 tion, as occurs in Statius's *Thebaid,* when Statius imagines that Jove assembles the gods and arranges the Theban war, and when he introduces Jove saying:

> Terrible old man! deserving are you, yes, deserving in your blindness to hope for Jove as your avenger. New strife will I send upon the guilty realm.

However, the digression begins at this verse:

At Iovis imperiis rapidi super atria celi etc.

25   Sunt enim quattuor cause digressionis faciende, ut ait Tullius in prima *Rethorica,* scilicet criminacio, similitudo, delectacio et amplificacio. Causa criminacionis, sicut Tullius ponit in *Verrinis,* qui cum cepisset accusare Verrem de adulterio, dimisso cursu oracionis sue, id est dimissa principali materia, utitur digressione, describens amenitatem loci in quo Verrem dicit comisisse adulterium, dicens "ibi fontes amenos, arbores veris dotibus insignitas, prata virencia et flore multiphario purpurata," et hoc ad commodum sue cause, ut scilicet, audita tanta loci amenitate sive pulcritudine, verisimile esset et quasi argumentum probabile auditori Verrem adulterium comisisse. Causa similitudinis, ut quando inducuntur comparaciones, ut habetur in versibus premissis: "Predecessoris etc." Causa delectacionis, ut quando inseritur aliquod ludicrum per quod auditores ex idemptitate materie precedentis torpentes reddantur attenti. Huius exemplum habemus in Alano, *De planctu Nature,* ubi postquam Natura tradidit epistolam Hymeneo, Nature nuncio, ut eam suo sacerdoti Genio deferat, statim auctor, quia prius quasi per totum librum in reprehencione viciorum immorabatur, ad removendum idemptitatis fastidium auditoribus, subito inducit diversa instrumenta musicalia,

But now by Jove's command in the spacious halls of the revolving heavens etc.

There are in fact four reasons for making a digression, as 25 Cicero says in his first *Rhetoric,* namely, accusation, comparison, amusement, and amplification. For the sake of accusation, as Cicero does in the *Verrines:* when he had begun to accuse Verres of adultery, having abandoned the course of his speech, that is, having abandoned the principal subject matter, he employs a digression, describing the pleasantness of the place in which he claims that Verres had committed adultery, saying "there the pleasant springs, the trees adorned with the gifts of spring, the meadows flourishing and arrayed with every kind of flower," and this for the advantage of his case, namely, that, having heard about the exceptional pleasantness or beauty of the place, it would be a plausible and, as it were, probable argument to the hearer that Verres had committed adultery. For the sake of comparison, as when comparisons are introduced, as occurs in the previously mentioned verses: "All things, John, would have mourned the calamities of your predecessor etc." For the sake of amusement, as when something playful is inserted by means of which listeners who are wearied by the sameness of the preceding matter are made attentive. We have an example of this in Alan of Lille's *The Plaint of Nature,* at the point immediately after Nature gave a letter to Hymen, Nature's messenger, so that he could bear it to her priest Genius, when the author, because up to then he had dwelled on the reprehension of vices more or less throughout the book, in order to relieve the readers of their dislike of sameness suddenly introduces various musical instruments, so that

quorum dulcedine diversitatis recreari poterit spiritus audientis. Et hoc facit Alanus hiis versibus:

> Iam tuba terribili bellum clangore salutans
> intonuit, cognata loquens preludia belli,
> mugitu simili similem signando tumultum.
> Aera ledebat mendaci vulnere cornu.
> Devia vox huius, vox huius anormala, nescit
> organicis parere modis artique favere
> spernit et effrenem miratur musica cantum. etc.

Vel aliter, ut ait Victorinus super Tullium: "Delectacionis causa fit digressio, ut si prata, nemora, fontes rivosve describas et hanc ipsam descripcionem ad causam applices." Causa amplificacionis, sicut habetur in Boecio, *De consolacione Philosophie,* in principio ubi, enumeratis multis argumentis persuadentibus ad tristiciam, describit mortem, que stulta miserorum opinione "mors felix" dicitur. Et hoc facit ut ostendat eo forcius tristiciam suam ampliari. Hec digressio habetur hiis versibus:

> Mors hominum felix que se nec dulcibus annis
>   inserit et mestis sepe vocata venit.
> Heu, heu quam surda miseros avertitur aure
>   et flentes oculos claudere seva negat.
> Dum levibus male fida bonis fortuna faveret,
>   pene caput tristis merserat hora meum.
> Nunc quia fallacem mutavit nubila vultum,
>   protrahit ingratas impia vita moras.

the listener's spirit might be refreshed by the sweetness of their variety. And Alan does this in these verses:

> Now the trumpet, heralding battle, gave forth its terrible blaring, uttering a warlike prelude to war, its roar the image of the roaring of war itself. The horn assailed the air with a feigned wound; its wavering voice, its formless voice gave no obedience to the modes of music and scorned to show kindness to art; music wondered at such uncontrolled song etc.

Or in other words, as Victorinus's commentary on Cicero says: "Digression is done for the sake of amusement, as if you were to describe meadows, groves, springs and brooks and apply this description to the case." For the sake of amplification, as occurs in Boethius, at the beginning of *The Consolation of Philosophy,* when, after many arguments conducing to sadness have been marshaled, he describes death, which in the foolish opinion of the wretched is called "happy death." And he does this so that he may show all the more forcefully his ever increasing sadness. This digression occurs in these verses:

> It is a happy death that comes not in the years of sweetness but often called to those who want to end their misery. Alas, alas, how it turns away from the wretched with deaf ear and cruelly refuses to close their weeping eyes. While fickle fortune favored me with fleeting gifts, such an hour of bitterness might have bowed my head. Now because her clouded, cheating face is changed my cursed life drags on its long, unwanted days.

Ex predictis igitur collige quod quociens fit digressio ex aliqua dictarum causarum, conveniens est et facit ad commodum cause.

26   Descripcio est alicuius rei vel persone dicenda sentencia diversis eius proprietatibus elongata. Ut cum dicenda sit hec brevis sentencia "Ista mulier est pulcra," ponatur descripcio pulcritudinis sue, ut fiat brevitas illa diffusa, sic:

Circinus est auctor capitis, flavescit in aurum
cerula forma come, parit ex se lilia frontis
lactea strata, suum vaccinia nigra colorem
appingunt ciliis, radiant in margine frontis
cristalli gemine, nasum moderata venustas
protrahit, in facie color est argenteus auro
mixtus in electrum, sintillant labra benigno
igne, color dentes investit eburneus; impar
nil habet inferius mulier formosa superne.

Ecce per descripcionem diffuse dicitur quod aliter brevissime diceretur.

27   Optimas descripciones exemplariter habemus in Alano, tam in *Anticlaudiano* quam in libro *De planctu Nature,* inter quas hec una precellens descripcio quam in libro *De planctu Nature* assignat expresse ponatur, et est descripcio veris, sic:

Floriger horrentem Zephirus laxaverat annum,
    extinguens Boree prelia pace sua.

From what has been said above, therefore, gather that whenever a digression is made for any of the said causes, it is appropriate and works to the advantage of the case.

Description is a judgment to be pronounced about some 26 thing or person that has been prolonged with the various characteristics of that person or thing. So that when this brief judgment is to be pronounced: "This woman is beautiful," a description of her beauty is supplied, so that the brevity becomes prolix, thus:

> A pair of compasses is the maker of her head, the dark appearance of her hair brightens into gold, the milky way of her forehead brings forth lilies from itself, dark blueberries paint their color on her eyelashes, crystals shine in the border of her double brow, a moderate beauty draws out her nose, in her face a silvery color has been mixed with gold into amber-hued electrum, her lips sparkle with beneficent fire, the color of ivory clothes her teeth; the woman who is beautiful above has nothing unequal below.

Note that by means of description what would otherwise be said very briefly is said in a prolix way.

By way of example we have excellent descriptions in Alan 27 of Lille, both in his *Anticlaudianus* and in his book *The Plaint of Nature*. Among them, one outstanding description that he includes in his book *The Plaint of Nature* clearly should be set down here, and it is a description of spring, thus:

> Zephyr, bringer of flowers, had calmed the fierceness of the year, quelling the assaults of Boreas by his peace-

Grandine perfusus florum pluit ille ligustra
    et pratis horum iussit inesse nives.
Ver, quasi fullo novus, reparando pallia pratis,
    horum succendit muricis igne togas.
Reddidit arboribus crines quos bruma totondit,
    vestem sic reparans quam tulit ipse prius.
Tempus erat quo larga suis expandit in agris,
    applausu driadum, gracia veris opes.
Quo dum maior inest virtus, infancia florum,
    alcius exsurgens, matre recedit humo.
Quo viole speculum, terre cunabula linquens,
    aeris afflatus postulat ore novo.
Tempus erat quo terra, caput stellata rosarum,
    contendit celo, sidere plena suo.
Quo vexilla gerens estatis amigdalus ortum
    predicat et veris gaudia flore notat.
Quo vitis gemmata, synus amplexa mariti
    ulmi, de partu cogitat ipsa suo.
Proscribit brume solaris cereus umbram,
    cogens exilium frigora seva pati.
Multis bruma tamen latuit fantastica silvis
    quam silve foliis fecerat umbra recens.
Iam flori puero Iuno dedit ubera roris
    quo primum partus lactet alumpna suos.
Tempus erat Phebi quo mortua semina virtus
    suscitat, e tumulis surgere cuncta iubens.
Quo mundum facies Iovialis leta serenat
    et lacrimas hyemis tergit ab ore suo,

ful influence. Brimming with a storm of blossoms he rained down white privets, and commanded their snows to cover the meadows. Spring, a fuller of a new kind, refurbishing the garments of the fields, set their robes ablaze with glowing purple. He gave back to the trees the tresses which winter had cut short, and so restored the garments which she had snatched away. It was the season when spring graciously diffuses its rich abundance through the fields, while the Dryads applaud; when the infant blossoms, as their strength increases, come forth and draw away from the nurturing soil; when the glowing violet, forsaking earth, its nursery, lifts its fresh face to seek the breeze. It was the season when earth, a stellar crown of roses on her head, seeks to rival heaven with this abundance of stars; when the almond tree, bearing the badges of summer, proclaims his coming, while his blossoms attest the joys of spring; when the budding vine, embracing the breast of its husband elm, thinks of giving birth.

The sun's candle banished the shadows of winter, forcing cruel cold to submit to exile, yet in many groves a phantom frost still lurked, because of the shade created by the trees' new leaves. Now Juno suckled the infant flower with dew, that she, as foster mother, might be the first to nurse the newborns. It was the season when the strength of Phoebus quickens the dead seeds, and bids all things rise from their tombs; when the happy countenance of Jove smiles on the world, and wipes away the wintry tears from her

aeris ut fidei se flos committere possit
  ne florem puerum frigoris urat hyemps.
Quo mundum Phebus hyemis torpore gementem
  visitat et leta luce salutat eum.
Pristina quo senium deponit temporis etas
  et mundus senior incipit esse puer.
Quo noctem Phebus propriis depauperat horis
  pigmeusque dies incipit esse gigas.
Quo parat hospicia Phebo solvendo tributum
  Frixeum gaudens hospite sole pecus.
Quo Philomena sui celebrat solempnia veris,
  odam melliti carminis ore gerens.
In cuius festo sua gutturis organa pulsat,
  ut proprio proprium predicet ore deum.
Quo dulci sonitu citharam mentitur alauda,
  convolat ad superos colloquiturque Iovi.
Splendor lascivos argenteus induit ampnes
  in fluviisque suum iusserat esse diem.
Discursus varii fontis garrire videres,
  prologus in sompnum murmur euntis erat.

28   Descripcio pulcritudinis in versibus plenius edocetur, ut
ibi: "Femineum plene etc." Si plura descripcionum exempla
videre placuerit, recurrite ad utrumque librum Alani vel ad
Matheum Vindosinensem, in libro de artificio versificatorie
discipline qui sic incipit: "Ne meas magnificare viderer fim-
brias," vel ad Bernardum Silvestrem, in libro *De Megacosmo et
Microcosmo,* vel—quod cetera opuscula modernorum multi-
plici colorum sidere prefulgurat—ad opusculum *Architrenii,*

face, that the flower may entrust itself to the protection of the air, and no wintry frost blight the tender blossom; when Phoebus revisits a world lamenting the lassitude of winter, and greets it with his joyous light; when the fresh youth of the season casts off old age, and a world grown old begins a new boyhood; when Phoebus deprives the night of hours that were his, and dwarfish day begins to be a giant; when Phrixus's ram does homage to Phoebus by offering hospitality, rejoicing to have the sun as guest; when Philomela celebrates her rites of spring, giving voice to her honey-sweet lyric song: she plays on her vocal instrument in this ritual way, that her voice may proclaim a divinity of its own; when the lark imitates the lyre with her sweet song, and flies into the heavens to hold converse with Jove. A silvery splendor enhanced the playful streams, and caused the rivers to give off a daylight of their own. One could behold the running chatter of a shimmering fountain, and the murmur of its flow was a prologue to sleep.

The description of beauty is amply illustrated in poetry, 28 as in that passage beginning: "In amplified form, a woman's etc." If it would please you to see many examples of such descriptions, you can turn to either of Alan of Lille's books or to Matthew of Vendôme, in his book on the craft of the art of versifying that begins thus: "Lest I seem to 'enlarge the borders of my garments,'" or to Bernard Silvestris, in his book *On the Megacosmus and the Microcosmus,* or—what outshines all other works of the moderns with the manifold star of its colors—to the work *Architrenius,* which John of

quod edidit eloquentissimus modernorum Iohannes Hauvillensis, de peregrino philosopho quem Architrenium nominat. Nec vos gravet si moremur in exemplis, ideo enim
difficilia proponimus ut obstupeant invidi, ideo multa ne
desperent instruendi. Quod si exempla prosaica videre placuerit, recurrite ad secundam epistolam Sidonii, ubi describit regem Theodoricum quantum ad habitum corporis,
quantum ad mensam, quantum ad ludum et quantum ad
alia. Et notandum quod in nulla materia fieri debet descripcio nisi serviat ad commodum cause et nisi talis sit ut ex ipsa
auditor aliquod eliciat argumentum.

29   Locus oppositorum est observacio duorum modorum
generalium quibus dici potest fere omnis sentencia. Unus
modus est assignare propositum in proposito, alius removere oppositum a proposito; id est, unus modus est affirma-
cionis, alius negacionis. Verbi gracia, dicturi hanc sentenciam "Ego loquor," dicam affirmando, sic: "Ego loquor."
Dicemus eandem sentenciam negando, sic: "Ego non taceo."
Postea coniungamus istas clausulas simul, preponendo nega-
tivam, subiungendo affirmativam, sic: "Ego non loquor, ego
taceo." Nec est curandum si verba exempli, causa evidencio-
ris doctrine, inornata sint et rudia, possunt enim venustari
per artificium sequens. Similiter pro hac sentencia "Ego sum
dives" potest dici "Non sum re tenuis set multis rebus

Hauville, the most eloquent of the moderns, produced, concerning a wandering philosopher whom he calls Architrenius. And it should not oppress you if we linger on examples, for we put forth difficult examples in order that the envious might be confounded, and many examples lest those who are to be instructed lose hope. Wherefore, if it pleases you to see examples in prose, turn to the second letter of Sidonius, where he describes King Theodoric with regard to his bodily condition, his table, his pastimes, and other things. And you should note that a description ought not to be employed in any subject matter unless it works to the advantage of the case and unless it is of such a sort that from it the listener extracts some kind of argument.

Collocation of opposites is the observation of two com- 29 mon methods by which it is possible to express almost any sentiment. One method is to highlight whatever has been proposed in what has been proposed, the other is to remove its opposite from what has been proposed; that is, one is a method of affirmation, the other of negation. For example, if we want to express the sentiment "I speak," I will say it by affirming it, thus: "I speak." We will express the same sentiment by negating it, thus: "I am not silent." Afterward, let us join these sentences together, putting the negative one first and adding the affirmative one, thus: "I do not speak; I am silent." And you ought not to worry if, for the sake of clearer instruction, the words of this example are unadorned and rough, for they can be beautified by means of the artifice that will follow. Similarly, in place of the statement "I am rich" one can say "I am not weak in property but abounding

abundans." Similiter pro hac sentencia "Ego sum vilis vel miser" potest dici "Non michi maiestas superest set honoris egestas."

30   Fit autem locus oppositorum duobus modis: uno modo per ipsas res opposito modo coniunctas, ut in premissis exemplis; alio modo per adiacencia rebus, quando scilicet proprietates enumeramus pro rebus quibus insunt vel ea que rem probant pro ipsa re probanda, sic:

> Non tumet immensi thesauri copia nobis;
> orrea non Cerere, non Bacho dolia turgent;
> non michi pastor oves curat nec mulio mulos;
> immo Ceres refugit, me Bachus destitit et grex
> arripitur nobis, muli peciere repulsam.

Et hoc totum nichil aliud est quam hoc: "Ego sum pauper." Et ibi species probant genus, id est illa que dicuntur in specie probant illa que dicuntur in genere. Nam cum dicitur "Ego sum pauper," in genere dictum est. Cum vero fit mencio defectus pecunie, granorum et pecorum, ostenduntur species probantes illud genus. Hunc modum habemus in secunda epistola Sidonii. Ubi dicturus est de quodam sene quod sanitatem habet iuvenilem, dicit quod non habet defectum senilem. Et hoc dicit hiis verbis: "Non illi cutis contrahitur, non hanelat pulmo, non cor concutitur, non riget lumbus, non spina curvatur set, sanitate preditus iuvenili,

in many things." Similarly, in place of the statement "I am worthless and wretched" one can say "Majesty does not abound in me but want of honor."

Moreover, collocation of opposites is done in two ways: 30 in one way by the same things expressed in opposite fashion having been joined together, as in the previous examples; in another way by what belongs to things, that is, when we list properties in place of the things in which they are present or we list those things that give proof of something in place of the thing to be proven itself, thus:

> Not for us does the abundance of a huge treasure expand; not with Ceres do our granaries, not with Bacchus do our jars swell; not for me does a shepherd watch sheep or a mule-keeper mules; but Ceres flees, Bacchus deserts me, the flock is snatched from us, and the mules have sought to reject us.

And all of this is to say nothing other than this: "I am poor." And here the species prove the genus, that is, those things that are said in terms of a species prove those that are said in terms of a genus. For when one says "I am poor," that is speaking in terms of the genus. But when mention is made of the lack of money, grain, and livestock, the species that prove that genus are shown. We encounter this method in the second letter of Sidonius. When he wants to say that a certain old man has the health of a young man, he says that he does not have the weakness of an old man. And he says this in these words: "His skin does not shrivel, his lungs do not pant, his heart has no spasms, his loins are not hardened, his spine is not curved; on the contrary, he is endowed with the healthiness of a young man, and the only attribute

solam sibi vendicat de senectute reverenciam." Simile habemus in *Anticlaudiano,* in descripcione paradisi terrestris, ubi
convenit Natura cum ceteris virtutibus ad fabricam illius be-
atissimi viri qui dicitur Antirufinus, ubi cum diceret auctor
quod "flores perpetue pulcritudinis gaudent privilegio," sic
usus est loco oppositorum:

> Non ibi nascentis expirat gracia floris
> nascendo moriens; nec enim rosa mane puella
> vespere languet anus set vultu semper eodem
> gaudens, eterni iuvenescit munere veris.
> Hic florem non urit hyemps, non decoquit estas.
> Non ibi bachantis Boree furit ira, nec illic
> fulminat aura Nothi nec spicula grandinis instant.
> Quicquid depascit oculos vel inebriat aures,
> seducit gustus, nares suspendit odore,
> demulcet tactum retinet locus iste locorum.

31   Igitur quando materia tractatur diffuse, aut ipsa diffusa
est in se aut brevis. Si diffusa sit, modis preassignatis iniciari
poterit et consummari. Quid autem si materia brevis sit?
Non dico tantum brevis, immo si brevissima materia fuerit?
Totidem modis et eisdem sumere possumus inicium et continuacionem sicut ante dictum est. Set quoniam predicti
octo modi prolongacionis materie non per se sufficiunt ad
prolongacionem brevissime materie, necesse est aliud assignare artificium quod serviat proposito.

of old age he can claim is reverence." We encounter the like in the *Anticlaudianus*, in the description of the earthly paradise, when Nature comes together with the rest of the virtues to fashion that most blessed man who is called Antirufinus, where the author, when he wanted to say that "the flowers delight in the privilege of perpetual beauty," used collocation of opposites, thus:

> Here the beauty of the newborn flower does not expire, dying even as it blooms; the maiden rose of morning does not become evening's weary old woman. With face ever the same she remains young, rejoicing in the gift of an eternal springtime. Here winter does not blast the flowers, nor summer parch them. The wrath of frenzied Boreas does not rage here, the breath of Notus brings no thunder, nor do shafts of hail harass them. Whatever feasts our sight, intoxicates our ears, seduces our palate, entrances our nostrils with its odor, is smooth to the touch; this place of all places contains it.

Now when a subject matter is treated in a prolix fashion, 31 it is either prolix in itself or brief. If it is prolix, it can be initiated and concluded with the methods previously indicated. However, what if the subject matter is brief? I say not only brief, but what if it is extremely brief? We can fashion the beginning and the continuation in just as many and the very same ways as have been mentioned above. But because the previously mentioned eight methods for extending the subject matter do not by themselves suffice for extending a very brief subject matter, it is necessary to specify another technique that can serve the purpose.

32   Sumatur igitur materia qua nulla potest minor assignari, scilicet talis que clauditur sentencia diccionis unius, ut est sentencia huius verbi "lego." Proposita tam brevi materia, statim ex ipsa elicienda sunt tria, scilicet principium, medium et finis, ut sumatur artificiale principium tum a medio, tum a fine, tum a proverbio tripliciter, tum ab exemplo tripliciter, et ita octo modi artificialiter. Sunt autem hec tria sumenda sic. Duo horum, scilicet principium et medium, in ipso verbo sunt sumenda. Tercium vero, scilicet finis, extrinsecus est sumendum. Set licet sit extrinsecus sumptum, semper tamen comitatur ipsum verbum. Principium vero et medium sic sumenda sunt in ipso verbo. Nam in verbo personali duo semper intelliguntur, scilicet persona verbi et res verbi, ut in hoc verbo "lego" persona verbi est "ego," res verbi "leccio." Sit igitur persona verbi quasi principium, res verbi quasi medium. Tercium, scilicet finis, extrinsece sic sumitur. Qualecumque sit verbum, sive transitivum, sive absolutum, adiciendum est tercium, scilicet tempus vel locus. Hec enim duo omnia consequuntur. Ait enim Boicius: "Tempus et locus sunt accidentales cause rerum." Verbi gracia: "Ego lego in tali tempore vel tali loco." Cum igitur tria elicuerimus ex unico verbo, negociandum est iuxta premissam doctrinam de principio materie, ut octo modos

Let us therefore take up a subject matter than which no ³² smaller may be specified, namely, such a one as is enclosed in the meaning of a single word, as is the meaning of the verb "I read." Once so brief a subject matter has been proposed, immediately three things must be extracted from it, namely, a beginning, middle, and end, so that an artificial beginning may be derived, whether from the middle or from the end or from a proverb in three ways or from an exemplum in three ways, and thus there will be eight methods of beginning artificially. Moreover, these three should be derived as follows. Two of them, namely, the beginning and middle, should be derived from within the verb itself. However, the third, namely, the end, should be derived from outside it; but although it has been derived from outside, nonetheless it always accompanies the verb itself. Now the beginning and the middle should be derived from within the verb itself in this way. Since two things are always understood in a personal verb, namely, the person of the verb and the matter of the verb, as in the verb "I read" the person of the verb is "I" and the matter of the verb is "reading," therefore, let the person of the verb be a kind of beginning and the matter of the verb a kind of middle. The third part, namely, the end, is derived extrinsically in this way. Of whatever sort the verb may be, whether it is transitive or absolute, a third element must be added, namely, time or place, for everything follows upon these two. For Boethius says: "Time and place are the accessory causes of things." For example: "I read at such a time or in such a place." Therefore, once we have extracted these three things from a single verb, we should operate in accordance with the earlier teaching concerning the beginning of the subject matter, so that we may bring forth eight

77

artificialium principiorum eliciamus. Quod alicui videbitur monstruosum et difficile cum in materia proposita sit, nisi unicum verbum profecto aliquid habet et subtilitatis et difficultatis.

33   Dicamus igitur circa hoc aliquid et rudia proponamus exempla, que licet non sint ornata, faciunt tamen ad exemplar doctrine. Verbi gracia, hec est materia nobis proposita: "Lego." In primis iuxta premissam doctrinam eliciamus tria ex hoc verbo, sic: "Ego lego in tali loco." Possumus igitur sumere principium artificiale tum a medio materie, scilicet a leccione, tum a fine, scilicet a loco.

34   A medio sic: "Istarum rerum leccio perutilis est et necessaria, quarum artificio non tantum exprimitur elegancia dicti set industria dicendi." Continuanda est materia iuxta premissam doctrinam per nomina relativa, sic: "Quarum exquisita commoditas meum invitat tam oculum quam animum, quorum uterque sic in ea pascitur ut nec oculus inspeccione nec animus delectacione sacietur."

35   A fine, scilicet a loco, sumitur artificiale principium sic: "Locus iste duplicem continet oportunitatem studii, tum sua iocundus pulcritudine, tum a strepitu semotus populari." Continuandum est iuxta premissam doctrinam, sic: "Cuius oportunitatis occasio, quoniam studencium

kinds of artificial beginnings. This will seem a strange and difficult task to anyone when it has to do with the sort of subject matter that has been proposed, unless indeed the single verb has some element both of subtlety and of difficulty.

Let us therefore say something about this and put forward rough examples, which, though they are not embellished, nonetheless serve as a model of the teaching. For example, this is the subject matter proposed for us: "I read." First of all, in accordance with the above teaching, let us extract the three elements from this verb, thus: "I read in such a place." Then we can derive an artificial beginning either from the middle of the subject matter, namely, from reading, or from the end, namely, from the place. 33

From the middle, thus: "Most useful and necessary is the reading of those things, by whose craft is expressed not only the refinement of what has been said but also the diligence of the speaking." In accordance with the earlier teaching, the subject matter should be continued by means of relative pronouns, thus: "Whose exquisite fitness invites my eye as much as my mind, each of which feeds on them in such a way that neither the eye in its looking nor the mind in its enjoying is satiated." 34

From the end, namely, from a place, an artificial beginning is derived thus: "This place encompasses a double opportunity for study, being, on the one hand, pleasing in its beauty and, on the other hand, far removed from the noise of people." In accordance with the earlier teaching, it should be continued thus: "The occasion of which opportunity, 35

79

concordat ocio, me totum invitat ad studium et in leccioni-
bus studiosis invenit studiosum."

36   A proverbio sumpto iuxta principium materie possumus
sic ordiri: "Cuius animus ad summe promocionis hanelat
fastigium, totus inhiat fructui et frequencie leccionum."
Continuandum est iuxta premissam doctrinam, sic: "Cuius
rei sum testis et argumentum, diligentissimus circa leccionem, ferventissimus ad promocionem."

37   A proverbio sumpto iuxta medium materie sic sumitur
artificiale principium: "Librorum inspeccio cum frequenti
revolucione recta methodus est ad lucrum sciencie, ut satis
innuit *Ethica* Catonis, illa scilicet paterna monicio 'Lege libros.'" Iuxta premissam doctrinam de continuacione materie, sic continuandum est: "Hoc enim familiariori doceor
testimonio. Flores enim in me producit sciencie commoditas, cum aura flaverit gracior, flores fructibus secuturis."

38   A proverbio iuxta finem, sic: "Legentibus et secretis
studencium ociis est accomoda solitudo locorum ab accessi-
bus hominum et strepitu linguarum absoluta." Iuxta premissam doctrinam sic continuandum est: "Argumentum huius
rei ex hoc loco satis elicitur, cuius oportunitas studentes eo
magis occupat, quo minus occupatur."

because it is conducive to the leisure needed by students, attracts me wholly to study and finds me studiously engaged in studious readings."

From a proverb employed with reference to the begin- 36 ning of the subject matter we can begin thus: "He whose spirit pants for the summit of supreme advancement longs with his whole being for the fruit and the abundance of readings." In accordance with the earlier teaching, it should be continued thus: "Of which fact I am myself a witness and further argument, being exceedingly diligent in reading, most burning for advancement."

From a proverb employed with reference to the middle of 37 the subject matter an artificial beginning is derived thus: "The perusal of books with the frequent turning over of their pages is the right way of proceeding toward the wealth of knowledge, as the *Ethics* of Cato sufficiently affirms, namely, that fatherly advice: 'Read books'." In accordance with the earlier teaching about the continuation of the subject matter, it should be continued thus: "Indeed, I am taught this by evidence that is most familiar. For the advantage of knowledge brings forth flowers in me, once its pleasing breeze has blown, with fruits to follow those flowers."

From a proverb related to the end, thus: "For those who 38 are reading and for the secluded leisure times of those who are studying, the solitude of places removed from the traffic of men and from the clamor of tongues is suitable." In accordance with the earlier teaching, it should be continued thus: "The proof of this matter is sufficiently drawn from this place, whose suitability occupies the studious all the more, the less it is occupied."

39 Ab exemplo sumpto iuxta principium sic sumitur artificiale principium: "De militari pendet officio in armorum excercicio dies exspendere et in hiis que miliciam respiciunt vires corporis excercere." Iuxta doctrinam continuacionis sic continuandum est: "Eiusdem racionis sunt opere studencium, quorum sollicitudo librorum inspeccionibus astringit animum et sue milicie totis viribus nititur indulgere."

40 Ab exemplo sumpto iuxta medium, sic: "Armorum frequens excercitacio, collativa probitatis, agilitatem inducit corporis et audaciam cordis." Iuxta premissam doctrinam sic continuandum est: "Eundem in modum assidua librorum revolucio, lucrativa sciencie, pariter inserit periciam et promptitudinem in mente."

41 Ab exemplo sumpto iuxta finem, sic: "Pro qualitate temporum variatur qualitas negociorum." Iuxta premissam doctrinam sic continuandum est: "Eiusdem condicionis est locus, cuius oportunitas requiritur iuxta qualitatem operis, ut ipsius congruitas animum invitet operantis."

42 Sic igitur habemus qualiter negociandum sit circa brevissimam materiam, ut scilicet unum verbum extendatur in tria, scilicet principium, medium et finem, et sic eliciantur octo principia artificialia et adaptentur sue continuaciones.

43 Adiungendum est et aliud generale documentum dictantibus, cum ignorent materiam tractare vel invenire, qualiter

From an exemplum employed with reference to the be- 39
ginning an artificial beginning is derived thus: "Military duty
entails spending one's days in the exercise of arms and exer-
cising the powers of the body in those things that have to do
with the craft of war." In accordance with the teaching
about continuation, it should be continued thus: "Of the
same account are the labors of the studious, whose solici-
tude binds their minds to the perusal of books and strives
with all its might to fulfill its own 'military service.'"

From an exemplum employed with reference to the mid- 40
dle, thus: "The frequent exercise of arms, productive as it is
of valor, induces agility of body and boldness of heart." In
accordance with the earlier teaching, it should be continued
thus: "In the same way, the continual reading over of books,
so profitable in knowledge, implants both skill and promp-
titude in the mind."

From an exemplum employed with reference to the end, 41
thus: "The character of activities varies according to the
character of the season." In accordance with the earlier
teaching, it should be continued thus: "Of the same condition is the place, whose suitability is sought out in accordance with the character of the labor, so that its appropriateness may stimulate the laborer's desire."

Thus we see how one should proceed with regard to a 42
very brief subject matter, namely, that one verb is extended
into three components—beginning, middle, and end—and
thus eight artificial beginnings are elicited and their contin-
uations are adapted to them.

Also worth adding is another general precept for students 43
of composition, when they do not know how to treat or generate subject matter, how the meaning of a single verb ought

sentencia unius verbi debeat eis sufficere. Ut ex modica scintilla possint ignem maximum suscitare, sic igitur ex unico verbo series dictaminis est elicienda. Inveniendum est quoddam proverbium in cuius altera parte ponatur sentencia illius unici verbi quod pro materia assignatur et in reliqua parte ponatur sentencia alterius verbi. Postmodum ex altera parte proverbii fiat narracio et ex reliqua formetur conclusio. Et sic elici poterunt tres clausule dictaminis: prima continens proverbium, secunda narracionem, tercia conclusionem. Set quoniam hec quantitas est exigua, possumus protrahere mediam clausulam, scilicet clausulam narracionis, et eam corroborare tum racionibus, tum racionum confirmacionibus et sic extendere dictamen in infinitum.

44   Documentum istud exemplo rudi declarabitur ut melius intelligatur. Ecce hoc verbum "doceo" proponitur pro materia. Sic enim ex isto verbo series dictaminis elicietur: "Qui scit, docere debet. Ego scio et hac causa doceo." In hac serie premittitur hoc proverbium "Qui scit etc.," in cuius altera parte ponitur verbum "docendi," cum dicitur "docere debet," et in reliqua verbum "sciendi," cum dicitur "Qui scit." Ita quod verbum unde elicitur proverbium semper sit in secunda parte proverbii et verbum unde deducitur narracio in prima parte eiusdem. Postea sequitur narracio, que sumitur ex prima parte proverbii, in qua narracione ponitur verbum

to be enough for them. Just as from a little spark they can kindle a great fire, so then may the sequence of their composition be drawn out from a single verb. A certain proverb should be found, in one part of which is placed the meaning of the single verb that is designated to stand for the subject matter and in another part is placed the meaning of another verb. Afterward, let the statement of facts be made from the one part of the proverb and let the conclusion be fashioned from the other. And in this way the three sentences of a composition may be derived, the first comprising the proverb, the second the statement of facts, and the third the conclusion. But since this quantity of text is meager, we can draw out the middle sentence, that is, the sentence containing the statement of facts, and strengthen it with arguments, on the one hand, and confirmations of arguments, on the other, and so extend the composition indefinitely.

This teaching will be clarified by means of a rough exam- 44 ple so that it may be understood better. Suppose that the verb "I teach" is put forward as the subject matter. Now the sequence of the composition may be derived from this verb, thus: "Whoever knows ought to teach. I know, and for this reason I teach." In this sequence the proverb "Whoever knows etc." is placed first, in one part of which is placed the verb of "teaching," when one says "ought to teach," and in the other the verb of "knowing," when one says "Whoever knows." For this reason, the verb from which the proverb is derived always should be in the second part of the proverb and the verb from which the statement of facts is drawn out should be in the first part of the same proverb. Later follows the statement of facts, which is taken from the first part of the proverb. The verb of "knowing" is placed in this state-

85

"sciendi" cum dicitur "Ego scio." Tercia et ultima est conclusio, que sumitur ex secunda parte proverbii, in qua ponitur verbum "docendi," cum sic subinfertur: "hac causa doceo."

45   Si autem velimus hanc seriem magis extendere, sumamus clausulam narracionis, scilicet hanc "Ego scio," et eam confirmemus racionibus et racionum confirmacionibus. Ecce raciones quibus confirmatur quod "Ego scio": "Quia multo tempore multam adhibui sciencie diligenciam et hoc inter peritos." Ecce confirmacionem racionis: "Revera inter peritos, quoniam inter Parisienses, ubi floret sciencia trivii, inter Tholetanos, ubi sciencia quadruvii, inter Salernitanos, ubi sciencia medicorum, inter Bononienses, ubi sciencia legum et decretorum."

Et sic ex modica maxima crescit aqua.

46   Sic igitur habemus exemplum rude formandi dictaminis: modo redigamus istam ruditatem in formam. Hoc et proverbium "Qui scit, docere debet" verbis elegancioribus sic explicetur: "In cuius animum fontes defluxerunt sciencie potum non neget sicientibus set fontes illi deriventur foras et aquas illas dividat in plateas." Hec narracio "Ego scio" sic ornacius exprimatur: "Hausi quidem fluenta sciencie, quibus humectavi siccitatem animi, quem ardenter sicientem in illis refrigeravi." Ecce racionem huius quod "Ego scio": "Nec mirum si sciencia sua michi communicet archana,

ment of facts when one says "I know." Third and last is the conclusion, which is taken from the second part of the proverb, in which the verb of "teaching" is placed when one adds the following: "for this reason I teach."

Now, if we wish to extend this sequence further, let us take the sentence containing the statement of facts, namely, "I know," and confirm it with arguments and confirmations of arguments. Here are some arguments that can be used to confirm that "I know": "Because for a considerable time I have diligently sought knowledge and done so among experts." Here is a confirmation of the argument: "Truly among experts, because I have studied at Paris, where knowledge of the trivium flourishes; at Toledo, where knowledge of the quadrivium flourishes; at Salerno, where knowledge of physicians flourishes; and at Bologna, where knowledge of the laws and decretals flourishes." 45

And thus much water rises where there was little.

So now that we have a rough example of the composition to be fashioned, let us render this roughness into a shape. The proverb "Whoever knows ought to teach" may be extended by means of more refined words, thus: "The one into whose mind the streams of knowledge have flowed should not refuse a drink to those who thirst, but those streams should be dispersed abroad and he should distribute those waters at the street corners." The statement of facts "I know" may be expressed more ornately, thus: "I have indeed drawn up the floods of knowledge, with which I have watered the dryness of my mind, which I have refreshed with them when it was burning with thirst." Here is an elaborated argument for "I know": "Nor is it strange if knowledge 46

cuius familiaritatem tam longi temporis obsequio promerui, cum crebris insultibus quadam violencia mentis extorsi. In laribus enim suorum conversatus familiarium continuavi vicennium, ubi me totum exuxit studium, lugubracione noctium diurnis continuata laboribus, et invenit me semper labor iste ferventem, raro respirantem, nunquam desidie vacantem. Precipuorum inhiabam discipline, locis eciam convenientibus et unicuique sciencie deputatis. Militabam enim Parisius in sciencia trivialium, Tholeti contemplator quadrivialium et Salerni rimabar raciones phisicalium, Bononie tandem instructus sciencia legum et decretorum. Ad hos autem fontes venit meus animus sitim suam extinguere, qui licet dulcescant aliunde, ex predictis fontibus dulciores bibuntur aque." Ecce conclusionem, scilicet hanc "hac causa doceo": "Hoc igitur quod habeo, distribuo et aquas quas undique collegi propino, pincerna diligens, animo sicienti."

47   Ecce habemus in exemplo predicto qualiter ex brevitate prolixitas generetur. Ibidem eciam videre possumus qualiter sentencia rudis quibusdam ornatibus informetur et qualiter sentencia facilis verborum difficultatibus aggravatur. Artem autem exornandi rudia et aggravandi facilia sequencia declarabunt.

reveals to me its secrets, she whose intimate acquaintance I have earned with prolonged deference and extorted with frequent assaults and a kind of intellectual violence. For I put together a span of twenty years dwelling in the haunts of her intimates, where study consumed me entirely and the candlelit toil of the nights continued in daytime labors, and this labor always found me burning, seldom catching my breath, never unoccupied in idleness. I attended eagerly to the instruction of distinguished experts and did so in the appropriate places that were allotted to a particular branch of knowledge. For I served at Paris in the science of the trivial arts, at Toledo I was a contemplator of the quadrivial, at Salerno I investigated the principles of medicine, and at Bologna, finally, I was taught the science of the laws and decretals. My mind came to quench its thirst from these springs, which, though they derive their sweetness from different places, nonetheless offer sweet waters indeed for the drinking." Observe the conclusion, namely, "for this reason I teach": "Therefore, this which I have I distribute and the waters that I have gathered from all quarters I—an attentive cupbearer—give the thirsty mind to drink."

Notice that in the above example we have the manner in [47] which prolixity is created from brevity. There we also can see how a rough sentiment can be made shapely with certain embellishments and how a facile sentiment is given weight by the difficulties of its words. However, subsequent chapters will make plain the art of embellishing what is rough and giving weight to what is facile.

De artificio epistolas componendi.

48 Set quoniam epistolas componentibus necessaria est ars prolongandi materiam, subiungamus et aliud artificium epistolis speciale. Quod artificium diligenter intuenti a premisso prolongacionis artificio non ex toto differre nec ex toto videbitur convenire. Est autem hoc artificium. In primis tria consideremus: qualitatem materie, qualitatem personarum, causam que excitat ad scribendum. Deinde aut iuxta principium, aut iuxta medium invenire debemus proverbium conveniens vel exemplum, quod est ceteris epistole partibus preponendum. Tale enim debet esse proverbium vel exemplum in quo duo verba vel unum verbum et unum participium situetur. Amplius, ex primo verbo proverbii vel exempli debet inveniri narracio, que probanda est causis, probabilibus racionibus et racionum effectibus et quibuscumque coniecturalibus argumentis que faciunt ad commodum cause. Ex quibus autem locis coniecturalia sumuntur argumenta posterius ostendetur, ubi de attributis persone et negocio est loquendum.

49 In narracione tamen is ordo servetur, ut scilicet sicut res se habent in maiori generalitate sic sibi vendicent prioritatem in ordine, ut scilicet magis generalia precedant et minus generalia sequantur. Consimiliter post proverbium vel exemplum, specialis sentencia declarativa proverbii vel exempli est deflectenda, que et serviat ad propositum et

CHAPTER 3

On the technique of composing letters.

But because an art of extending the subject matter is needed 48
by those who are composing letters, let us append still another technique that is particular to letters. To one paying
close attention, this technique will seem neither to differ
entirely from the previous technique for amplifying nor to
agree entirely with it. Here is the technique. First, let us pay
close attention to three things: the nature of the subject
matter, the nature of the persons involved, and the reason
that moves one to write. Next, with reference either to the
beginning or to the middle, we should find an appropriate
proverb or exemplum, which should be put before the other
parts of the letter. This proverb or exemplum ought to be
the sort in which two verbs are to be found, or one verb and
one participle. Furthermore, from the first verb of the proverb or exemplum one should generate the statement of
facts, which should be made credible by means of reasons,
probable arguments and effects of arguments, and certain
conjectural arguments that work to the advantage of the
case. The topics from which conjectural arguments are
taken will be shown later, when we speak about the attributes of persons and actions.

In the statement of facts, moreover, let this hierarchy be 49
observed, namely, that insofar as topics partake of greater
generality they should claim for themselves priority in order, so that the more general come first and the less general
follow. Similarly, after the proverb or exemplum, a special
sentiment that clarifies the proverb or exemplum also
should be deployed, so that it may both serve what has been

preparatoria sit ad negocium. Postea ex sentencia secundi verbi vel participii inveniri debet peticio et conclusio.

50 Et sic habentur quattuor partes epistole, scilicet exordium, id est proverbium vel exemplum, narracio, peticio et conclusio, quibus, si placuerit, poterimus salutacionem anteferre, in qua captatur benivolencia. Que salutacio quintam partem epistole perficit. Modernis tamen placet salutacioni supersedere et in dorso littere eam scribere. Nec tamen semper opus est hiis quinque partibus.

51 Debemus eciam videre quod per totam epistolam sit emptimematum plenitudo succincta et sentenciosa brevitas clausularum et, quantum poterimus, servare sentencie gravitatem. Gravis enim sentencia est que de facili moveat auditorem. Ad hoc autem ut sentencia sit gravis, id est motiva, invenienda est semper talis sentencia que convenienter respondeat materie qualitati. Ut si materia sit iocosa, inveniamus sentencias iocosas, que sua iocunditate auditorem moveant ad risum; si seriosa, inveniamus sentencias seriosas, que sua seriositate auditorem moveant ad devocionem vel, si oporteat, ad fletum. Et faciant voces ad quod de iure tenentur. Istud docet Oracius, in antiqua *Poetria,* sic:

> Non satis est pulcra esse poemata; dulcia sunto,
> et quocumque velint animum auditoris agunto.
> Ut ridentibus arrident, ita flentibus afflent

set forth already and prepare the way for the theme. Afterward, the request and conclusion should be generated from the meaning of the second verb or participle of the proverb or exemplum.

And thus the four parts of a letter are obtained—the exordium, that is, the proverb or exemplum; the statement of facts; the request; and the conclusion—before which, if it pleases, we may put the greeting, in which goodwill is secured. This greeting constitutes a fifth part of a letter, although our contemporaries prefer to omit the greeting from the body of the letter and write it on the back of the letter. Moreover, there is not always need for all five of these parts. 50

Also, we ought to see to it that throughout the entire letter there be concise abundance of enthymemes and pithy brevity of sentences, and we ought to preserve the weightiness of the sentiment as much as possible. Now a weighty sentiment is one that readily moves anyone who hears it. To insure that the sentiment is weighty, that is, persuasive, one always should find the sort of sentiment that corresponds fittingly to the nature of the subject matter. So, if the subject matter is humorous, we should find humorous sentiments, which with their humorousness may move the hearer to laughter; if it is serious, let us find serious sentiments, which with their seriousness may move the hearer to pious devotion or, if need be, to weeping. And let the words do what they are by right obliged to do. Horace teaches this in the old *Poetics,* thus: 51

> Not enough is it for poems to have beauty: they must
> have charm, and lead the hearer's soul where they will.
> As men's faces smile on those who smile, so they weep

humani vultus: si vis me flere, dolendum est
primum ipsi tibi: tunc tua me infortunia ledent.

52 Et quomodo carmina dictantis sua dulcedine moveant
auditorem idem Oracius in eodem subsequenter ostendit,
scilicet per attribucionem proprietatum unicuique rei de
qua nitimur aliquid persuadere. Quas proprietates Oracius
"colores operum" nominat, eo quod quodlibet opus sua gravitate purpurant et colorant. Set Tullius eas "attributa personis et negociis" esse dicit, eo quod personis et negociis sua
conveniencia tribuunt manifeste, de quibus seorsum plenius
est dicendum. Unde dicit Oracius:

Descriptas servare vices operumque colores
cur ego si nequeo ignoroque poeta salutor?

Sentencia est "Quare usurparem michi nomen poete si
ignorem colores operum?" (id est proprietates rerum quas
tractare volo), quasi diceret "Non sum dignus salutari ut
poeta." In cuius rei evidenciam Oracius quasi per totum librum suum invitat ad observacionem proprietatum.

53 Et quia, iuxta Aristotilem in sua *Poetria,* "omnis oracio
poetica in laude consistit et vituperio" et laus et vituperium
maxime concernunt personas hominum, ideo Oracius in
libro suo solum exprimit proprietates hominum. Set quia
proprietates hominum maxime inveniuntur ab illo attributo
quod dicitur natura, ideo Oracius precipue ostendit

at those who weep. If you would have me weep, you must first feel grief yourself: then will your misfortunes hurt me.

And the same Horace, in the same work, later shows how 52 the songs of a writer move the hearer with their sweetness, namely, by assigning the characteristics proper to each thing about which we strive to speak persuasively. Horace calls these characteristics "colors of poetic works," because with their weightiness they decorate and color any work whatsoever. But Cicero says that they are "attributes of persons and actions," because they openly assign to persons and actions their properties, concerning which we must speak in more detail in a separate chapter. For this reason Horace says:

If I fail to keep and do not understand these well-marked shifts and colors of poetic works, why am I hailed as poet?

The meaning is "Why should I usurp for myself the name of poet if I do not know the colors of poetic works?" (that is, the characteristics of the things that I wish to treat), as if to say "I am not worthy to be hailed as poet." In proof of which point, more or less throughout his book, Horace calls for the observation of characteristics.

And because, according to Aristotle in his *Poetics,* "every 53 poetic utterance rests on praise and blame," and because praise and blame mostly concern the characters of men, therefore in his book Horace portrays only the characteristics of men. But because the characteristics of men are discovered mostly from the attribute that is called nature, therefore Horace especially showed the characteristics that

proprietates que a natura sumuntur. Et quoniam proprietates a natura sumpte, iuxta Tullium, tripartite dividuntur, scilicet in illa que sumuntur a corpore et in illa que ab anima et in illa que ab extrinsecis, que vero corpori et anime insunt nociora sunt sensui, ideo exprimit Oracius proprietates que ab extrinsecis sumuntur. Considerantur hee a sex locis, scilicet a condicione, ut si est dominus vel servus; ab etate, ut iuvenis an senex; a sexu, ut vir vel mulier (et similiter ibi consideretur condicio); ab officio, id est statu, ut miles an mercator; a gente, ut Anglicus an Thetonicus; a patria, ut Romanus an Atheniensis.

54   Has proprietates ita ponit Oracius:

> Intererit multum Davusve loquatur an heros,
> maturusve senex an adhuc florente iuventa
> fervidus, an matrona potens an sedula nutrix,
> mercatorve vagus cultorve virentis agelli,
> Colcus an Assirus, Thebis nutritus an Argis.

Nam ubi dicit "Davus an heros," nominatur locus a condicione; ubi dicit "Maturusve senex an adhuc florente iuventa fervidus," nominatur locus ab etate; ubi dicit "an matrona potens an sedula nutrix," locus a sexu; ubi dicit "Mercatorve vagus cultorve virentis agelli," locus ab officio; ubi dicit "Colcus an Assirus," locus a nacione; ubi dicit "Thebis nutritus an Argis," locus a patria.

are taken from nature. The characteristics taken from nature, according to Cicero, are divided in three, namely, into those things that are taken from the body, those that are from the mind, and those that are from external circumstances. However, those that belong to the body and to the mind are better known to our understanding, and for that reason Horace portrays the characteristics that are taken from external circumstances. These are examined from six "places" or topics, namely, from social condition, as whether one is master or slave; from age, as whether a youth or an old man; from sex, as whether a man or a woman (and likewise where social condition is examined); from profession, that is, civil rank, as whether a soldier or a merchant; from race, as whether English or German; and from fatherland, as whether Roman or Athenian.

Horace lists these characteristics thus: 54

> Vast difference will it make, whether Davus or a hero speaks, a ripe old man or one still in the flower and fervor of youth, a dame of rank or a bustling nurse, a roaming trader or the tiller of a verdant field, a Colchian or an Assyrian, one bred at Thebes or at Argos.

For when he says "Davus or a hero," he cites the topic from social condition; when he says "a ripe old man or one still in the flower and fervor of youth," he cites the topic from age; when he says "a dame of rank or a bustling nurse," the topic from sex; when he says "a roaming trader or the tiller of a verdant field," the topic from profession; when he says "a Colchian or an Assyrian," the topic from race; and when he says "one bred at Thebes or at Argos," the topic from fatherland.

55 Amplius, quoniam inter has proprietates magis concernit
poetam distinguere inter proprietates annorum, ideo ostendit proprietates cuiuslibet etatis, dicens sic:

Etatis cuiusque notandi sunt tibi mores,
mobilibusque decor naturis dandus et annis.

Et quare debet talis fieri proprietatum distinccio idem Oracius paulo post subdit, dicens:

Ne forte seniles
mandentur iuveni partes pueroque viriles,
semper in adiunctis evoque morabimur aptis.

56 Et quia in epistolis semper oportet rebus et personis de-
bitas assignare proprietates, sciendum est quod quelibet
persona ab illo debet intitulari epiteto in quo maiorem fame
sortitur evidenciam et quod in eo pre ceteris dominatur,
iuxta illud Oracii:

Scriptor honoratum si forte reponis Achillem,
impiger, iracundus, inexorabilis, acer.
Sit Medea ferox invictaque, flebilis Yno,
perfidus Ixion, Yo vaga, tristis Horestes.

57 Consimiliter, in commendacione alicuius persone vel vituperio oportet multos proprietatum assignare articulos.
Non enim potest aliqua persona uno vel duobus vel paucis
sufficienter intitulari epitetis. Quia sicut parum prodest
rosam habere singularem, pluribus spinis suffocatam, et
unicam margaritam, pluribus oppressam paludibus, sic non

Moreover, since among these characteristics the poet is 55
especially concerned to distinguish among the characteristics of different stages of life, therefore he displays the characteristics of each age, speaking thus:

> You must note the manners of each age, and give a befitting tone to shifting natures and their years.

And a little later the same Horace adds the reason why such discrimination among characteristics should be made, saying:

> So, lest haply we assign a youth the part of old age, or a boy that of manhood, we shall ever linger over traits that are joined and fitted to the age.

And because in letters it is always fitting to assign the 56
proper characteristics to things and persons, one should know that every sort of person ought to be named by that epithet by virtue of which he is allotted the greatest proof of his reputation and that which dominates in him beyond all others, according to this statement of Horace:

> Writer, if you happen to bring back honored Achilles, let him be impatient, passionate, ruthless, fierce. Let Medea be fierce and unyielding, Ino tearful, Ixion forsworn, Io a wanderer, Orestes sorrowful.

Similarly, in commending or censuring any person it is fit- 57
ting to assign many subsets of characteristics, for no one is sufficiently described by one or two or even just a few epithets. For just as it is of little use to have a single rose that is choked by thorns or a singular pearl that is hidden in many a marsh, so it is not enough to proclaim a person's worth by

sufficit ad preconium unam vel paucas virtutes alicui persone assignari, cum forsan invideat uberior affluencia viciorum. Igitur ad comprobacionem multis debet intitulari epitetis, ut ubi

non prosunt singula, multa iuvent.

58   Amplius, sunt quedam epiteta que circa quasdam personas debent restringi, sunt et alia que circa plerasque debent
ampliari, sunt eciam aliqua que omnibus personis possunt
communiter assignari. Verbi gracia, in ecclesiastico pastore
fidei constancia, virtutis appetitus, illibata religio et blandimentum pietatis debent ampliari, iusticia siquidem debet
constringi, ne ex rigore iusticie ecclesiasticus videatur in ti-
rannidem emigrare. Eius enim epitetum, id est proprium,
est

parcere subiectis et castigare superbos.

Econverso, in imperatore, rege vel principe rigor iusticie as-
signandus est in augmento, tepor siquidem pietatis aliquan-
tulum in detrimento. Similiter et cetere proprietates circa
diversas personas diverso modo debent observari, scilicet ut

Singula queque locum teneant sortita decenter.

59   Set et quelibet persona sic describi debet ut ex descripcione maximum pretendatur fidei nutrimentum, ut de ea
vera vel verisimilia dicantur, iuxta illud Oracii:

assigning a single or merely a few virtues, when perhaps a host of vices may rival the scanty praise thus given. Therefore one who is praised ought to be commended with many epithets, so that where

things avail not singly, they help when they are many.

Furthermore, some epithets ought to be restricted to 58 certain types of persons, some ought to be attributed to a fair number of persons, and others ought to be attributed to all persons generally. For example, in describing the pastor of a church, one ought to stress his steadfast faith, his longing for virtue, his religious devotion, his sweet words of compassion, but his justice ought not to be enlarged upon, since too much emphasis on the churchman's rigorous justice might make him appear a tyrant. His epithet—that is, the one proper to him—is

to spare the humbled, and to punish the proud.

On the other hand, rigorous justice ought to be ascribed amply to an emperor, a king, or a prince, since the warmth of compassion would be a little to his disadvantage. Similarly, other qualities ought to be assigned in a variety of ways to other persons, so that

Each style keep the place becomingly allotted it.

And a person should be described in such a way that the 59 greatest attention is paid to the credibility of the description, so that what is said about the person either is true or seems to be true, in agreement with Horace's advice:

Aut famam sequere aut sibi conveniencia finge.

Fingere enim et invenire poterimus quicquid placuerit dummodo servetur materie uniformitas et simplicitas. Simplex materia est cui non implicatur aliquod vicium, ut interpretetur "simplex" quasi "sine plica," scilicet viciorum. Istud patet per Oracium, sic:

Denique sit quidvis, simplex dumtaxat et unum.

60   Invenire autem materiam possumus hac cautela. Excogitandum est iuxta qualitatem materie vel causam que excitat ad scribendum unum proverbium vel exemplum, quod toti materie anteponendum est sub ornata quadam serie verborum. Deinde inveniendum est causas, raciones, evidencias et argumenta ad commodum nostre cause, id est ad probacionem nostre intencionis, et talia inserere debemus, semper preponendo generaliora, ut ante dictum est. Est enim invencio probabilium argumentorum excogitacio ad commodum nostre cause, id est ad persuadendum illud quod intendimus. Est et "argumentum racio prestans probacionem, qua colligitur unum per aliud," ut ait Quintilianus, *De institucione oratoria.*

61   Ut autem hec doctrina quam premisimus evidencia lucescat exempli, hec materia nobis in medium veniat pro exemplo. Quidam idiota, cum ad nostrum veniret hospicium,

Either follow tradition or invent what is self-consistent.

For we can make up and invent whatever we please so long as the consistency and simplicity of the subject matter is preserved. A simple subject matter is one into which no vice is enfolded, so that "simple" may be understood etymologically as "without fold," namely without vices. This is evident in Horace, thus:

In short, be the work whatever it is, let it at least be simple and uniform.

Now we can generate the subject matter, with this pre- 60 caution. In accordance with the nature of the subject matter or the reason that drives us to write, we should think up a proverb or exemplum, which should be placed at the very head of the subject matter in a certain artful sequence of words. Then we should find causes, reasons, demonstrations, and arguments for the advantage of our case, that is, in support of our purpose, and we should incorporate these always by putting the more general first, as was said before. For invention is the devising of probable arguments for the advantage of our case, that is, for making persuasive what we mean to convey. And "an argument is a process of reasoning which provides proof and enables one thing to be inferred from another," as Quintilian says in *The Training of an Orator.*

But so that the teaching that we have already provided 61 may be illuminated by the clarity of an example, let the following subject matter take center stage by way of example. A certain ignoramus, when he had come to our hostel for

causa commorandi, audita quorundam sociorum fama laudabili, videns quod nemo sibi titulum laudis imposuit, tribus
in rebus se mendaciter pretulit universis, scilicet in redditi-
bus prediorum, in intellectu legum et in practica causarum.
Cum tamen ex toto sue pompositati veritas contradixit, tandem agnita veritate, cum pudore ab hospicio recessit. Nos
igitur rogati a consociis super hac materia epistolam ei mit-
tere, quam de facili non intelligeret nisi doctrina alterius sa-
pientis, ut sic sua pateret stoliditas, scripsimus invectivum.
Ex causa que excitat ad scribendum sive ex ipso negocio istud sumpsimus exemplum, imitando quod premisimus artificium: "Picta parietis superficies, cum ex longinquitate
temporis pictura senuerit, subiecte materie predicat vilita-
tem." Ex hoc exemplo, premissa salutacione, epistola floridis colorum tunicis adornata sequitur in hec verba:

62   "A. de B. salutacionem qua meruit salutari. Deaurati parietis ypocrisim, sue deauracionis senescente superbia, fidelis antifrasis, mencientis superbie communis expositor, fidelitatis sue mendacio exponit fideliter menciendo. Eodem
exposicionis officio, lingue superbientis yperbole superlativi
gradus mentita superbiam positivi palliando pauperiem,
antifrasice exposicionis fideli miraculo, in superlativum
degenerat positivans. Vere quam pecuniosa te reddituum
multitudo ditaverat, quam legum te sciencia precellens
instruxerat, quam subtilis causarum practica te cunctis

the purpose of lodging there, having heard about the praise-worthy reputation of certain of our companions and seeing that no one applied the title of praise to him, falsely set himself above everyone else in three things, namely, the incomes from his properties, his understanding of the laws, and his practice of legal cases. However, since truth utterly contradicted his boastful display, once the truth had been recognized, he left the hostel in shame. We, however, asked by our companions to send him a letter regarding this matter that he would not understand readily unless instructed by some other knowledgeable person, so that in this way his dullness would be clear, wrote an invective. From the reason that drove us to write or from the business itself we took this exemplum, by way of imitating the technique that we provided earlier: "The painted surface of a wall, when the picture ages with the passing of time, proclaims the baseness of the material that lies beneath it." From this exemplum, after the greeting has been put in front, there follows a letter adorned with the flowery garments of rhetorical colors, in these words:

"To A. of B. the greeting with which he deserved to be 62 greeted. The hypocrisy of a gilded wall, as the pride of its gilding ages, honest irony, the common exposer of lying pride, through the lie of its honesty exposes by lying honestly. By the same service of exposure, the lying hyperbole of a tongue that takes pride in a pride of the superlative degree by disguising a poverty of the positive degree, by the true marvel of ironic exposure, as it becomes positive degenerates superlatively. Truly, how the wealthy abundance of your incomes had endowed you, how exceptional knowledge of the laws had instructed you, how subtle practice of legal

pretulerat fame communis yronia proprie publicacionis auctentico dictamine loquitur deridendo. Nonne te sic erigendo deicis? Nonne sic sapiendo desipis? Nonne sic eloquendo mutescis? Nonne dictat vulgus:

Vincat opus verbum; minuit iactancia famam?

Quapropter, proscripta qualibet deaurate pompositatis ypocrisi, insolentis lingue succurras excessui, ne audientis fama populi fidem dederit antifrasice exposicioni."

63   In hac epistola videtur artificialis materie prosecucio, que est nebulosa fumositas in principio, exposicionis luce per sequentes clausulas lucide declarata. Artificialiter enim dictantes, ut sepe diximus, in principio sue materie preponunt conveniens proverbium vel exemplum continens obscure quod principaliter est intentum. Et quia latet intencio sub quadam obscuritate, debent sequentes clausule tales esse que patula sue lucis exposicione obscuritatis nebulam valeant lucidare, iuxta illud Oracii, quod dicit de commendacione Homeri, sic:

Non fumum ex fulgore, set ex fumo dare lucem
cogitat ut speciosa dehinc miracula promat,
Antifaten Scillamque et cum Ciclope Caribdim.

Sentencia est: Homerus non cogitat dare fulgidum principium et obscuram continuacionem in libro suo quem facit

cases had put you ahead of all others—these the ironic inversion of common rumor declares in the ludicrous, self-authored text of its very proclamation. Don't you cast yourself down by raising yourself up in this way? Don't you make yourself foolish by being wise in this way? Don't you grow dumb by speaking in this way? Don't the people proclaim:

Let the deed overcome the word; boasting lessens renown?

Wherefore, once you have banned any hypocrisy of gilded pomposity whatsoever, you should hasten to mend the transgression of an arrogant tongue, lest the gossip of the listening people lend credence to an ironic exposure."

In this letter one sees the artful elaboration of the subject 63 matter, which is a cloudy vapor in the beginning, clearly made plain by the light of exposition through the sentences that follow. For those who are composing artificially, as we have said often, place at the beginning of their subject matter an appropriate proverb or exemplum containing obscurely what is chiefly intended. And because the purpose lies hidden beneath a certain obscurity, the sentences that follow should be of such sort as can elucidate the mist of obscurity with the open exposition of their light, according to what Horace says in praise of Homer, thus:

Not smoke after flame does he plan to give, but after smoke the light, that then he may set forth striking and wondrous tales—Antiphates, Scylla, Charybdis, and the Cyclops.

The meaning is: Homer does not intend to provide a flashing beginning and an obscure continuation in his book that

de reditu Ulixis a Troia set ex fumido et obscuro principio cogitat dare lucidam continuacionem. Consimiliter, in hac epistola hoc exemplum "Deaurati etc." est quasi genus ad clausulas sequentes, continens earum mentem obscure, et ideo ceteris difficilior obscuriorque ordinatur, in quo ponitur unum verbum ("exponit") et unum participium ("deaurati"). Et quia participium in illo exemplo ponitur ante verbum, ex sentencia participii per similitudinem invenitur narracio, scilicet "Eodem exposicionis etc." Deinde sequitur racio narracionis, sic: "Vere quam etc." Deinde racionis confirmacio, sic: "Nonne te sic etc." Deinde sequitur peticio: "Quapropter etc.," que invenitur ex secundo verbo exempli, scilicet ex hoc verbo "exponit." Deinde conclusio, sic: "ne audientis etc." Et est pars peticionis et ex eodem verbo invenitur. Colores autem quibus exornatur epistola posterius ostendemus.

64   Set quoniam in epistola premissa verba nimium videntur phalerata, ponemus et aliam in verbis magis planam set in sentencia graviorem, cuius hec est materia. Quidam Arthurus nomine, cum in suum cognatum, regem Anglie, insidias et hostiles nequicias machinari presumpserit, incarceratus tandem per eundem regem, hanc epistolam, in qua movet regem ad misericordiam, destinavit:

65   "Reverendo domino suo Iohanni, Dei gracia regi Anglie, suus captivus tamen Arthurus, a tot nepotis miseriis

he composed about the return of Ulysses from Troy, but from a misty and obscure beginning he intends to provide a clear continuation. Similarly, in this letter the exemplum, "The hypocrisy of a gilded etc.," is a kind of origin for the sentences that follow, containing their intention obscurely, and therefore it is arranged to be more difficult and more obscure than the others. In it is placed one verb ("exposes") and one participle ("gilded"). And because the participle in this exemplum is placed before the verb, the statement of facts is generated from the meaning of the participle through a comparison, namely, "By the same service of exposure etc." Then follows the argument of the statement of facts, thus: "Truly, how etc." Then the confirmation of the argument, thus: "Don't you in this way etc." Then follows the request, "Wherefore etc.," which is derived from the second verb of the exemplum, namely, from the verb "exposes." Then the conclusion, thus: "lest of the listening etc." And this is a part of the petition and is derived from the same verb. However, we will show later the rhetorical colors with which a letter is embellished.

But because in the previous letter the words seem overly 64 embellished, we will supply still another letter, plainer in words but weightier in meaning, whose subject matter is this. A certain Arthur by name, who had presumed to plot an ambush and hostile villainies against his kinsman the king of England, when he had been jailed at last by the same king, dispatched this letter, in which he seeks to move the king to mercy:

"To John, his master most reverend, king by God's grace 65 of England, Arthur, albeit his captive, asks that you take pity on your nephew's abundant misfortunes. Royal wrath

colligere pietatem. Iras decet regias clemencia temperari punitque citra merita misericordia principalis. Merui, fateor, merui penam quam pacior. Quippe post dies patris mei, post vitam avi, post tempora patruorum in vobis tantum eram cognacionis et amicicie fiduciam habiturus. Set in tantum amicum impudenter presumpsi furores bellicos et hostiles insidias machinari, hostili quidem deceptus concilio. Non potui patrui, non potui patris, non potui vel proprii sanguinis recordari. Nunc autem celesti misericordie grates refero, que michi dedit et quid sim agnoscere et decepta stulticia penitere. Sic reddat michi Deus amiciciam vestram vel saltem vincula leniora. Nollem me penitus immunem hunc carcerem non sensisse, qui me patruo reddidit et a seductore gallico liberavit. Novit enim vestra discrecio quas penas hactenus sustinui; merui quidem, set parcite confitenti. Si pena michi transacta nondum vobis videatur meritis meis sufficiens et equalis, inspicite quid nepoti feceritis, quid captivo possitis. Quod si nec cognacio nec pene compassio, vestra saltem moveat gracia pietatem. Vere generose menti sufficit ad misericordiam potencia vindicandi."

66   Ecce in hac epistola sentencie gravitas iuxta quod exigit materie qualitas observatur. Invenitur autem hec gravitas ex huiusmodi locis quibus ad misericordiam moveatur animus auditoris.

67   Sic ergo tradita est sufficiens doctrina materiam prolongandi et epistolas artificialiter componendi.

should be tempered by clemency, and princely mercy punishes less precisely. I have earned, I confess, I have earned the penalty that I suffer. Indeed, after the days of my father, after the life of my grandfather, after the vicissitudes of my uncles, in you only would I have had the assurance of kinship and friendship. But against so great a friend I shamelessly presumed to plot warlike follies and insidious altercations, deceived to be sure by hostile suggestion. Not my uncle, not my father, not my own blood was I competent to remember. But now I give thanks to the mercy of heaven, which has granted me both to recognize what I am and to repent my deluded stupidity. So may God restore me to your friendship or at least provide me milder imprisonment. I would not wish that I, completely exempt, had not tasted this prison, which has brought me back to my uncle and freed me from the Gallic seducer. Your discretion knows what punishments I have suffered already: I have deserved them, to be sure, but spare the penitent who confesses. If you think the penalty inflicted on me not yet equal to my meriting nor sufficient, consider how you have treated a nephew, how you have handled a captive. But if neither kinship can do so nor compassion for suffering, at least let your graciousness engender some pity. To a mind truly noble the power of punishing suffices for mercy."

Observe in this letter that the weightiness of the sentiment is maintained in accordance with what the nature of the subject matter requires. Moreover, this weightiness is generated from the sorts of commonplaces by which the hearer's spirit may be moved to mercy. 66

Thus, sufficient instruction has been provided in extending the subject matter and composing letters artfully. 67

Capitulum 4

De septem modis abbreviandi materiam

Ad abbreviacionem materie quedam sunt vitanda, quedam observanda. Vitanda sunt omnia illa que prolixitatem inducunt, scilicet interpretaciones, circumlocuciones, comparaciones et cetere que premisse sunt in ultimo capitulo. Circumscriptis igitur omnibus illis, circa residuum, id est circa purum corpus materie, ita negociandum est. Dicenda sunt illa sola in quibus solis consistit vis materie et sine quibus plena sentencia haberi non potest.

2   Sunt autem dicenda per septem modos. Primus est emphasis, secundus articulus, tercius ablativus absolutus, quartus intellectus unius in alio, quintus dissolutum, sextus repeticionis vitacio, septimus sentencia multarum clausularum in una. Unde versus:

> Emphasis, articulus, casus sine remige liber,
> unius in reliquo nota callida, vincula dempta,

Chapter 4

On the seven ways of shortening the subject matter

In shortening the subject matter, certain things are to be avoided and certain things attended to. To be avoided are all those things that introduce prolixity, namely, interpretations, circumlocutions, comparisons and the others that have been set forth already in the last chapter. Having set aside all of these, therefore, one should proceed as follows concerning what is left, that is, concerning the essential body of the subject matter. Only those things should be said in which the heart of the subject matter remains even when they alone are present and without which its full meaning cannot be grasped.

These things, moreover, should be said by means of seven   2
methods. The first is emphasis, the second parataxis, the third ablative absolute, the fourth understanding one thing in another, the fifth asyndeton, the sixth avoidance of repetition, the seventh the meaning of many clauses contained in one. Hence the verses:

> Emphasis, parataxis, a case ungoverned, deft implica-
> tion of one thing in the rest, omission of conjunctions,

clausarum sensus multarum clausus in una,
septimus eiusdem verbi repeticio nulla.

3 Emphasis fit duobus modis: uno modo quando, locuturi
de re, loquimur de eius proprietate; alio modo quando rem
appellamus nomine sue proprietatis. Locuturi de re, loquimur de eius proprietate, ut dicturi de Scippione quod ipse
per prudenciam suam destruxit Cartaginem, dicimus "Scip-
pionis prudencia Cartaginem destruxit," id est Scippio per
suam prudenciam. Similiter dicitur: "Clemencia vestra sub-
veniat mee necessitati," id est "Vos per clemenciam vestram
subvenite michi habenti necessitatem." Rem appellamus
nomine sue proprietatis, ut hic: "Medea est ipsum scelus," id
est ita intense scelerosa quod nichil in ea invenitur preter
scelus. Tunc enim maxime utimur emphasi quando vel ad
laudem vel ad opprobrium innitimur personarum. Et convenit cum colore qui dicitur circuicio.

4 Articulus est quando dicciones in serie oracionis diversa
significantes sine coniunccione media proferuntur, ut hic:
"Ille, multis comitatus, hunc solum, inermem invasit, invenit, interfecit." Item et hic: "Acrimonia, voce, vultu adversarios terruisti."

5 Iste modus clausularum necessarius est in omni narracione facti, ubi scilicet narratur aliquod factum. Coniunccionis enim subtraccio materiam et breviat et exornat. Est
et iste modus aptissimus materiis inchoandis. Unde Symon
de bello Troiano libellum composuit, quem *Yliados* vel

the meaning of many clauses encompassed in one, seventh, no repetition of the same word.

Emphasis is done in two ways: in one way when, intend- 3
ing to speak of a thing, we speak of its characteristic; in another way when we call a thing by the name of its characteristic. Intending to speak of a thing, we speak of its characteristic, as when we want to say of Scipio that he destroyed Carthage through his prudence, we say "Scipio's prudence destroyed Carthage," that is, Scipio through his prudence. Likewise, one says: "Let your generosity relieve my need," that is, "Through your generosity, relieve me, who am in need." We call a thing by the name of its characteristic, as here: "Medea is sin itself," that is, so intensely sinful that nothing is found in her besides sin. Moreover, we use emphasis most when we are intent on either praising or blaming persons. And it coincides with the color that is called circumlocution.

Parataxis is when words that signify various things are 4
brought forth in a sequence of speech without a conjunction in between them, as here: "He, accompanied by many, came upon, found, killed him alone, unarmed." And likewise here: "By your harshness, voice, looks you have terrified your adversaries."

This way of handling clauses is needed in every narrative 5
of an action, namely, when an action is recounted. For removing a conjunction both shortens and adorns the subject matter. And this method is especially suitable for use when the subject matter is just getting started. So when Simon composed a book about the Trojan war, which he called

Auream capram nominat, in cuius principio utitur articulo, sic:

> Diviciis, ortu, specie, virtute, triumphis
> Rex Priamus clara clarus in urbe fuit.

6   Ablativus absolutus est qui absolvitur a regimine. Per quem materiam breviamus quando dicturi sumus aliquid per aliquod horum sex: si, quia, dum, cum, quando, postquam. Verbi gracia, quando dicendum sit "Postquam ipse hoc fecit, veni," dicimus "Hoc facto veni." Similiter, cum dicendum sit "Cum feceris finem narracionis tue quam incepisti, respondebo," dicimus "Narracionis tue fine facto, respondebo" vel "Finita narracione tua, respondebo." Hic modus utilissimus est in omni narracione.

7   Intellectus unius in alio est quando in aliquo consequenti suum intelligimus antecedens. Unde dicit Tullius: "Brevis erit narracio si ita dicetur, ut nonnunquam ex eo quod dictum sit illud quod non dictum sit intelligatur." Super quo textu dicit Victorinus: "ut posita aliqua secunda que sunt, sua prima declarent." Ut cum dicendum sit "Illuc ivit et reversus est," sufficit dicere "Reversus est." Hoc enim consequens dat intelligere suum antecedens, scilicet "ivit illuc." Similiter et hoc "secundum" dat intelligere "suum primum." Similiter, cum dicendum sit "Credidit michi centum libras et eas reddidi," dicimus "Reddidi centum libras." Unde notabiliter dicit Quintilianus, *De institucione oratoria:*

Iliados or *The Golden Goat,* he employed parataxis at the beginning, thus:

> For riches, birth, beauty, virtue, triumphs King Priam
> was famous in a famous city.

An ablative that is absolved from grammatical government is absolute. We shorten the subject matter by means of it when we want to say something with one of these six words: "if," "because," "while," "since," "when," "after." For example, when one needs to say "After he did this, I came," we can say "This done, I came." Likewise, when one needs to say "When you make an end of the account that you began, I shall answer," we can say "An end of your account having been made, I shall answer" or "Your account having been ended, I shall answer." This method is very useful in any narrative.

The understanding of one thing in another is when in a subsequent thing we understand its antecedent. About this Cicero says: "The narrative will be brief if it is told in such a way that at times something which has not been mentioned can be gathered from what has been said." Commenting on this text Victorinus says: "so that once some later events have been related, they make clear what came before them." As, when one wishes to say "He went there and returned," it suffices to say "He returned." For that which follows allows one to understand what comes before it, namely, "he went there." And similarly this "later event" allows one to understand "what came before it." Likewise, when one wishes to say "He loaned me one hundred pounds and I repaid them," we say "I repaid one hundred pounds." So Quintilian, in *The*

"Quociens exitus rei satis ostendit priora, debemus esse contenti eo quo reliqua intelliguntur." Ut cum dicendum sit "In portum veni, navem prospexi, quanti veheret interrogavi, de precio conveni, conscendi, sublate sunt anchore, solvimus horam, profecti sumus," pro hiis omnibus sufficit dicere "E portu navigavimus." In hoc enim exitu omnia illa priora intelliguntur: "In portum veni, navem prospexi, quanti veheret interrogavi etc."

8   Dissolutum est quociens clausule dissolvuntur, id est non ligantur vinculo coniunccionis, ut in premisso exemplo: "In portum veni, navem prospexi etc." Similiter et hic: "Prata luxuriant, floribus lasciviunt, ditantur veris opibus, aeris clemencia reviviscunt, amenitatis cultibus induuntur." Iuxta hunc modum videndum est quod in tantum debemus vitare prolixitatem rerum sicut et verborum. Quamvis enim in illo Quintilliani exemplo, "In portum veni, navem prospexi etc.," nichil posset dici brevius quam dicitur, quia tamen plures res quam oportet recitantur, quamvis in verbis breves sumus, in rebus longissimi reperimur. Unde dicit Tullius, in prima *Rethorica:* "Non minus rerum non necessariarum quam verborum multitudini supersedendum est." Et addit: "Multos enim decipit brevitatis imitacio, ut, cum se breves esse putent, longissimi sunt." Et hoc est cum res plures quam necesse est breviter proferamus. Et differt dissolutum ab articulo quia iste respectu diccionum, illud fit respectu oracionum.

Training of an Orator, notably says: "Whenever the conclusion gives a sufficiently clear idea of the premises, we must be content with that from which the rest is understood." As when one wishes to say "I came to the harbor, I saw a ship, I asked the cost of a passage, the price was agreed, I went on board, the anchor was weighed, we loosed our cable and set out," for all these it would have been sufficient to say "We sailed from the harbor." For in this ending all those things that went before are understood: "I came to the harbor, I saw a ship, I asked the cost of a passage etc."

Asyndeton is whenever the clauses are broken up, that is, are not bound with the chain of a conjunction, as in the previous example: "I came to the harbor, I saw a ship etc." Likewise also here: "The meadows luxuriate, they revel in flowers, they are endowed with spring's riches, they come back to life through the air's mildness, they put on the garments of delight." In accordance with this method you should see that, as much as possible, we ought to avoid prolixity of facts as well as of words. For although in that example of Quintilian's, "I came to the harbor, I saw a ship etc.," nothing can be said more briefly than it is said, nonetheless, because more facts are recited than is necessary, although we are short in words, we are found to be very long in facts. For this reason Cicero says, in the first *Rhetoric:* "One must refrain no less from an excess of superfluous facts than from an excess of words." And he adds: "For many are deceived by an appearance of brevity so that they are prolix when they think they are brief." And this happens when we bring forth, albeit briefly, more things than is necessary. Asyndeton differs from parataxis because the latter functions with respect to individual words, the former with respect to statements.

9   Repeticionis vitacio est quando unum quodque semel tantum dicitur. Unde nunquam incipiendum est ab eo in quo finimus, ut si diceres "Veni ad emulum meum et postquam veni convicia intulit et post convicia verberavit." Talis enim narracio viciosa est, eo quod hec duo "veni" et "convicia" inutiliter repetuntur. Debent et hic vitari omnes colores qui operantur circa repeticionem eiusdem vocis vel sentencie, ut sunt repeticio, conversio, complexio, traduccio, gradacio, interpretacio, conduplicacio, exclamacio, expolicio et consimiles.

10   Sentencia multarum clausularum in una est quando per participium vel gerundivum ex duabus clausulis unam conficimus, ut quando diversi actus eidem attribuuntur subiecto et alterum verbum in gerundivum convertimus vel participium, ut pro "Iste sedet et loquitur" dicemus "Iste sedendo loquitur" vel "Iste sedens loquitur." Similiter pro hac "Quidam venit ad me et osculatus sum eum" dicemus "Osculo suscepi venientem."

11   Et notandum quod addi possent plura alia precepta ad abbreviacionem quam premisimus, que Tullius enumerat in prima *Rethorica*. Que omnia nos sub uno precepto breviter ostendemus, quod est brevitatis sufficientissimum artificium, quod ideo ad extremum reservavimus, quoniam extremum dictum melius infigitur memorie. Septem alia que premisimus adiuvant set istud perficit brevitatem. Est autem hoc artificium. Proposita materia quam volumus breviare, circumscribende sunt omnes circumstancie, id est accidentalia materie, et colligenda sunt necessariarum rerum

The avoidance of repetition is when each particular thing 9
is said once only. For this reason we never should begin from
that on which we end, as if you were to say "I came to my rival and after I came he cast insults and after the insults he
struck me." Now such a narrative is faulty, because both "I
came" and "insults" are repeated uselessly. Here also should
be avoided all the colors that function through repetition of
the same word or thought, such as epanaphora, antistrophe,
symploce, polyptoton, climax, interpretation, reduplication, apostrophe, refining, and the like.

The meaning of many clauses contained in one is when, 10
by means of a participle or gerund, we make one clause out
of two clauses, as when various acts are attributed to the
same subject and we convert the second verb into a gerund
or a participle, so that instead of "This person sits and
speaks" we could say "This person speaks while sitting" or
"Sitting, this person speaks." Likewise, in place of this: "A
certain person came to me and I kissed him," we could say
"With a kiss I received the person coming."

Also, you should note that many precepts other than 11
those we have provided already could be added regarding
abbreviation, which Cicero enumerates in the first *Rhetoric*.
We will show all of these briefly under a single precept,
which is a very effective technique for brevity, and which for
that reason we have kept until last, since what is said last
sticks better in the memory. The other seven that we have
provided already only facilitate brevity, but this one accom-
plishes it. And this is the technique. Once the theme selected for abbreviation has been put forth, all the attendant
circumstances—that is, the "accidentals" of the theme—
should be edited out, and the names of the essential things—

nomina, illa scilicet sine quibus non staret materia et ipsius causa sunt. Deinde illis nominibus adiungenda sunt verba que faciunt ad propositum materie. Et quia volumus utriusque artificii exempla supponere, narremus unam fabulam iuxta observacionem septem modorum breviandi materiam. Deinde per hoc secundum artificium quam brevissime narrari poterit subiungamus.

12   Per septem modos sic metrice proceditur:

> Rebus in augendis longe distante marito,
> uxor mecha parit puerum. Post multa reverso
> de nive conceptum fingit. Fraus mutua. Caute
> sustinet. Asportat, vendit matrique reportans
> ridiculum simile, liquefactum sole refingit.

In hac enim materia omnes septem modi coincidunt. Primus modus est ubi dicit "fraus mutua"; secundus ibi: "sustinet, asportat etc."; tercius ibi: "rebus in augendis"; quartus ibi: "uxor mecha parit" (per hoc intelligitur ipsam concepisse); quintus, per totam materiam—nulla enim clausula ligatur cum alia; sextus, similiter per totam materiam, ubi nichil dictum iterum recitatur; septimus ibi: "reportans ridiculum simile, liquefactum sole refingit" pro "reportat et fingit."

13   Si autem hanc materiam breviare volumus secundum aliud artificium, colligenda sunt hec quinque nomina—vir, mulier, puer, sol, nix—et verbis convenientibus adiungantur, sic:

namely, those things without which the theme would not remain and that are its cause—should be gathered together. Then, to those nouns should be added verbs that are useful to the theme's intention. And because we wish to supply examples of each technique, we shall recount a tale by observing the seven ways of shortening the subject matter. Then we will subjoin an example of how briefly it can be narrated by means of this second technique.

By means of the seven methods one proceeds thus in 12 verse:

> Her husband abroad improving his fortunes, an adulterous wife bears a child. On his return after long delay, she feigns it begotten of snow. Deceit is mutual. Slyly he waits. He whisks off, sells, and—reporting to the mother a like ridiculous tale—counterfeigns the child melted by sun.

Now in this subject matter all seven methods coincide. The first method is where it says "Deceit is mutual"; the second here: "he waits, he whisks off etc."; the third here: "improving his fortunes"; the fourth here: "an adulterous wife bears" (by this it is understood that she had conceived); the fifth, through the entire subject matter—for no clause is linked with another; the sixth, likewise through the entire subject matter, where nothing said is recited again; the seventh here: "reporting a like ridiculous tale, feigns the child melted by sun" instead of "he reports and he feigns."

However, if we wish to shorten this subject matter by 13 means of another technique, these five nouns should be gathered together—man, woman, boy, sun, snow—and they should be joined to suitable verbs, thus:

De nive conceptum quem mater adultera finxit
sponsus eum vendens liquefactum sole refinxit.

Vel sic:

Vir, quia quem querit genitum nive femina finxit
vendit et a simili liquefactum sole refinxit.

14   Iam satis evidenter dictum est de prolongacione et abbreviacione, quorum utrumque sciri potest quamvis ne-
sciatur modus bene dicendi. Modi bene dicendi duo sunt:
unus est ornata difficultas, alius ornata facilitas, de quibus
sufficienter dicendum est. Set hoc primo notandum est,
quod nec difficultas ornata nec ornata facilitas est alicuius
ponderis si ornatus ille sit tantum exterior. Superficies enim
verborum ornata, nisi sana et commendabili fulciatur sentencia, similis est vili picture que licet placeat longius stanti,
tamen displicet propius intuenti. Sic et ornatus verborum
sine ornatu sentenciarum semel forte audienti placet, diligenter intuenti displicet. Talis enim ornatus, timens argutum iudicem, venire non audet in medium set querit in late-
bris habitare. Istud innuit Oracius, in antiqua *Poetria,* sic:

Ut pictura poesis: erit que si propius stes
te capiet magis et quedam si longius abstes.
Hec amat obscurum, volet hec sub luce videri,

A husband, selling him whom the adulterous mother feigned begotten of snow, in turn feigned him melted by sun.

Or thus:

Since his wife feigned one he questions begotten of snow, the husband sells him, and likewise counterfeigned him melted by sun.

Now we have spoken clearly enough about lengthening 14 and shortening, either of which can be known even if the method of speaking well is not known. The methods of speaking well are two: one is ornamented difficulty, the other ornamented facility, both of which must be spoken about adequately. But first this should be noted, that neither ornamented difficulty nor ornamented facility has any weight if that ornament is only on the outside. For the ornamented surface of words, unless it be supported by a sound and praiseworthy sentiment, is like a cheap picture that, though it may please one who stands at a distance, nevertheless displeases one who regards it up close. So also the ornament of words without the ornament of thoughts might please somebody hearing it only once but displeases someone who pays careful attention. For such ornament, fearing a shrewd judge, dares not venture into the open but seeks to lurk in the shadows. Horace suggests this, in the old *Poetics,* thus:

A poem is like a picture: one strikes your fancy more, the nearer you stand; another, the farther away. This courts the shade, that will wish to be seen in the light,

iudicis argutum que non formidat acumen;
hec placuit semel, hec decies repetita placebit.

Si autem sentencia laudabilis sit et honesta, laudabili et honesta verborum tunica vestiatur,

Ne pudeat matrona potens in paupere panno.

15   Ad ornatum autem verborum videndum est quod adiectiva epitetice, id est evidenter, proprie, sua respiciant substantiva et verba sua supposita. Quid sit epitetum posterius ostendetur. De qualitate verborum ita dicit Oracius, in antiqua *Poetria,* sic:

Tristia mestum
vultum verba decent, iratum plena minarum,
ludentem lasciva, severum seria dictu.

Multa sunt eciam alia que faciunt ad ornatum verborum, de quibus statim dicetur.

16   Patet igitur quod prius cogitandum est de ornata et gravi sentencia quam de florida verborum iunctura. Unde et Oracius dicit quod artifex dictaminis se debet habere in invencione sue materie ad modum illius qui portare mollitur aliquod grave onus, qui priusquam onus ferat, prudenter ponderis gravitatem examinat si viribus respondeat humerorum. Conformiter, qui pondus materie dictare proponit prius videre debet si gravitas materie viribus ingenii sui respondeat, ut, si materia talis fuerit cuius forte proprietates

and dreads not the critical insight of the judge. This pleased but once; that, though ten times called for, will always please.

However, if the sentiment is praiseworthy and honorable, let it be clothed with a praiseworthy and honorable garment of words,

Lest a noble lady feel shame in pauper's rags.

However, for the adornment of words you should see to it 15 that adjectives modify their substantives and their subjoined words epithetically, that is, vividly and appropriately. What an epithet is will be shown later. Horace says as much concerning the nature of words, in the old *Poetics,* thus:

Sad tones befit the face of sorrow; blustering accents that of anger; jests become the merry, solemn words the grave.

There are also many other things that contribute to the adornment of words, about which we will speak presently.

It is evident, then, that one should think about orna- 16 mented and weighty ideas before one thinks about florid constructions. For this reason Horace also says that when generating his subject matter the fashioner of a composition should behave like a person who is struggling to carry some heavy burden: before he bears the burden, he prudently tests the heaviness of its weight to see if it matches the strength of his shoulders. In the same way, one who intends to compose on a weighty subject matter should first see if the heaviness of the subject matter corresponds to the strength of his skill, since, if the subject matter should

agnoscit, bene potest talem materiam dictare. Si vero proprietates eius non agnoscit, non debet presumere eam dictare. Qui enim taliter materiam precogitat duo commoda consequetur, scilicet facundiam, id est verborum copiam, et parcium materie lucidum ordinem, id est quid in principio, quid in medio, quid in fine collocabit. Istud autem primum est preceptum quo instruit Oracius poetam in invencione sue materie, dicens:

> Sumite materiam vestris, qui scribitis, equam
> viribus et versate diu, quid ferre recusent,
> quid valeant humeri. Cui lecta potenter erit res,
> nec facundia deseret hunc nec lucidus ordo.

17 Per hoc eciam artificium vitare possumus incongruam digressionem. Et hec est causa quare talis facienda est materie premeditacio. Quia cum materia supra vires ingenii gravis eligitur et eam artifex secundum artis exigenciam ad finem debitum nescit perducere, statim ad quedam alia ibi locum non habencia inutiliter et viciose digreditur, que quia per se posita satis placere conspicit, ideo materie sue inconveniencius interponit. Talis enim modus dictandi comparatur vili vesti preciosis assute panniculis, cuius adventu vilitati vestis non defertur set honor, si quem habuit, summopere minoratur. Sic, qui materiam gravem quasi quibusdam ornatibus

happen to be the sort whose characteristics he is familiar with, he can compose well on such subject matter. However, if he is not familiar with its characteristics, he should not presume to compose on it. Whoever thinks through his subject matter ahead of time in this way will achieve two rewards, namely, fluency, that is, an abundance of words, and a clear order for the parts of the subject matter, that is, what he will place in the beginning, what in the middle, and what at the end. This indeed is the first precept with which Horace instructs the poet concerning the generation of his subject matter, saying:

> Take a subject, you who write, equal to your strength;
> and ponder long what your shoulders refuse, and what
> they are able to bear. Whoever shall choose a theme
> within his range, neither speech will fail him, nor clear-
> ness of order.

Also, through this technique we can avoid unsuitable digression. And this is the reason why such prior meditation on the subject matter is necessary. Because when a subject matter is chosen whose weight is beyond the powers of one's skill, and the craftsman doesn't know how to carry it through to its due conclusion in accordance with the demands of his art, at once he strays uselessly and faultily to some other matters that have no place there, which, because he perceives them to be pleasing enough when placed by themselves, he therefore inserts into his subject matter unfittingly. Indeed, such a manner of composing is comparable to a lowly garment that has been stitched with costly patches, through the addition of which the garment is not relieved of its baseness, but rather any nobility it might have

peregrinis assuerit, illam pocius dedecorat quam decorat, sicut facit ille qui descripciones inducit ineptas, ut qui describit lucum, id est silvam, vel altare Diane, id est Palladis, vel amenitatem alicuius fluvii aut arcum pluvialem, cum talia describere nichil conferat ad commodum cause.

18   Incongruam digressionem reprehendit Oracius per duas methaforas, quarum una est per picturam cipressi. Mos enim olim fuit afflictorum pericula in quadam tabula depingere in qua eorum gravedinem posset quilibet intentare. Contigit ut quidam, maris evadens naufragium, rogaret quemdam pictorem naufragium suum depingere precepitque pictori ut personam suam depingeret more alicuius natantis in periculo versus ripam. Pictor vero, in sola pictura cipressi arboris expertus, quesivit si vellet aliquid addi de cipresso. Unde dicit Oracius:

> Et fortasse cipressum
> scis similare: quid hoc,

(id est hec pictura, scilicet valet)

> si fractis enatat expers
> navibus ere dato qui pingitur?

(id est si ille qui pingitur postulat pingi navibus fractis pro pecunia data pictori pro mercede).

had is greatly diminished. Thus, whoever "stitches up" a weighty subject matter with some vagabond adornments, "disembellishes" rather than embellishes it. This is what a person who introduces unsuitable descriptions does—like someone who describes a grove (that is, a forest) or the altar of Diana (that is, Pallas) or the pleasantness of some stream or a rainbow, when describing such things contributes nothing to the advantage of the case.

Horace criticizes unsuitable digression by means of two metaphors, one of which is a picture of a cypress. For once upon a time it was the custom of people afflicted by ill fortune to depict their perils on a tablet so that everyone could see how serious they were. It happened that a certain person who escaped a shipwreck at sea asked a certain painter to depict his shipwreck and instructed the painter to depict him swimming toward the shore in great peril. But the painter, who knew only how to paint a cypress tree, asked if he would like something added having to do with a cypress. For this reason Horace says:

> Perhaps, too, you can draw a cypress. But what of that,

(that is, this picture; namely, what is it worth?)

> if you are paid to paint a sailor swimming destitute from his wrecked vessel?

(that is, if—in return for the money he had paid to the painter as a fee—the one who is being painted asked to be painted amid wrecked vessels).

19   Alia methafora est per fusorem qui, cum inceperat fundere amphoram, id est magnum vas, finaliter fecit urceum, id est minimum vas. Unde dicit Oracius:

> Amphora cepit
> institui: currente rota cur urceus exit?

Ecce versus Oracii testes eorum que dixi:

> Inceptis gravibus plerumque et magna professis
> purpureus, late qui splendeat, unus et alter
> assuitur pannus, cum lucus et ara Diane
> aut properantis aque per amenos ambitus agros,
> aut flumen Reni aut pluvius describitur arcus.
> Set nunc non erat his locus. Et fortasse cipressum
> scis similare: quid hoc, si fractis enatat expers
> navibus ere dato qui pingitur? Amphora cepit
> institui: currente rota cur urceus exit?

20   Ex predictis igitur collige quod primo excogitare debemus egregiam sentenciam et postea verborum honestam picturam. Unde in "Libro versuum" dicitur:

> Dives honoretur sentencia divite verbo,
> ne rubeat matrona potens in paupere panno.

Est igitur necessarium ut honestam sentenciam honesta verborum tunica vestiamus. Quia sicut in constitucione rei

The other metaphor is a metal-caster who, although he 19 had begun to cast a wine jar (that is, a large vessel), in the end made a pitcher (that is, a very small vessel). For this reason Horace says:

That was a wine jar when the molding began: why, as the wheel runs round, does it turn out a pitcher?

Here are the verses of Horace that testify to what I have said:

Works with noble beginnings and grand promises often have one or two purple patches so stitched on as to glitter far and wide, as when Diana's grove and altar, or "The winding stream a-speeding 'mid fair fields," or the river Rhine, or the rainbow is described. For such things there is a place, but not just now. Perhaps, too, you can draw a cypress. But what of that, if you are paid to paint a sailor swimming destitute from his wrecked vessel? That was a wine jar when the molding began: why, as the wheel runs round, does it turn out a pitcher?

From what has just been said, therefore, gather that first 20 we should devise an excellent sentiment and afterward a noble depiction of it through our words. Regarding this it is said in the "Book of Verses":

Let rich meaning be honored by rich diction, lest a noble lady blush in pauper's rags.

It is therefore needful that we clothe a noble sentiment in a noble garment of words. So just as the addition of a pearl or an emblem to a worthy garment will make the whole

materialis, ex apposicione alicuius margarite vel emblematis totum materiatum elegancius elucescit, sic in mediocri dictamine floridis figurarum tunicis vestita, materia celebriter festivatur et clarior rutilat expolita. Et sicut materia statue nullo venustatis precio insignita rudis est et nimia vilitate plebescens, sic in dictamine materia rudis est et inconcinna donec artificiali tunica cuiusdam scematis, tropi vel coloris rethorici splendide tunicetur, dicente Ysidoro, 8. *Ethimologiarum,* capitulo septimo: "Officium poete in eo est ut ea que vere gesta sunt in alias species obliquis figuracionibus cum decore aliquo conversa traducat," id est, ut ea que communiter facta sunt artificialiter eloquatur. Item Alanus, *De planctu Nature:* "Poete tamen aliquando historiales eventus ioculacionibus fabulosis quasi quadam eleganti sutura confederant, ut ex diversorum competenti iunctura ipsius narracionis elegancior pictura resultet."

21   Set ecce per exempla quomodo rudis materia diversis verborum ornatibus vestiatur. Hec rudis materia "Lana male filata processu temporis efficitur manifesta," sic poterit verborum floribus ornari: "Lane vicium, quod occultat nove filacionis infancia, erroris antiqui senium manifestat" vel sic: "Incongrue filacionis vicium, licet ad tempus ignorancie moriatur in tenebris, temporis sui adveniente senio, in communis noticie memoriam reviviscit" vel sic: "Si quid oblivio, noverca memorie, ab aure noticie communis incarceret,

costume seem more elegant, so in an ordinary composition that is clothed in the flowery garments of the figures, the subject matter frequently is enlivened and, having been refined, shines all the more brightly. And just as the material of a statue that is distinguished by no wealth of beauty is rough and made common by its extreme baseness, so in a written composition the subject matter is rough and inelegant until it is brilliantly clothed with the artful garment of some scheme, trope, or rhetorical color. As Isidore says, in *Etymologies* 8, chapter seven: "The duty of the poet consists in this, that he transfer those things which actually have been done into other kinds, once they have been transformed through indirect figures of speech with a certain grace," that is, that he express artfully those things that have been done in the ordinary way. Likewise Alan of Lille, in *The Plaint of Nature:* "Poets often join historical events to their own playful fabulations by a sort of elegant stitching, in order that from the artful conjoining of these diverse materials a more elegant narrative pattern may emerge."

But behold in some examples how a rough subject matter 21 may be clothed with various ornaments of words. This rough subject matter "Badly spun wool is made evident in the course of time" could be adorned with flowers of words thus: "The flaw of wool, which the infancy of recent spinning conceals, the old age of past error makes evident" or thus: "The flaw of unsuitable spinning, though it remain for a time in the shadows of ignorance, as the old age of its days approaches, returns to life in the memory of general notoriety" or thus: "If anything is locked away by forgetfulness, stepmother of memory, from the ear of general notoriety,

vulgaris fame fidelitas liberat et dissolvit." Unde dicitur:
"Sepe novum vetera faciunt peccata ruborem." Simili usus
est Bernardus artificio, cum diceret "Mentula impedit ne
genus humanum pereat," sic:

> Militat adversus Lachesim solersque renodat
> mentula Parcarum fila resecta manu.

Similiter et quidam elegantissime clericum quemdam luxu-
riosum ait hiis versibus:

> Hic est
> philosophus Veneris, quem mollis pagina lecti
> non libri reficit, qui dum magis approbat album
> incaustum tempusque nigrum, nocturna placere
> non lucis scriptura solet, rubeoque libello
> inspuitur calamo delectans litera ceco.

Similiter, Matheus Vindocinensis exprimit feditatem luxurie sic:

> Dactilici metri prior intrat sillaba, crebro
> concussu fedant menia feda breves.

Similiter, cum diceret "Iste pre timore pallet," ita dicit:

> Deflorat gravis ora metus pallorque ruboris
> exulis heredem se sine iure facit.

22   Et sciendum quod in hiis et similibus, quanto pluribus
ornatibus vel figuris vestiatur materia, tanto iocundius reficit auditorem. Verbi gracia, in hac locucione "Vestre

the fidelity of common rumor frees and releases it." Regarding this it is said: "Often old sins cause new shame." Bernard employed a similar technique when he wished to say "The phallus prevents humankind from perishing," as follows:

> The phallus wars against Lachesis and carefully rejoins the vital threads severed by the hands of the Fates.

Likewise, someone else says most elegantly that a certain cleric is lascivious in these verses:

> This one is a philosopher of Venus, whom the soft page of a bed, not a book, refreshes, whom nocturnal writing and not that of daylight is accustomed to please, since he favors more the white ink and the black time, and whose favorite text is spewed into a pink book by a blind pen.

Likewise, Matthew of Vendôme depicts the foulness of lust, thus:

> The hexameter's long syllable thrusts in, the two short syllables defile the foul ramparts with repeated pounding.

Likewise, when he wishes to say "This one grows pale from fear," he says:

> Grave apprehension deflowers her cheeks and pallor made itself the unlawful heir of exiled blushes.

And you should know that in these and the like, the more 22 the subject matter is clothed with many ornaments and figures, the more delightfully it refreshes the hearer. For example, in this expression "Let the reverence of your

discrecionis reverencia, vestre nobilitatis benignitas, vestre fidelitatis promissio parvitatis mee precibus faveat graciose," multiplex est figura. Est enim lepos in eo quod uni, causa reverencie, loquimur pluraliter cum dicitur "vestre." Est et emphasis in eo quod proprietas ponitur pro subiecto. Et est dyaliton in eo quod clausule plures ordinantur sine coniunccione. Est et repeticio in eo quod eadem diccio est principium plurium clausularum. Nec propter concursum tot figurarum est huiusmodi locucio reprehendenda set magis honore digna, quia sicut virtus non excludit virtutem, nec rosa lilium, nec iacinctus margaritam, set ubi

non prosunt singula, multa iuvant.

Consimiliter, nec color est exclusivus coloris, ymmo clarius rutilant congregati et relativo se invicem venustant beneficio.

23   Cum igitur, iuxta Tullium, omnis ornatus aut est verborum aut sentenciarum, quibus omnis locucio rudis artificiosa redditur. Rursus ornatus verborum quedam est difficultas ornata, quedam ornata facilitas. Nos primo de ornata difficultate dicamus.

discretion, the kindness of your nobility, the promise of your faithfulness graciously favor the prayers of my insignificance," the figure is manifold. For it is "lepos" (charm) in that we speak in the plural to a single person, for the sake of reverence, when "vestre" is used. It is also "emphasis" in that a characteristic is put in place of the subject. It is also "dialiton" in that several clauses are arranged without a conjunction. It is also "epanaphora" in that the same word is the beginning of several clauses. Nor is this sort of expression blameworthy because of the conjunction of so many figures, but rather it is worthy of honor, for just as one virtue does not exclude another, neither does a rose a lily, nor an amethyst a pearl, but where

things avail not singly, they help when they are many.

So one color does not exclude another. On the contrary, in a group they glitter more brightly, beautifying one another in turn by mutual favor.

Therefore, since, according to Cicero, every ornament either is of words or of thought, by these every rough expression is rendered artful. Then again, some ornaments of words involve ornamented difficulty, some ornamented facility. Let us speak first about ornamented difficulty. 23

Capitulum 5

De decem speciebus transumpcionis quibus ornata difficultas efficitur

Ornatam difficultatem decem potissime operantur, scilicet decem species transumpcionis. Est enim transumpcio recessus a propria potestate vocabuli, ut patet ex Tullio in secunda *Rethorica*. Recedimus enim a propria potestate vocabuli dupliciter, scilicet significacione et ordine. Significacione, quando vox deducitur a propria significacione ad alienam, ut hic: "Pratum ridet," id est "floret." Ordine, ut quando dicciones aliter ordinantur in serie oracionis quam in serie construccionis, ut "Vestram precor reverenciam." Set prius dicendum est de illis speciebus transumpcionis quibus receditur a propria potestate vocabuli gracia significacionis.

2   Novem sunt colores quibus transumitur diccio a propria significacione ad alienam, horum quattuor sunt species graviores et quinque leviores. Quattuor graviores sunt nominacio, pronominacio, permutacio, translacio, ut statim

Chapter 5

Concerning the ten kinds of transumption by means of which ornamented difficulty is produced

Ten things chiefly bring about ornamented difficulty, namely, the ten kinds of transumption. Transumption is a departure from the proper force of a word, as Cicero makes clear in his second *Rhetoric*. Now we can depart from a word's proper force in two ways, namely, in signification and in order. In signification when a word is led away from its own signification to that of another word, as here: "The meadow laughs," that is to say, it blooms. In order, as when words are placed in a different order in the sequence of our speech than they would be in the sequence of their grammatical construction, as "Your—I beseech—reverence." But first we should speak about those kinds of transumption in which one departs from a word's proper force with respect to its signification.

There are nine colors in which a word is shifted from its proper meaning to that of another word. Of these, four are the weightier varieties and five the lighter ones. The four weightier types are onomatopoeia, antonomasia, allegory, and metaphor, as will be explained shortly. Moreover, tran-

declarabitur. Fit autem transumpcio quattuor modis: primo modo, ab animato ad animatum; secundo, ab inanimato ad inanimatum; tercio, ab animato ad inanimatum; quarto, ab inanimato ad animatum.

3   Verbi gracia, ab animato ad animatum, ut quando quod proprium est uni animatorum attribuitur uni alii animato cui non est proprium, ut "Voce sua citharizat avis." Nam citharizare hominibus convenit proprie, avibus vero nisi transumptive.

4   Ab inanimato ad inanimatum, ut:

Pontum pinus arat, sulcum premit alta carina.

Hic enim attribuitur aque quod proprium est terre. Similiter et pinus, cum sit nomen arboris, transumitur ad significandum navem, quarum neutra animam habet.

5   Ab animato ad inanimatum, ut:

Murmurat in medio vox salientis aque.
In medio lacrimatur humus.

Nam et murmurare et lacrimari homini propria sunt: aque et humo transumptive assignantur.

6   Ab inanimato ad animatum, ut:

Floridus eloquio, veteranus marcidus evo.
Dum viret ingenio, senii pre tempore marcet.

Nam esse floridum et marcidum florum est vel foliorum: homini transumitur.

7   Artificium transumendi hoc est. Considerandum est verbum quod debet transumi, de quibus dicatur proprie; et si

sumption is done in four ways: the first way, from animate to animate; the second, from inanimate to inanimate; the third, from animate to inanimate; and the fourth, from inanimate to animate.

For example, from animate to animate, as when something that is proper to one of the animate beings is attributed to another animate being to whom it is not proper, as "The bird plays the lyre with its voice." For to play the lyre pertains to men properly but to birds only transumptively. 3

From inanimate to inanimate, as: 4

The pine plows the sea, the deep keel digs a furrow.

For here is attributed to water what is proper to earth. Likewise also "pine," although it is the name of a tree, is shifted to signify "ship," neither of which is animate.

From animate to inanimate, as: 5

In its midst the sound of leaping water murmurs. In its midst the earth weeps.

For both to murmur and to weep are proper to a man: they are assigned to water and earth transumptively.

From inanimate to animate, as: 6

Flowering in eloquence, an old man is withered in years. While he flourishes because of his skill, he withers because he is in the time of declining age.

For to be flowering and withered are properties of flowers or leaves: they are applied transumptively to a man.

The technique of transumption is as follows. Regarding the word that ought to be shifted, one should consider the things to which it may be applied in its proper meaning; and 7

ad aliam rem transumi debeat, videndum est quod inter illa sit conveniens similitudo. Omnes enim transumentes secundum aliquam similitudinem transumunt. Sic autem inveniri debet similitudo: perscrutandum est in verbo transumendo quoddam commune, quod pluribus convenit quam illud verbum, et quibuscumque aliis convenit illud commune proprie, conveniet transumenda diccio transumptive. Verbi gracia, hoc verbum "nasci" convenit solis animatis proprie. Et in hoc verbo intelligitur quoddam commune, scilicet incipere esse, quod pluribus convenit quam "nasci," scilicet omnibus que incipiunt esse. Igitur hoc verbum "nasci" conveniet omnibus illis transumptive, ut cum dicitur "Nascuntur flores in agris, in vite racemi," id est incipiunt esse. "Nata est malicia in diebus nostris," id est incipit esse. Hoc enim artificium est planissima via ad facilem transumpcionem. Reprobatur transumpcio turgida et opaca.

8   Est et alia cautela per quam, mediante predicto artificio, castigari poterit transumpcio, ne dura sit vel obscura, et est hec. De quacumque re loquimur, videamus apud nos quid de ea loqui intendimus, laudem scilicet an opprobrium, quoniam circa utrumque idem operatur artificium. Deinde per similitudinem videamus quid aliis rebus proprie conveniat secundum similem statum, id est secundum similem laudem vel simile vituperium, et idem dicetur de re proposita transumptive. Verbi gracia, dicturi de homine quod habeat

if the word should be shifted to some other thing, one should see to it that there is some fitting similarity between those two things. For all transumptions shift a word's meaning based on some similarity. Moreover, the similarity should be discovered thus: one should seek out a certain common feature in the word to be transumed, one which applies to more things than that single word designates, and to whatever other things that shared feature applies properly, the word being transumed will apply transumptively. For example, the verb "to be born" properly applies only to animate beings. And in this verb is understood a certain common feature, namely, to begin to exist, which applies to more things than "to be born" does, namely, to all things that begin to exist. Therefore this verb "to be born" will apply to all these things transumptively, as when one says "The flowers are born in the fields, the grape clusters on the vine," that is, they begin to exist. "An evil is born in our days," that is, it begins to exist. This technique is the smoothest road to easy transumption. Turgid and obscure transumption is to be rejected.

There is still another device by means of which, with the assistance of the previous technique, the transumption can be corrected so that it is neither harsh nor obscure, and it is this. Concerning whatever matter we speak about, we should mentally consider what we intend to say about it, namely, whether it is praise or blame, since the same technique works for both. Then, by analogy, we should see what suits other things properly from a similar standpoint, that is, according to a like praise or blame, and the same should be said transumptively about the matter we have chosen to present. For example, if we want to say about a man that he

8

albam faciem, rubias genas, glaucos crines, dulcem gustum, pulcra verba, dicamus "Homo iste liliatam habet faciem, genas purpureas, aureos crines, gustum mellitum, florida verba."

9   Hoc artificio usus est Alanus quasi per totum. Ait enim in descripcione Nature: "Frons vero, in amplam evagata planiciem, lacteo liliata colore, lilio videbatur contendere." Et alibi, de errore humano, sic: "Humanum namque genus, a sua generositate degenerans, in construccione generum barbarizans, Venereas regulas invertendo nimis irregulari utitur methaplasmo."

10   Et ut breviter concludam, fere quicquid floride elocucionis rutilanti prelucet sidere, transumpcionis beneficio promovetur. Nam in *Architrenio,* cuius multiplex ornatus cetera modernorum precellit opuscula, nichil fere sine transumpcione reperitur. Et sciendum, teste Gervasio de Saltu Lacteo, quod ubi habetur diccionum penuria, possumus satis licite novas dicciones invenire, nunquam prius forsitan auditas, ut "tantalizat," "tunicat," "tiresiat," "philomenat." Istud idem confirmat magister Johannes Hauvillensis fieri licere, auctoritate Oracii dicentis:

Licuit semperque licebit
signatum presente nota producere nomen.

Et exponit predictam auctoritatem Oracii sic: "licuit," id est licitum fuit quibuscumque dictantibus, et "semper licebit," id est licitum erit; "producere," id est in usum proferre,

has a white face, red cheeks, shining hair, a sweet taste, lovely words, let us say "This man has a lilied face, rosy cheeks, golden hair, a honeyed taste, flowery words."

Alan of Lille has used this technique virtually everywhere. 9 For he says in his description of Nature: "Her forehead extended to an ample breadth, and lilied in its milky whiteness seemed to rival the lily." And elsewhere, concerning human error, thus: "For the human race, fallen away from its noble origin, is barbarous in its construction of the genders, and practices a most irregular metaplasm that inverts the rules of Venus."

And as I would conclude in brief, just about anything that 10 shines forth with the glittering star of flowery style is augmented with the help of transumption. For in the *Architrenius,* whose manifold ornament surpasses all other works of the moderns, almost nothing is found to be without transumption. And you should know, as Gervase of Melkley attests, that where there is a shortage of words, we are able quite legitimately to invent new words, words perhaps never heard before, such as "he tantalizes," "she tunics," "he tiresiases," "she philomenizes." Master John of Hauville confirms that it is permitted to do this very thing, on the authority of Horace, who says:

It has ever been, and ever will be, permitted to produce names stamped with the mint mark of the day.

And he explicates the above quotation of Horace thus: "it has been permitted," that is, permission has been granted to whoever was composing, and "it ever will be permitted," that is, permission will continue to be granted; "to produce," that is, to bring forth for use, as it were, "to draw from afar

quasi "procul ducere," scilicet a non usu ad usum; "nomen," id est quamcumque diccionem nomen dico; "signatum nota presente," id est expressa racione invencionis presente. Unde non licet michi invenire hanc diccionem "buba" ad significandum hominem.

11 Notarum igitur alia exprimitur extrinsecus et intrinsecus, alia intrinsecus tantum. Extrinsecus et intrinsecus quando per principium ipsius diccionis patet racio sue invencionis, nichilominus tamen determinatur alia diccione significativa exprimente racionem sue invencionis, ut hic: "Ista mulier preliliat lilia," id est precellit lilia in candore. Unde Johannes Hauvillensis, de pulcritudine Tisbes:

Lilia vernifluo Tisbe preliliat ore,
preradiat radios prerosulatque rosas.

Hec autem, "Tisbe preliliat nivem," adeo viciosa esset quod nullo modo tollerabilis.

12 Intrinsecus tantum exprimitur nota ut hic: "Facies tua dumescit pilis." Hec diccio "dumescit" exprimit in se racionem sue invencionis. Patet enim per principium quod a "dumo" trahitur. Et est sensus "Faciei tue pili similes sunt dumo."

13 Quandoque autem exprimitur nota intrinsecus tantum set extrinsecus exprimitur significacio verbi inventi—non dico racio invencionis—ut hic: "Cristallantur aque glacie temporali." "Cristallus" nota est huius verbi "cristallantur"

(*procul ducere*)," namely, from nonuse to use; "a name," that is, I call any word whatsoever a name; "stamped with the mint mark of the day," that is, provided that a present rationale of the invention is expressed. For this reason I am not permitted to invent the word "buba" in order to signify "man."

Now some "mint marks" or new significations are expressed both externally and internally, others only internally. 11 Both externally and internally when from the origin of the word itself the rationale of its invention is clear, but nonetheless it is modified by another signifying word that expresses the rationale of its invention, as here: "This woman outlilies the lilies," that is, she surpasses the lilies in whiteness. So John of Hauville says about the beauty of Thisbe:

> In her face overflowing with springtime Thisbe outlilies the lilies, she outbeams the sunbeams and outroses the roses.

However, this: "Thisbe outlilies the snow" would be very faulty and in no way tolerable.

A new signification is expressed only internally, as here: 12 "Your face grows bushy with whiskers." This word "grows bushy" expresses in itself the rationale of its invention. For it is clear from its origin that it is taken from "bush." And the meaning is "The whiskers on your face are like a bush."

Sometimes, however, the new signification is expressed 13 only internally, but the meaning of the invented word is expressed externally, as here: "The waters are crystallized with seasonal ice." "Crystal" is the new signification of the verb "are crystallized," but the modifier "with seasonal ice" shows

set hec determinacio "glacie temporali" ostendit significacionem. Est enim sensus "Aque cristallantur," id est in cristallum mutantur. Si vero dicam "Cristallantur aque glacie perpetua," hec alia determinacio alium potest sensum exprimere, scilicet hunc: "cristallantur," id est fiunt cristallus.

14   Quandoque longe extra exprimitur significacio, ut hic:

Ut sol lucens in berillo
transit illum nec in illo
 repugnat integritas
set excrescit et augetur
qua decrescit et deletur
 frigoris immensitas,
sic est caro lucis orta
de puella, clausa porta,
 sic berillat virginem
incarnatus rex celestis:
viciorum tota pestis
 per hunc perit hominem.

Significacio huius diccionis "berillat" exprimitur per illud principium "Ut sol lucens in berillo." Notat enim non quod virgo fiat berillus set quod in hoc similis sit berillo.

15   Ornatissime eciam ex nominibus comparativi et superlativi gradus nova verba inveniuntur, ut "maiorat," "alciorat," "minorat," "peiorat," "maximat," "altissimat," "minimat," "pessimat." Similiter et participia sine verbis a quibus oriuntur, ut "viridans," "comans." Theodolus:

Ore columba suo ramum viridantibus ultro.

the meaning. For the meaning is "The waters are crystallized," that is, they are changed into crystal. But if I should say "The waters are crystallized with perpetual ice," this other modifier can express another meaning, namely, this: "they are crystallized," that is, they become crystal.

Sometimes the meaning is expressed quite externally, as here: 14

> As the sun, when it shines in a beryl, passes through it, and the gem's purity does not resist, but rather grows and is increased, whereby the immensity of its coldness shrinks and is removed, so was the flesh of light born from a maiden, a closed gate, so does he "berylize" a virgin, the incarnate King of Heaven: the whole plague of sins perished through this man.

The meaning of the verb "berylize" is expressed by that which comes first: "As the sun, when it shines in a beryl." For it indicates not that the virgin becomes a beryl but rather that in this one respect she is like a beryl.

New verbs also are invented most elegantly from nouns 15 of the comparative and superlative degree, such as "he greaters," "she highers," "he lessens," "she worsens," "he greatests," "she highests," "he leasts," "she worsts." And in like manner participles may be invented without there being verbs from which they derive, such as "greening," "hairing." Theodolus:

> From afar the dove carried back in its mouth a branch with greening leaves.

Similiter et inchoativa sine verbis a quibus veniant, ut "hillarescit," "iuvenescit," "dumescit," "plebescit." Quandoque eciam a nominibus substantivis contingit invenire comparativa vel superlativa, ut hic:

Qui sedet hac sede, ganimedior est Ganimede.

Set huiusmodi ludicra sunt et ab operibus auctenticis elimentur. In huius doctrine exemplum Iohannes Hauvillensis hunc composuit versum:

Petrior es petra, tigre tigrior, idrior idra.

Visa tamen doctrina Oracii hac, scilicet

dabiturque licencia sumpta pudenter,

predictum versum iussit abradi et hunc apponi:

Idra, tigris, petra plus idra, tigride, petra.

Nova enim verba quadam raritate et pudencia invenienda sunt. Invencionis enim raritas et dicendi puritas cum quadam pudencia veniam mereantur.

16   Ex Greco eciam dicciones licenter possumus extorquere, ut Bernardus extorsit hec nomina "Megacosmus," "Microcosmus," Iohannes Hauvillensis hoc nomen "Architrenius."

And in like manner inchoative verbs may be invented without verbs from which they come, such as "becomes happy," "grows young," "grows bushy," "becomes notorious." And sometimes it happens that comparatives or superlatives are invented from substantive nouns, as here:

The one who sits in this seat is "Ganimedier" than Ganimede.

But these sorts of things are jokes and should be stripped away from serious works. To illustrate this precept John of Hauville composed this verse:

You are "stonier" than a stone, "tigrier" than a tiger, "hydrier" than the hydra.

However, on the authority of Horace, namely,

and license will be granted, if used with modesty,

he ordered that the previous verse be erased and this one put in its place:

You are more hydra, tiger, stone than hydra, tiger, stone themselves.

For new words should be invented with a certain infrequency and with modesty. For infrequency of invention and purity of speaking, along with a certain modesty, can excuse a great deal.

And we also have license to extract words from Greek, as 16 Bernard extracted the names "Megacosmus" and "Microcosmus" and John of Hauville the name "Architrenius."

17   Et sciendum quod tam ars usitatas dicciones transumendi quam novas et inauditas inveniendi confirmatur auctoritate Oracii, hiis versibus:

> In verbis esto tenuis cautusque serendis
> dixeris egregie notum si callida verbum
> reddiderit iunctura novum. Si forte necesse est
> indiciis monstrare recentibus abdita rerum,
> fingere cinctutis non exaudita Cethegis
> continget dabiturque licencia sumpta pudenter;
> et nova fictaque nuper habebunt verba fidem si
> Greco fonte cadant, parce detorta. Quid autem
> Cecilio Plautoque dabit Romanus ademptum
> Virgilio Varroque? Ego cur, adquirere pauca
> si possum, invideor, cum lingua Catonis et Enni
> sermonem patrium ditaverit et nova rerum
> nomina protulerit? Licuit semperque licebit
> signatum presente nota producere nomen.

Ad quorum versuum noticiam intellige quod primo commendat Oracius artem transumpcionis et ad eam invitat, dicens "esto tenuis," id est subtilis, et "cautus," id est circum-
spectus, "in verbis serendis," id est in nova significacione
ponendis, quia tu "dixeris," id est dicere poteris, "egregie," id
est laudabiliter et ornate, "si callida iunctura," id est discreta
ordinacio, "reddiderit," id est fecerit, verbum "notum," per

And you should know that both the art of transuming   17
familiar words and that of inventing new and unheard-of
words is confirmed by the authority of Horace, in these
verses:

> Be tasteful and careful in weaving words together. You
> will express yourself most happily, if a skillful setting
> renders a familiar word new. If it is necessary to repre-
> sent abstruse things in novel terms, you will have a
> chance to fashion words never heard of by the kilted
> Cethegi, and license will be granted, if used with
> modesty; while words, though new and of recent make,
> will win acceptance, if they spring from a Greek fount
> and are modified therefrom but sparingly. Why indeed
> shall Romans grant this license to Caecilius and Plau-
> tus, and refuse it to Virgil and Varro? And why should I
> be grudged the right of adding, if I can, my little fund,
> when the tongue of Cato and of Ennius has enriched
> our mother speech and brought to light new names for
> things? It has ever been, and ever will be, permitted
> to produce names stamped with the mint mark of
> the day.

For the comprehension of these verses, understand that
Horace first praises the art of transumption and invites us to
practice it, saying "be tasteful," that is, subtle, and "careful,"
that is, circumspect, "in weaving words together," that is, in
positing a new meaning, because "you will express yourself,"
that is, you will be able to speak, "most happily," that is laud-
ably and elegantly, "if a skillful setting," that is a prudent ordering, "renders," that is, makes, a word that is "familiar,"

significacionem propriam, "novum," per significacionem transumptivam.

18   Secundo ostendit quod licitum est invenire verba nova, que scilicet prius nunquam erant audita, sic: "si forte necesse est," id est oportunum, "monstrare," id est exprimere, "abdita rerum," id est conceptus rerum qui in animo absconduntur, "recentibus indiciis," id est novis signis vel verbis. Est enim id quod est in voce nota vel signum eius quod est in mente, ut dicit Philosophus. Tunc "continget," id est contingens erit, et "licencia dabitur"—"licencia," dico, "sumpta pudenter," id est cum quadam pudencia et raritate. "Dabitur," inquam, "licencia fingere," id est ad fingendum vocabula "non exaudita Cithegis," id est illis Romanis qui nova verba maxime invenerunt. "Cithegis," dico, "cinctutis," id est cinctis, id est paratis, et est epentesis figura. Patet igitur quod invenire possumus que Cithegi nunquam audierunt.

19   Tercio ostendit quod ex Greco possumus extorquere dicciones et hoc per modicam immutacionem diccionis, ut ab hiis Grecis "tragodia," "comodia," "cristos," extorquentur ista notha "tragedia," "comedia," "Cristus." Similiter, Iohannes Hauvillensis, ab "archos" Grece, quod est "princeps" Latine, et "trene," "lamentacio," extorsit hoc nomen "Architrenius," id est "principaliter lamentans," et hoc per modicam mutacionem. Mutavit enim "archos" in "archi," "trene" in "trenius," ex quibus "Architrenius." Similiter et quilibet consimili potest uti artificio. Ego enim pro hac clausula "Duxisti tibi mulierem meretricem audacter"

through its proper signification, "new," through a transumptive signification.

In the second place, he shows that we are allowed to invent new words, that is, words that never were heard before, thus: "if it is necessary," that is, it is opportune, "to represent," that is, express, "abstruse things," that is, the concepts of things that are hidden in the mind, "in novel terms," that is, in new signs or words. For that which is in a word is a mark or sign of what is in the mind, as the Philosopher says. Then "you will have a chance," that is, the chance will be offered, and "license will be granted"—"license," I say, "if used with modesty," that is, with a certain modesty and infrequency. "There will be granted," I say, "license to fashion," that is, for inventing words "never heard of by the Cethegi," that is, by those Romans who invented new words to the greatest extent. "By the Cethegi," I say, who are "kilted," that is girt, that is, prepared (and this is the figure epenthesis). The sense is, therefore, that we can invent what the Cethegi never heard.

Third, he shows that we can extract words from the Greek, and this through a small modification of the word, as from these Greek words "tragodia," "comodia," "cristos," are extracted these hybrids "tragedy," "comedy," "Christ." In like manner John of Hauville extracted from "archos" in Greek, which is "prince" in Latin, and "trene," "lamentation," this word "Architrenius," that is, "one who principally laments," and this through a small change. For he changed "archos" into "archi" and "trene" into "trenius," from which comes "Architrenius." In the same way, anyone else can employ a similar technique. For in place of the sentence: "You have rashly taken a harlot as your wife" I might say: "You

dicerem: "Duxisti Thaidem panthomorpham," id est omni-
formem sive variabilem. "Panthomorphon" Grece "omni-
forme" significat. Dicit Oracius: "et verba novaque" pro, id
est, "nuper ficta," "habebunt fidem," id est auctoritatem, "si
cadant de Greco fonte," id est si deriventur a Greco, quod
fons est Latini, "verba," dico, "detorta," id est mutata,
"parce," id est per modicam mutacionem.

20   Quarto ostendit quod hec ars et licencia data est omnibus
in communi. Unde dicit "autem," pro set, "quid dabit Romanus," id est concedet, "Cecilio et Plauto," qui antiquissimi
sunt, "ademptum," id est ablatum vel negatum, "a Virgilio et
Varro," qui quasi moderni sunt. Hoc est, quam licenciam
extorquendi nova verba concedet Romanus Cecilio et
Plauto, quam non concedet Virgilio et Varro? (Quasi diceret
"nullam.") Et quod nos moderni non excludamur ostendit,
dicens "cur," id est qua racione, "ego," Oracius, "si possum
adquirere pauca," id est verba, "invideor," id est per invidiam
prohibeor (quasi diceret "non prohibeor"), "cum lingua Catonis et Enni," qui Latinum dicuntur primitus invenisse,
"ditaverit sermonem patrium," id est linguam Latinam, "et
protulerit nova nomina rerum," que inaudita prius fuerunt.

21   Quinto concludit: "Licuit semperque licebit producere
signatum presente nota." Hoc paulo ante expositum est. In
omni enim transumpcione hoc precipue attendendum est,
ut significacio diccionis transumpte ad significacionem

have married a pantomorphic Thais," that is, one who is omniform and changeable. "Pantomorphon" in Greek means
"omniform." Horace says: "and new words," that is, as those
"of recent make," "will win acceptance," that is, authority, "if
they spring from a Greek fount," that is, if they are drawn
from Greek, which is the source of Latin, "words," I say, that
"are modified," that is, have been changed, "sparingly," that
is, through a small change.

Fourth, he shows that this art and license have been 20
granted to all in common. For this reason he says "indeed,"
instead of "but," "why shall Romans grant," that is, allow it,
"to Caecilius and Plautus," who are most ancient, and "refuse," that is, take it away or deny it, "to Virgil and Varro,"
who are, as it were, moderns. This is to say, what license for
extracting new words will a Roman allow to Caecilius and
Plautus that he will not allow to Virgil and Varro? (As if to
say "none.") And he shows that we moderns are not excluded
when he says "and why," that is, for what reason, should "I,"
Horace, "if I can add my little fund," that is, of words, "be
grudged the right," that is, be forbidden through envy (as if
to say "I am *not* forbidden"), "when the tongue of Cato and
of Ennius," who are said to have invented Latin originally,
"has enriched our mother speech," that is, the Latin tongue,
"and brought to light new terms for things," which had not
been heard previously.

Fifth, he concludes: "It has ever been, and ever will be, 21
permitted to produce something stamped with the mint
mark of the day." This was explained a little earlier. Moreover, in every transumption one should pay special attention to this: the meaning of the word that has been transumed should be consistent with the meaning of a word in

159

diccionis cui fit transumpcio dependeat convenienter, ut "Iste inebriatur poculo amoris." Viciose enim diceretur "pane amoris."

22   Contingit eciam plerumque quod ex intencione transumentis diccionis transumpte significacio variatur. In huiusmodi enim transumpcione quandoque respicitur status ipsius cuius nomen transumitur, quandoque vicina convertibilitas terminorum—illius, scilicet, qui transumitur et illius pro quo transumitur. Status respicitur, ut si dicam "Iste est alter Tantalus," quia Tantalus fuit in diviciis quibus uti non potuit. Ideo transumo hanc diccionem "Tantalus" ad significandum idem quod "egenus in habundancia." Unde quidam:

> Inter opes multas, cum sit michi nulla facultas,
>   Parisius dego Tantalus alter ego.

Respicitur eciam vicina convertibilitas terminorum, ut si dicam "Pirotheus est alter Theseus." In hac enim non respicio statum Thesei set transumo hanc diccionem "Theseus" ad significandum idem quod hec vox: "volens omnia que Theseus," quia illi duo termini fere convertuntur. Patet igitur quod secundum diversam transsumentis intencionem, hec clausula potest dupliciter intelligi:

> Iste est alter Piramus.

relation to which the transumption is made, as in "This person is made drunk by the cup of love." For it would be faulty to say "by the bread of love."

Also, it frequently happens that the meaning of the transumed word varies according to the intention of the one who is doing the transuming. Indeed, in this sort of transumption, sometimes the focus is on the condition of an actual person whose name is being transumed, and sometimes it is on the near interchangeability of the terms involved— namely, of the term that is transumed and of the one in relation to which it is transumed. The condition of the person himself is the focus, as if I were to say "He is a second Tantalus," because Tantalus was surrounded by riches that he could not use. Thus I transume this name "Tantalus" to mean the same thing as "poor in the midst of abundance." So somebody says:

> Amid many riches, since I have no means of my own,
> in Paris I live as a second Tantalus.

The near interchangeability of terms also can be the focus, as if I were to say "Pirotheus is a second Theseus." For in this transumption I do not focus on the condition of Theseus but I transume this word "Theseus" so that it means the same thing as the phrase "wishing everything that Theseus wishes," because those two terms can practically be interchanged. Therefore it is clear that, according to the different intention of the one doing the transuming, the following sentence can be understood in two ways:

> He is a second Pyramus.

Si respiciatur status, sic: "Piramus," id est "amicus a voluntate." Unde illud:

> Vivit adhuc Piramus Tisbe dilectissimus.

Si convertibilitas, sic: "Piramus," id est "omnia volens que
Piramus." Unde illud:

> Nodus amoris eos constrinxit et altera Tisbe
> Piramus et Tisbe Piramus alter erat.

Hic enim modus transumpcionis ornatissimus iudicatur.
Unde propter hunc modum isti duo versus maxime com-
mendantur:

> Cum sit "ego" quod "nos" et cum sit "amo" quod
> "amamus,"
> Iunge licenter "amo nos" et "amamus ego."

23   Transumitur autem diccio triplici racione. Vel racione alicuius precedentis, ut hic: "In vernali deliciosa temperie procelle dormiunt, aer mansuescit, aura silet, aves citharizant,
rivi ludunt, rami pubescunt, agri floribus depinguntur." Ecce
omnia ista verba transumuntur racione precedencium no-
minativorum. Vel transumuntur racione sequentis, ut hic:
"Predicator verbi Dei verba seminat, quibus cibat animum,
inebriat aures et reficit totam mentem." Ecce omnia hec
verba transumuntur racione sequencium obliquorum. Vel
transumitur diccio racione utriusque, ut hic: "Studiosus
auditor ex ore docentis haurit doctrinam, qua et animus

If the focus is on condition, thus: "Pyramus," that is, "a friend deprived of his own will." And so we have that verse:

He lives still a Pyramus most loved by Thisbe.

If the focus is on interchangeability, thus: "Pyramus," that is, "wishing everything that Pyramus wishes." And so we have that verse:

The knot of love bound them together, and Pyramus was a second Thisbe and Thisbe a second Pyramus.

Now this method of transumption is considered most elegant. Thus, on account of this method, these two verses are accorded the greatest praise:

Since "I" is "we" and since "I love" is "we love," it is licit to join *amo* to *nos* and *amamus* to *ego*.

Moreover, a word is transumed in one of three respects. 23 Either with respect to something that precedes it, as here: "In the delightful temperateness of spring storms slumber, the air grows mild, the wind keeps silent, the birds play the lyre, the brooks play, the branches put forth the down of puberty, the fields are painted with flowers." Note that all these verbs are transumed with respect to the preceding nominatives. Or the words are transumed with respect to something that follows, as here: "The preacher of God's word sows words, with which he feeds the soul, intoxicates the ears, and refreshes the entire mind." Note that all these verbs are transumed with respect to the direct objects that follow them. Or a word is transumed with respect to both, as here: "The zealous listener draws from the teacher's mouth learning, by which the intellect is guided toward

promovetur ad scienciam et spiritus ad virtutem." Ecce hoc verbum "promovetur" transumitur racione huius precedentis "animus" et huius sequentis "ad scienciam," similiter et racione huius precedentis "spiritus" et huius sequentis "virtutem."

24   Nunc dicendum est de quattuor speciebus gravioribus transumpcionis, quarum prima est nominacio.

25   "Nominacio," secundum Tullium, "est que nos admonet ut cuius rei aut nomen non sit aut satis honestum non sit, eam nosmet verbo idoneo nominemus," id est quando aliquid vel caret nomine, cui per similitudinem nomen imponimus, vel habet nomen et illud honestiori nomine nominamus. Ei quod caret nomine nomen imponimus, ut cum dicimus:

"Iurgia" ventorum, "strepitus" maris, "ira" procelle.

Nam nec ventus pro iurgio, nec mare pro strepitu, nec ira pro procella nomen propriatum habet. Id quod habet nomen honestiori nomine nominamus, ut cum dicitur

Populi "fragor" impulit urbem,

id est tumultus populi. Fit autem duabus de causis, imitacionis scilicet et significacionis. Imitacionis, ut in premisso exemplo "iurgia ventorum etc." Significacionis, ut in illo exemplo "populi fragor impulit urbem" ad significandum magnum fuisse tumultum.

knowledge and the spirit likewise toward virtue." Note that the verb "is guided" is transumed with respect to the preceding word "intellect" and the subsequent phrase "toward knowledge," and in like manner with respect to the preceding word "spirit" and the subsequent word "virtue."

Now we should speak about the four weightier kinds of 24 transumption, of which the first is onomatopoeia.

"Onomatopoeia," according to Cicero, "is what suggests 25 to us that we should ourselves designate with a suitable word a thing which either has no name or has a name that is not quite appropriate," that is, when something either lacks a name, and we impose a name on it through similitude, or it possesses a name and we name it with a more appropriate name. We impose a name on that which lacks a name, as when we say:

The "quarreling" of the winds, the "crashing" of the sea, the "rage" of the storm.

For the wind has no proper name for its "quarreling," nor the sea for its "crashing," nor the storm for its "wrath." We name that which has a name by a more appropriate name, as when it is said that

The "thundering" of the populace assailed the city,

that is, the uproar of the populace. And this is done for two reasons, namely, for the sake of imitation and for the sake of meaning. Imitation, as in the prior example "the quarreling of the winds etc." Meaning, as in the example "the thundering of the populace assailed the city" to signify that the uproar had been great.

26   Et habet hic color locum in substantivis appellativis. Transumitur substantivum appellativum ad significacionem adiectivi sue proprietatis et hoc dupliciter. Quandoque sine determinacione, ut si pro hac "Hostes vestri non venient desides set feroces" dicam "Non venient vobis asini set leones." Hic modus aptissime fit quando substantivum transumptum alii substantivo iungitur per apposicionem. *Architrenius:*

Nascitur et puero vagit nova pagina versu,

ut intelligas "versu puero," id est "novo." Quandoque cum determinacione et hoc tripliciter. Tum preposicionis cum suo casuali, ut hic: "Bernardus Silvestris in dictamine prosaico psitacus, in metrico est et philomena." Tum ablativi per se, ut:

Iste est nanus corpore, mente gigas.

Tum genitivi, ut:

Succedet asinus nequicie.

Et sciendum quod quando substantivum transumitur sic ad significacionem adiectivi sue proprietatis verius est denominacio quam nominacio.

27   Pronominacio est que quasi cognomine quodam extraneo demonstrat illud quod suo nomine non potest appellari, id est quando attribuimus proprium nomen et extraneum alicui cum per eius nomen, ad laudem vel vituperium, non cognominetur. Ad laudem, ut de quodam dicitur:

And this color also has its place in appellative substan- 26
tives. An appellative substantive can be transumed to express the meaning of an adjective that signifies one of its
properties, and this in two ways. Sometimes without modification, as if in place of this: "Your enemies when they come
will not be idle but fierce" I were to say "It is not asses that
will come to you but lions." This method is used most fittingly when a transumed substantive is joined to another
substantive through apposition. As in the *Architrenius:*

A new work is born, and wails in infant verses,

so that you understand "in infant verses," that is, in new
verses. Sometimes with modification, and this in three ways.
At times by a preposition with its object, as here: "Bernard
Silvestris is a parrot in prose composition and in metrical
composition a nightingale." At times by an unaccompanied
ablative, as:

He is a dwarf in body, a giant in mind.

At times by a genitive, as:

Next will come the ass of wickedness.

And you should know that when a substantive is transumed
in this way to the meaning of an adjective that signifies one
of its properties, it is more precisely metonymy than onomatopoeia.

Antonomasia designates by a kind of adventitious epithet 27
a thing that cannot be called by its proper name, that is,
when we assign a name that is both proper and adventitious
to someone when he may not be named by his own name, in
praise or in blame. In praise, as is said of someone:

Ore Paris, fama Pelides, viribus Hector,
censu Cresus, avis Cesar Agenor erat.

Ad vituperium, ut de alio, scilicet Davo, dicitur:

Actibus Herodes, animo Nero, Birria verbis,
fraude Sinon, Protheus pectore Davus erat.

Et habet hic color locum in propriis nominibus ad propositum transumptis. Ideo dictum est ad propositum, quoniam
si transumatur proprium nomen ad contrarium permutacio
est, ut nunc dicam.

28   Permutacio est oracio aliud verbis, aliud in sentencia de-
monstrans. Et fit quattuor modis. Primo per similitudinem,
ut hic:

"Navem regit ille magister
et Tiphis noster" vel "Redam rusticus iste
ducit et Autemedon noster."

Tiphis enim optimus nauta et Autemedon optimus auriga
fuisse dicitur. Unde Ovidius:

Tiphis et Autemedon dicar amoris ego.

Secundo modo per contrarium, ut "Iste est Paris facie," id
est turpis et sic contrarius Paridi. Et hic modus inter tropos
yronia nominatur, id est hostilis derisio. Tercio modo
quando plures dicciones allegorice sunt transumpte, ut:

Pastores predantur oves,

Agenor was in face a Paris, in fame a Pelides, in strength a Hector, in wealth a Croesus, in ancestors a Caesar.

In blame, as is said concerning another, namely, Davus:

Davus was in deeds a Herod, in spirit a Nero, a Birria in words, in deceit a Sinon, a Proteus in heart.

And this color has its place in proper nouns that have been transumed in line with the stated theme. "In line with the stated theme" has been said because, if a proper noun is transumed to its contrary, then it is allegory, as I will now discuss.

Allegory is a manner of speaking that denotes one thing 28 by the letter of the words, but another by their meaning. And it is done in four ways. First, through similitude, as here:

"The captain steers the ship and is our Tiphys" or "This bumpkin drives the wagon and is our Automedon."

For Tiphys is said to have been the best sailor and Automedon the best charioteer. So Ovid says:

I shall be called the Tiphys and Automedon of Love.

The second way is through opposition, as "He is a Paris in face," that is, ugly and thus the opposite of Paris. And among the tropes this method is called irony, that is, hostile derision. The third way is when many words have been transumed allegorically, as:

Shepherds rob the sheep,

169

id est prelati subiectos. Quarto modo quando tota oracio transumitur et nulla pars sui, id est quando oracio accipitur pro eo quod ex ea sequitur, ut hic:

Litus aro lateremque lavo dum servio pravo,

id est inaniter laboro. Hoc enim sequitur ex premissis.

29   Translacio est cum verbum vel adiectivum, gracia convenientis similitudinis, a propria ad alienam traditur significacionem, ut "Pratum ridet," quando scilicet flores exeunt a foliis sicut dentes a labiis. Iste sermo est "succosus," "aridus," "exanguis," "durus" vel "strictus."

30   Nunc sequitur de quinque levioribus speciebus transumpcionis, quarum prima est circuicio.

31   Circuicio est oracio rem simplicem sumpta forma circumscribens, ut quando proprietas que est forma subiecti ponitur pro subiecto cuius est, ut flagicium pro flagicioso, gracia pro gracioso, ut superius dicitur ubi de emphasi dictum est.

32   Hic color optimus est pueris instruendis. Verbi gracia, sumatur aliqua rudis oracio, ut hec: "Tempus nocet segeti." Addatur utrique substantivo conveniens adiectivum, sic: "Tempus humidum nocet segeti nutriende." Et cum omne adiectivum copulans habeat substantivum preiacens, a quo denominative sumitur, mutetur utrumque adiectivum in substantivum et fiet circuicio utriusque. Oportet igitur

that is, the prelates rob their subjects. The fourth way is when the entire sentence is rephrased transumptively and not any one part of it, that is, when the sentence is received in place of that which follows from it, as here:

> I plow the shore and I wash brick while I serve a depraved man,

that is, I labor in vain. And this follows from what has been said before.

Metaphor is when a verb or an adjective is transferred   29
from its proper meaning to a different one by virtue of a relevant point of comparison, as in "The meadow laughs," that is, when the flowers emerge from the leaves like teeth from the lips. This sort of discourse can be "juicy," "dry," "bloodless," "hard," or "tight."

What now follows concerns the five lighter types of transumption, of which the first is periphrasis.   30

Periphrasis is a manner of speaking that uses a particular   31
feature to circumscribe a simple idea, as when a property that is a feature of a subject is put in place of the subject whose feature it is, as "disgrace" for "disgraceful," "grace" for "gracious," as is said above where emphasis was discussed.

This color is an excellent one for teaching boys. For example, let some rough sentence be selected, like this: "The   32
season does harm to the crop." Let a fitting adjective be joined to each substantive, thus: "The wet season does harm to the nourishing crop." And since each connecting adjective has a substantive that precedes it, and from which it is derived by metonymy, let each adjective be changed into a substantive and a periphrasis of both will be created. It is

mutare utrumque priorum substantivorum in genitivum, quod potest eciam fieri cum verbi mutacione, sic:

Temporis humiditas furatur segetis nutrimentum.

Tandem cuilibet substantivo conferre potes suum adiectivum, si placet, hoc modo: "Ventosi temporis infelix humiditas segetis spoliat nutrimentum."

33   Ornatissime fit circuicio quando actum verbi determinat diccio significans instrumentum vel locum vel tempus vel huiusmodi, ut hic: "Temporis humiditas sua manu furibunda furatur segetis nutrimentum." Unde diligenter intuendum est si unum tantum, duo vel plura sint subiecta in proposita materia. Si unum tantum, illud mutandum est in substantivum significans proprietatem. Si duo, potest alterum tantum vel utrumque mutari. Si plura quam duo, elegans ut maior pars mutetur. Set ut invenias substantivum significans proprietatem, adicias subiecto convenientissimum adiectivum et in substantivum significans proprietatem mutetur. Deinde et verbum per similitudinem mutetur et determinetur per diccionem instrumentum, tempus vel locum significantem vel huiusmodi. Verbi gracia, in hac rudi locucione "Aves ludunt," unum habes subiectum, scilicet "aves." Deinde adicias conveniens adiectivum, quod inveniatur per causam, sic: "Aves ludunt quia lascive." Deinde extrahe ab adiectivo "lascivia." Dic igitur "Avium lascivia ludit." Deinde

then necessary to change both of the original substantives into the genitive case, which also can be done in conjunction with a changing of the verb, thus:

The wetness of the season steals the nourishment of the crop.

Finally, if you wish, you can join to any substantive its adjective, in this way: "The infertile wetness of the windy season plunders the nourishment of the crop."

Periphrasis is most elegant when a word that designates 33 an instrument or a place or a time or the like modifies the action of the verb, as here: "The wetness of the season with its thieving hand steals the nourishment of the crop." In this connection one should take careful heed whether there is only one subject, two subjects, or many subjects in the proposed subject matter. If only one, that one should be changed into a substantive that designates a property. If two, only one of them can be changed or both of them. If more than two, it is elegant if the majority of them are changed. But in order to find a substantive that designates a property, first add to the subject a most fitting adjective and then let it be changed into a substantive that designates a property. Next let the verb both be changed through a similitude and modified by a word that designates an instrument, time or place or the like. For example, in the rough expression "The birds play," you have one subject, namely, "birds." Next add an appropriate adjective, which may be discovered through the cause of the action, thus: "The birds play because they are wanton." Next extract "wantonness" from the adjective. Say, therefore, "The wantonness of the

subde diccionem significantem instrumentum, tempus vel locum vel huiusmodi, sic:

Ludit in arboreis avium lascivia ramis.

Nec oportet hic mutare verbum, cum sit clausula conveniens.

34   Similiter in hac rudi locucione "Ego diligo Deum," habes duo subiecta, "Ego" et "Deum." Adicias utrique conveniens adiectivum, sic: "Ego devotus diligo Deum misericordem." Deinde muta utrumque adiectivum in substantivum, sic: "Mea devocio Dei diligit misericordiam." Ut autem perfeccius dicatur, muta verbum "diligit" per similitudinem, sic. Quid est diligere, vide per simile. Qui enim diligit, illum quem diligit amplectitur. Sume igitur "amplectitur" pro "diligit." Deinde subde instrumentum utriusque actus, diligendi et amplectendi. Instrumentum diligendi est cor, amplectendi brachium. Mutetur igitur instrumentum primi actus, scilicet cor, in genitivum et habes: "Mea devocio Dei misericordiam brachiis cordis amplectitur."

35   Fit autem hic color duabus de causis, scilicet causa rei ante oculos ponende et causa brevitatis. Causa rei ante oculos ponende, sic:

Hoc scelus, hec pestis, hec impietas, furor iste
nostrum concussit subita formidine regnum.

Causa brevitatis, sic:

Extinguit nostram successio principis urbem.

birds plays." Next supply a word that designates an instrument, time or place or the like, thus:

> The wantonness of the birds plays in the branches of the trees.

Here it is not necessary to change the verb, since the sentence is agreeable.

Likewise, in this rough expression "I love God," you have 34 two subjects, "I" and "God." Add a fitting adjective to each, thus: "Devout, I love merciful God." Next change each adjective into a substantive, thus: "My devotion loves God's mercy." But so that it may be expressed more perfectly, change the verb "loves" through a similitude, as follows. Through a comparison, see what it is to love. For one who loves embraces the one whom he loves. Therefore, use "embraces" in place of "loves." Next supply the instrument of each act, loving and embracing. The instrument of loving is the heart, of embracing the arms. Therefore, let the instrument of the first act, namely, the heart, be changed into a genitive and you have "My devotion embraces the mercy of God with the arms of my heart."

And this color is used for two reasons, namely, for the 35 sake of placing the thing before the reader's eyes and for the sake of brevity. For the sake of placing the thing before the reader's eyes, thus:

> This sin, this plague, this impiety, this madness has shaken our realm with sudden terror.

For the sake of brevity, thus:

> The succession of the prince has destroyed our city.

36 "Denominacio," secundum Tullium, "est que a rebus finitis et propinquis trahit oracionem qua possit intelligi res
que non suo vocabulo sit appellata." Que descripcio quia
difficilis est, ponamus et aliam huius sufficienter declarati-
vam. Denominacio est quociens illud ex quo, in quo vel per
quod ponitur pro eo quod vel e contrario. Quam descripcionem sic intellige: "illud ex quo," scilicet "aliquid est," ponitur pro "eo quod," scilicet "ex eo est," ut quando inventor
ponitur pro invento, efficiens pro effectu, materia pro materiato, causa pro causato, possessor pro possesso. "In quo," id
est quociens illud in quo aliud est ponitur pro eo quod, scilicet in illo est, ut quando continens ponitur pro contento,
subiectum pro proprietate, tempus pro eo quod est in tempore, maius commune pro minus communi et sic de similibus. "Per quod," id est quociens illud per quod aliud est ponitur pro eo quod, scilicet per illud est, ut utens pro utensili,
dominus pro ministro, antecedens pro consequente et sic de
consimilibus. "Vel e contrario," id est quociens illud quod ex
alio est ponitur pro eo ex quo est, ut quando inventum pro
inventore, effectus pro efficiente, materiatum pro materia,
causatum pro causa. Et consimiliter de aliis intellige, scilicet
"in quo" et "per quod."

37 Inventor pro invento, ut

CHAPTER 5

"Metonymy," according to Cicero, "is the figure which   36
draws from an object bounded or closely akin an expression
suggesting the object meant, but not called by its own
name." Because this description is difficult, let us provide
another that clarifies it adequately. Metonymy occurs whenever that from which, that within which, or that by means
of which is put in place of that which a thing is, or the reverse. Understand this description as follows: "that from
which" (something is) is put in place of "that which" (is from
it), as when the inventor is put in place of the invention, the
agent in place of the effect, the materials in place of what
was made from them, the cause in place of what was caused,
the owner in place of what was owned. "Within which," that
is, whenever "that within which something is" is put in place
of "that which" (is within it), as when the container is put in
place of the contained, the subject in place of the property, a
time in place of what takes place within the time, the more
common in place of the less common, and so on. "By means
of which," that is, whenever "that by means of which something is" is put in place of "that which" (is by means of it), as
the user in place of the utensil, the master in place of the
servant, the antecedent in place of the consequence, and so
on. "Or the reverse," that is, whenever "that which is from
something else" is put in place of "that from which it is," as
when the invention is put in place of the inventor, the effect
in place of the agent, what was made in place of the materials it was made from, what was caused in place of the cause.
And understand the others in the same way, namely, "within
which" and "by means of which."

The inventor in place of the invention, as   37

177

Sine Cerere et Libero friget Venus,

id est sine pane et vino friget luxuria. Item et hic:

In cratere meo Thetis est coniuncta Lieo.
Est dea iuncta deo set dea maior eo.

Id est, aqua mixta est vino in cipho meo set plus est de aqua quam de vino.

38   Econtra inventum pro inventore, sic:

Stultus qui segeti, stultus qui supplicat uve:
per segetem, Cererem, Bachum designo per uvam.

39   Efficiens pro effectu vel causa pro causato, quoniam sub simili conceptu utrumque comprehenditur, de facili patebit si quid sit causa, quid effectus cognoscas. Causa vel efficiens est illud ex quo vel per quod aliquid fit. Causatum vel effectus est quod fit ex aliqua causa vel per aliquam causam. Verbi gracia, "homines sunt tristes" et hoc ex aliqua causa. Tristantur enim homines non sine causa. Causa propter quam tristantur est tempus, bellum vel huiusmodi. Est igitur tempus, bellum vel huiusmodi causa vel efficiens, "homines" sunt causatum vel effectus. Constituitur igitur in talibus difficultas quando tempus, bellum vel huiusmodi ponitur pro hominibus, sic: "Tempus istud est triste," id est homines sunt tristes propter tempus. "Bellum est flebile," id est homines sunt flebiles propter bellum. Vel melius dicamus causa ponitur pro causato vel efficiens pro effectu quando adiectivo in

Without Ceres and Liber Venus freezes,

that is, without bread and wine lust is cold. Likewise here:

> In my drinking bowl Thetis is joined to Lyaeus. Thus is
> goddess united with god, but the goddess is greater
> than he.

That is, water has been mixed with wine in my cup but there
is more of water than of wine.

Conversely, the invention in place of the inventor, thus: 38

> He is stupid who prays to the grain, stupid who prays
> to the grape. By "grain" I signify Ceres, by "grape" Bac-
> chus.

The agent in place of the effect or the cause for what was   39
caused—since both are included under the same concept—
will be readily apparent if you recognize what is a cause,
what an effect. The cause or the agent is that from which or
by means of which something comes to be. What is caused
or the effect is that which comes to be from some cause or
by means of some cause. For example, "The men are sad,"
and this from some cause. For men do not become sad without cause. The cause of their becoming sad is the times, war,
or the like. The times, war, or the like is therefore the cause
or agent; "the men" are what was caused or the effect.
Therefore, the difficult situation of such persons is estab-
lished when the times, war, or the like is put in place of the
men, thus: "This time is sad," that is, "men are sad on account of the times." "War is tearful," that is, "men are tearful
on account of war." Or we might better say that cause is put
in place of what was caused or agent for effect when a word

quo notatur effectus cause iungitur diccio significans causam, sic: "Dies iste est letus," id est causa que facit letum vel
efficiens leticiam. "Iste cibus est eger," id est efficiens egrum
vel egritudinem. Ad hunc modum potest reduci illud Sancti
Thome:

O letus dolor in tristi gaudio,

id est dolor in principio efficiens leticiam in fine. Similiter et
hic: "O felix culpa que talem ac tantum meruit habere re-
demptorem," id est efficiens felicitatem per redempcionem.
Nunquam enim fuissemus redempti nisi fecissemus peccatum. "O necessarium Ade peccatum," id est peccatum efficiens redempcionem necessariam.

40   Econtra causatum pro causa vel effectus pro efficiente, ut
in principio *Anticlaudiani:*

Ne iaceat calamus scabra rubigine torpens.

"Scabra rubigine," id est inhonesta dissuetudine, nam ru-
bigo effectus est dissuetudinis; per dissuetudinem ferrum
trahit rubiginem. Similiter ubi dicitur "calamus" ponitur efficiens pro effectu, scilicet calamus pro scriptura vel modo
scribendi. Per hunc modum: "Iste frequenter sudat in libris,"
id est laborat. "Iste excandescit," id est irascitur. "Iste
erubescit," id est verecundatur. "Iste pallet," id est timet.
Est enim sudor effectus laboris. Excandere effectus est ire,
erubescere verecundie, pallere timoris.

41   Materia pro materiato, ut "Ferro suo vulneravit me," id
est gladio.

that signifies the cause is joined to an adjective in which the effect of a cause is designated, thus: "This day is joyful," that is, the day is a cause that makes one joyful or brings about joy. "This food is sick," that is, the food causes one to be sick or causes sickness. What has been said of St. Thomas Becket can be attributed to this method:

O happy sorrow in sad joy,

that is, sorrow in the beginning that produces joy in the end. And likewise here: "O happy fault that deserved to have such a great redeemer," that is, a fault that produces happiness through redemption. For we never would have been redeemed unless we had committed the sin. "O necessary sin of Adam," that is, sin that produces a necessary redemption.

Conversely, what was caused in place of the cause or the 40 effect in place of the agent, as in the beginning of the *Anti-claudianus:*

Lest my pen lie idle, coated with rust.

"Coated with rust," that is, through shameful disuse, for rust is the effect of disuse; through disuse iron attracts rust. Likewise, when "pen" is said, the agent is put in place of the effect, namely, the pen in place of the writing or the manner of writing. In the same way: "He frequently sweats over his books," that is, labors. "He grows hot," that is, gets angry. "He reddens," that is, feels ashamed. "He grows pale," that is, fears. For sweat is the effect of labor, to grow hot is the effect of anger, to redden that of shame, to grow pale that of fear.

Materials in place of what was made from them, as "With 41 his iron he wounded me," that is, with his sword.

Digitus lascivit in auro,

id est in annulo auri. Et Ovidius, *Methamorphoseos,* ostendens quod in aurea etate mundi homines non navigabant in terras alienas, ponit "pinum," que est arbor de qua fiebant naves, pro nave, sic:

Nondum cesa suis, peregrinum ut viseret orbem,
montibus in liquidas pinus descenderat undas.

42 Econtra, materiatum pro materia, sic:

Hec navis viruit, hec quondam floruit hasta,

id est lignum de quo fiebat navis et hasta.

43 Possessor pro possesso, continens pro contento, subiectum pro proprietate, quia hec multum similia videntur, ut in *Alexandreide* Galteri, de laude Alexandri:

Invalidusque puer gerit alto corde leonem,

id est audaciam leoninam. Et alibi in eodem: "Indue mente virum," id est audaciam vel probitatem virilem. Per hoc autem artificium pro "candore" ponitur "nix," "ebur" vel "lilium"; pro "rubore," "rosa"; pro "purpura," "murex"; pro suavi odore, "balsamus"; pro lacrimabili peticione, "lacrima." Et sic pro quibuscumque subiectis sue proprietates. Verbi gracia, pro hac: "Hec puella candidam habet faciem cum rubore depictam," dicendum est:

The finger rejoices in gold,

that is, in a ring made of gold. And Ovid, in the *Metamorphoses,* when he shows that in the golden age of the world men did not sail to foreign lands, puts "pine," which is the tree from which ships are made, in place of "ship," thus:

> Not yet had the pine tree, felled on its native mountains, descended thence into the watery plain to visit other lands.

Conversely, what was made in place of the materials from which it was made, thus: 42

> This ship was green, this spear once flowered,

that is, the wood from which the ship and the spear were made.

The owner in place of the possession, the container in place of what was contained, the subject in place of its property, because these seem very similar, as in Walter of Châtillon's *Alexandreis,* in praise of Alexander: 43

> And the weak boy bears the lion in his great heart,

that is, the lion's boldness. And elsewhere in the same work: "put on the man in your mind," that is, a man's boldness or valor. By means of this technique, moreover, "snow," "ivory," or "lily" can be put in place of "whiteness"; in place of "redness," "rose"; in place of "purple," "murex"; in place of "sweet odor," "balsam"; in place of "tearful plea," "tear." And thus in place of any subjects whatsoever, their properties. For example, in place of "This girl has a white face painted with red," you should say

Lilia nupta rosis faciem pinxere puelle.

Set notandum quod non fit competens transumpcio si pro hac clausula: "Albedo est color disgregativus visus" poneretur hec: "Ebur est color disgregativus etc." vel "Lilia sunt color etc."

44 Oportet igitur quod huiusmodi transumpcio determinetur vel proprie vel remote. Proprie, ut hic, de pulcritudine cuiusdam puelle:

Consona sunt aliis oris rosa, balsama naris,
    nix auris, menti lilia, dentis ebur.

Ecce quomodo adiuncti genitivi proprie determinant omnes istos nominativos. Remote, scilicet ex alia parte coniunccionis, ut in alio exemplo: "Lilia nupta rosis etc." Nam hec diccio "faciem" ex parte predicati determinat transumpcionem, que fit ex parte subiecti, quia per hanc diccionem "faciem" patet manifeste quod hec diccio "lilia" ponitur pro candore. Per hos modos poterit diligens lector alios huiusmodi coloris modos, quos propter prolixitatem omittimus, intelligere satis clare.

45 Superlacio est oracio manifestam superans veritatem, laudis augende minuendeve causa. Causa laudis augende, sic:

Virginis ad vultum marcet rosa, lilia pallent,
    languet luna, latent sidera, Phebus hebet.

Lilies married to roses paint the girl's face.

But you should note that a suitable transumption is not produced if, in place of the sentence: "Whiteness is a color that is divisive of sight," this is put: "Ivory is a color that is divisive etc." or "Lilies are a color etc."

Now this sort of transumption may be modified either   44
properly or remotely. Properly, as here, concerning the beauty of a certain girl:

> In harmony with the rest are the rose of the mouth,
> the balsam of the nose, the snow of the ears, the lilies
> of the chin, the ivory of the teeth.

Notice how the attached genitives properly modify all those nominatives. Remotely, namely, from another part of what is being conjoined, as in another example: "Lilies married to roses etc." For the word "face" modifies, from the part of the predicate, the transumption, which is made from the part of the subject, because through the word "face" it becomes abundantly clear that the word "lilies" is put in place of "whiteness." In these ways a diligent reader will be able to understand clearly enough other methods for producing this sort of color, which we leave out in order to avoid prolixity.

Hyperbole is a manner of speech exaggerating the plain   45
truth, whether for the sake of augmenting or diminishing praise. For the sake of augmenting praise, thus:

> Beside the maiden's face the rose withers, the lilies
> fade, the moon languishes, the stars are hidden, Phoe-
> bus is dull.

Hic enim coincidunt superlacio, dissolutum et gradacio. Causa laudis minuende, sic:

Ydra, tigris, petra plus ydra, tigride, petra.

Et reducitur ad yperbolen. Et est utilis in descripcionibus. Videndum tamen est ne fiat excessus immoderatus. Unde in "Libro versuum" dicitur:

Et placet excessus, quem laudat et auris et usus.

Unde satis exceditur veritas in fine "Libri versuum," ubi de papa sic dicitur:

Nec Deus es nec homo: quasi neuter es inter utrumque,
quem Deus elegit socium. Socialiter egit
tecum, partitus tibi mundum; noluit unus
omnia, set voluit tibi terras et sibi celum.

46   Intelleccio est cum res tota parva de parte cognoscitur aut de toto pars, id est cum per partem cognoscimus totum vel e contrario. Per partem cognoscimus totum, sic: "Hic moram feci per quattuor hiemes," id est per quattuor annos. Similiter: "Equora puppis arat," id est navis, cuius posterior pars "puppis" dicitur. Similiter fit hic modus si "gurges" pro mari accipiatur, sic: "Transcurso gurgite vade." Et tunc incidit figura taphinosis, id est humiliacio magne rei. Fit autem

And here hyperbole, asyndeton, and climax occur together. For the sake of diminishing praise, thus:

> You are more hydra, tiger, stone than hydra, tiger, stone themselves.

And the Latin *superlatio* can be equated with hyperbole. And it is useful in descriptions. However, one should take heed lest the exaggeration be immoderate. For this reason it is said in the "Book of Verses":

> And exaggeration is a source of pleasure when both ear and good usage commend it.

So the truth is exaggerated just enough at the end of the "Book of Verses," when the following is said about the pope:

> You are neither God nor yet man. You are neither—yet somewhere between the two: one whom God has chosen as his partner. He deals with you as an associate, sharing the world with you. It was not his will to possess all things—he alone; rather, he willed earth to be yours and heaven his own.

Synecdoche occurs when the whole is known from a 46 small part or a part from the whole, that is, when through a part we recognize the whole or the reverse. We recognize the whole through a part, thus: "Here I tarried for four winters," that is, for four years. Likewise: "The stern plows the sea," that is, the ship, whose rear part is called the "stern." Likewise, this figure is produced if "eddies" is taken in place of "sea," thus: "Having sailed across the eddies, go." And then occurs the figure tapinosis, that is, the humbling of a great thing. However, this is done more excellently when

magis egregie quando attribuitur aliquid parti gracia tocius, ut "Hec mulier castum habet oculum."

47 Per totum intelligimus partem, ut "Sol intrat domum," id est radius solis; "Annus iste frigidus est" propter hiemem frigidam. Et in Evvangelio: "Tulerunt Dominum meum et nescio ubi posuerunt eum." "Dominum" pro corpus Domini accipitur, ut dicit Beda. Magis egregie fit quando aliquid attribuitur toti gracia partis, ut "Cesar erat crispus," propter caput crispum.

48 Fit et aliter intelleccio, secundum alios, quando ponimus unum pro pluribus vel plura pro uno. Et sic incidit figura exallage, id est alienacio numeri vel aliena posicio numeri. Unum pro pluribus, ut:

"Stella polum pingit," "Hillaris flos purpurat agros."
Per "stellam," "stellas," per "florem" concipe "flores."

Plura pro uno, ut:

Virgineos vultus lacrimis undare videmus,

cum de una sola virgine dicatur. Inde forsan est quod plurale huius nominis "os, oris," scilicet "ora," frequenter pro facie singulariter accipitur. Boecius, *De consolacione:*

Et veris elegi fletibus ora rigant.

Sentencia est: "Versus facti de miseria faciunt faciem meam lacrimabilem." Est enim "elegus, -ga, -gum," id est "miser, -a,

something is attributed to a part for the sake of the whole, as "This woman has a chaste eye."

We understand a part through the whole, as "The sun enters the house," that is, a ray of the sun; "This year is cold," on account of a cold winter. And in the Gospel: "They carried away my Lord and I know not where they placed him." "Lord" is used in place of "the Lord's body," as Bede says. It is done more excellently when something is attributed to the whole for the sake of a part, as "Caesar was curly," on account of his curly head of hair. 47

Synecdoche is produced in still another way, according to others, when we put one in place of many or many in place of one. And thus occurs the figure exallage, that is, the transferring of number or the unfamiliar placement of number. One in place of many, as: 48

"A star paints the heavens," "A cheery flower adorns the fields." By "star," understand "stars," by "flower," "flowers."

Many in place of one, as:

We see virginal faces overflow with tears,

even though only one virgin is being spoken about. It is perhaps for this reason that the plural of the noun *os, oris,* namely, *ora,* frequently is taken in place of "face" in the singular. Boethius, in his *Consolation:*

And with unfeigned tears these elegies drench my face.

The meaning is: "Verses made concerning unhappiness make my face tearful." For the word is *elegus, -ga, -gum,* that

-um." Ponitur eciam plurale pro singulari, ut in Evvangelio: "Latrones qui pendebant iuxta crucem improperabant ei." "Latrones," id est alter latro, ut exponit Beda. Et convenit intelleccio cum figura synodoche.

49   Abusio est quando verbo simili et propinquo pro certo et proprio abutimur, ut si ponatur "longum" pro "magno," "breve" pro "parvo," "eternum" pro "continuo," ut "Iste est homo brevis stature set longi concilii." Nam inter longum et magnum, breve et parvum magna est in significacione propinquitas. Et convenit cum figura catacresi.

50   Nunc dicendum est de illa specie transumpcionis penes quam receditur a propria potestate vocabuli gracia ordinis, non significacionis, que a Tullio transgressio, a Donato yperbaton nominatur.

51   Transgressio est que verborum perturbat ordinem traieccione et perversione, id est que removet ea in ordine que propinqua sunt in construccione vel anticipat ea que sequi deberent, ut hic: "Quos humane deprimit impietatis calliditas divina reserat optatum gracia consolamen" et hic:

Sepe novum vetera faciunt peccata pudorem.

Et reducitur ad yperbaton et ab eo exceditur. Habet autem sub se duos colores: traieccionem et perversionem.

52   Traieccio est exclusa preposicione quarumcumque parcium oracionis quas vel ordo anteponit preposteracio vel

is, *miser, -a, -um* (unhappy). Again the plural is put in place of the singular, as in the Gospel: "The thieves who were hanging alongside the cross reproached him." "Thieves," that is, the second thief, as Bede explains. And the Latin *intellectio* corresponds to the figure synecdoche.

Catachresis is when we misuse a similar and neighboring word in place of the exact and proper one, as if "long" were put in place of "great," "short" in place of "small," "eternal" in place of "continuous," as "This is a man of short stature but long counsel." For there is great affinity in meaning between long and great and between short and small. And the Latin *abusio* corresponds to the figure catachresis.   49

Now we should talk about that type of transumption in which one departs from the proper force of a word with respect to the order, not the meaning, which is called *trangressio* by Cicero, "hyperbaton" by Donatus.   50

Hyperbaton upsets the word order by means of transposition and anastrophe, that is, it separates in the word order things that are near to each other in the grammatical construction or takes up in advance things that ought to follow, as here: "Those whom the cunning[a]—presses down[c]—of human impiety[b], to them—lays open[bb]—divine grace[aa]—the desired consolation[cc]" and here: 51

Often old[a]—make new shame[c]—sins[b].

The Latin *transgressio* is equivalent to hyperbaton but has a narrower reference. Moreover, it holds within it two colors: transposition and anastrophe.

Transposition is the reversed order or the slight shifting backward of any parts of a speech, except prepositions, that   52

construccio coniungit recessio moderata, ut "Vestram deprecor amiciciam."

53 Perversio est moderata divisio vel posteracio preposicionis cum suo casuali. Fit autem dupliciter. Uno modo quando preposicio preponitur genitivo, suo casuali sequente, ut "ad tue peticionis instanciam," "in tue dileccionis amicicia." Alio modo quando preposicio interponitur, ut "ea de re," "qua de causa."

54 In omni transgressione hoc diligenter attendendum est, ne dicciones coniungendas nimia disiungat distancia, que et confusionem generat et ledit spiritum audientis. Unde Tullius, in secunda *Rethorica:* "Item fugere oportet longam verborum continuacionem, que et auditoris aures et spiritum oratoris ledit." Maxime tamen caveri debet in metris et precipue in metro elegiaco. Unde Vindosinensis ad Bartholomeum Turonensem, versus finem libri sui de vita Tobie, ita scribit:

Non placet aut placeat elegis yperbaton, immo
    succincte brevitas enucleata patet.

Et postea subdit causam, sic:

Vocum congeries prolixa, noverca favoris,
    displicet, excurrit, labitur, auris abest;
digeritur cicius epulum per fragmina: plena
    luce minuciolis carmina cesa placent.

Debent igitur in artificioso dictamine clausule breves esse et succincte, ne fiat construccio suspensiva aut transgressio

either the normal order puts before or the grammatical construction joins together, as "Your[b]—I beseech[a]—friendship[c]."

Anastrophe is the slight separation or postplacement of a 53
preposition with respect to its object. It is done in two ways. In one way when the preposition is put before a genitive, with its object following, as: "through[a]—of your petition[c]—the force[b]," "in[a]—of your love[c]—the friendship[b]." In another way when the preposition is interposed, as "this[b]—about[a]—matter[c]," "this[b]—for[a]—reason[c]."

In every hyperbaton one should take careful heed lest too 54
great a distance separate the words that should be joined together, which both creates confusion and does violence to the spirit of the listener. For this reason Cicero says, in the second *Rhetoric:* "One should likewise avoid a long period, which does violence both to the ear of the listener and to the breathing of the speaker." Yet it should be avoided most especially in verse and above all in elegiac verse. For this reason Matthew of Vendôme, toward the end of his book on the life of Tobias, writes thus to Bartholomew of Tours:

> Hyperbaton does not or should not please in elegies, but brevity, succinctly set forth, is clear.

And afterward he supplies the reason, thus:

> A prolix heap of words, the stepmother of goodwill, displeases, runs rampant, falls flat, misses the ear; a feast is digested more readily in morsels: when full of light, succinct songs please with dainty details.

Therefore, in a skillful composition the sentences should be short and concise, lest the grammatical construction be left

inordinata. Inde est quod Matheus Vindocinensis, ubi describit versum, invitat ad brevitatem clausularum, que scilicet non diu pendeant, sub hiis verbis: "Versus est metrica oracio succincte et clausulatim progrediens venusto verborum matrimonio et sentenciarum flosculis picturata, que nichil diminutum, nichil in se continet ociosum." Et addit: "Non enim aggregacio diccionum, dinumeracio pedum, cognicio temporum facit versum, set elegans iunctura diccionum, expressio proprietatum et uniuscuiusque rei observatum epytetum."

55   Est et diligenter notandum, tam circa prosam quam metrum, quod omnis diccio aliam determinans diccionem respiciat quam determinat epitetice, id est proprie et evidenter, sive transumptive sive sine transumpcione, ut intelligas per proprie convenienter. Est enim epitetum attribucio alicuius accidentis alicui rei specialiter accomodata. Et interpretatur "appositivum" vel "suppositivum." Et additur ad determinacionem subiecti causa laudis vel vituperii. Causa laudis, ut "Hector fortis," "pulcher Paris," "fortis Achilles," "facundus Ulixes," "magnus Alexander." Hec enim accidencia predictis viris prerogative et specialiter accomodantur. Causa vituperii, ut "Birria segnis," "deformis Davus."

56   Epitetum enim ab omnibus poetis maxime observatur. Vix enim in Virgilio vel Ovidio tres versus simul invenies in quibus non habeatur conveniens epitetum. Ecce in principio *Georgicorum:*

dangling or the hyperbaton be excessive. So it is that Matthew of Vendôme, when he describes verse, encourages brevity of sentences—namely, that they should not linger in the air for a long time—with these words: "Verse is metrical discourse proceeding concisely and clause by clause and made charming by a graceful marriage of words and by flowers of thought. It contains in itself nothing deficient and nothing redundant." And he adds: "For it is not the accumulation of words, the counting of feet, and observance of meter that constitute verse but elegant combination of words, vivid presentation of relevant qualities, and carefully noted epithets of each single thing."

One should also note carefully, with regard to prose as much as to meter, that every word that modifies another word should stand in relation to the word that it modifies in the manner of an epithet, that is, properly and manifestly, whether it does so transumptively or without transumption, and by "properly" you may understand "fittingly." For an epithet is the attribution of some nonessential quality to something to which it is especially suited. And it means "placed before" or "placed after." And it is added in order to modify the subject for the sake of praise or blame. For the sake of praise, as "Hector the strong," "handsome Paris," "strong Achilles," "eloquent Ulysses," "great Alexander." For these nonessential qualities are suited to the above men in a privileged and special way. For the sake of blame, as "Birria the lazy," "misshapen Davus."

Now the epithet is very greatly esteemed by all poets. Indeed, in Virgil or Ovid you will hardly find three verses together in which there is not a suitable epithet. Notice at the beginning of the *Georgics:*

55

56

195

Quid faciat letas segetes etc.

Hoc enim adiectivum "letas," quamvis transumptive ponatur, respicit tamen hoc subiectum "segetes" epitetice.

57   Hoc autem eciam usus est Galterus in *Alexandreide,* ubi introducit Alexandrum, sub anno etatis sue duodecimo, conquerentem de oppressione patris sui Philippi per Darium regem Persarum, hiis verbis:

Heu, quam longa quies pueris! nunquamne licebit
inter funereas acies mucrone corusco
Persarum dampnare genus, profugique tiranni
cornipedem lentum celeri prevertere cursu?

Ecce qualiter hec sex adiectiva—"longa," "funereas," "corusco," "profugi," "lentum," "celeri"—determinant epitetice hec sex substantiva— "quies," "acies," "mucrone," "tiranni," "cornipedem," "cursu."

58   Et notandum quod adiectivum solam veritatem significans non facit epitetum, ut "Homo albus currit." Amplius, ornatissimum est epitetum quod substantivum determinat transumptive, ut "aurea cesaries," id est glaucus crinis, "nivea facies."

59   Fit autem epitetum aliquando per apposicionem et hoc ornatissime si sit apposicio transumptiva. *Architrenius:*

Cognatusque Necis Sopor et precursor inermis
Torpor Egestatis.

Et hic:

What makes the crops joyous etc.

For the adjective "joyous," although it is used transumptively, nonetheless stands in relation to the subject "crops" in the manner of an epithet.

So too did Walter of Châtillon use this technique in the 57 *Alexandreis,* when he introduces Alexander, in his twelfth year, complaining about the oppression of his father Philip by Darius, King of the Persians, in these words:

> Alas, how long is this repose of boyhood! Will I never be permitted to harm the race of Persians with a flashing sword amid the deadly squadrons and outrun the slow, horn-footed beast of the fleeing tyrant with swift galloping?

Notice how the six adjectives — "long," "deadly," "flashing," "fleeing," "slow," "swift" — modify, in the manner of epithets, the six substantives — "repose," "squadrons," "sword," "tyrant," "horn-footed beast," "galloping."

And note that an adjective that signifies nothing but the 58 truth does not make an epithet, as "The white man runs." Furthermore, the most elegant epithet is one that modifies a substantive transumptively, such as "golden tresses," that is, gleaming hair, or "snowy face."

Moreover, an epithet is sometimes produced through ap- 59 position, and this is done most elegantly if the apposition is transumptive. As in the *Architrenius:*

> Sleep, the brother of Death, and Listlessness, the herald of helpless Poverty.

And here:

Arbor, honor claustri, iacet obruta flatibus austri.

"Honor claustri" apposicio est.

60 Est et alius modus ornatissimus tam in omni transumpcione quam in epitheto, quando scilicet eadem diccio semel
posita proprie accipitur et transumptive. Galterus, de ani-
mositate Alexandri:

Effunditque prius animo quam dente cruorem.

Hoc verbum "Effundit" respectu huius ablativi "dente" proprie ponitur set respectu huius substantivi "animo" transumptive. Similiter in "Libro versuum":

Armat eos in corde fides, in corpore ferrum.

Et alibi:

Hic melius loquitur animus quam lingua.

Et hic: "Sedent in virgulto virgines tenentes flores in manibus et relucent ibi lilia facierum pariter et ortorum." Et hic:
"Pusillum habes et animum et oculum."

61 Ita dictum est de ornata difficultate.

A tree, the pride of the cloister, lies overthrown by the
blasts of the south wind.

"The pride of the cloister" is an apposition.

And there is another very elegant method, as relevant to 60
any transumption as to an epithet, namely, when the same
word, having been used once in its proper meaning, is also
taken transumptively. Walter of Châtillon, on the valor of
Alexander:

And the lion cub sheds blood with his valorous
thoughts before he can do so with his teeth.

The verb "sheds" is used properly with regard to the ablative
"teeth" but transumptively with regard to the substantive
"thoughts." Likewise in the "Book of Verses":

Faith arms their hearts, iron their bodies.

And elsewhere:

Here the mind speaks better than the tongue.

And here: "The virgins sit in the grove holding flowers in
their hands, and there the lilies of their faces and those of
the gardens shine equally." And here: "You have both little
courage and little eyes."

And so we have discussed ornamented difficulty. 61

Capitulum 6

De hiis in quibus omnis ornatus attenditur et in quibus diccionibus melior sit ornatus

Teste Tullio in secunda *Rethorica,* omnis perfecta elocucio tria habere debet: eleganciam, composicionem et dignitatem. Elegancia est ornatus sentencie qua unumquodque "pure et aperte dici videatur": "pure," sine vicio, ut sunt barbarismus, solecismus et decem vicia eis annexa; "aperte," evidenter, plane, et hoc attribuendo cuilibet rei suas proprietates.

2   Composicio est superficialis verborum ornatus tali ornatu qui non causatur ex aliquo scemate, tropo vel colore rethorico. Et consistit in fuga viciorum et eleccione virtutum. In fuga viciorum, ut si vitemus crebras vocalium concursiones, labdacismum, methacismum et iotacismum. In eleccione virtutum, ut si dicciones ornatas ad materiam adaptemus. Unde, teste Vindosinense, ornate dicciones "sunt quasi gemmarum vicarie, quarum artificiosa posicione dictamen solempnius festivatur: earum enim multiformis

Chapter 6

Concerning the things with which all ornament is concerned and in which words the best ornament consists

According to Cicero in the second *Rhetoric,* every finished style should have three things: taste, artistic composition, and distinction. Taste is ornamentation of the meaning such that every single thing "seems to be expressed purely and openly": "purely," that is, without fault, such as barbarism, solecism, and the ten faults connected to them; "openly," that is, manifestly, plainly, and this is done by attributing to each thing its proper characteristics.

Artistic composition is the superficial ornamentation of 2 words with the sort of ornament which is not brought about through some scheme, trope, or rhetorical color. And it consists in the avoidance of faults and the pursuit of virtues. In avoidance of faults, as when we eschew the frequent collision of vowels, labdacism, metacism, and iotacism. In the pursuit of virtues, as when we fit elegant expressions to the subject matter. Thus, according to Matthew of Vendôme, elegant expressions "are akin to gemstones, whose artful deployment makes a solemn composition charming. Their

ornatus aliis diccionibus collateralibus sue venustatis imperciuntur beneficium et quasi socialiter cuiusdam festivitatis accomodant blandimentum."

3   Cuiuslibet enim ornatus prerogative dicciones, quedam sunt adiectiva, quedam verba. Nec tamen ab ornatu substantiva secluduntur, set quia numerus adiectivorum preponderat, de substantivis parciorem, de adiectivis pleniorem facimus mencionem. Quare autem adiectiva et verba maiorem habent ornatum quam cetere partes hec est racio. Adiectiva enim et verba sunt maxime determinativa proprietatum, in quarum observancia, teste Oracio in sua *Poetria,* prerogativa dictandi perpenditur elegancia.

4   Set adiectivorum sex sunt terminaciones que maxime faciunt ad ornatum, scilicet -alis, -osus, -atus, -ivus, -aris, -ior, de quibus per ordinem, ad maiorem evidenciam, pauca ponantur exempla.

      (-alis)
Pastoris signum est officiale pedum.
Amplificat cultus materiale bonum.
Sceptrum pontifices imperiale gerunt.
Est forme vicium collaterale Venus.
      (-osus)
Vernat maiestas imperiosa ducum.
Pauperat oris opes deliciosus amor.
Coniectura parit suspiciosa metum.
Sors variare studet insidiosa fidem.

manifold ornament, moreover, grants the gift of its beauty to neighboring expressions and, as it were, sociably bestows the blessing of a certain charm."

Now among the privileged words of any ornament, some 3 are adjectives, some are verbs. Nor, for that matter, are substantives excluded from ornament; but because the number of adjectives is greater, we mention substantives less and adjectives more. And here is the reason why adjectives and verbs possess greater ornament than the other parts of speech. Adjectives and verbs are most effective in designating proper characteristics, on the observance of which, according to Horace in his *Poetics,* special elegance in composition depends.

Now there are six endings of adjectives that are most 4 conducive to ornament, namely, *-al, -ous, -ate, -ive, -ar, -er.* For greater clarity, let a few examples of these be set forth in order.

(-al)
The shepherd's *official* symbol is his crook.
Cultivation improves *material* goods.
Pontiffs wield the *imperial* scepter.
Lust is the *collateral* defect of beauty.
(-ous)
The *imperious* splendor of rulers flourishes.
Delicious love impoverishes the richest vocabulary.
Suspicious guesses pave the way for terror.
An *insidious* oracle causes one to lose faith.

(-atus)

Materie precium materiata beant.

Rex est nobilibus intitulatus avis.

Lex titubat, pietas intumulata iacet.

Nulla timenda timet illaqueatus amor.

(-ivus)

Iusta relativo gaudet honore fides.

Est nocue mentis expositiva manus.

Cristus adoptiva nos pietate fovet.

Continuativo federe gaudet amor.

(-aris)

Succurrit miseris particulare bonum.

Est exemplaris altera vita michi.

Ypocrite gratus est popularis honor.

Obsequium nescit vir famulare pati.

(-ior)

Disputat in vultu candidiore rubor.

Ver picturat humum floridiore coma.

Terram luna rigat humidiore rota.

Lampade respirat lucidiore dies.

Similiter et in aliis adiectivis proprietates convenienter determinantibus est ornatus set in sex premissis precipue.

5   De verbis autem specialis regula per determinaciones non est danda set generaliter quecumque verba convenienter proprietates determinant. Faciunt ad ornatum sive epitetice, sive antitetice. Quid sit antitheta posterius ostendetur. Verborum enim precipuus est ornatus eorum

(-ate)

Fabricated things increase the value of their materials.

A king is *celebrated* for his noble ancestors.

When the law falters, duty lies *prostrate.*

Captivated love fears nothing that it ought.

(-ive)

True friendship rejoices in honors *relative* to one's merit.

The hand is *expositive* of a deceitful mind.

Christ nurtures us with *adoptive* kindness.

Love takes pleasure in a *progressive* liaison.

(-ar)

A *particular* good aids the unfortunate.

The lives of others are *exemplary* to me.

Popular acclaim pleases the hypocrite.

No true man tolerates *overfamiliar* flattery.

(-er)

A blush vies for mastery in a *whiter* face.

Spring decorates the earth with *ampler* foliage.

The moon bedews the earth with its *moister* cycle.

The day glows with a *brighter* luster.

There is likewise ornament in other adjectives that suitably designate proper characteristics, but especially in the previous six types.

For verbs, in contrast, a special rule for designations can- 5 not be given; but, in general, all verbs whatsoever suitably designate proper characteristics. They can create ornament either through epithets or through antitheses. What an antithesis is will be shown later. Peculiarly ornamental are

que sunt prime coniugacionis, de quibus hec exempla ponantur.

Pilleat insignes aurea mitra comas.
Prosperat adversas sors variata vices.
Prospera sors nescit perpetuare fidem.
Pauperat elatas prodiga mensa domos.
Festivant humiles aurea vasa cibos.
Purpurat assiduus grata labella rubor.
Intitulat nocuum nobilis actor opus.
Sincopat in coitu mentula crebra sonos.
Confiscare solet rex populare bonum.
Alterat humanos sors inimica status.
Virginis optate fedus adoptat amans.
Illaqueat victrix libera colla Venus.
Importat dampni significata dolor.
Malleat innocuum victima sacra bovem.
Versificatoris scema venustat opus.
Quod complere nequis primiciare cave.

Similiter et in aliis verbis cuiuscumque coniugacionis et precipue in verbis prime coniugacionis.

6   Amplius, generaliter quecumque dicciones de novo inveniuntur dictamen excellenter exornant, ut "roseare," "li-
liare," "optimare," "herbidare," "reverenciare" et huiusmodi,
de quibus dictum est. Unde Servius: Demostenes rogatus ut
pro re publica os suum aperiret, ait: "Non possum. Squinancem pacior." Cui quidam prudens respondit: "Non squinancem set arginancem." Acceperat enim, ut putabatur, argentum tacendi causa. Ecce quam egregie invenit novam
diccionem "arginancem."

those verbs that belong to the first conjugation, of which let the following examples be provided.

A golden covering *caps* distinguished tresses.
Fickle fortune *prospers* contrary changes.
Prosperous fortune cannot *conserve* faith.
Lavish tables *empauper* noble houses.
Golden tableware *embellishes* humble meals.
A constant redness *adorns* pleasing lips.
A noble doer *dignifies* a harmful deed.
In coupling a swift-pounding penis *syncopates* its sound.
A king is wont to *confiscate* his subjects' property.
Hostile fate always *alters* men's condition.
A lover *craves* union with the girl he longs for.
Venus the conqueror *ensnares* unattached hearts.
Sorrow *conveys* the signs of misfortune.
A religious sacrifice *clubs* the harmless ox.
A versifier's figure of speech *beautifies* a poem.
Do not *inaugurate* something you cannot finish.

Likewise also in other verbs of whatever conjugation and especially in verbs of the first conjugation.

Moreover, in general, whatever expressions are newly in- 6 vented excellently adorn a composition, as "to rose," "to lily," "to besten," "to grassify," "to honorize," and the like, concerning which we have spoken already. As Servius says: "Demosthenes, when asked that he open his mouth for the republic, said: 'I cannot. I have a sore throat.' To which a certain wise man responded: 'Not a sore throat but a sore groat.' For it was thought that he had accepted silver for the sake of keeping silent." Notice how cleverly he invents the new expression "sore groat."

7   Dignitas est qualitas dicendi verborum et sentenciarum floribus purpurata. Consistit enim in coloribus verborum et sentenciarum, de quibus posterius plenius est loquendum. Ex predictis igitur collige quod in elocucione primo precedit ornatus sentencie, deinde sequitur ornatus verborum, tercio qualitas dicendi. Siquidem nonnulla racio huius ordinis poterit assignari. Etenim, sicut in prefata divisione primo precedunt sentencie, secundo ornata verba sequuntur, tercio qualitas dicendi subiungitur, similiter in artificioso dictamine, primo precedit ymaginacio sensus, secundo sequitur sermo interpres et expositor intellectus, tercio subiungitur qualitas dicendi, id est verborum et sentenciarum florida disposicio. Primo enim est sentencie concepcio, secundo verborum ornata composicio, tercio in qualitate dicendi egregia ordinacio. Horum trium declarativum potest esse quod de sancto Thoma legitur: "Clamat cunctis Thome constancia. Omne solum est forti patria." Hic enim, quantum ad primum membrum, est ornatus interioris sentencie ex generali dicto seu proverbio; quantum ad secundum, verba sunt satis festiva; quantum ad tercium, est ornatus in qualitate dicendi. Est enim denominacio in eo quod possessum ponitur pro possessore, cum dicitur "Thome constancia," id est "Thomas constans," vel circuicio in eo quod proprietas ponitur pro subiecto. Nec, licet hec tria concurrant, derogatur honor dictaminis; set horum concursus, quasi trium gemmarum prerogativa dignitas,

CHAPTER 6

Distinction is a quality of speaking that has been adorned   7
with flowers of speech and thought. For it consists of the
colors of words and thoughts, which are spoken about more
fully later. From what has been said earlier, therefore, gather
that in style first comes the elegance of the meaning, then
follows the elegance of the words, and third the quality of
the expression. And indeed some reason may be given for
this order. For just as in the division referred to earlier,
meanings come first, ornamented words follow second, and
the quality of expression is given as the third member, so in
artful composition the conceptual realization of meaning
comes first, then language, the interpreter and expounder of
understanding, follows second, and third is added the quality of expression, that is, the flowery arrangement of words
and thoughts. Thus the conception of meaning comes first,
second the ornamented composition of words, and third an
excellent arrangement in the quality of expression. The lines
concerning St. Thomas Becket can help elucidate these
three things: "The constancy of Thomas calls out to all. To
one who is strong every land is his native country." For here,
as regards the first part, there is ornament of the inner
meaning from a general maxim or proverb; as regards the
second, the words are sufficiently elegant; as regards the
third, there is ornament in the quality of speaking. For there
is metonymy, in that what is possessed is put in place of the
possessor, when "the constancy of Thomas" is said, that is,
"constant Thomas," or else periphrasis, in that a property is
put in place of the subject. Nor is the dignity of the composition diminished, even though these three occur together;
but their concourse, like the special distinction of three

preciose picture cultibus ornatusque triplici precio dictamen purpurat et depingit. Istud per similitudinem patere
potest. Nam sicut in homine possumus contemplari vitalem
spiritum, corporee venustatem materie et legitimam vivendi
qualitatem, nec tamen unum est alterius exceptivum, immo
coniuncta melius comparantur et graciorem habent effica-
ciam, similiter in dictamine venustas interioris sentencie et
superficialis verborum ornatus et qualitas dicendi sese invicem hospitaliter recipiunt et unum sine consorcio alterius
vix aut raro solitariam sortitur posicionem.

jewels, adorns and decorates the composition with the refinements of a precious painting and triple the value of ornament. This can be made clear by means of a comparison. For just as in a man we can consider mind, physical beauty, and propriety of lifestyle, and, to be sure, one does not exclude the other, but rather they show to better advantage taken one with the other and have a greater power of pleasing, likewise in a composition the beauty of the inner meaning and the exterior elegance of the words and the quality of the expression gracefully reinforce each other and scarcely does any one of these characteristics take its place alone without the company of another.

Capitulum 7

De ornata facilitate et de determinacione, que est potissimum elocucionis condimentum, et de coloribus verborum et sentenciarum

Ornatam facilitatem due profecto res operantur, scilicet determinacio et qualitas dicendi per 36 colores verborum et 19 sentenciarum. Precurramus igitur artificium determinacionis. Determinantur autem duo, nomen scilicet et verbum.

2   Preloquamur de determinacione nominis. Nomen igitur aut est proprium aut appellativum. Nomen proprium tripliciter determinatur: tum per obliquum, tum per adiectivum, tum per verbum.

3   Quando determinatur per obliquum, aut determinatur per genitivum aut per ablativum. Per genitivum, ut "Marcia Catonis," id est uxor, et tunc subaudiendum est nomen appellativum in illo casu in quo ponitur proprium nomen determinatum, sic: "Marcia uxor Catonis." Est enim regula apud gramaticos: quando nomen proprium determinatur

Chapter 7

On ornamented facility and on determination, which is the principal seasoning of style, and on the colors of words and thoughts

Two things produce ornamented facility, namely, determination and the quality of speaking by means of the thirty-six colors of words and the nineteen colors of thoughts. Accordingly, let us first run through the technique of determination. Two things can be determined, namely, a noun and a verb.

Let us first speak about the determination of a noun. A noun is either proper or appellative. A proper noun is determined in three ways: sometimes by an oblique noun, sometimes by an adjective, and sometimes by a verb.

When a proper noun is determined by an oblique noun, it is determined either by a genitive or by an ablative. By a genitive, as in "Cato's Marcia," that is, his wife, and then you should understand this as if there were an appellative noun in the same case as the proper noun that has been determined, thus: "Marcia, wife of Cato." For there is a rule among the grammarians: when a proper noun is determined

per genitivum, subaudiendum est nomen appellativum in illo casu in quo ponitur proprium determinatum a quo regatur genitivus determinans. Et notandum quod in tali posicione sufficit unica determinacio ad ornatum. Sapit enim hec sola determinacio "Marcia Catonis," quamvis non sit ibi inculcacio similium, quod alias in determinacionibus raro continget. Fere enim ubique alias determinacionum inculcacio facit ornatum, non unica determinacio per se, nisi forte diccio determinans ponatur transumptive, ut "Ridet ager." Tunc enim unica determinacio exornat per se. Est enim inculcacio induccio similium vel determinacionum florida multitudo, similitudo similitudinis est augmentum.

4   Proprium determinatur per ablativum, sic:

> Tullius ore, Paris facie, Cato moribus, Hector
> viribus, etate Partonopheus erat.

5   Proprium determinatur per adiectivum, sic:

> Sit Medea ferox invictaque, flebilis Yno,
> perfidus Ixion, Yo vaga, tristis Horestes.

Hoc est exemplum Oracii. Similiter in Ovidio magno, ubi Ovidius enumerat aquas que convenerant ad consolandum Peneum dolentem de amissione filie sue Daphnes, que conversa fuerat in laurum, propria nomina aquarum determinantur per adiectiva, sic:

by a genitive, you should understand it as if there were an appellative noun in the same case as the determined proper noun by which the determining genitive is governed. And you should note that in such a placement one determination is enough to produce ornamentation. For this single determination, "Cato's Marcia," adds zest, even though there is no inculcation of similes in it—a thing that otherwise occurs only rarely in determinations. For nearly everywhere else it is the inculcation of determinations that creates ornamentation, and not a single determination by itself, unless the determining word happens to be used transumptively, as in "The field laughs." For then the single determination adorns all by itself. Whereas inculcation is the introduction of similes or a flowery multitude of determinations, this simile is an augmentation of a simile.

A proper noun is determined by an ablative, thus: 4

He was a Cicero in his mouth, a Paris in his face, a Cato in his morals, a Hector in his strength, a Parthenopaeus in his youth.

A proper noun is determined by an adjective, thus: 5

Let Medea be fierce and unyielding, Ino tearful, Ixion forsworn, Io a wanderer, Orestes sorrowful.

This is an example from Horace. Likewise in the "Great Ovid," in the place where Ovid lists the streams that come together to console Peneus, who was grieving over the loss of his daughter Daphne, who had been transformed into a laurel, the proper names of the streams are determined by adjectives, thus:

Populifer Spercheus ac irrequietus Enimpheus
Eridanusque senex lenisque Amphiris et Oas.

Similiter et in illo loco ubi enumerat canes Acteonis dilace-
rantes dominum suum mutatum in cervum. Ecce exemplum
domesticum:

Te presente tremit muliebris Gallia, textrix
   Flandria, pannosa Scocia, teste fuga.

6   Proprium determinatur per verbum dupliciter. Uno
modo sic quod nichil interveniat nominativum et verbum,
sic:

Invictam ferri, mitti recipique monetam.
Misit Guido, tulit Hugo, recepit Adam.

Alio modo sic quod aliquid interveniat, sicut adverbium similitudinis, ut habemus in Sydonio, in illa epistola in qua
commendat personam Claudiani, hiis verbis: "Explicat ut
Plato, implicat ut Aristotiles, . . . simulat ut Crassus, dissi-
mulat ut Cesar." Ecce quod premisimus de inculcacione, scilicet quod determinacionum inculcacio facit ornatum, non
unica per se determinacio. Non enim ad ornatum sufficit
dicere "Misit Guido," set hec inculcacio facit ornatum:

Misit Guido, tulit Hugo, recepit Adam.

7   Utrumque istorum modorum habemus in *Anticlaudiano*.
Primum in descripcione Fortune, sic:

The poplar-fringed Spercheus, the restless Enimpheus, hoary Eridanus, gentle Amphiris and Oas.

And likewise in the place where he lists the dogs of Actaeon
who tore apart their master, after he had been transformed
into a stag. Here is a homemade example:

In your presence effeminate France, cloth-making
Flanders, ragged Scotland tremble, as witness their
flight.

A proper noun is determined by a verb in two ways. In 6
one way so that nothing comes between the nominative and
the verb, thus:

That unconquered money be carried, sent, and received. Guido sent, Hugo carried, Adam received it.

In a different way so that something comes between, such
as an adverb of similitude, as we find in Sidonius, in the letter in which he praises the character of Claudianus, in these
words: "He unfolds like Plato, he enfolds like Aristotle, . . .
he simulates like Crassus, he dissimulates like Caesar." This
illustrates what we said before about inculcation, namely,
that it is the inculcation of determinations that creates ornamentation, and not a single determination by itself. For it
is not enough to produce ornamentation to say "Guido
sent," but this inculcation creates ornamentation:

Guido sent, Hugo carried, Adam received it.

We find both of these methods in the *Anticlaudianus*. The 7
first in the description of Fortune, thus:

Marcessit laurus, mirtus parit, aret oliva.

Et sequitur:

Hic raro philomenat avis, citharizat alauda.

Secundum modum habemus ubi commendat turbam septem arcium, quas puellas vocat parantes currum Prudencie,
sic:

Ut Zeusis pingit chorus hic, ut Milo figurat,
ut Fabius loquitur, ut Tullius ipse perorat.

8   Ita dictum est de nomine proprio. Sequitur de appella-
tivo. Nomen appellativum aut est substantivum aut adiectivum. Substantivum tripliciter determinatur: aut per verbum
aut per adiectivum aut per casum quem regit.

9   Quando substantivum determinatur per verbum, vel
plura appellativa determinantur per plura verba vel unum
per plura vel plura per unum. Non adicio quartum membrum, scilicet ubi unum determinatur per unum, quia, ut
diximus, unica determinacio non facit ad ornatum set inculcacio determinacionum.

10 Plura appellativa determinantur per plura verba, ut hic:
"Non illi cutis contrahitur, non hanelat pulmo, non cor
concutitur, non riget lumbus, non spina curvatur." Et hic:

The laurel withers, the myrtle bears fruit, the olive is parched.

And it continues:

Here Philomela's song and the music of the lark are rare.

We find the second method where he praises the throng of the seven arts, which he calls the maidens preparing the chariot of Prudence, thus:

This sisterhood paints like Zeuxis, sculpts like Milo, speaks like Fabius, pleads like Cicero himself.

And so the proper noun has been discussed. What fol- 8 lows concerns the appellative. An appellative name is either a substantive or an adjective. A substantive is determined in three ways: by a verb, by an adjective, or by the case that it governs.

When a substantive is determined by a verb, either sev- 9 eral appellatives are determined by several verbs or one appellative is determined by several verbs or several appellatives are determined by one verb. I do not add a fourth category, namely, when one appellative is determined by one verb, because, as we have said, a single determination does not produce ornamentation but rather the inculcation of determinations does.

Several appellatives are determined by several verbs, as 10 here: "His skin does not shrivel, his lungs do not pant, his heart has no spasms, his loins are not hardened, his spine is not curved." And here:

Flatus dispergit, oblivio perdidit, ira
  iecit, pes trivit, sors mala rupit opus.

11   Unum appellativum determinatur per plura verba, sic:
"Anima mundi est quidam vigor naturalis quo corpora vege-
tantur et crescunt, animalia moventur et senciunt, racionalia iudicant et discernunt, spiritus sciunt et intelligunt."
Ecce aliud exemplum:

Unde superbit homo? Sitit, esurit, estuat, alget,
  flet, ridet, metuit, sperat, habundat, eget.

12   Plura appellativa determinantur per unum verbum, sic:
"O ter quaterque beatum, de cuius culmine datur amicis leticia, lividis pena, posteris gloria, desidibus et pigris incita-
mentum, vegetis et alacribus exemplum." Ecce exemplum
Stacii:

Iam clipeo clipeus, umbone repellitur umbo,
  ense minax ensis, pede pes et cuspide cuspis.

Ecce aliud exemplum Ovidii:

Phillida Demophon leto dedit hospes amantem;
  ille necis causam prebuit, illa necem.

Exemplum domesticum est hoc:

Vexatur gladius sanguine, strage solum.

The wind scattered, forgetfulness obliterated, anger cast down, the foot trampled upon, an ill fate destroyed the work.

One appellative is determined by several verbs, thus: 11 "The world's soul is a certain natural force by means of which bodies quicken and grow, animals move and feel, rational beings judge and discern, spirits know and understand." Here is another example:

Whence comes man's pride? He thirsts, hungers, feels hot, feels cold, weeps, laughs, fears, hopes, abounds, lacks.

Several appellatives are determined by one verb, thus: "O 12 thrice and four times blessed, whose elevation gives joy to your friends, pain to the envious, glory to your descendants, a spur to the indolent and lazy, an example to the lively and active." Here is an example from Statius:

Then shield thrusts against shield, boss upon boss, threatening sword on sword, foot against foot and lance on lance.

Here is another example, from Ovid:

Demophoon—her guest—killed Phyllis, who loved him. He supplied her death's cause, she the death itself.

This is a homemade example:

The sword is vexed with blood, the ground with carnage.

13   Et notandum quod quando idem verbum pluribus clausulis respondet, zeuma est, ut in premissis exemplis. Fit autem, ut ait Hisidorus, tripliciter: a superiori, ab inferiori, a
medio. A superiori quando verbum, in superiori—id est
prima—clausula positum, respondet omnibus que sequuntur. Et vocatur a Tullio "adiunctum," ut in Ovidio:

> Frigida pugnabant calidis, humencia siccis,
> mollia cum duris, sine pondere, habencia pondus.

Ab inferiori quando verbum, in ultima clausula positum, refertur ad clausulas precedentes. Et vocatur a Tullio similiter
"adiunctum," ut hic:

> Tu dominus, tu vir, tu michi frater eras.

A medio quando verbum nec in prima nec in ultima clausula
set in aliqua media situatur et refertur tam ad precedentes
quam ad clausulas subsequentes. Et vocatur a Tullio "coniunctum," ut in premisso exemplo Stacii "Iam clipeo clipeus
etc." Quando vero singulis clausulis suum verbum attribuitur, ypozeusis est et contrariatur zeumati. Et vocatur a Tullio "disiunctum," ut hic:

> Bella cupit laxatque genas et temperat ungues.

Et hic:

> Penalopen morum festivat gracia, forme
> purpura declarat, ditat acervus opum.

And you should note that when the same verb corre- 13
sponds with several clauses, that is zeugma, as in the foregoing examples. As Isidore says, it is accomplished in three
ways: from the previous, from the latter, and from the middle. From the previous when a verb that has been placed in
the previous—that is, the first—clause corresponds with all
of those that follow. And this is called "adjunction" by Cicero, as in Ovid:

> Cold things strove with hot, moist with dry, soft with
> hard, weighty with weightless.

From the latter when a verb that has been placed in the last
clause refers to the preceding clauses. And this is likewise
called "adjunction" by Cicero, as here:

> You my master, you my husband, you my brother were.

From the middle when the verb is placed neither in the first
nor in the last clause but in a clause in the middle and refers
equally to the preceding and the following clauses. And this
is called "conjunction" by Cicero, as in the previous example
from Statius: "Then shield against shield etc." But when to
each of several clauses its own verb is assigned, that is hypozeuxis and is the opposite of zeugma. And this is called "disjunction" by Cicero, as here:

> She yearns for war, and she loosens her jaws and trims
> her talons.

And here:

> Gracious conduct marks Penelope, regal form distin-
> guishes her, great wealth enriches her.

14   De zeumate et ypozeusi ideo specialem facimus mencionem, quia sunt duo elegantissima scemata tractandi et
metrice et prosaice et ceteris scematibus ad ornatum facilem specialius amicantur. Hiis enim duobus utuntur omnes
artificialiter dictantes et succincte et maxime Vindocinensis, in libro de vita Tobie.

15   Sub ypozeusi invenitur et aliud scema satis elegans, et vocatur "singula singulis." Et fit quando, inculcatis determinacionibus, prima primis, secunda secundis, tercia terciis, et
sic de ceteris conformantur, ut in hoc exemplo:

Celum, terra, fretum volucres, pecuaria, pisces
    tollit, alit, celat aere, farre, lacu.

Similiter et Vindocinensis, ubi commendat Tobiam, sic
utitur singula singulis:

Odit, amat, reprobat, probat, execratur, adorat
crimina, iura, nephas, fas, simulacra, Deum;
seminat, auget, alit, exterminat, arguit, arcet
dogmata, iura, decus, scismata, probra, dolos.

16   Quando substantivum determinatur per adiectivum, similiter triplex est variacio: aut enim plura substantiva determinantur per plura adiectiva, aut unum per plura, aut plura
per unum. Plura substantiva per plura adiectiva, ut in secunda epistola Sydonii, in qua describit mensam Theodorici
regis hiis verbis: "Videas ibi eleganciam Grecam, abundan-
ciam Gallicanam, celeritatem Ytalicam, publicam pompam,

We make special mention of zeugma and hypozeuxis be- 14
cause they are two very elegant figures for both metrical and
prose composition and are especially compatible with the
other figures for the purposes of ornamented facility. For everyone who composes artfully and succinctly uses these
two, and above all Matthew of Vendôme in his book about
the life of Tobias.

Under hypozeuxis is found yet another rather elegant fig- 15
ure, and it is called "each to each." And it occurs when, after
determinations have been inculcated in a series, the first
items are matched up with the first, the second with the second, the third with the third, and so on for the rest, as in this
example:

> Sky, earth, sea the birds, beasts, fishes
> lifts, feeds, conceals with air, grain, gulf.

And likewise Matthew of Vendôme, when he praises Tobias,
employs each to each, thus:

> He hates, loves, reproves, approves, curses, adores
> crimes, laws, wrong, right, idols, God; he sows, in-
> creases, nourishes, stamps out, censures, prevents
> teachings, laws, honor, schisms, abuses, deceptions.

When a substantive is determined by an adjective, the 16
variations are likewise threefold: for either several substantives are determined by several adjectives or one substantive
by several adjectives or several substantives by one adjective. Several substantives by several adjectives, as in the
second letter of Sidonius, in which he describes King Theodoric's table in these words: "You can find there Greek elegance, Gallic plenty, Italian briskness, public pomp, private

225

disciplinam privatam, regiam diligenciam." Similiter in Vegecio Renato, *De re militari,* circa principium libri, ubi ostendit qualis debeat esse bonus miles hiis verbis: "Sit autem adolescens Martis operi deputatus vigilantibus oculis, erecta cervice, lato pectore, humeris musculosis, valentibus digitis, longioribus brachiis, ventre modico, exilior cruribus, suris et pedibus non multa carne distentis set nervorum duricia collectis." Ecce exemplum domesticum:

> Tibia feminea, tuba mascula, timpana rauca,
> cimbala preclara, concors symphonia, dulcis
> fistula, sompnifere cithare vituleque iocose.

17 Unum substantivum determinatur per plura adiectiva, ut "Mensa nostra pauper erat et immunda, mensale sordidum et antiquum, fercula grossa et insipida, servientes illepidi et inculti, omnia incompta et indecencia." Aliter eciam determinatur unum per plura quando non interponitur adiectivis hec coniunccio "et" set hec coniunccio "set," sic:

> Parva domus set prava fuit, res apta set arta,
> facta set infecta pluribus illa modis.

Et notandum quod per hanc coniunccionem "set" incidit color correccio, de quo posterius. Et multum iuvat color iste quando miscetur colori qui dicitur agnominacio. Est enim correccio agnominacioni mixta in premisso exemplo, ubi dicitur "Parva set prava, apta set arta, facta set infecta."

discipline, regal diligence." Likewise in Vegetius Renatus, *On Military Science,* near the beginning of the book, where he shows how a good soldier ought to be, in these words: "Let the youth destined for the work of Mars have watchful eyes, a straight neck, a broad chest, muscular shoulders, strong fingers, rather long arms, a moderate-sized belly, slender legs, calves and feet not swollen with a lot of flesh but drawn together with firm sinews." Here is a homemade example:

> The feminine flute, the masculine trumpet, the hollow
> drum, the shining cymbals, the mellow symphonia, the
> sweet-sounding pipe, the sleep-bringing lyres, and the
> merry fiddles.

One substantive is determined by several adjectives, as in 17 "Our table was poor and untidy, the tablecloth was filthy and old, the food was coarse and tasteless, the servers were rude and uncultivated, everything was inelegant and unseemly." Also, one substantive is determined by several adjectives in another way when the conjunction "and" is not placed between the adjectives but rather the conjunction "but," thus:

> The house was humble but jumbled, something right
> but tight, one built but unbuilt in many ways.

And you should note that by means of this conjunction "but" there occurs the color "correction," which will be treated later. And this color is very pleasing when it is mingled with the color that is called "paronomasia." For correction has been mixed with paronomasia in the previous example, where one says "humble but jumbled, right but

Similiter et hic: "Leta set lenta procedit oracio." Similiter et hic:

Non alleluia ructare set allia queris;
   plus in salmone quam Salomone legis.

Hic enim et in consimilibus unica determinacio facit ornatum. Suavius tamen redolet determinacio inculcata. Alio
modo determinatur unum per plura quando nulla coniunccio intericitur adiectivis set punctatim proferuntur, sic:
"Mulier habet animum vagum, errantem, varium, subdolum,
malignantem."

18   Plura substantiva determinantur per unum adiectivum,
sic: "Eque fui diligens, discens et docens." Ita dictum sit
qualiter substantivum determinatur per adiectivum.

19   Quando substantivum determinatur per casum quem regit, aut determinatur per genitivum aut per dativum aut per
ablativum. Per genitivum, ut in *Anticlaudiano,* de laude Beate
Virginis:

Hec est stella maris, vite via, porta salutis,
regula iusticie, limes pietatis, origo
virtutis, venie mater thalamusque pudoris.

Per dativum, ut in eodem, similiter de Beata Virgine:

tight, built but unbuilt." Likewise also here: "The pleasing but plodding speech goes on." Likewise also here:

> You seek to belch forth not Gloria in Excelsis, but garlic in excess; you speak more of salmon than of Solomon.

Here and in similar instances only one determination creates the ornamentation. Nonetheless, an inculcated determination would produce a sweeter effect. One substantive is determined by several adjectives in another way when no conjunction is inserted between the adjectives but they are brought forth one after another, thus: "Woman has a mind that is inconstant, wandering, changeable, cunning, malicious."

Several substantives are determined by one adjective, 18 thus: "I was equally diligent as student and teacher." And so we have discussed how a substantive is determined by an adjective.

When a substantive is determined by a case that it gov- 19 erns, it is determined either by a genitive, a dative, or an ablative. By a genitive, as in the *Anticlaudianus,* in praise of the Blessed Virgin:

> She is the star of the sea, the way to life, the port of salvation, the standard of justice, the pathway of piety, the source of virtue, the mother of mercy and chamber of chastity.

By a dative, as in the same work, likewise concerning the Blessed Virgin:

Spes miseris, medicina reis, tutela beatis,
proscriptis reditus, erranti semita, cecis
limes, deiectis requies, pausacio fessis.

Per ablativum, sic:

Femina, fraude quidem vulpes, ausu leo, facto
vipera, se velat simplicitate sua.

20   Est adhuc et quartus modus per quem determinatur substantivum aliter quam in premissis, scilicet per oracionem
constantem ex preposicione et obliquo accusativo vel ablativo. Accusativo, ut in Alano:

Cuius ad adventum redit etas aurea mundo,
post facinus pietas, post culpam gracia, virtus
post vicium, pax post odium, post triste iocosum.

Ablativo, sic: "Lepus es in bello, leo in hospicio, homo in
ocio, nemo in negocio." Ita sufficienter dictum est de determinacione substantivi appellativi.

21   Adiectivum determinatur dupliciter: tum per obliquum
quem regit, tum per oracionem constantem ex preposicione
et obliquo. Quando determinatur per obliquum, per omnes
casus contingit ipsum determinari, excepto vocativo, quia
vocativus non regitur. Adiectivum determinatur per genitivum, sic: "Cupidus es pecunie, parcus tue, prodigus aliene."
Per dativum, sic: "Tu soli deditus es malignitati, maliciosus

Hope for the wretched, cure for the sinful, safeguard for the blessed, return for the exile, path for the wanderer, way for the blind, ease for the downtrodden, rest for the weary.

By an ablative, thus:

Woman, a very fox in fraud, a lion in bold action, a viper in deed, veils herself with her innocence.

There is still another, fourth way in which a substantive is 20 determined, different from the previous ways, namely, by a phrase that consists of a preposition and an oblique, in either the accusative or the ablative case. In the accusative, as in Alan of Lille:

At her coming the golden age returned to the world, piety after wickedness, grace after guilt, virtue after vice, peace after hatred, laughter after sorrow.

In the ablative, thus: "You are a rabbit in war, a lion in hospitality, a human being in leisure, nobody in action." Thus, enough has been said about determination of an appellative substantive.

An adjective is determined in two ways: sometimes by an 21 oblique case that it governs, sometimes by a phrase that consists of a preposition and an oblique case. When it is determined by an oblique case, it is possible for it to be determined by any case, except a vocative, because a vocative is not governed. An adjective is determined by a genitive, thus: "You are desirous of money, sparing of your own, prodigal of another's." By a dative, thus: "You are devoted to malice alone, malicious to others, worse to your own, worst to

aliis, peior tuis, pessimus tibi." Determinatur eciam unum adiectivum per diversos dativos respectu diversorum, ut in hiis versibus Hildeberti Cenomanensis episcopi:

Est igitur proba iuncta probo, formosa decoro,
callida censato, religiosa pio.

Ecce hoc adiectivum "iuncta" determinatur per diversos dativos respectu diversorum. Determinatur enim per hunc dativum "probo" respectu huius adiectivi "proba" et per hunc dativum "decoro" respectu huius adiectivi "formosa" et sic de aliis. Adiectivum determinatur per accusativum, sic: "Diversis efflorescis virtutibus, velox intelligenciam, efficax racionem, tenax memoriam, disertus sermonem, speciosus vultum, urbanus gestum, robustus membra, coadiutus agilitate corporis et ceteris dotibus Graciarum." Et notandum quod nunquam construitur adiectivum proprie cum accusativo, nisi per synodochen, nisi fuerit participium verbi regentis accusativum. Ornaciorem vero facit oracionem figura ipsa quam ipsa proprietas. Determinatur eciam non per accusativum set per oracionem constantem ex preposicione et accusativo, sic: "Animus tuus totus effluit in maliciam, in superiores tumidus, in inferiores inhumanus, intollerabilis in pares, maliciosus in omnes." Adiectivum determinatur per ablativum, sic: "Beata Katerina, lilio candens pudicicie, iuvencula tempore, regia nacione, preacuta scienciis arcium et armis corroborata virtutum, contra philosophos pro fide

yourself." One adjective is also determined by diverse datives with respect to diverse things, as in these verses by Hildebert, Bishop of Le Mans:

> Therefore an upright woman is joined to an upright man, a beautiful one to a handsome one, a clever one to an intelligent one, a religious one to a pious one.

Note how this adjective "joined" is determined by diverse datives with respect to diverse things. For it is determined by the dative "upright" with respect to the adjective "upright" and by the dative "handsome" with respect to the adjective "beautiful" and so forth. An adjective is determined by an accusative, thus: "You flourish with various virtues, quick in intelligence, powerful in reason, tenacious in memory, fluent in speech, handsome in countenance, refined in carriage, strong in limbs, assisted by bodily agility and the other gifts of the Graces." And you should note that an adjective is never constructed with an accusative in proper usage but only by means of synecdoche, unless the accusative happens to be a participle of the governing verb. However, using the said figure makes an utterance more ornate than following the said rule of proper usage. An adjective also is determined not by an accusative but by a phrase that consists of a preposition and an accusative, thus: "Your entire mind flows forth in malice, puffed up toward your superiors, inhuman toward your inferiors, intolerable toward your equals, malicious toward all." An adjective is determined by an ablative, thus: "Blessed Katherine, shining with the lily of modesty, young in time, regal in birth, most acute in knowledge of the arts and strengthened by the arms of the virtues, fighting for the faith against the philosophers, gained

dimicans, victis lucrata victoriam, pro Christo morientibus mortem commutavit in vitam." Et hic:

Femina dulce suum semper respergit amaro,
plena malo, verbo dulcis, amara dolo.

Determinatur enim adiectivum aliter, scilicet per oracionem constantem ex preposicione et ablativo, sic: "Nobilis es in expensis: strictissimus in propriis, largissimus in alienis." Ita dictum sit de adiectivo.

22 Verbum dupliciter determinatur: tum per adverbium, tum per diccionem casualem. Per adverbium, sic: "Tessaras colligit rapide, inspicit sollicite, volvit argute, mittit instanter, ioculanter compellit, pacienter exspectat." Hoc dicit Sydonius de Theodorico rege. Et addit: "In bonis iactibus tacet, in malis ridet, in neutris irascitur, in utrisque philosophatur."

23 Quando verbum determinatur per diccionem casualem, aut determinatur per nominativum, genitivum, dativum, accusativum aut ablativum. Per nominativum quando nominativus ponitur adverbialiter, ut "Incedo supinus," id est "supine." Et tunc fiet talis inculcacio: "Circa leccionem assistimus intenti, speculamur solliciti, recurrimus assidui, laboramus studiosi." Aut determinantur plura verba per plures nominativos: quando, scilicet, semel positum pertinet ad diversos nominativos, sic:

victory for the vanquished and converted death into life for those dying for Christ." And here:

Woman always sprinkles her sweet with bitter, filled with evil, sweet in word, bitter in fraud.

An adjective is determined in yet another way, namely, by a phrase that consists of a preposition and an ablative, thus: "You are renowned for your expenditures: very tight with what is yours, very liberal with what is another's." And so we have discussed the adjective.

A verb is determined in two ways: sometimes by an adverb, sometimes by an inflected word. By an adverb, thus: "He picks up the dice quickly; he examines them anxiously, spins them elegantly, throws them eagerly; he addresses them jestingly and awaits the result calmly." Sidonius says this about King Theodoric, and he adds: "If the throw is lucky, he says nothing; if unlucky, he smiles; in neither case does he lose his temper, in either case he is a real philosopher." 22

When a verb is determined by an inflected word, it is determined either by a nominative, a genitive, a dative, an accusative, or an ablative. By a nominative when a nominative is used adverbially, as "I advance, supine," that is, "supinely." And then an inculcation of this sort will be produced: "Intent, we attend the lecture; excited, we watch; constant, we hurry back; zealous, we labor." Or several verbs are determined by several nominatives, namely, when what is used once pertains to various nominatives, thus: 23

Rex tuus est speculum quo te speculata superbis,
sidus de cuius rutilas fulgore, columpna.

Verbum determinatur per genitivum, sic: "O ridiculosam
magnitudinem, quam nec sue pudet ignorancie nec penitet
negligencie nec temporis iacture." Per dativum, sic: "Iste in
corde (et corde) loquens concordat fraudi, discordat sibi,
detrahit absenti, blanditur assistenti." Per accusativum, sic:
"Divine dispensacionis misericordia penitentem admittit,
peccata remittit, debita dimittit, punienda pretermittit."
Hec sunt verba Cenomanensis episcopi, in suis epistolis.
Ecce exemplum domesticum:

Perdita restituo, dispersa recolligo, fracta
consolido, lapsa surrigo, rupta suo.

Contingit eciam unum verbum determinari per plures accusativos respectu diversorum, sic:

Respuit in primis lacrimosas arida, blandas
aspera, clamosas surda puella preces.

Ecce hoc verbum "respuit" determinatur per hunc accusativum "lacrimosas" respectu huius nominativi "arida" et sic de
ceteris. Determinatur eciam verbum per oracionem constantem ex preposicione et accusativo, sic: "Filius iste nequicie preliatur in socios, desevit in subditos, murmurat in
prelatos, malignatur in universos." Per ablativum determinatur verbum dupliciter: uno modo quando unum verbum

Your king is the mirror in which, seeing yourself, you take pride; the star, with whose radiance you shine; the pillar.

A verb is determined by a genitive, thus: "O laughable greatness, which neither is ashamed of its ignorance nor repents of its neglect nor of the loss of time." By a dative, thus: "This person, speaking in his heart (and with his heart), assents to deceit, dissents from himself, disparages those absent, flatters those present." By an accusative, thus: "The mercy of divine dispensation admits the penitent, remits sins, cancels debts, overlooks what deserves punishment." These are the words of the Bishop of Le Mans, in his letters. Here is a homemade example:

I restore what has been lost, I gather what has been scattered, I make whole what has been broken, I raise up what has fallen, I sew what has been torn.

It is also possible for one verb to be determined by several accusatives with respect to various things, thus:

Dry-eyed, the maiden especially rejected tearful pleas; harsh, she rejected gentle pleas; deaf, she rejected noisy pleas.

Notice this verb "rejected" is determined by the accusative "tearful" with respect to the nominative "dry-eyed" and so forth. A verb is also determined by a phrase that consists of a preposition and an accusative, thus: "This son of iniquity fights against comrades, rages against subordinates, mutters against rulers, works malice against everyone." A verb is determined by an ablative in two ways: in one way when one

determinatur per plures ablativos, alio modo quando plura verba determinantur per plures ablativos. Unum per plures ablativos, sic: "Acrimonia, voce, vultu adversarios terruisti." Et tunc incidit color quem premisimus in abbreviacione materie, scilicet articulus. Plura verba per plures ablativos, sic:

Non animo solo set et ore malignus et actu
fervet mente, fremit ore nocetque manu.

Determinatur eciam verbum per oracionem constantem ex preposicione et ablativo, sic: "Iste in convivio predicat, in ecclesia iocatur, in cubiculo dampnat, in questione dormitat."

24 Ex premissis constat qualiter facienda est verbi determinacio uniformiter inculcata, scilicet tum per adverbia, tum per genitivos, tum per dativos, tum per accusativos, tum per ablativos, tum per oracionem constantem ex preposicione et suo accusativo vel ablativo.

25 Commixta fit eciam determinacio, scilicet difformiter: in eadem clausula vel diversis. In eadem quando verbum clausule dupliciter determinatur, scilicet vel per diversos casus vel per unum casum et oracionem constantem ex preposicione et suo casu accusativo vel ablativo. Et utrobique facienda est inculcacio talium clausularum, quoniam ex inculcacione pendet vis elegancie. Et precipue facilitatis ornate verbum clausule recipit diversas determinaciones secundum diversos casus, sic:

verb is determined by several ablatives, in another when several verbs are determined by several ablatives. One verb is determined by several ablatives, thus: "With sharp talk, voice, face you frightened the opponents." And then there occurs a color that we treated previously under abbreviation of the subject matter, namely, parataxis. Several verbs are determined by several ablatives, thus:

> Wicked not in spirit alone but also in mouth and deed,
> he rages in mind, roars in mouth, and harms with hand.

A verb also is determined by a phrase that consists of a preposition and an ablative, thus: "This one preaches at a banquet, jokes in a church, condemns in a bedroom, and sleeps at a trial."

From the above it is evident how one should go about 24 creating a determination of a verb inculcated in one particular way, namely, sometimes by adverbs, sometimes by genitives, sometimes by datives, sometimes by accusatives, sometimes by ablatives, and sometimes by a phrase that consists of a preposition and its accusative or ablative.

A determination can also be mixed, namely, in two ways: 25 in the same clause or in several clauses. In the same clause when the verb of that clause is determined in two ways, namely, either by several cases or by one case and a phrase that consists of a preposition and its accusative or ablative case. And in both instances an inculcation of such clauses should be created, since the power of refinement depends on this inculcation. And the verb in a clause of ornamented facility, in particular, admits various determinations with respect to various cases, thus:

Liriopes triplicem producit formula florem:
crine crocum, facie lilia, fronte rosam.

Ecce in hac clausula "formula Liriopes producit crocum crine," hoc verbum "producit" dupliciter determinatur, scilicet per hunc accusativum "crocum" et hunc ablativum "crine." Et sic idem verbum determinatur per diversos casus.

26   Verbum clausule dupliciter determinatur, scilicet per unum casum et oracionem constantem ex preposicione et casu, sic: "Agis sine iactancia litteratum, sine scurrilitate facetum, sine superbia nobilem, sine malicia potentem, sine popularitate communem." Ecce in hac clausula "agis sine iactancia litteratum," hoc verbum "agis" dupliciter determinatur, scilicet per hunc accusativum "litteratum" et per hanc oracionem "sine iactancia." Et sic de ceteris.

27   In diversis clausulis commiscentur diverse determinaciones sic, scilicet quod in una clausula ponatur unus modus determinandi, in alia alius, in tercia tercius et sic deinceps, ut in hiis versibus:

Hinc ferus, hinc rigidus, utrinque severus, utrique
congruus, utrumque nactus, utroque potens.

Ecce in hac clausula "utrimque severus" determinatur hoc adiectivum "severus" per hoc adverbium "utrinque," in sequenti clausula hoc adiectivum "congruus" per dativum "utrique," in alia aliud adiectivum per accusativum, in alia aliud per ablativum. Hec autem diversitas casuum sumitur

The beauty of Liriope brings forth a triple flower: a
crocus in her hair, a lily in her face, a rose in her forehead.

Notice in the clause "the beauty of Liriope brings forth a
crocus in her hair" the verb "brings forth" is determined in
two ways, namely, by the accusative "crocus" and by the ablative "hair." And thus the same verb is determined by various cases.

The verb of a clause is determined in two ways, namely, by   26
one case and by a phrase that consists of a preposition and a
case, thus: "You do without bragging what is learned, without scurrility what is courteous, without pride what is noble,
without malice what is powerful, without populism what is
communal." Notice in the clause "you do without bragging
what is learned" the verb "you do" is determined in two
ways, namely, by the accusative "what is learned" and by the
phrase "without bragging." And so for the others.

Various determinations are mixed in various clauses in   27
this way, namely, that one method of determining is used in
one clause, another in the second, and a third in the third,
and so forth, as in these verses:

Here wild, there inflexible, strict on both sides, suited
to each, having obtained each, powerful in each thing.

Notice in the clause "strict on both sides" the adjective
"strict" is determined by the adverb "on both sides," in the
following clause the adjective "suited" is determined by the
dative "to each," in another clause another adjective is determined by the accusative, and in another clause another
adjective is determined by the ablative. But this diversity of

ab eadem diccione et sic incidit color traduccio. Aliter eciam commiscentur diverse determinaciones in diversis clausulis, scilicet quando sic inculcamus clausulas quod in una clausula est alius modus determinandi verbum quam in ceteris, quamvis non in omni clausula varietur modus determinandi, ut hic: "Invitavit nos ad mensam apparatus ferculorum, expectacionem fames ipsa non sustinuit, set cum cibis et potibus veloces inivimus concilium et ventri satisfacto properavimus ad recessum." Ecce aliud exemplum: "Cum essemus omnes in lumbis Ade, maculam contraximus ex macula materie; in ramos diffusum est vicium radicis; in membra declinavit dolor capitis; in filios successit iniquitas parentis; iure hereditario descendit pena in posteros; in tenebris obvoluit ergastulum inferni ramos cum radice, membra cum capite, filios cum parente." Ecce in propositis exemplis, non in omni clausula variatur iste modus determinandi verbum, nec in omnibus observatur. Sic igitur habemus omnes determinacionis modos qui accidere possunt.

28   Et notandum quod ideo diximus inculcacionem facere ad ornatum quia inculcacio per se oracionem exornat, quamvis sine subsidio figure vel coloris. Qui igitur voluerit gaudere clausularum inculcacione, expedit ei memoriter tenere artificium quod premisimus materiam prolongandi, et semper pre manibus habeat interpretaciones, circumlocuciones, descripciones et precipue locum oppositorum.

cases is taken from the same word, and thus occurs the color polyptoton. In still another way various determinations may be mixed in various clauses, namely, when we inculcate the clauses in such a way that in one clause the way of determining the verb is different than in the others, although the method of determining is not varied in every clause, as here: "The splendid preparation of the dishes invited us to the table, hunger itself did not tolerate any waiting, but with food and drink we quickly held counsel and, having satisfied our belly, we hastened to retire." Here is another example: "Since we all were in Adam's loins, we contracted his stain from the stain in our substance; the vice of the root has spread into the branches; the head's pain diverged into the limbs; the parent's evil passed down into the children; by the law of inheritance the penalty fell to the descendants; the prison house of hell has shrouded in shadows the branches with the root, the limbs with the head, the children with the parent." Notice that in the proffered examples this method of determining the verb is not varied in every clause, nor is it observed in all of them. So therefore we have every method of determination that can possibly occur.

And it should be noted that we said that inculcation produces ornamentation because inculcation by itself adorns the discourse, even if it lacks the support of a figure or a color. Therefore, it will profit anyone who might wish to revel in the inculcation of clauses to hold in his memory the technique of extending the subject matter that we provided earlier, and at all times he should have ready to hand interpretations, circumlocutions, descriptions, and especially the collocation of opposites. 28

29   Ita dictum sit de prima parte facilitatis ornate, scilicet determinacione. Nunc sequitur de secunda, scilicet de qualitate dicendi per colores verborum et sentenciarum.

30   Quoniam omnes colores et verborum et sentenciarum ad ornatam facilitatem faciunt, exceptis decem coloribus verborum penes quos receditur a propria potestate vocabuli (de quibus sufficienter expeditum est), nunc distinguemus inter colores verborum et sentenciarum, deinde singulorum descripciones assignabimus qualitercumque. Color verborum, ut dicit Tullius, est "ipsius sermonis insignita perpolicio." Sunt quidam colores tante proprietatis ut et non intelligentes alliciunt ad auditum, ut puta similiter cadens, similiter desinens, agnominacio. Color sentenciarum est qui sentencia vendicat dignitatem qui et plenius excitat intellectum. Prius igitur de 36 coloribus verborum dicendum est.

31   Repeticio est cum eandem diccionem ponimus in principio plurium clausularum, ut in *Architrenio:*

Tu patris es verbum, tu mens, tu dextera: verbum
expediat verbum, mens mentem, dextera dextram.

32   Conversio est contraria priori, cum eadem diccio ponitur in fine plurium clausularum, sic:

Te virtus ditat, laus ditat, gracia ditat.

Et hic: "Ab hoc regno concordia sublata est, prosperitas sublata est, liberalitas sublata est."

And so we have discussed the first part of ornamented fa- 29
cility, namely, determination. Now follows the second part,
namely, the quality of speaking by means of the colors of
words and the colors of thoughts.

Since all colors, both of words and of thoughts, produce 30
ornamented facility, except the ten colors of words in which
the proper potency of the word is abandoned (which have
been treated sufficiently), now we will distinguish between
colors of words and of thoughts and then we will provide descriptions of each and every one of them. A color of words,
as Cicero says, is "the fine polish of the language itself."
There are certain colors of such appropriateness that they
lead even those who do not understand them to listen: for
instance, homoeoptoton, homoeoteleuton, and paronomasia. A color of thoughts is one that claims its merit from a
sentiment and that more fully stirs the intellect. Let us
therefore speak first about the thirty-six colors of words.

Epanaphora is when we put the same word at the begin- 31
ning of several clauses, as in the *Architrenius:*

You are the word, you are the mind, you are the right
hand of the Father: may that word sustain my word,
that mind my mind, that right hand my right hand.

Antistrophe is the opposite of the preceding color, when 32
the same word is placed at the end of several clauses, thus:

You virtue enriches, praise enriches, grace enriches.

And here: "From this kingdom concord has been removed,
prosperity has been removed, generosity has been removed."

33   Complexio est unius diccionis in principio et alterius in fine multarum clausularum posicio frequentata. Et componitur ex duobus coloribus premissis, sic:

Sperne voluptates mundi, sperne spectacula mundi.

34   Traduccio est eiusdem diccionis crebra posicio in eadem significacione vel diversa. Eadem, sic: "Hunc hominem vocas, qui si fuisset homo, nunquam tam crudeliter vitam hominis petisset." Diversa, sic:

Virtutum flores si carpseris, ut rosa flores.

35   Contencio est opposita fronte contrariorum posicio, ut: "Amicis te implacabilem, inimicis te placabilem prebes." Et reducitur ad figuram que dicitur antitheta. Est autem antitheta sentencia continens contrarias dicciones falsitatis set et quandoque impossibilitatis apparenciam pretendentes. Intellectu tamen subtilis investigatoris solucio delitescit, sic:

Nimia humilitas superbia est.

Sensus est: "Nimia humilitas in apparencia superbia est in existencia." Similiter:

Nichil michi donat qui omnia donat michi.

Sensus est: "Nichil michi donat in effectu qui omnia donat in promisso." Et hoc ideo dicitur quia large promittencium est parum dare. Similiter in premisso exemplo de sancto

Symploce is the repeated placement of one word at the 33
beginning and another at the end of multiple clauses. And it
is made up of the two preceding colors, thus:

Reject the pleasures of the world, reject the spectacles
of the world.

Polyptoton is the frequent placement of the same word 34
in the same or a different meaning. The same meaning, thus:
"You call him a man, who, had he been a man, would never
so cruelly have sought another man's life." A different meaning, thus:

If you plucked the flowers of virtues, you would flower
like a rose.

Antithesis is the placement of contraries face to face, as: 35
"To friends you show yourself implacable, to enemies conciliatory." And the color called *contentio* in Latin is equivalent to the figure that is called antithesis in Greek. However,
the figure antithesis is a sentiment that contains opposed
words that assert what has the appearance of falsehood and
sometimes even impossibility. But to a subtle inquirer's understanding a solution nonetheless lies hidden, thus:

Too much humility is pride.

The meaning is: "Too much humility in appearance is pride
in reality." Likewise:

He gives me nothing who gives me everything.

The meaning is: "He gives me nothing in effect who gives
me everything in promise." And this is said because it is the
practice of those who promise a lot to give little. Likewise,

Thoma: "O letus dolor in tristi gaudio." Huius figure varietates plenissime ostendit Gervasius de Saltu Lacteo, qui elegancias tam prosa quam metro speciales tractat perfecte.

36   Exclamacio superius describitur ubi de apostrophacione locutum est. Huius exemplum habetur in "Libro versuum," sic:

> O dolor! O plus quam dolor! O mors! O truculenta
> mors! Utinam esses, mors, mortua! Quid meministi . . . ?

37   Interrogacio est que, enumeratis hiis que obsunt cause adversariorum, superiorem confirmat oracionem, sic: "Nonne te sic erigendo deicis? Nonne sic sapiendo desipis? Nonne sic eloquendo mutescis?," ut superius habetur.

38   Raciocinacio est interrogacionum enumeracio et earundem responsio subsecuta, sic:

> Dives avarus eget. Quare? Quia cum petit usus,
> tangere parta timet. Cur? Ne minuatur acervus.

39   Sentencia est oracio sumpta de vita que aut quid sit aut quid esse oporteat in vita breviter ostendit. Et est quasi proverbium, sic:

> Sepe novum vetera faciunt peccata pudorem.

Et hic:

in the preceding example of St. Thomas Becket: "O happy sorrow in sad joy." Gervase of Melkley, who treats the particular refinements in both prose and meter completely, shows the varieties of this figure in fullest detail.

Exclamation is described above where apostrophe was 36 discussed. There is an example of it in the "Book of Verses," thus:

> O sorrow! O greater than sorrow! O death! O truculent death! Would you were dead, O death! How dare you recall...?

Rhetorical question is the color which, when the points 37 against the adversaries' cause have been summed up, reinforces the argument that has just been delivered, thus: "Don't you cast yourself down by raising yourself up in this way? Don't you make yourself foolish by being wise in this way? Don't you grow dumb by speaking in this way?," as is found above.

Reasoning by question and answer is the enumeration of 38 questions and the answer to each in a close series, thus:

> The covetous man is needy. How so? Because when need requires, he fears to touch what has been obtained. Why? Lest his hoard be reduced.

Maxim is a saying drawn from life, which shows concisely 39 either what happens or what ought to happen in life. And it is like a proverb, thus:

> Often old sins cause new shame.

And here:

In facie legitur hominis secreta voluntas.

40 Contrarium est quod ex duabus rebus alteram breviter et facile confirmat, sic:

Qui sibi non parcit, michi vel tibi quomodo parcet?

Et differt a contencione quia istud confirmat, aliud non.

41 Membrum oracionis est res breviter absoluta sine tocius sentencie demonstracione, que denuo alio membro excipitur. Cum autem ex duobus membris constare possit, commodissime fit ex tribus, ut ait Tullius, ut hic. "Et inimico consulebas et amicum ledebas et tibi ipsi nocebas."

42 Articulus superius describitur in abbreviacione materie. Eius exemplum est hoc:

Prompta, pudica, timens, humilis, facunda, fidelis,
  docta, potens, locuples, nobilis Yo fuit.

43 Continuacio est densa et continens verborum frequentacio cum absolucione sentenciarum. Fit autem tripliciter: in sentencia, in contrario, in conclusione. In sentencia, sic: "Ei non multum potest obesse fortuna qui sibi firmius in virtute quam casu presidium collocavit." In contrario, sic: "Nam si quis spei non multum collocarit in casu, quid est quod ei casus magnopere obesse possit?" In conclusione, sic: "Quodsi in eos plurimum fortuna potest qui suas raciones omnes in

A man's hidden desire is read in his face.

Reasoning by contraries is the color that neatly and di- 40
rectly proves one of two statements, thus:

Who does not spare himself, how will he spare me or
you?

And it differs from antithesis because this color proves
something, but the other does not.

Colon is a sentence member, brief and complete, which 41
does not express the entire thought, but is in turn supplemented by another colon. Although it can consist of two
cola, Cicero says it is most suitably made from three, as
here: "You were consulting the best interests of your enemy,
you were hurting your friend, and you were injuring yourself."

Comma is described above under abbreviation of the 42
subject matter. This is an example of it:

Io was prompt, modest, fearful, humble, fluent, faith-
ful, learned, powerful, wealthy, noble.

Period is a close-packed and uninterrupted group of 43
words embracing a complete thought. It is accomplished in
three ways: in a maxim, in a contrast, and in a conclusion. In
a maxim, thus: "Fortune cannot much harm him who has
built his stronghold more firmly upon virtue than upon
chance." In a contrast, thus: "For if a person has not placed
much hope in chance, what great harm can chance do him?"
In a conclusion, thus: "But if Fortune has her greatest power
over those who have cast all their plans to chance, we should

casu intulerint, non sunt omnia committenda fortune, ne
magnam nimis in nos habeat dominacionem."

44   Compar est distinccio clausularum quasi ex equali numero sillabarum, sic:

> Turba colorum, vis violarum, pompa rosarum
> induit ortos, purpurat agros, pascit ocellos.

45   Similiter cadens est diccionum casualium in eadem construccione verborum similis exitus, sic: "Hominem laudas
egentem virtutis, abundantem felicitatis." Hic color maxime invenitur in quodam opusculo de bello Troiano quod sic
incipit:

> Pergama flere volo, fato Danais data solo.

46   Similiter desinens est diccionum casu carencium similis
exitus, sic: "Turpiter audes facere, nequiter studes dicere;
vivis invidiose, delinquis studiose, loqueris odiose."

47   Commixtum est quando predicti duo colores commiscentur, ut dictum est in premisso exemplo: "Perditissima
racio est etc." Hunc colorem non ponit Tullius set dicit quod
similiter cadens et similiter desinens quandoque miscentur.
His tribus coloribus in opere auctentico non decet uti nisi
casualiter eveniant, cuilibet enim brevi materie, ut puta epi-
taphiis et proverbiis, deputantur. Quidam tamen sub huiusmodi coloribus voluit epitaphium Phillidis componere, scilicet sic:

> Phillida Demophon leto dedit hospes amantem;
>   ille necis causam prebuit, illa necem.

not entrust our all to Fortune, lest she gain too great a domination over us."

Isocolon is division into clauses of about the same number of syllables, thus: 44

A crowd of colors, a host of violets, a parade of roses
clothes the gardens, adorns the fields, feasts the eyes.

Homoeoptoton is the similar ending of inflected words 45
in the same period, thus: "You praise a man lacking in virtue,
abounding in good fortune." This color is found especially
in a certain work on the Trojan War that begins thus:

For Troy I wish to moan, handed over to the Greeks by
fate alone.

Homoeoteleuton is the similar ending of words that lack 46
a case, thus: "You dare to act dishonorably, you strive to talk
despicably; you live jealously, you sin zealously, you speak
odiously."

Mixture is when the previous two colors are mixed, as 47
was said in an earlier example: "A most depraved principle it
is etc." Cicero does not include this color but he says that
homoeoptoton and homoeoteleuton are sometimes mixed.
It is not proper to use these three colors in an authoritative
work, unless they occur by chance, since they are reserved
for all sorts of brief subject matter, such as epitaphs and
proverbs. Someone indeed chose to compose the epitaph of
Phyllis by means of such colors, namely, thus:

Demophoon—her guest—killed Phyllis, who loved
him. He supplied her death's cause, she the death itself.

Et notandum quod hii tres colores et agnominacio, de quo immediate agemus, si rarissime hiis utamur, oracionem egregiant et illustrant, si vero frequenter, puerili videbimur elocucione delectari, teste Tullio in secunda *Rethorica,* ubi agit de agnominacione.

48   Agnominacio est diccionum fere similium in voce elegans ordinacio, sic: "Nichil magis quam Cupido homini cupido placere potest." Bernardus:

Fronduit in plano platanus, convallibus alnus.

Fit autem et hic color multis modis, ut patet in secunda *Rethorica* Ciceronis, set ex premissa descripcione clarius elucescunt.

49   Subieccio superius describitur in apostrophacione. Cuius exemplum est istud Laurencii Dunelmensis, in suo *Yponasticon,* de Adam peccante, sic:

O pater! O quid agis? Deus est quem spernis etc.,

sicut prius.

50   Gradacio est descensus vocis ad seipsam superius anticipatam. Fit autem dupliciter, scilicet inflexione eiusdem vocis et resumpcione. Inflexione, ut in Vindocinensi:

Fama creat laudem, laus premia, premia mentem,
    mens studium, studium carmina, carmen opus.

And it should be noted that these three colors and paronomasia, which we will treat next, distinguish and embellish
our speech if we employ them very sparingly; but if we use
them frequently, "we shall seem to be taking delight in a
childish style," according to Cicero in his second *Rhetoric,*
where he treats paronomasia.

Paronomasia is the elegant arrangement of words that   48
are almost alike in sound, thus: "Nothing can please a cupid-
inous man more than Cupid." Bernard Silvestris:

> The plane tree flourishes on the plain, the alder in val-
> leys.

As is evident in Cicero's second *Rhetoric,* this color also is
produced in many ways, but they are clearly evident from
the previous description.

Hypophora is described above under apostrophe. An ex-   49
ample of that color is the one by Lawrence of Durham, in
his *Hypognosticon,* concerning the sinning Adam, thus:

> O father! O what are you doing? It's God whom you
> scorn etc.,

as quoted previously.

Climax is a word's going back to the very same word,   50
which appeared immediately before it. And it is accomplished in two ways, namely, by changing the inflection and
by repeating the same word. By changing the inflection of
the same word, as in Matthew of Vendôme:

> Fame begets praise, praise reward, reward reflection,
> reflection inspiration, inspiration poetry, poetry a fin-
> ished work.

Si quis autem ad denarium numerum huiusmodi versuum in die pervenerit versificatorem reputat expeditum. Resumpcione, sic:

> Me dolor infestat, infestat me dolor intra
> et latitat plaga, plaga salute carens.

51 Diffinicio est que breviter et absolute alicuius rei complectitur proprietates, demonstrando quod ipsa res est, sic: "Maiestas rei publice est in qua continetur amplitudo et dignitas civitatis."

52 Transicio est que postquam quid dictum sit breviter ostendit, proponit breviter quid sequatur (et vocatur "epilogus"), sic: "Modo in patrem cuiusmodi fuerit audistis; nunc qualis ipse parens extiterit considerate."

53 Correccio est cum tollitur quod dictum est et pro eo magis ydoneum ordinatur, sic:

> Hic homo pars hominis; non pes set pars pedis; ymmo
> parte pedis minor est; non minor ymmo nichil.

54 Occupacio est cum dicimus nos preterire aut nescire aut nolle dicere illud quod maxime dicimus, sic: "Non intendo dicere quomodo virginem devirginasti."

55 Disiunctum, coniunctum et adiunctum sunt tres distincti colores quos plenius tetigimus ubi de zeumate et ypozeusi locuti sumus.

56 Conduplicacio quid sit et quot modis et ex quibus causis

Moreover, anyone who could manage ten such verses per day he counts as an agile versifier. By repeating the same word, thus:

> Sorrow me vexes, vexes me sorrow within, and there
> lies hidden a wound, a wound lacking remedy.

Definition in brief and clear-cut fashion encompasses the 51 characteristic properties of some thing by showing what the thing itself is, thus: "The sovereign majesty of the republic is that which comprises the grandeur and dignity of the state."

Transition is the color which, after it briefly recalls what 52 has been said, briefly sets forth what is to follow next (and it is also called "epilogue"), thus: "You have just heard how he has been conducting himself toward his father; now consider what kind of parent he was himself."

Correction is when what has been said is retracted and 53 something more suitable is put in its place, thus:

> This man is but part of a man; not even a foot but part
> of a foot; nay, he is less than a part of a foot; or not less,
> but nothing at all.

Paralipsis is when we say that we are passing over or do 54 not know or refuse to say that which precisely we are saying, thus: "I do not intend to tell how you deprived a virgin of her virginity."

Disjunction, Conjunction, and Adjunction are three sep- 55 arate colors that we touched upon more fully when we spoke about zeugma and hypozeuxis.

What reduplication is and how many ways it can be 56

habeat fieri satis plene ostensum est superius in prolongacione materie, ubi scilicet de apostrophacione actum est.

57   Interpretacio superius describitur in prolongacione materie. Est enim primus prolongacionis modus, sicut ibidem
sufficienter ostensum est.

58   Commutacio est cum due sentencie inter se discrepantes
ex traieccione ita efferuntur ut ex priori posterior priori
contraria perficiatur, sic: "Esse oportet ut vivas, non vivere
ut edas."

59   Permissio est cum nos aliquam rem ex toto ad alicuius
concedimus potestatem, sic: "Quoniam in necessitatis articulo michi vestre succurrit benignitatis auxilium, hec pauca
que michi de multis relicta sunt vobis et vestre tribuo volun-
tati."

60   Dubitacio superius describitur in capitulo prolongacionis materie, ubi de apostrophacione actum est. Cuius exemplum habetur in "Libro versuum," sic:

> Volucrum rimaberis aure
> murmura? vel motus oculo? vel cetera?

61   Expedicio est cum, racionibus pluribus enumeratis quibus aliqua res aut fieri aut non fieri potuerit, cetere tolluntur
et una relinquitur quam intendimus, ut in "Libro versuum,"
sic:

> Expedit humani generis qui vicerit hostem
> ut sit homo purus aut angelus aut Deus. Esse
> purus non posset, quia purus prompcior esset
> lapsurus possetque leves incurrere lapsus.

accomplished and from which motives has been shown fully enough above under prolongation of the subject matter, namely, where apostrophe was treated.

Interpretation is described above under prolongation of 57 the subject matter. For it is the first method of prolonging, as is shown sufficiently in that place.

Reciprocal change occurs when two discrepant thoughts 58 are so expressed by transposition that the latter is completed by the former although contradictory to it, thus: "You must eat to live, not live to eat."

Surrender is when with regard to some matter we put 59 ourselves entirely in someone's power, thus: "Because the aid of your benignity hastens to relieve me in my state of need, I grant to you and to your will these few things that remain to me from among many."

Indecision is described above in the chapter on prolonga- 60 tion of the subject matter, where apostrophe was treated. There is an example of it in the "Book of Verses," thus:

Will your ear interpret the singing of birds—or their movements your eye? or (etc.)?

Proof by elimination is when we have enumerated the 61 several ways by which something either could have been or could not have been accomplished, and all are then discarded except the one on which we are insisting, as in the "Book of Verses," thus:

The one who vanquished mankind's foe had to be pure man, or an angel, or God. Pure man he could not be, because pure man straightway was fallible and could easily fall into sin. Angel you could not be, for since the

> Angele non poteras: quia, cum natura ruisset
> propria, non stares in nostra. . . .
>> Convenit ergo
> ut Deus esset homo, cuius sapiencia plena . . .

62   Dissolutum vel dissolucio superius describitur in abbreviacione materie. Et convenit cum figura que vocatur asintheton.

63   Prescisio est cum dictis quibusdam reliquum quod incep-
tum est dici relinquitur iudicio audientis vel prescisio est
incepte narracionis retractio, ut hic:

> Fles? Fleo. Nonne taces? Non. Vado vocare magistrum.
> Vade. Mavisne vocem? Que michi cura? Voca!

Item magister Johannes de Hauvilla introduxit Caunum in-
terrogantem et Biblidem pavide respondentem, cum inve-
nisset eam Caunus dolentem, sic:

> Quis te lesit? A. Quis? Amor.

Et iterum, cum ipsa vexaret eum:

> Quid michi vis? Quod a. Quid? Quod ama. Quid vis?
>   Quod amare.
> Quid? Quod amare ve. Quid vis? Quod amare velis.

Et sic plerumque fit hic color sub dyalogo.

64   Conclusio est que brevi argumentacione ex hiis que ante
dicta sunt aut facta conficit id quod necessario consequatur,
sic:

angelic nature had fallen you would not stand firm in ours. . . . It was fitting, therefore, that God become man—God whose fullness of wisdom. . . .

The color called *dissolutum* or *dissolutio* in Latin is de- 62 scribed above under abbreviation of the subject matter. And it coincides with the figure that is called asyndeton in Greek.

Aposiopesis is when something is said and then the rest 63 of what the speaker has begun to say is left to the discretion of the hearer, or aposiopesis is the taking back of a narration that has been started, as here:

> Are you crying? I am crying. Will you be quiet? No.
> I'm going to call the teacher. Go. Do you want me to call? What do I care? Call!

Likewise, master John of Hauville introduced Caunus inquiring and Biblis responding fearfully, when Caunus had found her grieving, thus:

> Who harmed you? L. Who? Love.

And again, when she was annoying him:

> What do you want from me? That l. What? That lo.
> What do you want? That love. What? That y. love.
> What do you want? That you love.

And this color is frequently accomplished like this through dialogue.

Conclusion deduces by means of a brief argument the 64 necessary consequences of what has been said or done before, thus:

Non est certa dies mortis: re cercior omni
  mors est, et mortis ergo relinque viam.

65   Ita dictum sit de 36 coloribus verborum. Sequitur de 19
      coloribus sentenciarum.

66   Distribucio est quando per plures res aut personas di-
      versa negocia disperguntur. Per res, sic:

Flet natura, silent mores, proscribitur omnis
  orphanus a veteri nobilitate pudor.

Per personas, sic:

Iudicis est punire malos, regis dare leges,
  vulgi iura sequi, questoris querere causas.

67   Licencia est maiores non offendens faceta reprehensio.
      Et habet sub se tres species, ut dicit Tullius, quarum prima
      sic describitur. Licencia est expressa reprehensio alicuius
      maioris cum mitigacione, id est quando maior reprehenditur
      ne persona reprehensa pro reprehencione aspera moveatur,
      sic: "Miramini, Quirites, quod ab omnibus vestre raciones
      deserantur? quod causam vestram nemo suscipiat? quod
      nemo vestri se defensorem profiteatur? Illud attribuite
      vestre culpe atque istud desinite mirari." Ecce ex hiis verbis
      reprehensivis de facili possent Quirites ad iracundiam pro-
      vocari et ideo subiungi debet talis mitigacio laudis: "Me-
      mentote quante nobilitatis duxistis originem, quantam lau-
      dem obtinuistis, vestris exigentibus meritis," etc.

The day of one's death is not certain: death is more certain than anything, and so abandon the path of death.

And so we have discussed the thirty-six colors of words. 65
The nineteen colors of thoughts follow.

Distribution is when various actions are dispersed among 66
a number of things or persons. Among things, thus:

Nature weeps, morality is silenced; modesty, an orphan, is wholly banished from her once noble station.

Among persons, thus:

It pertains to the judge to punish the wicked, to the king to give laws, to the common folk to obey laws, to the magistrate to try cases.

License is clever reproof that does not offend one's bet- 67
ters. And it contains within it three kinds, as Cicero says,
the first of which is described thus: License is reproof of
someone superior with a qualification, that is, when a superior is reproved in such a way that the person reproved is not
angered by harsh reproof, thus: "You wonder, fellow citizens, that everyone abandons your interests? That no one
undertakes your cause? That no one declares himself your
defender? Blame this upon yourselves; cease to wonder at
it." Notice that the Roman citizens might easily be provoked to anger by these words of reproof, and therefore
qualifying praise of this sort should be added: "Remember
how great the dignity from which you sprung, how great the
praise you won because your merits demanded it etc."

68   Secunda licencia describitur sic. Licencia est obiurgacio
facta alicui persone per talia in quibus delectat obiurgari,
sic: "Nimium, Quirites, animis estis simplicibus et mansue-
tis; nimium creditis unicuique. Estimatis unumquemque
eniti ut perficiat que vobis pollicitus sit. Erratis et falsa spe
diu frustra detinemini. Stulticia est vestra: id quod erat in
vestra potestate ab aliis petere quam ipsi sumere maluistis."

69   Tercia sic describitur. Licencia est significacio timoris dicendi ea in quibus tamen delectat animus auditoris vel cum
reprehendimus per id quod nos timemus quomodo re-
prehensus accipiat, sic: "Michi cum isto, iudices, fuit amicicia, set ista tamen amicicia, tametsi vereor quomodo accep-
turi sitis, tamen dico, vos me privastis." Fit eciam dupliciter,
aperte scilicet et occulte. Aperte, ut quando ea quibus reprehendimus exprimuntur, ut in "Libro versuum":

Si fas est, accuso Deum etc.

Occulte, quando ea quibus reprehendimus conceptui relin-
quuntur, sic: "Domine, salva reverencia, verba vestra non faciunt ad effectum."

70   Diminucio est eius quod in nobis vel in aliis scimus egregium ad vitandum arroganciam attenuacio, sic: "Non paucas
tribulacionum gravedines passi fuimus pro re publica et
iniuste." Huic colori respondet figura liptote et interpretatur "minus dicens et magis significans."

The second kind of license is described as follows. Li- 68
cense is rebuking some person for the sorts of things for
which he enjoys being rebuked, thus: "Fellow citizens, you
are of too simple and gentle a character; you place too much
trust in every one. You think that every man strives to per-
form what he has promised you. You are mistaken, and have
now for a long time been kept back by false and groundless
hope. The fatuity is yours: you have chosen to seek from
others what lay in your power, rather than take it yourselves."

The third kind is described as follows. License is when we 69
say that we fear to mention things that actually will please
the hearer's spirits or when we reprove someone with something while worrying about how the one who is reproved
will take it, thus: "I enjoyed a friendship with this person,
men of the jury, yet of that friendship—although I fear how
you are going to receive what I shall say, yet I shall say it—
you have deprived me." Also, this is accomplished in two
ways, namely, openly and covertly. Openly, as when the
things we reprove are expressed, as in the "Book of Verses":

If heaven allow it, I chide even God etc.

Covertly, when the things we reprove are left to thought, as:
"My lord, with all due respect, your words have no effect."

Understatement is the lessening of what we know to be 70
outstanding in ourself or in others for the purpose of avoiding arrogance, thus: "We had endured not a few oppressive
afflictions on behalf of the state, and these unjustly." To this
color corresponds the figure litotes, and it is translated as
"saying less and meaning more."

71   Descripcio superius exponitur in prolongacione materie.
Est enim septimus modus materiam prolongandi, ut ostensum est prius.

72   Divisio est que rem semovens a re utramque absolvit subiecta racione, sic:

> Hinc decor, inde pudor duplici te laude venustant.
> Ridet in ore decor; pudor est in corpore florens.

73   Frequentacio est cum res in tota causa disperse, ut aut
gravior aut acrior aut criminosior oracio fiat, breviter col-
liguntur, sic: "A quo tandem abest iste vicio? Quid est cur
iudices velitis eum liberare? Sue pudicicie proditor est, in-
sidiator aliene; cupidus, intemperans, petulans, superbus;
impius in parentes, ingratus in amicos, infestus cognatis; in
superiores contumax, in equos et pares fastidiosus, in inferiores crudelis; denique in omnes intollerabilis."

74   Expolicio est cum in eodem loco manemus et aliud atque
aliud dicere videmur. Fit autem dupliciter, loquendo scilicet
eandem rem vel de eadem re. Eandem rem, id est eandem
sentenciam, loquemur non eodem modo—quia hoc obtun-
dere auditorem est et non sentenciam expolire—set eam
commutare oportet. Commutabimus eandem sentenciam
tribus modis: verbis, pronunciando, tractando.

75   Verbis commutabimus eandem sentenciam quando aliqua sentencia semel dicta bis vel sepius aliis verbis que idem

Vivid description is explained above under prolongation 71
of the subject matter. Namely, it is the seventh method of
prolonging the subject matter, as was shown earlier.

Division separates one thing from another and resolves 72
each by means of a reason subjoined, thus:

> Here beauty and there modesty adorn you with double
> praise. Beauty smiles in your face; modesty is flour-
> ishing in your body.

Accumulation occurs when the points scattered through- 73
out the whole cause are tied up together concisely, so as to
make the speech more impressive or sharp or accusatory,
thus: "From what vice, I ask finally, is this defendant free?
What grounds have you members of the jury for wishing to
release him? He is the betrayer of his own chastity, and a
conspirator against that of others; covetous, intemperate,
irascible, arrogant; disloyal to his parents, ungrateful to his
friends, troublesome to his kin; insulting to his betters, dis-
dainful of his equals and peers, cruel to his inferiors; in short
he is intolerable to everyone."

Refining consists in dwelling on the same topic and yet 74
seeming to say something ever new. Now this is accomplished in two ways, namely, by repeating the same thing or
by speaking about the same topic. We shall repeat the same
thing, that is, the same thought, not in the same way—for
that would weary the hearer and not refine the thought—
but rather it befits us to vary it. We will vary the same theme
in three ways: in words, by delivery, and in treatment.

We will vary the same theme in words when, having ex- 75
pressed some thought once, we articulate it twice or more
often in different words that mean the same thing. So Alan

significant demonstratur. Unde Alanus, in *Anticlaudiano,* in descripcione paradysi terrestris, dicit istam sentenciam tribus vicibus sub diversis verbis, scilicet "In medio paradisi scaturit fons purissimus," sic:

> In medio lacrimatur humus fletuque beato
> producens lacrimas, fontem sudore perhenni
> parturit et dulces potus singultat aquarum.

76   Pronunciando commutabimus eandem sentenciam quando tum ima voce, tum alta, tum alio genere vocis seu gestus eadem sentencia pronunciatur. Set quia hic modus sola vocis prolacione ostenditur et nulla vox scribi potest, exemplariter non monstratur.

77   Tractando commutabimus eandem sentenciam dupliciter: sermocinacione aut exuscitacione. Sermocinacio est color de quo protinus est loquendum. Quantum vero ad presens propositum pertinet est locucio in qua constituitur alicuius persone racio accomodata ad dignitatem, hoc modo, ut, quo facilius res cognosci possit, ne ab eadem sentencia recedamus, sic: "Sapiens qui omnia rei publice causa suscipienda putabit pericula. Sepe ipse secum loquitur dicens 'Non michi soli set eciam atque alio usui multo pocius natus sum patrie; vita, que fato debetur, saluti patrie potissimum detur. Aluit hec me; tute atque honeste produxit usque ad hanc etatem; munivit meas raciones bonis legibus, optimis moribus, honestissimis disciplinis. Quid est quod a me satis ei persolvi possit unde hec accepta sunt?' Quare sic loquitur

of Lille, in the *Anticlaudianus,* in his description of the earthly paradise, repeats three times in different words the same theme — namely, "In the midst of paradise there gushes forth the clearest of springs," thus:

> At the center of the glade the earth is weeping. Producing a blessed stream of tears, with unending sweat it gives birth to a fountain, and it sobs forth sweet drafts of water.

We will vary the same theme by delivery when we pronounce the same thought now with a low voice, now with a high voice, and now with some other kind of voice or gesture. But because this method can be demonstrated only through an utterance of the voice, and no voice can be put in writing, it cannot be illustrated with an example. 76

We will vary the same theme in treatment in two ways: by dialogue and by arousal. Dialogue is a color that has to be discussed a little further on. But insofar as it is relevant to the present topic, dialogue is speech in which is put a thought process that is appropriate to the character of some person, in such a way that, for the sake of greater clarity, we do not abandon the original thought, thus: "Wise is the man who thinks that for the common weal he ought to undergo every peril. Often he speaks to himself, saying: 'Not for self alone was I born, but also, and for quite another use, for the fatherland. Above all, let me give my life, which is owed to fate, for the salvation of my country. She has nourished me. She has in safety and honor reared me to this time of life. She has protected my interests by good laws, the best of customs, and a most honorable training. How can I adequately repay her from whom these blessings have been received?' 77

sapiens secum sepe, ego in periculis rei publice nullum ipse periculum fugi."

78 Exuscitacio est cum nos commoti aliquid dicimus quo auditoris animum commovemus, sic: "Quis est tam tenui cogitacione preditus, cuius animus tantis angustiis invidie continetur, qui non hunc hominem studiosissime laudet et sapientissimum iudicet, qui pro salute patrie, pro incolumitate civitatis, pro rei publice fortuniis quamvis magnum atque atrox periculum studiosissime suscipiat et libenter subeat?" Unde in "Libro versuum":

Quisnam tam cerebri vacuus etc.

79 De eadem re loquemur septem modis. Primus modus est cum res simplex ponitur cum racione subiecta; secundus cum res simplex ponitur sine racione subiecta; tercius in quo ponitur res duplex cum racione; quartus quando inducitur color contrarium, de quo predictum est; quintus quando inducitur similitudo; sextus quando inducitur exemplum; septimus quando inducitur color qui dicitur conclusio, de quo similiter dictum est. De hiis septem planissima ponuntur exempla in "Libro versuum." Ubi scribitur "Prudens ita papa laborem etc.," habetur primus modus, in quo ponitur res simplex cum racione subiecta. Res ponitur ubi dicitur "Prudens ita papa etc." Racio subicitur cum dicitur "quia tanta potestas etc." Secundus modus incipit ubi dicitur "quia sic Deus etc."; tercius modus ibi: "Ergo remissus in

Because the wise man often speaks thus to himself, when the republic is in danger, I myself have shunned no danger."

Arousal is when, moved by emotion ourselves, we say 78 something to stir up the emotions of the hearer, thus: "Who is possessed of reasoning power so feeble, whose soul is bound in such straits of envy, that he would not heap eager praise upon this man and judge him most wise, a man who for the salvation of the fatherland, the security of the state, and the prosperity of the republic eagerly undertakes and gladly undergoes any danger, no matter how great or terrible?" So also in the "Book of Verses":

Who is so void of wit? etc.

We will speak about the same theme in seven ways. The 79 first way is when a simple matter is put forward with a subjoined reason; the second is when a simple matter is put forward without any subjoined reason; the third is that in which a double matter is put forward with a reason; the fourth is when the color "reasoning by contraries" is introduced, which has been discussed previously; the fifth is when a comparison is introduced; the sixth is when an exemplum is introduced; the seventh is when the color that is called "conclusion" is introduced, which likewise has been discussed. Very clear examples of these seven have been put forward in the "Book of Verses." Where it says "So a prudent pope bases all his efforts etc.," there is the first method, in which a simple matter is put forward with a subjoined reason. The matter is put forward when it says "So a prudent pope." The reason is subjoined when it says "because such great power." The second method begins where it says "since God etc."; the third method here: "Therefore if he is

hoc" (racio subicitur ibi: "nam pariter suus est et publicus hostis"); quartus ibi: "An melius etc."; quintus ibi: "Memento notare"; sextus ibi: "Phisicus et pastor etc."; septimus ibi:

Ergo nephas sepeli, pie papa, subambule Petri, etc.

80   Commoracio est cum in loco firmissimo quo tota causa continetur diucius manemus et eodem sepius reditur, id est quando quis, ut moveat auditores, plura argumenta inducit ad commodum sue cause et ad id in quo maxima vis est sepe revertitur, sic: "Unusquisque propria viciorum sorde oblinitur. Te solum symonie vicium pregravat. Hec unica labes causa est ruine proprie."

81   Contencio est per quam contrariarum sentenciarum clausule referuntur, id est quando sentencie contrarie proponuntur, sic: "Vos huiusmodi incomodis lugetis, iste rei publice calamitate letatur." Et differt a contencione colore verborum in hoc quod illa contrarietatem verborum circa eandem rem ostendit, ista contrarietatem sentencie circa diversas res ex quadam comparacione producit.

82   Similitudo est oracio traducens ad rem quampiam aliquod simile ex re dispari, id est quando quis ad commodum sue cause inducit aliquam similitudinem per quam conveniens eliciat argumentum, ut in *Alexandreide* Galteri, ubi introducitur Aristotiles informans Alexandrum, sic:

remiss in this" (the reason is subjoined here: "for he is his own enemy and the public's as well"); the fourth here: "Is it better etc."; the fifth here: "Take heed and remember"; the sixth here: "Physician and shepherd etc."; the seventh here:

Suppress wickedness then, holy Father, successor of Peter etc.

Dwelling on the point occurs when we remain rather long 80 upon, and often return to, the strongest topic, on which the whole cause rests, that is, when someone brings in multiple arguments to the advantage of his cause, in order to move the hearers, and often returns to the argument that has the greatest force, thus: "Each person has been smeared with his very own stain of vice. The single vice of simony burdens you in the extreme. This one fault is the cause of your own ruin."

Antithesis is the color by means of which clauses with op- 81 posite meanings are brought together, that is, when contrary ideas are put forward, thus: "While you deplore these sorts of troubles, this knave rejoices in the ruin of the state." And the color of thought antithesis differs from the color of words antithesis insofar as the latter displays an opposition of words pertaining to the same thing, while the former creates an opposition of meaning pertaining to different things by means of some analogy.

Comparison is a manner of speech that carries over an el- 82 ement of likeness from one thing to a different thing, that is, when, for the advantage of his cause, someone introduces some comparison by means of which he can draw forth a suitable argument, as in Walter of Châtillon's *Alexandreis,* when Aristotle is introduced instructing Alexander, thus:

Consultor procerum servos contempne bilingues
et nequam, nec quos humiles natura iacere
precipit exalta, nam qui pluvialibus undis
intumuit torrens, fluit acrior ampne perhenni.

Et statim reducit similitudinem ad suum propositum, sic:

Sic partis opibus et honoris culmine servus
in dominum surgens, truculencior aspide surda,
obturat precibus aures, mansuescere nescit.

Fit autem quattuor modis et quattuor de causis: per contrarium, per negacionem, per collacionem, per brevitatem.
Unde ad unamquamque causam sumende similitudinis ac-
comodabimus singulos modos pronunciandi.

83   Causa ornandi sumitur similitudo per contrarium, sic:
"Non enim, quemadmodum in palestra qui tedas ardentes
accipit celerior cursu est continuo quam iste qui tradit, ita
melior imperator novus qui accipit exercitum quam iste qui
dedit; propterea quod defatigatus cursor integro facem, hic
peritus imperator imperito excercitum tradit."

84   Causa probandi sumitur exemplum per negacionem, sic:
"Neque equus indomitus, quamvis bene natura compositus
sit, ydoneus potest esse ad eas utilitates et aptus ad ea que

Consult with leaders, despising deceitful and depraved slaves, and do not raise up lowborn men whom nature instructs to grovel, for the torrent that has become swollen with rainwater flows more violently than a steady stream.

And immediately he directs the comparison back to his theme, thus:

Thus the slave, once he has procured wealth and the eminence of honor, rises against his master, and, fiercer than a deaf asp, he closes his ears to entreaties and knows not how to become gentle again.

Comparison is accomplished in four ways and for four different purposes: by contrast, by negation, by detailed parallel, and by abridged comparison. So to each single aim in the use of comparison we shall adapt the corresponding form of presentation.

In the form of a contrast, comparison is used for the purpose of embellishing, thus: "Unlike what happens in the palaestra, where he who receives the burning torch is swifter in the relay race than he who hands it on, the new general who receives command of an army is not superior to the general who gave up its command. For in the one case it is an exhausted runner who hands the torch to a fresh athlete, whereas in this it is an experienced commander who hands over the army to an inexperienced." 83

In the form of negation, a comparative exemplum is used for the purpose of proof, thus: "Neither can an untrained horse, however well built by nature, be fit for the services 84

desiderantur ab equo; neque homo indoctus, quamvis sit in-
geniosus, ad virtutem poterit pervenire."

85   Causa apercius dicendi sumitur similitudo per brevitatem, sic: "In amicicia gerenda, sicut in certamine currendi,
non ita convenit excerceri ut quoad necesse sit venire possis, set ut productus studio et viribus ultro facile procurras."

86   Causa rem ante oculos ponendi sumitur similitudo per
collacionem, sic: "Uti citharedus cum prodierit optime ves-
titus, palla inaurata indutus, cum clamide purpurea coloribus variis intexta, et cum corona aurea magnis fulgentibus
gemmis illuminata, citharam tenens exornatissimam auro et
ebore distinctam, ipse preterea forma et specie sit et statura
apposita ad dignitatem, si, cum magnam populo commove-
rit expectacionem, repente, silencio facto, vocem emittat
acerbissimam cum turpissimo corporis motu, quo melius
exornatus sit et quo magis fuerit expectatus, eo magis contemptus et derisus eicietur; ita si quis in excelso loco et in
magnis ac locupletibus copiis collocatus fortune muneribus
et nature commodis omnibus abundabit, si virtutis et arcium, que virtutis magistre sunt, egebit, quo magis ceteris
rebus erit copiosus et illustris et expectatus, eo vehemen-
cius derisus et contemptus ex omni conventu bonorum
eicietur."

and prepared for those things desired of a horse, nor can an uncultivated man, however well endowed by nature, attain to virtue."

In the form of an abridged comparison, a comparison is 85 used for the purpose of greater clarity, thus: "In maintaining a friendship, as in a footrace, you must train yourself not only so that you succeed in running as far as is required, but so that, extending yourself by will and sinew, you easily run beyond that point."

In the form of a detailed parallel, a comparison is used for 86 the purpose of vividness, thus: "Let us imagine a player on the lyre who has presented himself on the stage, magnificently garbed, clothed in a gold-embroidered robe, with purple mantle interlaced in various colors, wearing a golden crown illumined with large gleaming jewels, and holding a lyre covered with golden ornaments and set off with ivory. Further, he has a personal beauty, presence, and stature that impose dignity. If, when he has roused a great expectation in the public, he should in the silence he has created suddenly give utterance to a rasping voice, and this should be accompanied by a repulsive gesture, he is the more forcibly thrust off in derision and scorn, the richer his adornment and the higher the hopes he has raised. In the same way, a man of high station, endowed with great and opulent resources, and abounding in all the gifts of fortune and the emoluments of nature, if he yet lacks virtue and the arts that teach virtue, will so much the more forcibly in derision and scorn be cast from all association with good men, the richer he is in the other advantages, the greater his distinction, and the higher the hopes he has raised."

87 Exemplum est alicuius facti vel dicti preteriti cum certi auctoris nomine propositio. Et fit eisdem causis quibus et similitudo, ut in "Libro versuum":

> Vix tamen esse potest ut homo sine crimine vivat.
> Ethicus unde Cato: "Nemo sine crimine vivit."

88 Ymago est forme cum forma cum quadam similitudine collacio, aut vituperii aut laudis causa. Causa laudis, sic: "Ibat in prelium gigas iste ferocissimus impetu leonis acerimi, cuius ictibus nullus resistere potuit inimicus." Causa vituperii, sic:

> Cotidie tamquam rapidus draco circuit hostis,
>   querens quem devoret, quem truci dente terat.

Et differt a similitudine quia illa inducit rem similem, non ponendo unam rem pro alia quomodo ista facit.

89 Effeccio est forme corporis alicuius expressio manifesta, sic: "Hunc, iudices, dico, rubrum, brevem, incurvum, canum, subcrispum, cesium, cui sane magna est in mento cicatrix, si quomodo potest vobis in memoriam venire. Hunc diligenter, queso, aspicite."

90 Notacio est cum alicuius natura certis signis describitur, que sicuti quedam note, nature sunt attributa, sic: "Istumne videtis qualiter anulis incedit gemmatis, ferrum lateri

Exemplification is the citing of something done or said in   87
the past, along with the definite naming of the doer or author. And it is used for the same purposes as a comparison,
as in the "Book of Verses":

> Yet it can hardly be that a man may live without fault,
> whence Cato the moralist says: "No one lives without
> fault."

Simile is the comparison of one figure with another, im-   88
plying a certain resemblance between them, for the purpose
of censure or praise. For the purpose of praise, thus: "This
most ferocious giant entered the combat with the impetu-
osity of the fiercest lion, whose blows no enemy could withstand." For the purpose of censure, thus:

> Every day the enemy prowled about like a swift ser-
> pent, seeking whom he would devour, whom he would
> destroy with his savage teeth.

And simile differs from comparison because the latter introduces a thing that resembles another, but not by putting
the one thing in place of the other, as the former does.

Portrayal is the explicit representation of some person's   89
bodily form, thus: "I mean him, men of the jury, the ruddy,
short, bent man, with white and rather curly hair, blue-gray
eyes, and a huge scar on his chin, if perhaps you can recall
him to memory. I ask you to look carefully at this man."

Character delineation consists in describing a person's   90
character by the definite signs which, like distinctive marks,
are attributes of that character, thus: "Do you see how this
man parades about in jewel-covered rings, how he attaches a

confederat, in modum leonis caput elevat quam superbe?"
Similiter in "Libro versuum":

Scisne pigri morem? etc.

91   Sermocinacio est cum alicui persone sermo attribuitur et
is exponitur cum racione dignitatis, sic: "Cur tam maliciosus
es ut boni te spernant, socii te fugiunt et tecum ceteri mali
non appetunt conversari?"

92   Conformacio est eadem cum prosopopeia: nec eam excedit nec ab ea exceditur. Unde de ea dictum est in prolongacione materie. Huius coloris habes exempla quasi per totum
in libro qui dicitur "Esopus in apologis."

93   Significacio est que plus relinquit in suspicione quam positum est in oracione. Fit autem quinque modis. Per exupe-
ranciam, quando causa suspicionis augende plus dicitur
quam ipsa veritas admittat, sic:

De tantis opibus quibus olim floruit iste
non superest illi vas in quo deferat undam.

Per ambiguum, cum illud quod dicitur potest in pluribus
sensibus accipi set accipitur tantum in eam partem quam
vult is qui dixit, sic:

Aio te, Eiacidem, Troianos vincere posse.

Per consequenciam, cum res que sequantur aliquam rem
dicuntur, ex quibus tota res relinquitur in suspicione; ut si
filio salsamentarii dicas: "Quiesce tu, cuius pater cubito se

sword to his side, how proudly like a lion he raises his head?"
Likewise, in the "Book of Verses":

Do you know the habit of the lazy man? etc.

Dialogue consists in assigning to some person language   91
which as set forth conforms with his character, thus: "Why
are you so wicked that good people spurn you, comrades flee
you, and even other bad people have no desire to consort
with you?"

Personification is the same as prosopopoeia: it has nei-   92
ther broader nor narrower reference. For this reason it has
been discussed under prolongation of the subject matter.
You have examples of this color virtually everywhere in the
book that is called "Aesop's Fables."

Emphasis is the color which leaves more to be suspected   93
than has been actually asserted. And it is produced in five
ways. Through hyperbole, when more is said than truth
strictly allows, so as to give greater force to suspicion, thus:

Of the extensive riches in which this man once
abounded there remains to him not even a pitcher in
which he could carry water.

Through ambiguity, when what is said can be taken in several senses but is taken only in that sense which the speaker
intends, thus:

I say that you, Eiacides, the Trojans can conquer.

By logical consequence, when one mentions the things that
follow from a given circumstance, thus leaving the whole
matter to be inferred; for example, if you should say to the
son of a fishmonger: "Quiet, you, whose father used to wipe

emungere solebat." Per abscisionem, quando incipimus aliquid dicere et sermonem prescindimus et hoc quod diximus relinquitur in suspicione, sic:

> Hic color, hic sexus, hec etas, illa figura.
> Nuper in alterius thalamo . . . set dicere nolo.

Per similitudinem, cum similitudinem introductam nec exponimus nec ad propositum reducimus set per eam quid intendimus subtiliter denotamus, ut in "Libro versuum":

> Magnus Alexander, cum bella etc.

Similiter, in sexto apologi Esopi, hic modus invenitur, sic:

> Femina dum nubit furi, vicinia gaudet.
>   Vir bonus et prudens talia verba movet:
> Sol pepigit sponsam. Iovis aurem terra querelis
>   perculit et causam, cur foret egra, dedit:
> Sole necor solo; quid erit, si creverit alter?
>   Quid paciar? Quid aget tanta caloris hiemps?

94 Brevitas est res verbis tantum necessariis expedita, id est quando tantum ea que sunt necessaria ad materiam inseruntur, sic: "Christus conceptus est de Spiritu Sancto, natus ex Maria virgine, passus sub Poncio Pilato, crucifixus, mortuus et sepultus."

95 Demonstracio est cum res ita verbis exprimitur ut geri negocium et res ante oculos esse videatur. Hic, secundum

his nose with his forearm." Through aposiopesis, when we begin to say something and we cut our speech short and what we have said is left to be inferred, thus:

This complexion, this sex, this age, that figure. Just lately, in another's chamber . . . — but I will say nothing of that.

Through analogy, when we introduce some analogue and neither expound it nor relate it to the topic, but by its means we subtly indicate what we have in mind, as in the "Book of Verses":

When Alexander the Great declared war etc.

Likewise, this method is found in the sixth fable of Aesop, thus:

When a woman marries a thief, the neighborhood rejoices; but a good and wise man utters the following words: "The sun took a bride. Then the earth assailed Jove's ear with her complaints and explained why she was troubled: 'I am slain already by a single sun; what will it be like if another sun is born? What will I have to endure? What will so great a heat storm do?'"

Conciseness is the expressing of an idea by the very mini- 94 mum of essential words, that is, when one includes only what is absolutely necessary to the subject matter, thus: "Christ was conceived of the Holy Spirit, born of the Virgin Mary, suffered under Pontius Pilate, was crucified, died, and was buried."

Ocular demonstration is when an event is so described in 95 words that the business seems to be enacted and the subject

Tullium, tria sunt necessaria—scilicet triplex administracio, scilicet ante rem, cum re, post rem. De triplici administracione loquemur ubi de attributis negocio agemus. Huius coloris satis egregium exemplum ponit Matheus Vindocinensis, sic:

> Risus, amor coitus, ventris concepcio triplex
> indicium lese virginitatis habent.

Nam ubi dicitur "risus," est administracio ante rem; ubi dicitur "amor coitus," in re; et ubi dicitur "ventris concepcio," post rem.

96   Ita dictum sit de 19 coloribus sentenciarum.

to pass vividly before our eyes. Here, according to Cicero, three things are necessary—in other words, a triple handling, namely, what preceded the event, what accompanied the event, and what followed the event. We will speak about this triple handling when we deal with the attributes of an action. Matthew of Vendôme provides a quite outstanding example of this color, thus:

> Flirting, pleasure in intercourse, pregnancy—these are the threefold sign of virginity's loss.

For where it says "flirting," that is what happened before the event; where it says "pleasure in intercourse," that is what accompanied the event; and where it says "pregnancy," that is what happened after the event.

And so we have discussed the nineteen colors of thoughts. 96

Capitulum 8

De officio omnium colorum et quomodo figure coloribus reducuntur

Colorum tam verborum quam sentenciarum distincta sunt officia. Quidam enim specialiter faciunt ad prolongacionem, quidam ad abbreviacionem, quidam ad difficultatem, quidam ad facilitatem, quidam ad iocum excitandum, quidam cuilibet materie indifferenter adaptantur. Nec obstat quod de predictis tactum est, quoniam ibi de principalioribus, hic vero de adiuvantibus demonstramus.

2 Ad prolongacionem materie faciunt repeticio, conversio, complexio, traduccio, exclamacio, interrogacio, raciocinacio, membrum oracionis, continuacio, subieccio, gradacio, diffinicio, transicio, correccio, occupacio, conduplicacio, interpretacio, commutacio, dubitacio, expedicio, licencia, diminucio, descripcio, divisio, expolicio, commoracio, contencio, similitudo, exemplum, ymago, affeccio, notacio, sermocinacio, demonstracio. Ad abbreviacionem faciunt contrarium, articulus, disiunctum, coniunctum, adiunctum, dissolutum, prescisio, distribucio, frequentacio, brevitas.

Chapter 8

On the function of all the colors and how the figures are related to the colors

The functions of colors, both of words and of thoughts, are diverse. For some serve especially for prolongation, some for abbreviation, some for difficulty, some for facility, some for provoking mirth, and some are suited equally to any sort of subject matter. It is not a problem that the aforesaid functions of colors have been treated already, since there we explain the major ones but here the subsidiary ones.

Those that serve to prolong the subject matter are epanaphora, antistrophe, symploce, polyptoton, apostrophe, rhetorical question, reasoning by question and answer, colon, period, hypophora, climax, definition, transition, correction, paralipsis, reduplication, interpretation, reciprocal change, indecision, proof by elimination, license, understatement, vivid description, division, refining, dwelling on the point, antithesis, comparison, exemplum, simile, portrayal, character delineation, dialogue, and ocular demonstration. Those that serve to abbreviate are reasoning by contraries, comma, disjunction, conjunction, adjunction, asyndeton, aposiopesis, distribution, accumulation, and

Ad difficultatem valent decem species transsumpcionis, de quibus plenius dictum est, ad facilitatem omnes colores et verborum et sentenciarum, exceptis transumpcionis speciebus. Ad iocum suscitandum prescisio et occupacio specialiter accomodantur. Ad omnem materiam indifferentes sunt sentencia, compar, similiter cadens, similiter desinens, commixtum, agnominacio, permissio, conclusio, significacio. Sunt et alia specialia officia quorumdam colorum de quibus sparsim prelocutum est.

3   Nunc dicendum est quomodo figure coloribus reducuntur vel e converso. Sicut ait Gervasius de Saltu Lacteo, in libro de eleganciis, "Vicia, figure et rethorici colores quadam similitudine vestiuntur et sunt in multis ex equo sibi respondencia, in multis excedencia pariter et excessa. Verbi gracia, Donatus dicit barbarismum fieri "per immutacionem littere, ut 'olli' pro 'illi.'" Idem consequenter, in tractatu methaplasmi, dicit: "Antithesis est littere pro littera posicio, ut 'olli' pro 'illi.'" Qui modus in coloribus 'mutacio' vocatur, ut 'predones' pro 'precones.' Potest igitur in huiusmodi vicium latere sub umbra virtutis et ideo difficilimum est expressissimas inde differencias assignare."

4   Sunt enim tria figurarum genera: methaplasmus, scema, tropus. De methaplasmo nichil pertinet presenti negocio.

5   "Scema" Grece, Latine "figura" vel "ornatus" interpretatur. Fit enim per varias verborum et sentenciarum formas,

conciseness. For difficulty the ten varieties of transumption are effective, concerning which we have spoken more fully, and for facility all the colors of words and thoughts are effective except the varieties of transumption. Aposiopesis and paralipsis are especially suited to arouse mirth. Those equally suited to every subject matter are maxim, isocolon, homoeoptoton, homoeoteleuton, mixture, paronomasia, surrender, conclusion, and emphasis. There are also other special functions of certain colors that have previously been spoken about here and there.

Now we should talk about how figures are related to colors and vice versa. As Gervase of Melkley says in the "Book of Refinements," "Faults, figures, and rhetorical colors are clothed in a certain resemblance and in many cases correspond to each other exactly, in many cases have broader or narrower reference than each other. For example, Donatus says that a barbarism is caused by the changing of a letter, like 'thee' in place of 'they.' The same author accordingly says, in his treatment of metaplasm: Antithesis is putting one letter in place of another letter, like 'thee' in place of 'they.' Among the colors this method is called 'change,' like 'preyers' in place of 'prayers.' Thus, in this sort of thing a vice can hide beneath the shadow of a virtue, and therefore it is extremely difficult to draw hard and fast distinctions there." 3

There are three kinds of figures: metaplasm, scheme, and trope. Regarding the metaplasm there is nothing relevant to present concerns. 4

"Scheme," in Greek, translates "figure" or "ornament" in Latin. Now it is accomplished by means of various arrangements of words and thoughts, for the purpose of 5

propter eloquii ornamentum. Sub scemate continentur omnes figure, et verborum et sentenciarum, penes quas propria potestas vocabuli observatur. Et sciendum est quod quandoque ex equo respondet colori, quandoque eum excedit, quandoque ab eo exceditur. Ex equo respondet, ut "intelleccio" color et "synodoche" figura, quoniam tot modis accidit color iste sicut ista figura et econtraria. Excedit colorem, ut "paranomasia" figura "agnominacionem" colorem, in eo quod comprehendit consonanciam finalem cum iniciali et media, agnominacio solam inicialem et mediam. Exceditur a colore, ut "methonomia" a "denominacione." Et sic de similibus.

6   "Tropus" Grece, "conversio" Latine. Per tropos enim vulgarem modum loquendi vertimus in ornatum. Sub tropo comprehenduntur omnes species transumpcionis. Et quandoque excedit et exceditur et ex equo respondet, ut de scemate dictum est.

ornamenting speech. Under scheme are included all the figures, both of words and of thoughts, in which the proper meaning of the word is observed. And you should know that sometimes a scheme or figure corresponds exactly to a color, sometimes it has broader reference, and sometimes it has narrower reference. It corresponds exactly, like the color *intellectio* with the figure synecdoche, since this color occurs in as many ways as this figure and vice versa. It has broader reference than the color, as the figure paronomasia does the color *adnominatio,* in that the former includes final along with initial and medial agreement of sounds, while *adnominatio* includes only initial and medial agreement of sounds. It has narrower reference than the color, as metonymy relative to *denominatio.* And thus with similar cases.

"Trope," in Greek, is "turning," in Latin, for by means of 6 tropes we turn a common manner of speaking into an ornate one. Under trope are included all the varieties of transumption. And sometimes one has broader or narrower reference or corresponds exactly with its counterpart, as was said of a scheme.

Capitulum 9

De arte inveniendi ornata verba
quibus locucio rudis
venustatur egregie

Ars inveniendi ornata verba potissime penes permuta-
cionem attenditur. Est enim mutacio partita: una verborum
et non sentenciarum, altera verborum et sentenciarum set
retenta sensus equipollencia.

2   Verborum et non sentenciarum plerumque fit permutacio per figuram que dicitur "synonima," et est quando in
connexa oracione pluribus verbis unam rem significamus. Et
reducitur ad "interpretacionem" rethoricum colorem, ut
hic: "Nichil agis, nichil moliris, nichil cogitas" et hic: "Non
feram, non paciar, non sinam."

3   Permutacio verborum et sentenciarum set retenta sensus
equipollencia fit plerumque per tropum qui dicitur "perifra-
sis," id est "circumlocucio." Fit autem tropus bipertito: aut
enim feditatem circuitu devitat aut veritatem splendide

Chapter 9

On the art of generating ornamented words by means of which uncouth speech is made exceptionally beautiful

The art of generating ornamented words is observed especially in terms of permutation. And this sort of change is twofold: one kind is change of words only and not of meanings and the other is change of words and meanings with an equivalent sense retained.

Permutation of words but not of meanings often may be 2 accomplished through the figure that is called "synonymy," and this is when we signify one thing through many words in a linked utterance. And it is related to the rhetorical color "interpretation," as here: "You do nothing, you undertake nothing, you plan nothing" and here: "I will not bear it, I will not suffer it, I will not permit it."

Permutation of words and meanings with an equivalent 3 sense retained may often be accomplished by means of the trope that is called "periphrasis," that is, "circumlocution." This trope may be executed in two ways: it either avoids foulness by a roundabout statement or it embellishes the bare truth with ornamentation. It avoids foulness by a

producit. Feditatem circuitu devitat, ut Vindocinensis ponit feditatem luxurie in versibus preallegatis:

Dactilici metri prior intrat sillaba, crebro
concussu fedant menia feda breves.

Hoc autem tropo usus est Alanus fere per totum in libro suo *De planctu Nature,* ubi plurium viciorum fetorem palliat eleganter. Et quare hoc faciat, ipse in eodem ostendit, sic: "Consequens enim est predictorum viciorum scoriam deauratis locucionibus purpurare viciorumque fetorem verborum odore inbalsamare mellifluo, ne si tanti sterquilinii fetor in nimie promulgacionis auras evaderet plerosque ad indignacionis vomitum invitaret." Veritatem splendide producit, ut in Virgilio:

Et iam prima novo spargebat lumine terras
Titanis croceum linquens Aurora cubile,

ut sit sensus: "Iam diescebat," et in Vindocinensi:

Doctrine pater est usus: doctrina scolaris
interscisa perit, continuata viget,

ut sit sensus: "Usus facit magisterium."

4   Amplius, retenta sensus equipollencia, sentencie et verba permutantur quando simplex et parcialis intellectus per clausulas vel oraciones suppletur et econverso, ut si pro parciali intellectu huius verbi "rubet" dicatur "purpurat ora

roundabout statement, as when Matthew of Vendôme represents the shamefulness of lust in the previously cited verses:

The hexameter's long syllable thrusts in, the two short syllables defile the foul ramparts with repeated pounding.

Alan of Lille employed this trope almost everywhere in his book *The Plaint of Nature,* where he elegantly veils the shamefulness of many vices. And in the same work he himself shows why he should do this, thus: "For it is appropriate to decorate the dross of the vices we have named with gilded terms, and to sweeten their vicious foulness with the scent of honeyed words, lest the stench of this great dung heap be spread too far abroad by the breeze, and cause many to vomit in indignation." Circumlocution embellishes the bare truth with ornamentation, as in Virgil:

And now early Dawn, leaving the saffron bed of Tithonus, was sprinkling her fresh rays upon the earth,

so that the meaning is: "Now it was day," and in Matthew of Vendôme:

Practice is the father of learning: interrupted learning perishes, continued learning grows strong.

The sense of this is simply: "Practice produces mastery."

Further, an equivalent sense is retained while meanings and words are changed when a simple and incomplete understanding is expanded by clauses or sentences and vice versa, so that for the incomplete understanding of the verb "she blushes" one may say "a blush reddens her face." 4

rubor." Similiter, pro "luget" "fletibus ora rigat." Similiter, pro "irascitur" "pullulat ira minax." Talis autem permutacio celeberima est apud omnes egregie dictantes. Et fit dupliciter: vel mutacione indeclinabilium parcium vel declinabilium.

5   Primo ergo de permutacione parcium indeclinabilium ostendamus. Partes indeclinabiles hac arte permutande sunt: considerandum est quid significetur per partem indeclinabilem et exprimendum est vel per nomen vel per verbum. Verbi gracia, dicturi "Tunc" vel "Cras veniet amicus," videamus quid significetur per hec adverbia: per "cras" "dies crastina," per "tunc" "illa dies demonstrata," "aliqua certa die." Dicamus igitur "Crastina dies" vel "Illa dies transmittet venientem." Similiter, pro hac "Huc veniet" dicamus "Hic locus admittet venientem" vel hec: "Hic locus erit hospicium venienti." Similiter, pro hac "Vado pro socio" dicamus "Est socius michi causa vie." Et pro hac "Sum inter vos" dicamus "Sum medius vestrum" vel "Hospitor in medio vestrum." Et pro hac "Iste vadit circa domum" dicamus "Circuit iste domum." Et pro hac "Nobilis es et probus" dicamus "Tua nobilitas nubit probitati," ut hec coniunccio "et" mutetur in hoc verbum "nubit." Et pro hac "Heu michi" dicamus "Dolore afficior."

Likewise, for "he mourns" one may say "he floods his face with tears." Likewise, for "he grows angry" one may say "a menacing wrath burgeons in him." Indeed, this sort of permutation is very much celebrated among all those who compose well. And it may be accomplished in two ways: by changing either indeclinable parts of speech or declinable ones.

So let us first demonstrate permutation of indeclinable 5 parts of speech. Indeclinable parts of speech should undergo permutation in this way: one should consider what is meant by the indeclinable part of speech and then express it either by a noun or by a verb. For example, if we mean to say "Then" or "Tomorrow a friend will come," let us first see what is signified by these adverbs: by "tomorrow" is signified "the day of the morrow," by "then" is signified "that day indicated" or "some definite day." Let us say, therefore, "The day of the morrow" or "That day will deliver the one who is coming." Likewise, in place of this: "He will come here," let us say "This place will receive the one who is coming" or this: "This place will be a guest house for the one who is coming." Likewise, in place of this: "I go on behalf of a comrade," let us say "A comrade is the cause of my journey." And in place of this: "I am among you," let us say "I am in your midst" or "I dwell in the midst of you." And in place of this: "This one goes around the house," let us say "This one circles the house." And in place of this: "You are noble and honest," let us say "Your nobility is wedded to your honesty," so that the conjunction "and" is transformed into the verb "is wedded." And in place of this: "Woe is me," let us say "I am afflicted by sorrow."

6   Sequitur de arte permutandi declinabilia. Parcium declinabilium tria permutari solent ut fiat ornatus: nomen substantivum, adiectivum et verbum. Nomen substantivum aut
ponitur in recto aut in obliquo. Si in recto, mutetur in aliud
nomen nominativi casus per artem transumpcionis, ut pro
hac "Tumultus populi impulit civitatem" dicamus "Populi
fragor impulit urbem." Si substantivum sit in obliquo, mutetur in nominativum suum vel alium similis significacionis,
cum verbo conveniente. Nec intellige quod verbum activum
mutetur in passivum, quia licet hoc valeat in metro, in prosa
nichil valet. In metro valet sic:

Torquet amor superos, superi torquentur amore.
Ars puerum flectit, flectitur arte puer.

Talis enim in prosa resiprocacio raro valet.

7   Set qualecumque verbum, fuerit personale vel imperso-
nale, mutetur in aliud verbum, sive proprie sive transumptive. Verbi gracia, in hac locucione "Video rem illam" ponitur obliquus post verbum activum. Mutetur ergo sic: "Res
illa se presentat" vel "offert aspectui meo" vel "Res oculis
imminet illa meis." Similiter et hec "Sedeo in hoc loco" potest sic mutari: "Iste locus sedem michi prestat" vel "Me locat

Now follows the art of applying permutation to declin- 6
able words. Three of the declinable parts of speech are cus-
tomarily changed in order to produce ornamentation: the
substantive noun, the adjective, and the verb. A substantive
noun is put either in the nominative case or in an oblique
case. If it is in the nominative case, it is changed into another noun of the nominative case through the art of transumption, so that in place of this: "The uproar of the populace assailed the city," we might say "The thundering of the
populace assailed the city." If a substantive is in an oblique
case, let it be changed into its own nominative or the nominative of another substantive with a similar meaning, with
an appropriate verb. Do not take this to mean that an active
verb should be changed into a passive one, because, although this is effective in meter, it does not work in prose.
It is effective in meter, thus:

> Love torments the gods above; even the gods are tor-
> mented by love. Cunning sways a boy; a boy is swayed
> by cunning.

Yet this kind of alternation rarely is effective in prose.

But any kind of verb, whether it is personal or imper- 7
sonal, may be changed into another verb, either literally or
transumptively. For example, in the expression "I see that
thing" an oblique case is placed after an active verb. Therefore, let it be changed thus: "That thing presents itself" or
"offers itself to my sight" or "That thing appears before my
eyes." Likewise also this: "I sit in this place" can be changed
thus: "This place supplies me a seat" or "This place accom-
modates me and refreshes me with a seat." Likewise also

et sede recreat iste locus." Similiter et hec "Per vultum intelligimus mentem hominis" potest sic mutari:

In facie legitur hominis secreta voluntas.

In hoc ergo precepto potest unusquisque proficere, cuiuscumque sciencie fuerit. Quia si magne sciencie est, cum converterit verbum, adinveniet verbum convenientissimum, sive proprie sive transumptive; si modice, adinveniet verbum puerile; si mediocris, verbum adinveniet mediocre.

8   Aliud documentum est hoc. Proposito verbo in quacumque perfecta locucione, sive aliquid sequatur sive nichil, considera ad quam rem pertineat verbum et de illa fiat sermo et ei quod suum est attribue. Ut in hac locucione "Ego lego," in qua nichil sequitur verbum, ponitur hoc verbum "lego," quod pertinet ad leccionem. Fiat igitur sermo de leccione et ei quod suum est attribue, sic: "Leccio me pascit commoditate sua." Set quia leccio tum docentis est, tum discentis (ut in scola, ubi unus docet et alius discit), tum recitantis (ut in ecclesia vel mensa, ubi recitamus verba sanctorum), tum inspicientis (ut in claustro vel thalamo, ubi libros inspicimus), attribuendum est leccioni diversas proprietates, diverso respectu. Si ergo dicendum est de docente quod legat, secundum hoc leccioni quod suum est attribue, sic: "Leccio mea rem aliis clausam aperit et involutam evolvit." Si de discente, secundum hoc leccioni quod suum est

this: "We understand the mind of a man through his countenance" can be changed thus:

A man's hidden desire is read in his face.

Thus anyone can succeed in this teaching, whatever his state of knowledge may be. Because, if he is a person of great knowledge, when he converts the verb he will produce another verb that is most apt either literally or transumptively; if he is a person of small knowledge, he will produce a childish verb; if he is a person of average knowledge, he will produce a middling verb.

Another lesson is this one. When you have put forward a 8 verb in some expression that is complete, whether something follows it or nothing follows it, think about the thing to which the verb pertains and let your speech be about that thing and attribute to it what belongs to it. So in the expression "I read," in which nothing follows the verb, we find the verb "read," which pertains to reading. Therefore let the speech be about reading and attribute to it what belongs to it, thus: "Reading nourishes me with its benefits." But because reading sometimes belongs to a teacher, sometimes to a student (as in a school, where one teaches and another learns), sometimes to a reciter (as in a church or a refectory, where we recite the words of the saints), sometimes to a peruser (as in the cloister or bedchamber, where we peruse books), one should attribute different properties to reading in different contexts. Thus, if it is to be said of a teacher that he reads, attribute to the reading what belongs to it accordingly, thus: "My reading opens a thing that is closed to others and unfolds what is enfolded." If it is to be said of a student, attribute to the reading what belongs to it accordingly,

attribue, sic: "Leccio mea luce sua purgat in me tenebras ignorancie." Si de recitante, secundum hoc leccioni quod suum est attribue, sic: "Leccio mea recitatorie verbis subservit aliorum." Si de inspiciente, secundum hoc leccioni quod suum est attribue, sic: "Leccionis speculum oculos meos moratur et animum."

9   Item, quocumque respectu dicatur "Ego lego," communiter potest dici "Leccio est opus meum." Et sicut ostendimus in hac locucione "Ego lego," in qua nichil sequitur verbum, idem artificium invenietis et si aliquid sequatur verbum, ut "Ego lego librum istum" vel "rem illam," "in illo loco," "in illo tempore" vel "coram illis." Et non solum tunc uti possumus hoc documento set eciam precedente, quod docet convertere obliquum in nominativum, ut hec "Ego video illum" potest sic mutari: "Visus meus se flectit in illum" vel "In illum se meus defigit intuitus." Similiter et hec "Ego scribo," in qua nichil sequitur verbum, potest sic mutari: "Sollicitat scriptura manum." Vel aliter, cum verbum positum in perfecta locucione converteris in substantivum, pone illud substantivum in quocumque casu et, adiunctis aliis verbis, invenies sentenciam que equivaleat sentencie illius perfecte locucionis que proposita est, ut, proposita hac "Ego scribo," mutetur "scribo" in "scriptura" et ponatur in quocumque casu et inveniatur sentencia equivalens huic "Ego scribo." In nominativo potest sic dici: "Sollicitat scriptura manum." In genitivo, sic: "Stilus meus fungitur officio scripture." In dativo, sic: "Manus invigilat scripture." In accusativo, sic:

thus: "With its light my reading clears away the darkness of ignorance in me." If it is to be said of a reciter, attribute to the reading what belongs to it accordingly, thus: "My reading, in the guise of a reciter, acts as servant to the words of others." If it is to be said of a peruser, attribute to the reading what belongs to it accordingly, thus: "The mirror of reading detains my eyes and my mind."

Also, in whatever context "I read" may be said, it is generally possible to say "Reading is my task." And just as we have shown in the expression "I read," in which nothing follows the verb, so you will encounter the same technique even if something should follow the verb, such as "I read this book" or "that thing," "in that place," "at that time," or "in the presence of those persons." And then we can use not only this lesson but also the previous one, which teaches how to convert an oblique case into a nominative, so that this: "I see him" can be changed thus: "My sight directs itself onto him" or "My gaze fixes itself on him." Likewise also this: "I write," in which nothing follows the verb, can be changed thus: "Writing preoccupies my hand." Or alternatively, when you convert a verb placed in a complete expression into a substantive, put that substantive in whatever case and, when you have added other verbs, you will generate a thought that is equivalent to the thought of the complete expression that has been put forth. So when this: "I write" has been put forth, let "I write" be changed into "writing" and let it be put in whatever case and a thought may be generated that is equivalent to this: "I write." It can be said in the nominative case, thus: "Writing preoccupies my hand." In the genitive, thus: "My stylus performs the task of writing." In the dative, thus: "My hand pays constant heed to writing." In the

"Concilio manuum mearum res progreditur in scripturam."
In ablativo, sic: "Manus mea non desinit a scriptura."

10   Adiectivum simili artificio cum verbo mutatur. Sicut
enim verbum vertitur in substantivum rei verbi, ita verten-
dum est adiectivum in substantivum istius adiectivi, ut hoc
adiectivum "albus" debet mutari in hoc substantivum "albedo," "candor," "nix," "lac," "lilium" et huiusmodi, que pertinent ad rem illius adiectivi, ut "Hec facies est pulcra" sic
potest mutari: "Informat candor faciem" vel sic: "In facie
pulcra lac, nix et lilia certant" vel "In facie pulcra lactis lascivit ymago." Similiter hec "Iste est pulcher" potest sic mutari: "Istius faciem signavit sigillum pulcritudinis." Similiter
hec "Iste est facundus" potest sic mutari: "Potavit torrente
suo facundia linguam" vel "Dos est facundia lingue."

11   Et notandum quod in hiis duobus documentis ultimo
propositis, quorum unum est convertere obliquum in nominativum, reliquum adiectivum et verbum in substantivum,
cum hac cautela negociandum est. In primo documento sic
negociare. Cum enim converteris obliquum in nominativum, invenies iterum in ista conversione alium obliquum et
istum similiter convertas in nominativum, et sic deinceps
donec in aliquam iuncturam incideris elegantem. Ut hac
proposita "Ego video istam rem," sic poteris vertere obliquum in nominativum: "Res ista se presentat aspectui meo."

accusative, thus: "Through the counsel of my hands the matter proceeds into writing." In the ablative, thus: "My hand does not desist from writing."

An adjective can be changed by means of a technique   10 similar to the one used with a verb. For just as a verb is turned into a substantive expressing the matter of the verb, so an adjective should be turned into a substantive expressing the matter of that adjective. So the adjective "white" should be changed into the substantive "whiteness," "brightness," "snow," "milk," "lily" and the like, which all pertain to the matter of that adjective. So "This face is beautiful" can be changed thus: "Brightness characterizes this face" or thus: "In this beautiful face milk, snow, and lilies contend" or "In this beautiful face the likeness of milk frolics." Likewise this: "He is handsome" can be changed thus: "The seal of beauty has stamped his face." Likewise this: "He is eloquent" can be changed thus: "Eloquence has given his tongue to drink from its stream" or "Eloquence is the dowry of his tongue."

And you should note that in applying the two lessons that   11 have just been set forth, one of which is to convert an oblique case into a nominative, the other to convert an adjective and a verb into a substantive, you should proceed with the following caution. In applying the first lesson, proceed as follows. When you convert an oblique case into a nominative, you will again generate in this conversion another oblique case and you may likewise convert this into a nominative, and so on until you arrive at some attractive combination. So when you have set forth this: "I see this thing," you will be able to turn the oblique case into a nominative, thus: "This thing presents itself to my vision."

Ecce iterum in hac conversione alium obliquum, scilicet "aspectui meo." Mutetur igitur in nominativum, sic: "In rem istam oculorum meorum declinat intuitus." Et sic descendendum est donec inveniat animus in quo sibi complaceat. Nec est instandum in prima conversione, sive fuerit conveniens iunctura verborum, sive non. Quia si non fuerit conveniens, non est standum set procedendum ad competentem inveniendam; si conveniens, adhuc procedendum ad competenciorem inveniendam, ut ex duobus competentibus magis competens eligamus.

12   In secundo documento, quod docet convertere verbum vel adiectivum in substantivum, similiter negociare. Cum enim converteris adiectivum vel verbum in substantivum, invenias iterum in hac conversione aliud verbum vel adiectivum et istud vertas similiter in substantivum, et sic deinceps donec incideris in clausulam elegantem. Ponamus ergo exemplum de verbo. Proposita hac "Ego studeo," sic poteris vertere verbum in substantivum: "Studium sollicitat animum." In hac conversione verte similiter verbum "sollicitat" in substantivum, sic: "Est studium mentis sollicitudo mee" vel "In mentem studii sollicitudo venit" vel "Me secum studii sollicitudo trahit." Similiter, hac proposita "Ego ludo," sic verte verbum in substantivum: "Ludus delectat animum." In hac similiter verte verbum "delectat," sic: "Sua dulcedine solatur animum delectacio ludorum." In hac adhuc verte verbum "solatur," sic: "Animi mei quedam respiracio est et solacium iocunditas ludorum." Similiter, hac proposita "Ego

Behold once again in this conversion another oblique case, namely, "to my vision." Therefore, let it be changed into a nominative, thus: "The gaze of my eyes shifts onto this thing." And so one should proceed until the mind generates something that pleases it. And one should not rest content with the very first conversion, whether it is an apt combination of words or not. Because, if it is not apt, then one should not stop but should proceed to discover a suitable one; even if it is apt, still one should proceed in order to generate something still more suitable, so that from two suitable combinations we may choose the more suitable one.

In the second lesson, which teaches us to convert a verb or an adjective into a substantive, you should proceed in similar fashion. For when you convert an adjective or a verb into a substantive, you should generate once again in this conversion another verb or adjective and change this likewise into a substantive, and so on until you arrive at an elegant sentence. Let us therefore give an example of a verb. When you have set forth this: "I study," you will be able to turn the verb into a substantive, thus: "Study preoccupies my mind." In this conversion likewise turn the verb "preoccupies" into a substantive, thus: "Study is the preoccupation of my mind" or "The preoccupation of study comes into my mind" or "The preoccupation of study sweeps me along." Likewise, when you have set forth this: "I play," turn the verb into a substantive, thus: "Play delights my mind." In this likewise change the verb "delights," thus: "With its sweetness the delight of play comforts my mind." In this further change the verb "comforts," thus: "The pleasantness of play is a kind of rest and relaxation for my mind." Likewise, when you have set forth this: "I grieve," turn the verb

12

doleo," sic verte verbum in substantivum: "Pungit animum aculeus doloris." Et iterum verte verbum "pungit," sic: "Medullas cordis penetrat punctura doloris."

13   Nunc de adiectivo similiter vertendo ponamus exempla. Hac proposita "Tu es morigeratus," sic verte adiectivum in substantivum: "Animus tuus conditus est moribus." Verte iterum hoc adiectivum "conditus," sic: "Tuum inbalsamavit animum moralitatis condimentum" vel "Animo tuo suam infudit dulcedinem ethice condimentum." Ecce aliud exemplum. Proposita hac "Tu es sapiens et eloquens," sic poteris hec duo adiectiva in substantiva mutare: "Sapiencia tibi contulit animum aureum et eloquencia linguam argenteam." Similiter et hec duo adiectiva "aureum" et "argenteam" sic verte: "Os tuum argento lucet eloquencie et animus auro rutilat sapiencie." Ecce adhuc et aliud exemplum. Hac proposita "Tu es pulcher," sic verte adiectivum "pulcher": "Facies tua sigillata est pulcritudine." Similiter, adhuc verte hoc adiectivum "sigillata," sic: "Faciem tuam signavit sigillum pulcritudinis."

14   Sic igitur tradita est sufficiens doctrina de arte inveniendi ornata verba. Set hoc notabiliter attendendum, quod in omni conversione laudabilius est mutare obliquum, verbum et adiectivum in nomen transumptum quam proprie sumptum. Nam laudabilius est mutare "doleo" in "gemitus," "lacrima," "questus" vel "suspirium" quam in hoc nomen "dolor." Similiter et "albus" in "lac," "nix" vel "lilium" quam in "albedo," quia, ut sepe diximus, quanto plures figure vel

into a substantive, thus: "The needle of grief pricks my mind." And once again convert the verb "pricks," thus: "The prick of grief penetrates the depths of my heart."

Now let us give examples of converting an adjective in like fashion. When you have set forth this: "You are moral," turn the adjective into a substantive, thus: "Your mind has been seasoned with morals." Once again change this adjective "seasoned," thus: "The seasoning of morality perfumes your mind" or "The seasoning of ethics pours its sweetness into your mind." Here is another example. When you have set forth this: "You are wise and eloquent," you will be able to change these two adjectives into substantives, thus: "Wisdom has granted you a golden mind and eloquence a silver tongue." In like fashion, also convert these two adjectives "golden" and "silver," thus: "Your mouth shines with the silver of eloquence and your mind glows with the gold of wisdom." Here is still another example. When you have set forth this: "You are beautiful," convert the adjective "beautiful," thus: "Your face is ensealed with beauty." Likewise, further convert this adjective "ensealed," thus: "The seal of beauty has stamped your face."

Thus, sufficient instruction in the art of generating ornamented words has been conveyed. But you should pay special attention to the fact that in every conversion it is more praiseworthy to change an oblique case, a verb, and an adjective into a noun taken transumptively than into one taken in its literal sense. For it is more praiseworthy to change the verb "grieve" into the noun "groan," "tear," "complaint," or "sigh" than into the noun "grief." Likewise, it is also better to change the adjective "white" into the noun "milk," "snow," or "lily" than into the noun "whiteness," because, as we have

colores in dictamine combinentur, tanto solempnius illud egregiant et venustant. Verbi gracia, Alanus, *De planctu Nature,* dicturus "Agri et valles erant splendidi de liliis," non mutavit hoc adiectivum "splendidi" in suum proprium substantivum "splendor" set in hoc substantivum transumptum, scilicet "argentum," ut sua materia solempnius festivetur, sic:

Argentoque suo nobile lilium
preditavit agros imaque vallium.

15   Et notandum quod in omni conversione specialiter iuvat artificium quod premisimus in descripcione coloris qui dicitur "circuicio." Amplius, si in conversione ponatur nomen substantivum transumptive, cuius determinacio non plene sufficiat removere obscuritatem, si quam habeat verbum, adiectivum debet substantivo adiungi epithetice, tale scilicet quod plene removeat nubem et verbum suo splendore illuminet. Verbi gracia, in hac sentencia "Iura mollescunt vel iura rigent," transumitur hoc substantivum "iura," quod non satis elucidat verbum. Ut igitur luceat significacio verbi, adiunge adiectiva substantivis, sic: "Iura districta rigent; iura dispensatoria mollescunt." Consimiliter et si nulla sit obscuritas in verbo, negociandum est ut ex dupplici splendore verbi claritas geminetur. Nam in hac "Tellus potavit aquam excessive et imber demisit eam temere," verbi significacio per se splendeat. Melius tamen dicitur si hiis

said often, the more figures or colors are combined in a composition, the more ceremoniously they distinguish and beautify it. For example, when Alan of Lille, in *The Plaint of Nature,* intended to say "The fields and the valleys were bright with lilies," he did not change the adjective "bright" into its literal substantive "brightness" but into this meta-phorical substantive, namely, "silver," so that his subject matter might be celebrated more ceremoniously, thus:

> And the noble lily bestowed its silver on the fields and deep valleys.

And note that in every conversion the technique that we provided earlier, in our description of the color called "pe-riphrasis," is especially helpful. What is more, if you place a substantive noun in a conversion transumptively, and what modifies it does not suffice to remove its obscurity com-pletely, and if the verb also has some obscurity, then an ad-jective should be joined to the substantive as an epithet, namely, the sort of adjective that can remove the cloud en-tirely and light up the verb with its brightness. For example, in this sentence: "The laws soften or the laws stiffen," the substantive "laws" is given a transumptive sense, which the verb does not make sufficiently clear. Therefore, so that the meaning of the verb may shine forth, add adjectives to the substantives, thus: "Strict laws stiffen; generous laws soften." In like fashion, even if there is no obscurity in the verb, you should proceed in this way so that the clarity of the verb is twinned with a double brightness. For in this: "The earth drank water excessively and the rain shower let it fall heedlessly," the meaning of the verb shines forth by itself. However, it is better said if adjectives are added to

substantivis "tellus" et "imber" epithetice addantur adiectiva, sic:

Ebria tellus
plus equo rorem celi potavit et imber
dispensavit eum temere.

16   Hec dicta ad artem inveniendi ornata verba sufficiant.

these substantives "earth" and "rain shower" as epithets, thus:

The drunken earth drank the dew of heaven more than is right and the rain shower dispensed it heedlessly.

These statements suffice for the art of discovering orna- 16 mented words.

Capitulum 10

De execucione materie illibate

Ut unamquamque materiam laudabiliter tractemus et honeste, duo preter premissa sunt necessaria, scilicet ut sciamus exequi quamcumque materiam iuxta suam exigenciam. Materia igitur tractanda aut est illibata aut communis. In materia illibata, consuetudinarios rerum eventus, quantum poterimus, emulemur, ut scilicet vel vera dicamus vel verisimilia, per septem circumstancias que in hoc versu continentur:

Quis, quid, ubi, quibus auxiliis, cur, quomodo, quando.

Ad has enim, ut ait Boicius in *Topicis,* omnia attributa persone et negocio reducuntur. In quantum eciam poterimus, vulgi opinionem sequamur, ut scilicet ita de qualibet re loquamur sicut vulgariter homines opinantur. Unde Oracius:

Aut famam sequere aut conveniencia finge.

2   Hoc quidem artificio usus est magister Iohannes de

Chapter 10

On developing an original subject matter

So that we may treat any sort of subject matter in a praiseworthy and becoming fashion, namely, so that we know how to develop each kind of subject matter according to its requirement, two things are necessary besides those that have been mentioned already. For a subject matter that is worth treating is either original or common. In treating an original subject matter, we should imitate, as much as we can, the usual outcomes of things, namely, so that we say either what is true or what is plausible, by means of the seven circumstances that are contained in this verse:

> Who, what, where, with what aids, why, how, when?

For, as Boethius says in his *Topics,* all the attributes of a person and an action can be reduced to these. Also, as much as we can, we should follow the opinion of the majority, namely, so that we speak about any matter whatsoever just as men popularly believe one should. Thus Horace says:

> Either follow tradition or invent what is self-consistent.

Indeed, master John of Hauville used this technique in   2

Hauvilla in libro suo de peregrino philosopho, quem *Architrenium* vocat. Fingit enim ibi quemdam philosophum Architrenium omnia loca mundi visitantem, ut Naturam inveniat, cuius presencie suam exponat mentem de miseria humane condicionis. Et per totum librum observat artificialiter septem circumstancias, cuilibet rei suas attribuens proprietates. Huius libri, ut ait Gervasius, in elocucionis artificio "sola sufficit inspeccio studiosa rudem animum informare."

3   Debemus eciam in illibata materia procedere ad imitacionem aliorum quos digna memorie commendat auctoritas, ut si de bello tractaremus, imitacione Lucani procedamus, si de materia iocosa, imitacione Terencii. Istud innuit Oracius, dicens:

> Ex noto fictum carmen sequar, ut sibi quivis
> speret idem, sudet multum frustraque laboret
> ausus idem: tantum series iuncturaque pollet,
> tantum de medio sumptis accedet honoris.

4   Ceterum non prodest immo nocet brevitatis imitacio sine artis poetice adminiculo. Unde Oracius:

> In vicium ducit culpe fuga, si caret arte.

Ut ergo in unaquaque re perfeccionem habeamus, tria necessario requiruntur, ut ait Tullius in principio secunde *Rethorice:* ars et imitacio et usus vel excercitacio. "Ars est

his book about the wandering philosopher, which he calls the *Architrenius*. For he invents there a certain philosopher Architrenius who is visiting all the places of the world in search of Nature, so that in her presence he might speak his mind about the misery of the human condition. And throughout the book he skillfully observes the seven circumstances, attributing to each thing its own characteristics. As Gervase of Melkley says, "diligent examination" of this book "suffices on its own to form the unformed mind" in skill of expression.

In original subject matter, too, we should proceed to imitate others whom venerable authority calls to mind, so that if we were treating of war, we would proceed by imitation of Lucan, if of mirthful subject matter, by imitation of Terence. Horace suggests this, saying: 3

> My aim shall be poetry, so molded from the familiar that whoever may hope for the same success, may sweat much and yet toil in vain when attempting the same: such is the power of order and connection, such the beauty that will crown the commonplace.

Moreover, imitation of brevity without the support of poetic art does not advance but rather impairs. Thus Horace says: 4

> Shunning a fault may lead to error, if there be lack of art.

Therefore, so that we may achieve perfection in each and every thing, three things are required of necessity, as Cicero says at the beginning of his second *Rhetoric*: theory, imitation, and experience or practice. "By theory is meant a set of

precepcio, que dat certam viam racionemque dicendi. Imitacio est qua impellimur, cum dicendi racione, ut alicui in dicendo similes volumus esse. Excercitacio est assiduus usus consuetudoque dicendi." Ars enim artificem facit certum, imitacio aptum, excercitacio vel usus promptum. Unde et in "Libro versuum" hec sentencia Tullii ita tangitur:

> Rem tria perficiunt: ars, cuius lege regaris;
> usus, quem serves; meliores, quos imiteris.
> Ars certos, usus promptos, imitacio reddit
> artifices aptos, tria concurrencia summos.

rules that provide a definite method and system of speaking. Imitation stimulates us to desire, in accordance with a method of speaking, to be like a certain model in speaking. Practice is assiduous exercise and experience in speaking." For theory makes the craftsman sure, imitation makes him versatile, practice or experience makes him ready. Now this opinion of Cicero's is also touched upon in the "Book of Verses," as follows:

> Three things perfect a work: artistic theory, by whose law you may be guided; experience, which you may keep in reserve; and superior writers, whom you may imitate. Theory makes the craftsman sure; experience makes him ready; imitation makes him versatile; the three together produce the greatest craftsmen.

Capitulum 11

De execucione materie communis

In execucione materie communis cauti simus observando quinque modos quos assignat Oracius in *Poetria.* Dicit enim Oracius laudabilius et magis artificiosum est convenienter tractare communem materiam quam materiam illibatam. Difficilius enim est et artificiosius bellum Illiacum, id est Troianum, decenter exequi quam novam materiam ab omnibus inauditam. Hoc dicit Oracius hiis verbis:

> Difficile est proprie communia dicere; tuque
> rectius Illiacum carmen deducis in actum,
> quam si proferres ignota indictaque primus.

Set quamvis communem materiam bene tractare sit difficile, est tamen possibile si quinque modos, ut diximus, observemus.

2 Primus modus est ne moremur ubi moram faciunt alii, set ubi moram faciunt transeamus. Et intelligere debemus hanc moram quantum ad digressiones, descripciones vel huiusmodi, quoniam in materia communi, si digrediantur ad

Chapter 11

On developing common subject matter

In developing a common subject matter let us be careful to employ the five methods that Horace assigns us in his *Poetics*. For Horace says that it is more praiseworthy and more artful to treat common subject matter appropriately than to treat original subject matter. Indeed it is more difficult and requires more art to rehearse becomingly the war of Ilium, that is, of Troy, than a new subject matter that has not been heard by everybody. Horace says this in these words:

> It is hard to treat in your own way what is common:
> and you are doing better in spinning into action a song
> of Troy than if, for the first time, you were giving the
> world a theme unknown and unsung.

But though it may be difficult to treat a common subject matter well, it is nonetheless possible, as we said, if we employ the five methods.

The first method is that we do not pause where others make a pause, but where they make a pause we move on. And we should understand this pause as having to do with digressions, descriptions or the like, since, in a common subject matter, if they digress to something or describe

aliquod vel describant aliquod, ut ita moram faciant in materia, non debemus ibidem morari set illum locum materie breviter transilire.

3   Secundus modus est ne sequamur vestigia suorum verborum. Et hoc intelligendum est quantum ad corpus materie. Quia si ceteri qui tractant communem materiam prius hanc partem exprimant, secundo secundam, tercio terciam et sic deinceps, nos non debemus hec vestigia verborum sequi, scilicet ut istam partem quam premittunt premittamus et quam secundo ponunt secundam ponamus et sic eorum semper incedamus passibus, set universitatem materie speculantes, ibi dicamus aliquid ubi ipsi nichil dixerunt, et ubi ipsi aliquid, nos nichil; quod eciam ipsi prius, nos posterius ordinemus.

4   Tercius modus est ut de materia non transeamus ad talem articulum unde ad materiam regredi nesciamus, quemadmodum multi faciunt. Ita namque per digressiones elongantur a materia quod pene ad eam nesciunt revenire.

5   Quartus modus est ne premittamus tale principium quod sit nimis arrogans et superciliosum, quale est illud Ennii de bello Troiano:

Fortunam Priami cantabo et nobile bellum.

In cuius derisionem invehitur Alanus in *Anticlaudiano,* sic:

CHAPTER II

something, so as to create a pause in the subject matter, we should not pause in the same place but briefly pass over that place in the subject matter.

The second method is that we not follow in the footsteps 3 of their words. And this should be understood as having to do with the body of the subject matter. Because if the others who treat a common subject matter express this part first, a second second, a third third and so on, we should not follow in the footsteps of their words, in the sense that we put first the part that they put first and we put second what they put second and thus we walk always in their footsteps; but, looking over the entirety of the subject matter, let us say something in that place where they have said nothing, and where they have said something, let us say nothing; also, what they put first in order, let us put last.

The third method is that we not depart so far from the 4 subject matter that we do not know how to return to it, in the way that many do. For by means of digressions they wander so far from the subject matter that they scarcely know how to come back to it.

The fourth method is that we not offer as preface the 5 sort of beginning that is too pompous and haughty, an example of which is the one employed by Ennius concerning the Trojan War:

Of Priam's fate and famous war I'll sing.

Alan of Lille heaps scorn upon this in the *Anticlaudianus,* thus:

Illic pannoso plebescit carmine noster
Ennius et Priami fortunas intonat. Illic etc.

Tanta enim in principio verborum festivitate usus est et dicendi arrogancia quod nulla terminacio proporcionaliter videatur principio respondere.

6   Quintus modus est ut non sumamus principium materie a loco a materia nimis remoto, sicut fecit quidam qui, incipiens describere reditum Ulixis a bello Troiano, incepit ubi Tideus, pater Diomedis, interfecit fratrem suum Meleagrum et postea in Greciam fugiit et ibi Adrastus filiam suam Deyfilem sibi in matrimonio copulavit, ex qua Deyphile Meleager genuit Dyomedem, qui longo tempore post bellum Thebanum ad Troie excidium profectus est et decem annis ibidem moratus, tandem reversus est. Similiter, qui describeret bellum Troianum non inciperet ab eo loco quo Iupiter concubuit cum Leda in specie cigni et ex ea genuit duo ova, ex quorum altero creati fuerunt duo fratres Castor et Pollux et ex reliquo Elena, per quam fuit Troia subversa.

7   Hiis igitur quinque modis observatis, communem materiam specialiter et egregie poterimus pertractare. Quattuor primos modos ostendit Oracius hiis novem versibus:

Publica materies privati iuris erit, si
non circa vilem patulumque moraberis orbem,
nec verbum verbo curabis reddere fidus
interpres, nec desilies imitator in artum,
unde pedem proferre pudor vetet aut operis lex,

Here our modern Ennius fashions patchwork verse in
a low style, bellowing about the fortunes of Priam.
There etc.

For he has employed such great ceremoniousness of diction
and haughtiness of speech at the beginning that no ending
would seem to correspond in scale to the beginning.

The fifth method is that we do not take the beginning of 6
the subject matter from a place that is too far removed from
that subject matter, as a certain person did who, beginning
to describe the return of Ulysses from the Trojan War, began
when Tydeus, the father of Diomedes, killed his brother
Meleager and afterward fled to Greece, and there Adrastus
joined his daughter Deiphyle to him in marriage, from
which Deiphyle Meleager begot Diomedes, who long after
the Theban War set out for the siege of Troy and, after having remained in that place for ten years, at last returned.
Likewise, one who would describe the Trojan War would not
begin from that place where Jupiter lay with Leda in the
form of a swan and from her begot two eggs, from one of
which the two brothers Castor and Pollux were born and
from the other Helen, through whom Troy was overthrown.

Therefore, when we have employed these five methods, 7
we will be able to treat a common subject matter in a fashion that is both excellent and suited to its kind. Horace indicates the first four methods in these nine verses:

In ground open to all you will win private rights, if you
do not linger along the easy and open pathway, if you
do not seek to render word for word as a slavish translator, and if in your copying you do not leap into the
narrow well, out of which either shame or the laws of

nec sic incipies ut scriptor Cidicus olim:
"Fortunam Priami cantabo et nobile bellum."

Et statim reprehendit eum Oracius de arrogancia principii hiis verbis:

Quid dignum tanto feret hic promissor hiatu?
Parturient montes, nascetur ridiculus mus.

Primum modum ostendit ubi dicit "Non circa vilem patulumque moraberis orbem," quoniam vilescit locus ille qui omnibus patulus est et in quo omnes morantur. Secundum modum ostendit ibi: "Nec verbum verbo etc." Tercium ibi: "nec desilies imitator etc." Quartum ibi: "Nec sic incipies ut scriptor etc." Quintum modum ostendit ubi dicit "Nec reditum Diomedis ab interitu etc."

8   Set antequam ad quintum modum perveniat, commendat Homerum de humili principio, qui historiam de reditu Ulixis a Troia ita egregie incepit quod ex fumido et humili principio fulgidum facit finem. Quam historiam sic inchoat Homerus:

Dic michi, Musa, virum, capte post tempora Troie
Qui mores hominum etc.

Prius ergo ponamus versus Oracii et inde exposicionem:

Quantoque rectius hic, qui nil molitur inepte:
"Dic michi, Musa, virum, capte post tempora Troie
qui mores hominum multorum vidit et urbes."

your task will keep you from stirring a step. And you are not to begin as the Cydic poet of old: "Of Priam's fate and famous war I'll sing."

And immediately Horace criticizes him for the pomposity of the beginning in these words:

What will this boaster produce in keeping with such mouthing? Mountains will labor, to birth will come a laughable mouse!

He indicates the first method when he says "you do not linger along the easy and open pathway," since that place becomes worthless which is open to all and in which all linger. He indicates the second method here: "nor word for word etc." The third here: "in your copying you do not leap etc." The fourth here: "And you are not to begin as the poet etc." He indicates the fifth method when he says "nor Diomede's return from the death etc."

But before he comes to the fifth method, he praises Homer for a modest beginning, who excellently began his account of Ulysses's return from Troy in such a way that from a "smoky" and modest beginning he made a shining ending. Homer begins his account thus:

Sing, Muse, for me the man who on Troy's fall, the ways of men etc.

Therefore, let us first provide the verses of Horace and then their explanation:

How much more rightly he who undertakes nothing ineptly: "Sing, Muse, for me the man who on Troy's fall saw the ways and cities of many men." Not smoke after

Non fumum ex fulgore, set ex fumo dare lucem
cogitat, ut speciosa dehinc miracula promat,
Antifaten Cillamque et cum Ciclope Caribdim.

Isti sex versus sunt de commendacione Homeri.

9   Sequuntur ergo septem alii in quibus ostendit Oracius
quintum modum tractandi materiam communem, sic:

Nec reditum Diomedis ab interitu Meleagri,
nec bellum gemino Troianum orditur ab ovo:
semper ad eventum festinat et in medias res
non secus ac notas auditorem rapit, et que
desperat tractata nitescere posse, relinquit,
atque ita mentitur, sic veris falsa remiscet,
primo ne medium, medio ne discrepet imum.

Exponenda est littera sic: et "quanto rectius," id est melius,
ille "qui nil molitur inepte," id est inartificialiter, scilicet incepit, quasi multo rectius incepit Homerus quam "scriptor
Cidicus." Interrogative loquitur. Nomen Homeri tacuit, set
per principium historie Homerum intelligere se demonstrat, qui sic incipit: "Dic michi, musa, etc." Non enim iacti-
tat se canere reditum Ulixis arroganter in principio, sicut
Ennius, qui sic incepit: "Fortunam Priami," set invocat sa-
pienciam ad illud ostendendum. Littera satis plana est ad illum versum "Antifaten Cillam etc." Antifates rex erat Lestri-
gonum qui unum de sociis Ulixis devoravit. Cilla et Caribdis

flame does he plan to give, but after smoke the light, that then he may set forth striking and wondrous tales—Antiphates, Scylla, Charybdis, and the Cyclops.

These six verses are in praise of Homer.

Then follow seven others in which Horace indicates the 9 fifth method of treating a common subject matter, thus:

Nor does he begin Diomede's return from the death of Meleager, or the war of Troy from the twin eggs. Ever he hastens to the issue, and hurries his hearer into the story's midst, as if already known, and what he fears he cannot make attractive with his touch he abandons; and so skillfully does he invent, so closely does he blend facts and fiction, that the middle is not discordant with the beginning, nor the end with the middle.

The literal text should be explained thus: "how much more rightly," that is, better, that man "who undertakes nothing ineptly," that is, inartfully, namely, who began, which amounts to saying that Homer began much more rightly than "the Cydic poet." He is speaking in the interrogative. He did not mention Homer's name, but he shows that Homer is to be understood through the opening words of his story, which begins thus: "Sing, Muse, for me etc." For in his opening words he does not boast pompously that he sings the return of Ulysses, like Ennius, who began thus: "Of Priam's fate," but calls upon wisdom to reveal that to him. The literal text is straightforward enough at this verse: "Antiphates, Scylla etc." Antiphates was the king of the Laestrygones who ate one of the companions of Ulysses. Scylla and

sunt pericula marina. Ciclops, id est Polifemus, gigas erat unum oculum habens in fronte, quem telo suo Ulixes eruit. Quasi diceret Oracius de Homero: "Ita humiliter et egregie incepit Homerus, ut dehinc ostendat speciosa miracula que passus fuit Ulixes, scilicet Antifaten, Cillam etc." Vitando eciam remotum principium, Homerus incipit a medio materie. Unde dicit Oracius: Homerus "semper festinat ad eventum," id est finem, et "rapit auditorem in medias res" ipsius materie. "Res" dico "non secus," id est non aliter, "ac," id est quam, "notas." Et ille Homerus "relinquit" illa "que tractata desperat posse nitescere," id est illa que nec faciunt ad commodum sue cause, nec ad eius decenciam penitus pretermittit.

10   Notandum est igitur quod quando materiam prosequimur, observande sunt proprietates rerum ipsius materie in quibus specialiter est immorandum, quoniam in assignacione proprietatum pendet et difficultas et tractandi artificium. Unde Oracius, ceteris preceptis anteponens proprietatum observanciam, ad eam non semel set sepissime invitat. Dicit enim quod magis delectatur animus auditoris in fabula que nullius est ponderis, si debitis proprietatibus sit distincta, quam in gravi et fructuosa materia, proprietatibus indistincta. Iubet igitur ut inspiciamus mores et conversacionem humane vite, ex quibus poterimus elicere proprietates, dicente Catone:

Charybdis are perils of the sea. Cyclops, that is, Polyphemus, was a giant who had a single eye in his forehead, which Ulysses tore out with his weapon. In effect, Horace says of Homer: "Homer began so modestly and excellently so that he might subsequently depict the striking wonders that Ulysses experienced, namely, Antiphates, Scylla etc." Also, avoiding a remote beginning, Homer starts from the middle of the subject matter. For this reason Horace says: Homer "ever hastens to the issue," that is, the ending, and "hurries his hearer into the midst" of this same subject matter. "The story," I say, "just exactly," that is, not otherwise, "as," that is, than, "already known." And that same Homer "abandons" those things "which he fears he cannot make attractive with his touch," that is, those things that do not work to the advantage of his project but that he does not leave out entirely for the sake of its fitness.

Now you should notice that when we develop the subject 10
matter we should observe the characteristics of those elements of the subject matter on which we must dwell in particular, since both the difficulty and the skill of the treatment depend on assigning proper characteristics. Therefore Horace, who places the observation of characteristics before the rest of his precepts, urges this not once but very frequently. For he says that the mind of the hearer takes more pleasure in a fiction that has no weight, if it has been embellished with proper characteristics, than in serious and fruitful subject matter that is not so embellished. He therefore commands us to examine the customs and the conduct of human life, from which we will be able to elicit the proper characteristics, as Cato says:

Vita est nobis aliena magistra.

Istud ostendit Oracius hiis sex versibus:

Respicere exemplar vite morumque iubebo
doctum imitatorem et vivas hinc ducere voces.
Interdum speciosa locis morataque recte
fabula nullius veneris, sine pondere et arte,
valdius oblectat populum meliusque moratur
quam versus inopes rerum nugeque canore.

Littera sic est intelligenda: "ego iubebo doctum imitatorem," id est scriptorem, qui ut materiam proprietatibus
distinguat, imitatur facta hominum, "respicere exemplar
vite humane et morum" et iubebo eum "ducere," id est elicere, "hinc," id est de illo exemplari, "vivas voces," id est ex-
pressas, que scilicet proprietates exprimant ita, scilicet, ut
emphatica materie execucio videatur rem materialiter informare et ut conceptum mentis exponat expressio verborum.
Taliter enim verbis proprietates exprimentibus quelibet materia debet exprimi qualiter in ymaginarie descripcionis
preconcipitur argumento. Postea subdit Oracius huius pre-
cepti causam, sic: quia "interdum fabula nullius veneris," id
est nullius venustatis, et "sine pondere," id est sine gravitate,
et "sine arte," id est artificio elocucionis, sicut est fabula de
rusticano et urbano mure quam narrat Esopus in apologis, si
fuerit "speciosa locis," id est decorata proprietatibus in locis

CHAPTER II

Another's life is a teacher for us.

Horace shows this in these six verses:

> I would advise one who has learned the imitative art to look to life and manners for a model, and draw from there living words. At times a fiction marked by attractive commonplaces and characters fitly sketched, though lacking in charm, though without force and art, gives the people more delight and holds them better than verses void of thought, and sonorous trifles.

The literal text should be understood thus: "I would advise one who has learned the imitative art," that is, the writer, who imitates the deeds of men in order to distinguish his subject matter with the proper characteristics, "to look to life and manners for a model" and I will command him "to draw," that is, to elicit, "from there," that is, from that model, "living words," that is, expressive speech, namely, that expresses the characteristics in such a way that the emphatic performance of the subject matter may seem to give the idea material shape and the uttering of the words may expose the thought of the mind. For any subject matter should be expressed by means of words that express its characteristics exactly as it is preconceived through the symbolic representation of a description in the imagination. Afterward Horace inserts the reason for this precept, thus: because "at times a fiction lacking in charm," that is, of no beauty, and "without force," that is, without seriousness, and "without art," that is, skill in expression, as is the tale of the country mouse and the city mouse, which Aesop tells in his fables, if it happens to be "marked by attractive

debitis, et "recte morata," id est recte expectata—semper enim in proprietatibus immorari debemus, "valdius oblectat populum," id est placet populo, et "melius moratur," id est detinet ad audiendum, "quam versus inopes rerum," id est vacui proprietatum, et quam "nuge canore." "Nugas canoras" vocat versus in quibus nulla est sentencia, saltem proprietatibus distincta, set sonus tantum, sicut frequenter est et fere semper in versibus modernorum, qui in solis versibus leoninis seu consonanciam habentibus delectantur.

commonplaces," that is, adorned with proper characteristics in the appropriate places, and "characters fitly sketched," that is, fitly awaited—for we always should linger on the characteristics, "gives the people more delight," that is, pleases the people, and "holds them better," that is, detains them for the purpose of hearing, "than verses void of thought," that is, devoid of characteristics, and than "sonorous trifles." He calls "sonorous trifles" those verses in which there is no thought, at least none adorned with proper characteristics, but only sound, as is frequently the case and almost always in the verses of the moderns, who delight only in leonine verses or verses that rhyme.

Capitulum 12

De attributis persone
et negocio

Duo sunt de quibus agitur in rethorica questione, persona scilicet et negocium, ex quibus coniecturalia eliciuntur argumenta. Persona, ut ait Boicius in *Topicis,* est ille vel illa qui vel que propter aliquod dictum vel factum in causam trahitur, id est ille vel illa quem vel quam propter aliquod dictum vel factum reprehendere volumus vel laudare. "Omnis enim oracio poetica est laudacio vel vituperacio," ut ait Aristotiles in *Poetria.* Negocium est dictum vel factum propter quod aliquis vel aliqua trahitur in causam, id est dictum vel factum propter quod aliquem vel aliquam vel reprehendimus vel laudamus.

2   Prius ergo attributa persone breviter percurramus. Undecim, teste Tullio, sunt attributa persone, scilicet nomen, natura, convictus, fortuna, habitus, studium, affeccio, concilium, casus, oracio, factum. Que satis egregie ostendit Alanus in *Anticlaudiano,* sic:

Chapter 12

On the attributes of a person and an action

Two things are dealt with in a rhetorical case, namely, a person and an action, from which conjectural arguments are derived. A person, as Boethius says in his *Topics,* is that man or woman who is brought to trial because of something he or she said or did, that is, that man or woman whom we wish to praise or reprehend because of something he or she said or did. "For every poetic utterance is either praise or blame," as Aristotle says in his *Poetics.* An action is something said or done on account of which some man or woman is brought to trial, that is, something said or done on account of which we praise or reprehend some man or woman.

Therefore, let us first briefly run through the attributes 2 of a person. According to Cicero, there are eleven attributes of a person, that is to say, name, nature, way of life, fortune, habit, interest, feeling, counsel, accidents, speech, achievement. Alan of Lille indicates these quite excellently in the *Anticlaudianus,* thus:

> Quomodo personis accomoda roboris arma
> dant argumentis, set falso robore mutant
> nomen, natura, victus fortunaque vultus
> pretendens dubios, habitus, affeccio, fallax
> concilium, studium, casus, oracio, factum.

3   Nomen primum est attributum. Argumentum sive locus a nomine est quando per significacionem, interpretacionem vel nominis ethimologiam, aliquid de persona laudis vel vituperii persuadetur, ut Vindocinensis commendat Cesarem, sic:

> Cesar ab effectu nomen tenet: omnia cedens
> nominis exponit significata manus.

Similiter quidam iocose composuit epithafium cuiusdam defuncti, cui nomen erat Iohannes Calf, sic:

> O Deus omnipotens, vituli miserere Iohannis,
> quem mors preveniens noluit esse bovem.

4   Natura hic accipitur pro naturalibus que insunt homini. Hoc enim attributum, iuxta Tullium, tripartite dividitur in illa que a corpore sumuntur et in illa que ab anima et in illa que ab extrinsecis. A corpore, ut sunt longitudo stature, brevitas stature, fortitudo, debilitas, forma, deformitas. A naturalibus corporis traxit argumentum Stacius, loquens de Pollinice:

> Celsior ille gradu procera in membra etc.

How the attributes of personal character lend strong arms to an argument, whereas name, nature, way of life and fortune which displays changeable faces, habit, feeling, uncertain counsel, interest, accidents, speech, achievement change with the false appearance of strength.

Name is the first attribute. The argument or common- 3 place from name is when through the meaning, an interpretation, or the etymology of a name one argues something persuasively in praise or blame of a person, as Matthew of Vendôme praises Caesar, thus:

Slayer Caesar lives up to his name; his hand slaying all things makes clear the significance of his name.

Likewise, in jest, someone composed an epitaph for a certain dead person, whose name was John Calf, thus:

O almighty God, have mercy on John the calf, whom premature death did not want to be a bull.

Nature is here taken to mean the qualities that are pres- 4 ent in a man by nature. For this attribute, according to Cicero, is divided three ways, into those things that derive from the body, from the mind, and from externals. From the body, like tallness in stature, shortness in stature, strength, weakness, beauty, ugliness. Statius drew his argument from natural qualities of the body when speaking of Polynices:

Taller he, with long stride and towering limbs etc.

Nam celsitudo et membrorum proceritas attributa sunt corpori. Hoc enim attributum in descripcionibus personarum frequentissime reperitur.

5   Ab anima, ut ingeniositas, hebetudo, sapiencia, stulticia, memoria, oblivio, facecia, curialitas, pietas, benignitas, favor, amor, odium et similia. A naturalibus anime traxit argumentum Stacius, loquens de Tideo, sic:

> Set non et viribus infra
> Tidea fert animus totosque effusa per artus
> maior in exiguo regnabat corpore virtus.

Similiter Vindocinensis, in descripcione pape, sic:

> Disputat in papa virtutum concio, virtus
> certat virtutis anticipare locum.

6   Ab extrinsecis, ut sunt hec quinque que nos ante memoravimus, scilicet cognacio, sexus, patria, nacio, etas. Quibus adiungit Oracius sextum, id est condicionem, et septimum, scilicet officium. Pretermittit tamen cognacionem. Set hec duo, condicio et officium, attributa fortune verius estimantur, sicut superius diximus, allegando hos versus:

> Intererit multum Davusne loquatur an heros etc.

7   A cognacione trahitur argumentum, ut in Stacio, ubi Adrastus quesivit a Pollinice unde natus esset, Pollinices respondit:

For height and length of limbs are attributes of the body. Indeed, this attribute is found very frequently in descriptions of persons.

From the mind, as cleverness, dullness, wisdom, stupidity, memory, forgetfulness, wittiness, courtliness, piety, benignity, goodwill, love, hatred, and the like. Statius drew his argument from the natural qualities of the mind when speaking of Tydeus, thus:

> Yet was Tydeus in strength and spirit no whit the less, and though his frame was smaller, greater valor in every part held sway.

Likewise Matthew of Vendôme, in his description of the pope, thus:

> A whole assembly of virtues contends within the pope; virtue vies with virtue for the place of honor.

From externals, as are those five that we mentioned earlier, namely, kinship, sex, fatherland, nation, age. To these Horace adds a sixth, that is, social condition, and a seventh, namely, civil rank. However, he leaves out kinship. But these two, social condition and civil rank, are rather to be considered attributes of fortune, as we said above, while citing these verses:

> Vast difference will it make, whether Davus or a hero speaks etc.

An argument is drawn from kinship, as in Statius, when Adrastus asked Polynices where he had been born, Polynices responded:

Cadmus origo patrum,

et statim sumpsit argumentum a patria, sic:

tellus Mavorcia Thebe.

8   A sexu, ut in Virgilio:

Eya, rumpe moras: varium et mutabile semper femina etc.

et in Iuvenali:

Femina non sentit pereuntem prodiga sensum.

9   A patria, ut in premisso exemplo Stacii:

Proles Mavorcia Thebe

et hic:

Militat in pateris Vindosinense genus.

10   A nacione, ut in Ovidio:

Vix bene barbarica Greca notata manu.

Nam "Grecus" et "barbarus" ad nacionem pertinent. Inter patriam et nacionem hoc distat, quod nacio per genus lingue, patria secundum locum originalem consideratur.

11   Ab etate, ut in Ovidio:

A iuvene et cupido credatur reddita virgo?

Cadmus was the ancestor of my sires,

and then immediately derived an argument from fatherland, thus:

> my land Mavortian Thebes.

From sex, as in Virgil: 8

Ho! break off delay! A fickle and changeful thing is woman ever etc.

and in Juvenal:

An extravagant woman has no awareness of her failing judgment.

From fatherland, as in the earlier example from Statius: 9

My race Mavortian Thebes.

and here:

Vendôme's tribe wages battle at the punch bowl.

From nation, as in Ovid: 10

Scarce charactered in Greek by her barbarian hand.

For "Greek" and "barbarian" pertain to nation. Between fatherland and nation there is this difference, that nation is defined by the nature of one's language, fatherland by the place of origin.

From age, as in Ovid: 11

Is it to be thought she was returned a virgin, by a man young and eager?

Proprietates etatum ponit Oracius eleganter et primo proprietates puericie, hiis tribus versibus:

> Reddere qui voces iam scit puer et pede certo
> signat humum, gestit paribus colludere, et iram
> colligit ac ponit temere et mutatur in horas.

Proprietates iuventutis ostendit hiis quinque versibus:

> Imberbis iuvenis, tandem custode remoto,
> gaudet equis, canibus et aprici gramine campi,
> cereus in vicium flecti, monitoribus asper,
> utilium tardus provisor, prodigus eris,
> sublimis, cupidus et amata relinquere pernix.

Proprietates virilitatis ostendit hiis tribus versibus:

> Conversis studiis etas animusque virilis
> querit opes et amicicias, inservit honori,
> commisisse cavet quod mox mutare laborat.

Proprietates senectutis ostendit hiis sex versibus:

> Multa senem circumveniunt incommoda, vel quod
> querit et inventis miser abstinet ac timet uti,
> vel quod res omnes timide gelideque ministrat,
> dilator, spe longus, iners, avidusque futuri,
> difficilis, querulus, laudator temporis acti
> se puero, castigator censorque minorum.

Horace sets down the proper characteristics of ages skill-fully, starting with the characteristics of childhood in these three verses:

> The child, who by now can utter words and set firm step upon the ground, delights to play with his mates, flies into a passion and as lightly puts it aside, and changes every hour.

He shows the characteristics of youth in these five verses:

> The beardless youth, freed at last from his tutor, finds joy in horses and hounds and the grass of the sunny Campus, soft as wax for molding to vice, peevish with his counselors, slow to make needful provision, lavish with money, spirited, of strong desires, but swift to change his fancies.

He shows the characteristics of manhood in these three verses:

> With altered aims, the age and spirit of the man seeks wealth and friends, becomes a slave to ambition, and is fearful of having done what soon it is eager to change.

He shows the characteristics of old age in these six verses:

> Many ills encompass an old man, whether because he seeks gain, and then miserably holds aloof from his store and fears to use it, or because, in all that he does, he lacks fire and courage, is dilatory and slow to form hopes, is sluggish and greedy of a longer life, peevish, surly, given to praising the days he spent as a boy, and to reproving and condemning the young.

Quare talis fiet distinccio proprietatum ostendit, dicens:

> Ne forte seniles
> mandentur iuveni etc.

12   Victus hic appellatur nutritura. Hoc attributum Tullius tripartito dividit in apud quos, cuius arbitratu, quo more. Apud quos, id est in cuius domo vel curia vel familia, sicut in Lucano dicit Cesar, de Pompeio loquens:

> Solitus Sillanum lambere ferrum.

In quo significavit quod Pompeius fuerat de familia Sille, qui cives Romanos occidere consuevit. Similiter Salustius contra Tullium: "Numquid apud Marcum Pisonem hanc immoderatam eloquenciam iactura pudicicie perdidicisti?" Et in hoc significavit Tullium apud impudicissimum fuisse nutritum ideoque ipsum esse similiter impudicum. Considerandum est in victu quo more quis nutriatur, id est consuetudine cuius patrie, et cuius arbitratu, id est quos vivendi habuit preceptores. Similiter a victu trahit argumentum Vindocinensis, sic:

> Est grave consueto viciis desuescere, vergit
> noxius ad solite noxietatis iter.

13   Fortuna est status vite quem quis adipiscitur vel ex proprio arbitrio vel ex casu temporis vel ex hominum institucione. Ex proprio arbitrio, ut si quis sponte sua de divite se

He shows why there should be such differentiation of characteristics, saying:

So, lest haply we assign a youth the part of old age etc.

Way of living is here called upbringing. Cicero divides 12 this attribute three ways: among whom, by whose direction, and in what tradition. Among whom, that is, in whose house or court or entourage, as Caesar says in Lucan, when speaking of Pompey:

He once was wont to lick the sword of Sulla.

By this he means that Pompey had belonged to the entourage of Sulla, who was in the habit of killing Roman citizens. Likewise, Sallust against Cicero: "Did you not learn all your unrestrained eloquence under Marcus Piso at the expense of your chastity?" And by this he meant that Cicero had been brought up by a most immodest person and therefore was himself similarly immodest. Under way of living one should consider in what tradition someone is brought up, that is, by the customary practice of what fatherland, and by whose direction, that is, who were those who taught him how to live. Likewise, Matthew of Vendôme draws an argument from way of life, thus:

It is difficult for one so accustomed to abandon vice; being evil himself, he slips into the rut of his habitual evil.

Fortune is the position in life that someone attains either 13 through his own control or through a moment's chance or through social convention. Through his own control, as if someone by his own agency were to transform himself from

347

faciat pauperem ut spirituales divicias adquirat, sicut faciunt religiosi. Ex casu temporis, ut si quis casualiter oppressus cadat in pauperiem vel factus victor elevetur in aliquam dignitatem. Ex hominum institucione, sicut homines instituerunt servos, cum omnes simus liberi a natura. In fortuna ergo consideratur servitus, libertas, felicitas, infelicitas, prosperitas, adversitas, fama, infamia et huiusmodi. A fortuna trahit argumentum Virgilius, sic:

"Vade," ait, "o felix nati pietate."

Unde scias quod habere filios nature est set habere tales vel tales filios fortune est. Similiter et Vindocinensis, in descripcione Davi, sic:

Nequicia rabiem servilem predicat, actu
    enucleat serve condicionis opus.

14   Habitus, secundum Tullium, est "animi aut corporis in aliqua re constans," id est diuturna, "et absoluta," id est plena, "perfeccio, non natura set studio et industria comparata," ut sapiencia, facundia, eloquencia, religio, sanctitas, devocio, pietas et similia. Unde Victorinus, distinguens inter victum, habitum et affeccionem, ita scribit: "Scire aliquid perfecte et nolle quod scitur excercere habitus est; deinde aliquid non plene scire neque id quocumque modo excercere affeccio est; verum uniuscuiusque rei et habitus et affeccio si excerceantur et in actu sint, victus est." "Industria" autem hic

rich to poor so that he could acquire spiritual riches, as do those who take vows of asceticism. Through a moment's chance, as if someone, surprised by a chance occurrence, were to fall into poverty or, made victor, were raised to some high rank. Through social convention, just as men created slaves, since we all are free by nature. To fortune, therefore, are referred servitude, liberty, happiness, unhappiness, prosperity, adversity, renown, ill repute and the like. Virgil draws an argument from fortune, thus:

"Fare forth," he cries, "blessed in thy son's love."

From this you may know that to have sons pertains to nature but to have sons of this or that sort pertains to fortune. Likewise also Matthew of Vendôme, in his description of Davus, thus:

By his wickedness he proclaims his slave-like frenzy,
and by his acts he shows himself a slave girl's creation.

Habit, according to Cicero, is "a stable," that is, long last- 14
ing, "and absolute," that is, full, "completion of mind or body in some particular, which has been produced not by nature but by careful training and application," such as wisdom, fluency, eloquence, piety, sanctity, devotion, charity and the like. Whence Victorinus, when distinguishing among way of life, habit, and feeling, writes as follows: "To know something perfectly and to be unwilling to practice what is known is habit; then not to know something fully and not to practice it in any way is feeling; but if the habit and the feeling of any particular thing are practiced and are present in performance, that is way of life." Moreover, a

dicitur providencia quedam quare aliquid scire vel facere volumus. Ab habitu sumit Ovidius argumentum, sic:

Non formosus erat set erat facundus Ulixes.

Similiter si dicas: "Iste de facili non noceret cuiquam, quoniam religiosus est, nec de facili poterit convinci, quoniam sapiens est."

15   Affeccio est subita animi aut corporis mutacio cito recedens, ut si quid boni nobis subito nuncietur et incipiamus esse leti, vel grave et incipiamus esse molesti. In affeccione ergo consideratur leticia, tristicia, ira, timor, amor, odium et huiusmodi. Ab affeccione sumitur argumentum, sic:

O quam difficile est crimen non prodere vultu!

et hic:

In facie legitur hominis secreta voluntas.

16   Studium est assidua et vehemens animi ad aliquam rem cum magna voluntate applicacio, ut studium philosophie, geometrie, poetrie. Unde Victorinus, distinguens inter studium, affeccionem et victum, dicit: "Si quid vehementer aut cum magna voluntate volumus, studium est; deinde si quod volumus aliqua ex parte consequamur, affeccio est; si autem quod plenum et perfectum est tenemus, habitus est. Quod si ipsum plenum vel semiplenum excercere voluerimus, victus est." A studio trahitur argumentum sic: "Iste non est luxuriosus, quia multum studiosus est." Similiter Oracius:

kind of forethought whereby we wish to know and to do something is here called "application." Ovid derives an argument from habit, thus:

Ulysses was not comely, but he was eloquent.

Likewise, if you were to say: "This one would not easily hurt anyone, since he is religious, nor could he be easily persuaded, since he is wise."

Feeling is a sudden change of the spirit or body that goes 15 away quickly, as if something of benefit to us were suddenly announced and we began to be cheerful, or something grievous and we began to be troubled. Therefore, to feeling are referred happiness, sadness, anger, fear, love, hate, and the like. An argument is derived from feeling, thus:

O how hard it is not to betray a guilty conscience in the face!

and here:

A man's hidden desire is read in his face.

Interest is the diligent and energetic application of the 16 mind to some matter with great commitment of will, like an interest in philosophy, geometry, or poetry. Whence Victorinus, when distinguishing among interest, feeling, and way of life, says: "If we want something passionately and with great commitment of will, that is interest; then if to some extent we achieve what we want, that is feeling; but if what we have is full and complete, that is habit. If we wish to practice what itself is full or half-full, that is way of life." An argument is drawn from interest, thus: "This one is not licentious, because he is very studious." Likewise, Horace:

Conversis studiis etas animusque virilis
querit opes etc.

17 Concilium est aliquid faciendi vel non faciendi vere excogitata racio. "Racio," id est "discrecio," "vere excogitata," id
est "veraciter inventa." Vel secundum Vindocinensem:
"Concilium est recompensacio iuris libramine, ad fugam et
eleccionem excogitata discrecio." A concilio trahit argumentum Lucanus: Brutus ad Catonem, sic:

> Tu mente labantem
> dirige me, dubium certo tu robore firma.

Claudianus:

> Mentemque domet respectus honesti.

Similiter et hic: "Difficile est contra talem inire bellum, quoniam promptus est in concilio."

18 Casus est consuetudinarius calamitatis eventus, per quem
aliquid convincitur de persona, vel casus est consuetudo
male accidendi alicui. Casus differt a fortuna in hoc, quod
casus est inopinatus et consuetudinarius rei eventus ex causis confluentibus, fortuna vero est status vite etc., ut dictum
est. A casu trahit argumentum Boicius, *De consolacione,* sic:

> Qui cecidit, stabili non erat ille gradu.

Similiter et Vindocinensis:

With altered aims, the age and spirit of the man seeks
wealth etc.

Counsel is a truly deliberate plan for doing or not doing 17
something. "Plan," that is, judgment by discretion; "truly
deliberate," that is, truthfully discovered. Or according to
Matthew of Vendôme: "Counsel is the balanced weighing of
an action in the scales of justice, a careful sorting out of
which alternatives to reject and which to choose." Lucan
draws an argument from counsel: Brutus to Cato, thus:

Guide me in my weakness with your mind, in my doubt
with your unwavering strength.

Claudian:

And let regard for duty control your mind.

Likewise also here: "It is difficult to go to war against such a
one, since he is quick in counsel."

Accident is the ordinary occurrence of adversity, through 18
which we can see something of men's characters, or accident
is the habit of things turning out badly for someone. Accident differs from fortune in this, that accident is the unex-
pected and ordinary occurrence of a thing from a conflu-
ence of causes, but fortune is a position in life etc., as has
been said. Boethius, in his *Consolation,* draws an argument
from accident, thus:

Anyone who has fallen never stood firm.

Likewise also Matthew of Vendôme:

Vix miser emergit, vix letos migrat in usus
quem premit irate prosperitatis hiemps.

Unde scias quod casus est transitorius quasi ex toto, fortuna
vero paulo permanencior et maioris efficacie.

19   Oracio est assidua consuetudo loquendi vel consuetudo
dicendi—et intelligendum est tale dictum quod est preter
negocium—et per quod aliquid de persona persuadetur. Ab
oracione trahit Oracius argumentum, sic:

Omne supervacuum pleno de pectore manat.

Similiter et hic:

Est orare ducum species violenta iubendi,
et quasi nudato supplicat ense potens.

Similiter in Vindocinensi, ubi describit papam, sic:

Papa docenda docet, prohibet prohibenda, reatus
castigat, ceptrum spirituale tenet.

Est enim hic triplex attributum: nam ubi dicitur "papa docenda docet," attributum est ab oracione; ubi dicitur "reatus
castigat," a facto; ubi "ceptrum spirituale tenet," a fortuna.

20   Factum est consuetum alicuius persone excercicium vel
consuetudo faciendi, scilicet quicquid persona consuevit

CHAPTER 12

Only with difficulty does the wretched man emerge or
find joy who is buffeted by the wintry winds of an angry fortune.

From this you may know that accident is almost entirely
transitory, while fortune is somewhat longer lasting and of
greater effect.

Speech is a customary way of speaking or one's habitual 19
manner of talking—and here you should understand the
sort of speech that occurs beyond the confines of the action
at issue—which reveals something about a person. Horace
draws an argument from speech, thus:

Every word in excess flows away from the full mind.

Likewise also here:

The prayer of leaders is a violent kind of ordering, and
the powerful man begs, as it were, with a naked sword.

Likewise in Matthew of Vendôme, when he describes the
pope, thus:

The pope teaches what ought to be taught, prohibits
what ought to be prohibited, punishes sin, holds spiritual sway.

Indeed, here there is a triple attribute: for where he says
"the pope teaches what ought to be taught," the attribute is
from speech; where he says "he punishes sin," from accom-
plishment; where "he holds spiritual sway," from fortune.

Achievement is the customary practice of some person or 20
his habitual actions, namely, whatever the person has been
accustomed to practicing. And understand that what has

355

excercere. Et intellige factum esse omnino extra negocium. A facto trahit argumentum Lucanus, loquens de Cesare, sic:

Cesar in arma furens nullas nisi sanguine fuso
gaudet habere vias etc.

21   Attributorum negocio quattuor sunt genera. Quedam sunt continencia cum negocio, quedam in gestione negocii, quedam adiuncta negocio, quedam consequencia negocium. Que quattuor Alanus, in *Anticlaudiano,* sic ostendit:

Eventum que contineant, quid gestio facti
contineat, facto que sunt adiuncta vel ipsum,
ut res deposcit, solito de more sequatur.

Horum quattuor generum duo prima presenti negocio sunt necessaria; duo vero ultima magis conveniunt oratori, quare eis ad presens supersedendum est et de duobus primis est dicendum.

22   Continencia cum negocio sunt ea que semper videntur esse affixa ad rem, nec ab ea possunt separari. Sunt autem tria genera continencium cum negocio, scilicet summa negocii, causa negocii et triplex administracio, scilicet ante rem, cum re, et post rem. De hiis per ordinem doceamus.

23   Summa negocii est illud quod Tullius appellat "brevem ipsius negocii complexionem," scilicet nomen ipsius vel diffinicio, ut "prodicio patrie." Et valet ad auxesim criminis, id est ad ampliandum magis quam ad probandum, ut dicit

been done is entirely beyond the confines of the action at issue. Lucan draws an argument from achievement when he is speaking of Caesar, thus:

> Caesar, frantic for war, rejoices to find no passage except by shedding blood etc.

There are four kinds of attributes of an action. Certain 21 ones are coherent with the action, certain ones are in the performance of the action, certain ones are joined to the action, certain ones follow from the action. Alan of Lille shows these four in the *Anticlaudianus,* thus:

> What comprise the circumstances, what the performance of the deed includes, what things are adjunct to the deed, or follow upon it, as the case requires, according to normal procedure.

Of these four kinds, the first two are necessary to our present purpose; but the last two are more suitable for the orator, wherefore we should pass over them for the moment and discuss the first two.

Coherent with the action are those things which seem al- 22 ways connected with it and which cannot be separated from it. There are three kinds of attributes that are coherent with the action, namely, the gist of the action, the cause of the action, and the triple handling of the action, namely, before the fact, with the fact, and after the fact. Let us explain these in order.

The gist of the action is that which Cicero calls "a brief 23 summary of the action itself," that is to say, its name or definition, such as "betrayal of country." And this is effective in the heightening of the charge, that is, more for expanding

Victorinus. A summa negocii trahit argumentum Lucanus, loquens de Cesare, sic:

> O mundi domitor, rerum fortuna mearum,
> miles, etc.

Similiter Vindocinensis, in descripcione Davi, sic:

> Scurra vagus, parasitus edax, abieccio plebis
> est Davus, rerum dedecus, egra lues.

24 Causa duplex est, racionativa scilicet et impulsiva. Causa racionativa est quando, propter aliquam rem iam in animo provisam, aliquid facimus ut aut commodum adquiramus aut incomodum devitemus. Ut commodum adquiramus, ut in Lucano:

> Nescius interea capti ducis arma parabat
> Magnus, ut inmixto firmaret robore partes;

et in Oracio:

> Ex noto fictum carmen sequar, ut sibi quivis
> speret idem etc.

Ut incommodum devitemus, ut in Oracio:

> Ne forte seniles
> mandentur iuveni partes puerove viriles;

et in Vindocinensi:

than for proving, as Victorinus says. Lucan draws an argument from the gist of the action, when speaking of Caesar,
thus:

O soldier, conqueror of the world, on whom my des-
tiny depends etc.

Likewise Matthew of Vendôme, in his description of Davus,
thus:

A roaming buffoon, a gluttonous parasite, an offscour-
ing of the masses, Davus is a sickening pest, a disgrace
to the world.

Cause is twofold, namely ratiocinative and impulsive. A 24
cause is ratiocinative when, because of some matter already
foreseen in the mind, we do something so that we either
gain an advantage or avoid a disadvantage. So that we gain
an advantage, as in Lucan:

Magnus meanwhile, unaware that his commander had
been made prisoner, was taking the field, in order to
encourage his adherents by an addition of strength;

and in Horace:

My aim shall be poetry, so molded from the familiar
that whoever may hope for the same success etc.

So that we avoid a disadvantage, as in Horace:

Lest haply we assign a youth the part of old age, or a
boy that of manhood;

and in Matthew of Vendôme:

Ne languescat amor, ut amans pociatur amato,
 vota replere studet seu prece sive dato.

Et est hic utrumque ut incommodum devitemus, cum dicitur "Ne languescat amor," ut commodum adquiramus, cum dicitur "ut amans pociatur amato."

25 Causa impulsiva est quando repentina animi commocione in aliquod factum precipitamur. Unde dicit Victorinus: "quecumque causa ex confessione veniam meretur causa impulsiva est." Ut in Ovidio:

Audacem faciebat amor

et Iuvenalis:

Greculus esuriens: in celum iusseris, ibit.

Utrumque enim istorum, et amor et paupertas, causa est impulsiva. Similiter et de Iove, qui coactus est dare vaccam Iunoni causa removende suspicionis:

Dat vitulam nec dat, quia cogitur; immo rapinam,
 quod non sponte datur, equiparare potest.

26 Set videtur forsan alicui quod causa racionativa sit concilium et ita attributum persone esset attributum negocio. Ideo dicendum est que sit inter ea differencia. Differunt enim in modo agendi. Si enim concilium sic inducatur in

> So as to possess what he loves and not let love cool, the
> lover strives to achieve his goal with entreaties or gifts.

And here it is both so that we avoid a disadvantage, when we
say "and not let love cool," and so that we gain an advantage,
when we say "so as to possess what he loves."

A cause is impulsive when we are compelled to rush into 25
some action by a sudden commotion of the mind. Whence
Victorinus says: "any cause that earns pardon by virtue of
confession is an impulsive cause." As in Ovid:

> Love made her bold;

and Juvenal:

> Your hungry Greekling: tell him to go to heaven and
> he will.

For the cause of each of these, on the one hand love and on
the other poverty, is impulsive. Likewise also in the case of
Jove, who was forced to give Juno a heifer to allay her suspicion:

> He gives the calf and yet he does not give it; he is
> forced to. Indeed, his surrendering the calf was like
> the maiden's surrendering her honor; neither gave will-
> ingly.

But perhaps it may seem to someone that a ratiocinative 26
cause is the same thing as counsel and that therefore what is
an attribute of a person would also be an attribute of an action. Therefore, we should say what the difference between
them is. For they differ in the method of proceeding. For if
counsel is adduced as an argument in such a way that a

argumentum ut notetur qualitas persone, id est qualis persona sit in concilio, tunc est argumentum a concilio in attributis persone, ut si dicas: "Non est tutum contra illum inire bellum, quoniam promptus est in concilio" vel "quia vir magni concilii est." Ecce quomodo hic notatur qualis sit persona in concilio. Si vero concilium ita inducatur in argumentum, ut non notetur qualitas persone set ut demonstretur quare aliquid factum est, tunc licet concilium inducatur in argumentum, non erit argumentum a concilio set pocius a causa racionativa, ut si dicas: "Bene poterit sibi cavere, quoniam concilio sapientum utitur." Ecce hic ostenditur causa facti, quare scilicet poterit sibi cavere, nec ostenditur qualis est persona. Ideo argumentum est a causa racionativa. Vide igitur quod non tantum attendendum est quid in argumentum ducatur, quantum qualiter inducatur, ut ex modo argumentandi cognoscere possis ex quo attributo sumitur argumentum. Una enim et eadem res sic induci potest ut nunc ex uno loco sumatur argumentum, nunc ex alio, propter diversum modum inducendi, ut dictum est. Unde dicit Victorinus: "In omni narracione attendendum est quid propter quid dicatur. Sepe enim persona describitur ut negocium patefiat, sepe eciam gesta narrantur ut qualis sit persona videatur."

27   Rursus affeccio potest esse causa impulsiva quare aliquid fiat (subita namque ira affeccio est), set in modo argumentandi differunt, ut de concilio et causa racionativa dictum

quality of a person is indicated, that is, what sort of person he is in his counsel, then it is an argument from counsel among the attributes of a person, as if you were to say: "It is not safe to go to war against that one, since he is quick in counsel" or "because he is a man of great counsel." Notice how the sort of person he is in counsel is indicated here. If, on the other hand, counsel is adduced as an argument not so as to indicate a quality of a person but to show why something has been done, then, even though counsel has been adduced as an argument, it will not be an argument from counsel but rather from ratiocinative cause, as if you were to say: "He will be able to look out for himself well, since he takes the counsel of wise men." Notice here the cause of the deed is shown, namely, why he will be able to look out for himself, and it is not shown what sort of person he is. Therefore, the argument is from ratiocinative cause. Notice, therefore, that you should pay attention not only to what is adduced as an argument, but also how it is adduced, so that from the method of arguing you are able to recognize from which attribute the argument is derived. For one and the same thing can be adduced in such a way that now the argument is derived from one place, now from another, on account of a different method of adducing, as has been said. Whence Victorinus says: "In every statement of facts one should pay attention to what is said for what reason. For often a person is described so that the action is revealed; often, too, deeds are recounted so that what sort a person is may be seen."

Moreover, feeling can be an impulsive cause whereby 27 something is done (for sudden anger is a feeling), but in method of arguing they differ, as has been said about counsel

est. Si enim affeccio sic inducatur ut notetur qualitas persone, velut si dicas "Iracundus est," tunc est argumentum ab affeccione in attributis persone; si vero sic inducatur ut non notetur qualitas persone set cur aliquid factum sit, erit argumentum a causa impulsiva, ut si dicas "Ira commotus, occidit eum."

28   Administracio negocii triplex est: ante rem, cum re et post rem. Administracio negocii ante rem est quod fit ad negocium melius aggrediendum, ut "quoniam armavit se." Administracio negocii in re est quod fit ad negocium perpetrandum, ut "quoniam fortiter percussit." Administracio negocii post rem est quod fit ad melius exeundum de negocio, ut occisum in abdito sepelire. Vide igitur quod summa negocii et causa videntur esse affixa ad rem, id est rei adherencia; administracio enim non videtur posse separari: sine administracione nichil fieri potest; et hoc est quare dicuntur continencia cum negocio, quia vel semper negocio adherent vel ab eo non possunt separari. De triplici administracione trahit Vindocinensis argumentum, sic:

Risus, amor coitus, ventris concepcio triplex etc.,

ut predictum est. Ita dictum est de continentibus cum negocio.

29   In gestione negocii sunt ea que in ipso negocio gerendo sunt necessaria. Et sunt quinque: locus, tempus, occasio,

and ratiocinative cause. For if feeling is adduced in such a way that the quality of a person is indicated, as if you were to say "He is irascible," then the argument is from feeling among the attributes of a person; but if it were adduced not so as to indicate a quality of a person but why something was done, then the argument will be from impulsive cause, as if you were to say: "Stirred by anger, he killed him."

The handling of an action is threefold: before the fact, 28 within the fact, and after the fact. The handling of an action before the fact is what is done so that the action is undertaken more effectively, as "because he armed himself." The handling of an action within the fact is what is done to carry out the action, as "because he struck violently." The handling of an action after the fact is what is done to get out of the action effectively, as hiding a slain person in a secluded place. Notice, therefore, that the gist and the cause of an action seem to be attached to the matter, that is, adhering to the matter—for the handling does not seem capable of being separated: without handling nothing can be done—and this is why they are called attributes that are coherent with the action, because they always either adhere to the action or cannot be separated from it. Matthew of Vendôme draws an argument from the triple handling of an action, thus:

> Flirting, pleasure in intercourse, pregnancy—these are the threefold etc.,

as was said earlier. And so we have discussed the attributes that are coherent with an action.

The attributes that are in the performance of an action 29 are those that are necessary in the actual performing of the action. And they are five: place, time, occasion, manner, and

modus, facultas. De quibus per ordinem nos loquamur, et primo de loco.

30   Locus enim in se nichil valet ad probandum set semper probat secundum oportunitatem quam habet ad negocium administrandum. Probat autem aut ex qualitate aut ex quantitate aut ex habitudine. Qualitas loci est quod locus sit speciosus, planus, saxosus vel tumultuosus vel huiusmodi. Habitudo loci est comparacio loci ad alium locum. Quantitas est loci capacitas. A loci qualitate trahit Stacius argumentum, volens verisimiliter probare per qualitatem loci unde pugnabat Tideus quod solus ipse potuit plures occidere. Ait enim de ipso Tideo, cum insidiantes ei nequam incursum facerent:

> que sola medendi
> turbata racione via est, petit ardua dire
> spingos et abscisis infringere cautibus uncas
> exuperat iuga dira manus, scopuloque potitus,
> unde procul tergo metus et via prona nocendi,
> saxum ingens, . . .
> rupibus avellit etc.

Ecce ex eo quod ostendit qualis erat locus unde pugnabat, fecit verisimile quod solus plures potuit occidere. Ex quantitate eciam loci potest sumi argumentum, ut si aliquis te dicat alicubi ut insidias alicui faceres cum centum militibus latuisse et possis dicere: "Nec locus ille viginti posset capere." Ex habitudine loci sumitur argumentum, ut si dicas locum aliquem aptum esse insidiis, quoniam remotus est ab

means. Let us speak of these in order, and first concerning place.

A place in itself does not suffice to prove anything but always proves something according to the opportunity it offers for managing an action. It proves something either from the quality, quantity, or character of the place. The quality of a place is that the place may be lovely, level, stony, noisy, or the like. The character of a place is a comparison of the place to another place. Quantity is the capaciousness of a place. Statius draws an argument from the quality of a place when he wishes to offer plausible proof, based on the quality of the place where Tydeus was fighting, that he could have killed so many all by himself. For he says of this same Tydeus, when ambushers launched a wicked attack on him:

> He makes for the heights of the dire Sphinx—the only
> path of safety in his bewilderment—and tearing his
> nails upon the sheer cliff he scales the dreadful steep
> and gains mastery of the rock, where he has security
> behind and a clear downward range of harm. Then he
> tears away from the rocks a huge boulder etc.

Notice here that, because he describes the nature of the place where Tydeus was fighting, he made it seem plausible that he could have killed so many all by himself. An argument also can be derived from the quantity of a place, as if someone were to say that you had hidden somewhere with one hundred soldiers so that you could launch an ambush on someone, and you could say: "That place could not hold twenty." An argument is derived from the character of a place, as if you were to say that some place was suitable for an ambush, since it is distant from the city, just as Statius,

urbe, sicut Stacius, cum describeret quinquaginta milites contra Tideum insidias posuisse, ita dicit:

Fert via per dumos propior, qua calle latenti
precellerant denseque legunt compendia silve.
Lecta dolis sedes: gemini procul urbe malignis
faucibus urgentur colles, etc.

Ecce in hoc quod dixit "procul ab urbe," sumpsit argumentum a loci habitudine.

31 Tempus, secundum quod rethoribus convenit, est quedam pars eternitatis cum alicuius annui, menstrui, diurni, nocturnive spacii certa significacione. A tempore trahit argumentum Virgilius:

Omnia nunc florent, nunc formosissimus annus.

32 Occasio est oportunitas faciendi aliquid nata ex qualitate temporis, ut "quoniam multa oportunitate possent fieri nocte, cunctis dormientibus, que non possent fieri cunctis vigilantibus." Inter tempus et occasionem hoc interest, quod tempus dicitur ipsum temporis spacium, occasio est ipsa oportunitas temporis. Dividitur autem occasio in tria, scilicet publicum, commune, singulare, non quia quodlibet istorum sit occasio set quoniam ex hiis nascitur occasio. Publicum est quod ad totam pertinet civitatem, ut dies festus, communis ludus. Inde sic sumitur argumentum: "Bene fieri potuit ut illud illa die furaretur aliquis, quoniam omnes ad

when he was describing how fifty soldiers had set an ambush for Tydeus, says as follows:

> A nearer road leads them through copses, where by a hidden path they make the better speed and travel by a shortcut through the dense woods. It was a choice spot for a stratagem: at a distance from the city two hills bear close upon each other with a grudging gulf between etc.

Notice that in saying "at a distance from the city" he derived his argument from the character of the place.

Time, insofar as it pertains to rhetoricians, is a part of 31 eternity definitely indicated as being of a certain length, a year's, month's, day's, or night's. Virgil draws an argument from time:

> Now all things are in bloom, now the year is at its fairest.

Occasion is the opportunity for doing something that is 32 brought into being through the quality of the time, as "because many things could be done opportunely at night, when all are asleep, that could not be done when all are awake." Between time and occasion there is this difference, that "time" is said to be the actual length of time, while "occasion" is the actual opportunity that the time affords. Now occasion is divided into three categories, namely, public, common, and individual, not because any one of these is an occasion but because occasion arises from these. Public is that which pertains to the entire city, like a feast day or a communal festival. An argument is derived from this source, thus: "It could easily be that someone could have stolen that

ludum exierant." Commune est quod omnibus accidit eodem fere tempore, ut vindemie. Inde sic sumitur argumentum: "Nimirum si subito fuit destructa civitas, omnes enim exierant ad vindemias." Singulare est quod ad unum aliquem privatim pertinet, ut funus, exequie. Inde sic sumitur argumentum: "Nimirum si omnia de domo eius sublata sint, quoniam omnes exierant ad exequias."

33   Modus est qualitas facti secundum intencionem agentis, id est maneries ipsius facti. Inde sumit argumentum Oracius, sic:

> Atque ita mentitur, sic veris falsa remiscet,
> primo ne medium, medio ne discrepet imum.

Virgilius, in *Buccolicis:*

> An michi cantando victus non redderet ille,
> quem mea carminibus meruisset fistula caprum?

Vindocinensis:

> Credulitas festina nocet, consuevit habere
> effectus fragiles impetuosa manus.

Unde Ovidius:

> Difficiles aditus impetus omnis habet.

34   Facultas est auxilium aliquod sine quo non potest aliquid fieri vel per quod aliquid potest facilius fieri. Et sciendum

on that day, since everyone had gone out to the festival."
Common is that which happens to everyone at about the
same time, like the grape harvest. An argument is derived
from this source, thus: "It is no wonder that the city had
been destroyed suddenly, for everyone had gone out to the
grape harvest." Individual is that which privately pertains to
some one person, like funeral rites or a funeral procession.
An argument is derived from this source, thus: "It is no wonder that everything has been taken from his house, since all
of them had gone to a funeral."

Manner is the quality of a deed according to the inten- 33
tion of the one who does it, that is, the manner of the deed
itself. Horace derives an argument from this source, thus:

> And so skillfully does he invent, so closely does he
> blend facts and fiction, that the middle is not discor-
> dant with the beginning, nor the end with the middle.

Virgil, in the *Eclogues:*

> Did I not beat him in singing, was he not to pay me the
> goat my pipe had won by its songs?

Matthew of Vendôme:

> Quick credulity harms, a hasty hand is apt to have
> flimsy effects.

Whence Ovid:

> Impetuous force is always hard to face.

Means is some kind of aid without which something 34
cannot be done or by means of which something can be

quod quandocumque sumitur argumentum a facultate, semper probatur quibus auxiliis factum sit. A facultate sumit argumentum Ovidius, sic:

> Fallere credentem non est operosa puellam
>   gloria etc.

Similiter Vindocinensis:

> Est facilis falli mens nescia fallere: falli
>   simplicitas facili credulitate solet.

35 Ita dictum sit de hiis que sunt in gestione negocii. Reliqua duo genera attributorum negocio oratori specialiter tribuuntur. Unde de eis nichil ad presens. Nunc restat dicendum quomodo premissa persone et negocio attributa ad has septem circumstancias reducuntur:

> Quis, quid, ubi, quibus auxiliis, cur, quomodo, quando?

36 Sicut dicit Boicius in quarto *Topicorum,* septem sunt circumstancie, que in hoc versu continentur:

> Quis, quid, ubi, quibus auxiliis, cur, quomodo, quando?

Dicuntur autem attributa persone et negocio "circumstancie," quoniam "circa" causam "stant" et eam "stare" faciunt. Harum septem circumstanciarum prima, scilicet "quis," omnia undecim attributa persone continet, quoniam unumquodque attributum persone probat quis fecerit aliquid vel non fecerit. Omnia igitur attributa persone sunt hec una circumstancia "quis," quia omnia uno modo stare faciunt

done more readily. And you should know that whenever an argument is derived from means, it is always proved from the aids with which the action was accomplished. Ovid derives an argument from means, thus:

To beguile a trustful maid is glory but cheaply earned.

Likewise, Matthew of Vendôme:

It is easy to deceive the mind that knows not how to deceive, for simplicity with its ready credulity is easily misled.

And so we have discussed the attributes that are in the 35 performance of an action. The remaining two kinds of attributes of an action are assigned to the orator in particular. And so we will say nothing about these for the moment. Now it remains to say how the foregoing attributes of a person and an action are reduced to these seven circumstances:

Who, what, where, with what aids, why, how, when?

As Boethius says in the fourth book of his *Topics,* there are 36 seven circumstances, which are contained in this verse:

Who, what, where, with what aids, why, how, when?

The attributes of a person and an action are called "circumstances" because they "stand around" the case and they cause it "to stand." The first of these seven circumstances, namely, "who?," contains all eleven attributes of a person, since each and every attribute of a person proves who did or did not do something. Therefore, all the attributes of a person are this one circumstance "who?," because all of them

causam, et hoc ideo quia omnia comprobant quis fecit. Inde est quod quodlibet attributum persone per se est hec circumstancia "quis" et omnia simul sunt hec eadem. Secunda circumstancia, scilicet "quid," includit summam negocii et triplicem administracionem: hec enim duo ostendunt quid sit factum. Tercia, scilicet "cur," includit causam racionativam et impulsivam: utrumque enim ostendit cur aliquid factum sit. Quarta, scilicet "ubi," includit locum: locus enim ostendit ubi aliquid factum sit. Quinta, scilicet "quando," includit tempus et occasionem, quoniam utrumque istorum probat quando quid fieri potuit. Sexta, scilicet "quomodo," includit modum: modus enim ostendit quomodo quid factum sit. Septima, scilicet "quibus auxiliis," continet facultatem, quia facultas ostendit quibus auxiliis quid factum sit.

37   Ita de attributis persone et negocio et quomodo ad circumstancias reducuntur ostensum est.

cause the case to stand in one fashion, and this is because all of them demonstrate who did it. Thence it is that each and every attribute of a person is in itself this circumstance "who?" and all of them together are this same circumstance. The second circumstance, namely, "what?," encompasses the gist of the action and the triple handling of the action, for these two show what has been done. The third, namely, "why?," encompasses the ratiocinative and the impulsive cause, for each of these shows why something has been done. The fourth, namely, "where?," encompasses place, for place shows where something has been done. The fifth, namely, "when?," encompasses time and occasion, since each of these proves when something could have been done. The sixth, namely, "how?," encompasses manner, for manner shows how something has been done. The seventh, namely, "with what aid?," encompasses means, because means shows with what aids something has been done.

And so we have shown what are the attributes of a person 37 and an action and how they are reduced to the circumstances.

Capitulum 13

De stilis poeticis et modernis
et eorum proprietatibus

Stilos alii "figuras," alii "caractares" appellarunt. Gravis vel altus, mediocris, humilis vel attenuatus. Gravis vel altus stilus est qui constat ex verborum gravium magna et ornata construccione. Mediocris est qui constat ex humili neque tamen ex infima et pervulgatissima verborum dignitate, id est non multum gravitati nec multum planitudini insistit. Humilis est qui dimittitur usque ad usitatissimam puri consuetudinem sermonis. Cuilibet enim stilo duplex vicium est annexum, ut statim dicetur cum de viciis ostendemus. Sequitur de aliis stilis modernorum.

2   Preter tres stilos de quibus iam dictum est, sunt alii quattuor stili modernorum, scilicet Tullianus, Gregorianus, Hillarianus, Hisidorianus. In stilo Tulliano non est attendenda diccionum cadencia set sola sentencie gravitas et verborum florida exornacio. Quo utuntur antiquiores tam prosaice quam metrice scribentes, sicut Salustius, Quintilianus,

Chapter 13

On the poetic and the modern styles and their characteristics

Some call styles "figures," others "characters." The poetic styles are the grand or high, the middle, and the low or simple. The grand or high style consists of a large and ornate arrangement of impressive words. The middle style consists of words that are of a low yet not of the lowest and most colloquial class of words, that is, it does not depend for the most part on grandeur nor for the most part on simplicity. The low style is brought down even to the most current idiom of standard speech. To each style, moreover, a double fault is linked, as will be explained presently when we expound on the faults. What follows now concerns the other styles of the moderns.

Beyond the three styles about which we have just spoken, 2 there are four other styles of the moderns, namely, the Ciceronian, the Gregorian, the Hilarian, and the Isidorian. In the Ciceronian style one should not pay attention to the rhythm of phrases but only to the weightiness of the thought and the flowery adornment of the words. The more ancient writers used this style, whether writing in prose or meter, such as Sallust, Quintilian, Seneca, Martianus,

Seneca, Marcianus, Sidonius, Virgilius, Varro, Oracius, Ovidius, Lucanus, Stacius, Claudianus et plures alii quos celsa commendat auctoritas.

3   In stilo Gregoriano consideranda est diccionum cadencia et pedum ordinacio armonica et qualitas terminacionis. Unde sciendum quod omnis diccio monasillaba dicitur semispondeus, id est dimidius spondeus, nulla discrecione facta de accentu. Similiter omnis diccio dissillaba, absque discrecione temporis, dicitur spondeus. Similiter omnis diccio polisillaba, que scilicet duas sillabas excrescit, quotquot sillabarum fuerit, cognoscitur secundum suam penultimam. Nam si illa brevis fuerit, tres ultime sillabe illius diccionis faciunt dactilum, remanentes sillabe, quecumque fuerint, binario numero designate, faciunt spondeum. Si vero penultima longa fuerit vel acuta, omnes sillabe, binario numero designate, faciunt spondeos. Unde, ut servetur melior armonia, in hoc stilo plures dactali debent rarissime commisceri; spondei vero frequenter possunt collocari. Similiter in hoc stilo plerumque considerare oportet ut ultima diccio clausule super quam fit periodus cum diccione super quam fit coma conveniat in ultima sillaba et disconveniat in penultima.

4   Colores eciam verborum frequenter in hoc stilo ponuntur set colores transumpcionis magis raro. Hoc autem stilo maxime utuntur qui attinent curie Romane. Set notandum quod iste stilus magis oblectaret auditorem si partim cum stilo Tulliano misceretur, sicut in prima epistola quam premisimus. Et hoc modo scribendi maxime usus est Alanus,

Sidonius, Virgil, Varro, Horace, Ovid, Lucan, Statius, Claudian, and many others whom lofty authority commends.

In the Gregorian style one needs to observe carefully the 3 rhythm of phrases and the harmonious arrangement of feet and the nature of the ending. Now you should know that every monosyllabic word is called a semi-spondee, that is, half of a spondee, with no distinction being made based on accent. Likewise, every bisyllabic word, without distinction of duration, is called a spondee. Likewise, every polysyllabic word, namely, one that extends beyond two syllables, however many syllables there may be, is identified by its penultimate syllable. For if that happens to be short, the last three syllables of that word make a dactyl, while the remaining syllables, of whatever sort they may be, marked out in pairs, make a spondee. If, however, the penultimate syllable happens to be long or acute, all the syllables, marked out in pairs, make spondees. And so that harmony may be better preserved, in this style only very rarely should many dactyls be mingled together; but spondees can be put alongside one another frequently. Likewise, in this style one often needs to take heed that the last word of the clause that completes a period corresponds in its final syllable with the word that completes a comma and does not correspond with that word in its penultimate syllable.

Also, the colors of words are frequently included in this 4 style, but the colors involving transumption more rarely. Those who belong to the Roman Curia employ this style most of all. But you should note that this style would delight the hearer even more if it were mixed in part with the Ciceronian style, as in the first letter that we provided earlier.

De planctu Nature: maxime enim ibi tropicis locucionibus usus est, in quibus tocius eloquencie floridior est ornatus. Inde est quod libro *Architrenii,* propter tropicarum locucionum celebrem precellenciam, nullus liber modernorum similis invenitur, quamvis Bernardus Silvestris "in prosaico" dicatur "psitacus, in metrico philomena."

5   In stilo Hillariano similiter observanda est pedum cadencia set aliter quam in stilo Gregoriano. Semper enim in hoc stilo pedes ordinandi sunt hoc ordine: primo enim precedunt duo spondei et semispondeus et postea dactalus et iterum duo spondei et dimidius et dactalus. Et sic quater ordinandum est. Et post quartum dactalum, scilicet ad punctum periodalem, subditur dispondeus, id est duplex spondeus. Est autem hic stilus, propter suam dignitatem, apud multos in usu. Cuius exemplum est hoc: "Sepe furtivis gressibus surrepit infortunium, quod ad felicem exitum opus humanum invidet pervenire."

6   In stilo Hisodoriano plerumque ordinandi sunt pedes sicut in stilo Gregoriano et plerumque non, set semper ita distinguende sunt clausule quod in fine similem habeant consonanciam et videantur pares esse in sillabis, quamvis sint dispares, sicut dictum est in exposicione coloris qui dicitur compar. Est autem stilus iste valde motivus, quo utitur Hisidorus in libro *Soliloquiorum.* Huius stili exemplum est hoc: "Pre pudore genus humanum obstupeat, de communi dampno quilibet abhorreat, admirentur servi, stupescant

And Alan of Lille, in *The Plaint of Nature,* employed this style extensively: for there he especially employed expressions that use tropes, in which the ornamentation of eloquence as a whole is most florid. For this reason no book of the moderns is found to be a match for the book of the *Architrenius,* due to the notable excellence of its expressions that use tropes, even if Bernard Silvestris may be called "a parrot in prose, a nightingale in verse."

In the Hilarian style the cadence of prosodic feet is like- 5 wise to be observed but in a different way than in the Gregorian style. For in this style the feet are always to be arranged in this order: first come two spondees and a semi-spondee and afterward a dactyl and once again two and a half spondees and a dactyl. And this sequence should be repeated four times. And after the fourth dactyl, namely, at the point of the period, a dispondee, that is, a double spondee, is inserted. On account of its excellence, this style is in use among many writers. This is an example of it: "Often, with furtive steps, up creeps misfortune, which begrudges human efforts to arrive at a happy conclusion."

In the Isidorian style the feet often should be arranged 6 just as in the Gregorian style and often not, but the clauses always should be separated in such a way that they have a similar consonance at the end and seem to be equal in syllables, even if they happen to be unequal, just as has been said in the explanation of the color that is called isocolon. This style, which Isidore uses in his book of *Soliloquies,* is very moving. This is an example of this style: "With shame let the human race be stupefied, at this communal harm let each be horrified, let bondsmen be awed, free men be slack-jawed,

liberi, dum vocantur ad cathedram elingues pueri, conformant se magistris qui vix sunt discipuli, dum causa studendi favor est populi, prius legunt quam sillabicent, prius volant quam humi cursitent."

7   Ita dictum est de stilis.

when speechless boys are called to the chair, they act like masters who scarce students are, when studying's cause is the people's applause, they lecture before they spell a sound, they fly before they run on the ground."

And so we have discussed the styles.   7

Capitulum 14

De sex viciis capitalibus in dictamine quolibet evitandis

Sex sunt vicia circa sentenciam cuiuscumque dictaminis principaliter evitanda: primum, incongrua parcium materie posicio; secundum, inutilis digressio; tercium, obscura brevitas; quartum, incompetens stilorum mutacio; quintum, prodigialis variacio; sextum, inconveniens conclusio. Hec enim sex vicia inter omnia alia in scena, id est in theatro ubi recitabantur scripta poetarum, maxime dampnabantur, ut innuunt isti versus:

> Crimina sunt sena cur spernit carmina scena:
> thematis ignara series, digressio prava
> obscurumque breve, stilus alternatus inepte—
> vult comes esse malis variacio prodigialis,
> fine sedens imo conclusio dissona primo.

2   Incongrua parcium materie posicio est quando principium, medium et finis materie non bene coherent, ut si quis materiam iocosam vel comediam scriberet, in qua partes deberent observari ad lasciviam pertinentes, et transferret

Chapter 14

On the six chief faults to be avoided in any kind of composition

Six faults that affect the meaning of any kind of composition must be avoided above all: first, improper placement of the elements of the subject matter; second, useless digression; third, obscure brevity; fourth, inept change of styles; fifth, excessive variation; sixth, a discordant conclusion. Indeed, among all others these six faults were the ones most condemned on the stage, that is, in the theater where the writings of poets were recited, as these verses affirm:

> Six offenses cause the stage to reject poetic compositions: an ignorant sequence of topics, perverse digression and obscure brevity, style shifted ineptly, (excessive variation wants to be the companion of these ills), and, sitting at the very end, a conclusion that is discordant with the beginning.

Improper placement of the elements of the subject matter is when the beginning, middle, and end of the subject matter do not form a coherent whole, as if someone were to write a mirthful piece or a comedy, in which those elements should be heeded that have to do with lightheartedness, and

se ad partes tragedie, que sunt de gravibus personis et earum proprietatibus, et sic poneret in iocosa materia partem vel partes gravis materie. Hoc vicium dampnat Oracius per similitudinem a pictore sumptam, hiis 13 versibus:

Humano capiti cervicem pictor equinam
iungere si velit, et varias inducere plumas
undique collatis membris, ut turpiter atrum
desinat in piscem mulier formosa superne,
spectatum admissi risum teneatis, amici?

Et statim reducit similitudinem ad propositum, sic:

Credite, Pisones, isti tabule fore librum
persimilem cuius, velut egri sompnia, vane
fingentur species, ut nec pes nec caput uni
reddatur forme. "Pictoribus atque poetis
quidlibet audendi semper fuit equa potestas."
Scimus, et hanc veniam petimusque damusque vicissim;
set non ut placidis coeant immicia, non ut
serpentes avibus geminentur, tigribus agni.

Littera sic est intelligenda: "si pictor velit iungere cervicem equinam humano capiti," id est capiti mulieris, hoc dico: "membris" illius picture "collatis," id est collectis, "undique," id est ex diversis animalibus. Exponit quomodo: "ut mulier formosa superne," id est in superiori parte (et est

he were to shift his attention to the elements of tragedy, which concern serious persons and their characteristics, and thus insert within a mirthful subject matter an element or elements of a weighty subject matter. Horace condemns this fault by means of a comparison taken from a painter, in these thirteen verses:

> If a painter chose to join a human head to the neck of a horse, and to spread feathers of many a hue over limbs picked up now here now there, so that what at the top is a lovely woman ends below in a black and ugly fish, could you, my friends, if favored with a private view, refrain from laughing?

And immediately he applies the comparison to the issue at hand, thus:

> Believe me, dear Pisos, quite like such pictures would be a book, whose idle fancies shall be shaped like a sick man's dreams, so that neither head nor foot can be assigned to a single shape. "Painters and poets," you say, "have always had an equal right in hazarding anything." We know it: this license we poets claim and in our turn we grant the like; but not so far that savage should mate with tame, or serpents couple with birds, lambs with tigers.

The literal text should be understood thus: "if a painter chose to join the neck of a horse to a human head," that is, to the head of a woman, I say this: "the limbs" of this picture have been "picked up," that is, assembled, "now here now there," that is, from different animals. He explains how: "so that what is a lovely woman at the top," that is, in the upper

adverbium), "desinat," id est finiat, "turpiter," id est mon-
struose, "in piscem atrum," id est turpem. Ecce quomodo
partes illius picture discoherent. Est enim caput pulcre mulieris, pedes piscium, medium corpus de diversis animalibus
colligitur. O "Pisones," "amici" (alloquitur eos gracia quorum composuit librum suum), "admissi," id est recepti,
"spectatum," id est ad spectandum talem picturam, "teneatis," id est tenere potestis, "risum," ut, scilicet, non rideatis,
quasi diceret "non." Nunc reducit istam picturam ad dictamen viciosum, cuius partes discoherent, sic: O vos "Pisones,
credite librum," id est dictamen (continens pro contento),
"fore persimilem," id est valde similem, "isti tabule," id est
picture (similiter, continens pro contento). Et ne incertum
esset de quo dictamine loqueretur, subdit "cuius species," id
est partes, scilicet principium, medium et finis, "fingentur
vane," id est discoherentes, "velut sompnia egri," scilicet
sunt vana. Egro enim videtur quandoque quod videat ymagi-
nem habentem caput equinum, corpus vitulinum, tibias hu-
manas. Et exponit quomodo partes dictaminis sunt vane,
sic: "ut nec pes," id est finis, "nec caput," id est principium,
"reddatur," id est fiat, "uni forme" (et est figura themesis).
Tunc respondet antipofore, id est tacite obieccioni contra
illa que dixit. Posset quis sic obicere: "Equa potestas semper
fuit pictoribus atque poetis audendi," id est audacter

part (and this is an adverb), "ends," that is, terminates, "in an ugly," that is, unnatural, "and a black," that is, repulsive, "fish." Notice how the elements of this picture disagree, for the head is that of a beautiful woman, the feet those of fishes, and the middle of the body is assembled from different animals. "Dear Pisos," "my friends" (he addresses those for whose sake he composed his book), "if you were favored with," that is, allowed, "a private view," that is, to look at such a picture, "could you refrain," that is, would you be able to hold back, "from laughing," that is to say, would you be able not to laugh, which is as much as to say "no." Now he brings this picture back to a faulty composition whose elements disagree, thus: O you "Pisos, believe me that a book," that is, a composition (container in place of contents), "would be quite like," that is, extremely like, "such pictures," that is, paintings (likewise, container in place of contents). And so that it is not unclear which composition he is speaking about, he adds: "whose fancies," that is, elements, namely, the beginning, middle, and end, "shall be shaped idly," that is, disagree with each other, "like a sick man's dreams," that is, they are empty of meaning, for sometimes it seems to a sick person that he sees a shape that has the head of a horse, the body of a calf, and the legs of a human. And he explains how the elements of the composition are devoid of meaning, thus: "so that neither the foot," that is, the end, "nor the head," that is, the beginning, "can be assigned," that is, belong, "to a single shape" (and this is the figure tmesis). Then he responds to the anthypophora, that is, the silent objection to what he has said. Someone could object thus: "Painters and poets have always had an equal right in hazarding," that is, in beginning boldly, "anything,"

incipiendi, "quidlibet," id est quicquid vellent. Ad hoc respondet sic: Nos "scimus, et petimus hanc veniam"—artis licenciam (venia enim, quando precessit malefactum, ponitur pro indulgencia, quando vero non precessit, ponitur pro licencia)—"et damus vicissim," id est vicario modo, hanc licenciam, "set non ut immicia coeant," id est misceantur, "placidis," propter repugnanciam. Et exponit hoc: "non ut serpentes geminentur avibus" vel "agni tigribus." Per "serpentes" humiles res vel personas intelligamus, per "aves" graves, per "tigrides" immites vel crudeles, per "agnos" mansuetos.

3 Inutilis digressio est quando digredimur vel in materia vel ad aliud extra materiam, cum tamen digredi non faciat ad commodum cause. Sunt enim quattuor cause quare facienda est digressio, ut prius dictum est. Inutiliter igitur quis digreditur quando ex nulla dictarum causarum digreditur. Et sicut diximus, talis digressio provenit ex materia supra vires ingenii gravi, quam inceptam artifex ignorat artificialiter terminare. Hoc vicium dampnat Oracius hiis versibus quos premisimus:

Inceptis gravibus plerumque et magna professis
purpureus, late etc.

4 Obscura brevitas est quando quis adeo brevitati innititur, quod ea que sunt materie sue necessaria pretermittit. Unde gravis generatur obscuritas auditori. Nos autem artificium abbreviandi materiam plenius assignavimus, ultra quod si

that is, whatever they might wish. To this he responds thus: "We know it: this license we claim"—the license of art (for pardon is granted by indulgence when a misdeed comes before, but when a misdeed does not come before, then pardon is granted by license)—"and we grant" this license "in our turn," that is, in return, "but not so far that savage should mate," that is, mingle, "with tame," because of their opposite natures. And he explains this: "or serpents couple with birds" or "lambs with tigers." By "serpents" we should understand lowly things or persons, by "birds" grand ones, by "tigers" savage or cruel ones, by "lambs" mild ones.

Useless digression is when we digress either within the subject matter or to something outside the subject matter, even though it would not benefit our case to digress. For there are four reasons why a digression should be made, as has been said earlier. Therefore, someone digresses uselessly when he digresses for none of the said reasons. And, as we said, such a digression emerges from a weighty subject matter that is beyond the powers of one's talent, a digression that, once started, the craftsman does not know how to finish skillfully. Horace condemns this fault in these verses, which we provided earlier:

> Works with noble beginnings and grand promises often have one or two purple patches so stitched on as to glitter far and wide etc.

Obscure brevity is when someone strives for brevity to such an extent that he passes over those things that are necessary to his subject matter. From this a grievous obscurity is created for the hearer. However, we have treated the technique for abbreviating the subject matter quite thoroughly;

quis materiam breviare conetur, in obscuram incidet brevitatem. Hoc vicium maxime incidimus sub specie recti, quando scilicet plures res quam oportet in materia recitamus. Istud innuit Oracius, dampnando obscuram brevitatem, sic:

> Maxima pars vatum, pater et iuvenes patre digni,
> decipimur specie recti: brevis esse laboro,
> obscurus fio etc.

5   Incompetens stilorum mutacio est quando quis non observat stili sui proprietates vel quando in uno stilo inserit alterius proprietates contra artem. Sunt enim tres stili, de quibus dictum est, et eorum cuilibet est annexum duplex vicium, unum in sentencia, aliud in verbis.

6   Humili stilo annexum est duplex vicium, scilicet aridum et exangue: aridum ex parte sentencie, exangue ex parte verborum. Aridi enim sumus quando in tantum floridis et phaleratis verbis innitimur, quod saporem et succum sentencie non habemus. Unde vicium dicitur aridum ubi sentencia non est sapida vel succosa. Exangues sumus quando sentenciam divitem et honestam verbis honestis et floridis non ornamus, set vilibus verbis et nimium communibus eius reverencie derogamus. Unde vicium exangue dicitur quia est sine sanguine, id est sine fulgido colore.

7   Alto stilo annexum est eciam duplex vicium, scilicet turgidum et inflatum: turgidum in verbis, inflatum in sentencia. Turgidi enim sumus quando vel ignotis vel dure transumptis utimur verbis, ut sic curiositatem et iactanciam

if anyone should attempt to abbreviate the subject matter beyond that, he will fall into obscure brevity. We fall into this fault mostly under the semblance of truth, namely, when we recite more things than we should in the subject matter. Horace affirms this, when condemning obscure brevity, thus:

> Most of us poets, O father and sons worthy of the father, deceive ourselves by the semblance of truth. Striving to be brief, I become obscure etc.

Inept change of styles is when someone does not heed the characteristics of his style or when he grafts onto one style the characteristics of another, in opposition to the rules of art. For there are three styles, concerning which we have spoken, and to each of them a double fault is linked, one in the thought, the other in the words. 5

A double fault is linked to the low style, namely, the dry and the bloodless: the dry with respect to thoughts, the bloodless with respect to words. For we are dry when we strive for florid and elaborate words to such an extent that we have no "flavor" and "juice" of thought. Whence the fault is called "dry" when the thought is not "tasty" or "juicy." We are bloodless when we fail to adorn rich and becoming thought with becoming and flowery words, but with words that are cheap and too common we detract from its dignity. So this fault is called "bloodless" because it is without blood, that is, without brilliant color. 6

A double fault also is linked to the high style, namely, the turgid and the inflated: the turgid in words, the inflated in thought. For we are turgid when we employ either unknown words or words that have been awkwardly transferred from 7

ostendamus. Inflati sumus quando inaniter laboramus nimium esse curiosi, quasi ab aliis intelligi dedignemur.

8   Mediocri stilo annexum est similiter duplex vicium, scilicet fluctuans et dissolutum: fluctuans in verbis, dissolutum in sentencia. Fluctuantes sumus quando in stilo mediocri vel nimium ascendimus ad verba alto stilo appropriata vel nimium descendimus ad verba stilo humili attributa, et sic nescimus mediocris stili temperiem moderari. Dissoluti sumus quando ad sentencias accomodatas gravi stilo nimium ascendimus vel humili stilo nimium declinamus. Et sic fluctuamus in verbis et in sentencia dissolvimur, dum nescimus mediocris stili temperiem moderari.

9   Et notandum quod non sic appropriantur istis tribus stilis predicta vicia quod in aliis non inveniantur. Nam vicium aridum et exangue potest incidere in omni stilo, quia in omni stilo poterimus uti vili et contemptibili levitate, tam ex parte verborum quam sentenciarum. Similiter vicium fluctuans et dissolutum potest esse in omni stilo, nam in omni stilo possumus inconvenienter inserere alterius proprietates. Similiter vicium turgidum et inflatum potest esse in omni stilo, nam in omni stilo poterimus, tam in verbis quam in sentencia, esse nimium curiosi.

10   Dicuntur tamen predicta vicia predictis stilis esse annexa, quia principaliter et frequencius in illis contingunt. Ista vicia predicta dampnat Oracius, dicens:

their proper meaning, so that in this way we can show off our overly subtle knowledge and boastfulness. We are inflated when we labor pointlessly to be too recondite, as if we cared not whether we were understood by others.

Likewise, a double fault is linked to the middle style, 8 namely, the wavering and the loose: the wavering in words, the loose in thought. We are wavering when in the middle style we either ascend too high, to words that are suited to the high style, or descend too low, to words that are fit for the low style, and thus we do not know how to regulate the moderate blend of the middle style. We are loose when we ascend too high, to thoughts that are appropriate only for the weighty style, or we sink too low, to thoughts that are appropriate only for the low style. And thus we waver in words and loosen in thought when we do not know how to regulate the moderate blend of the middle style.

And note that the above faults are not assigned to these 9 three styles in such a way that they are not found in the others. For the dry and the bloodless fault can occur in every style, because in every style we may employ cheap and contemptible levity with respect to words as much as thoughts. Likewise, the wavering and the loose fault can be present in every style, for we may graft unsuitably onto every style the proper characteristics of another. Likewise, the turgid and the inflated fault can be present in every style, for in every style we may be too recondite, in words as much as in thought.

Nevertheless, the above faults are said to be linked to the 10 above styles because they occur there chiefly and more frequently. Horace condemns these aforementioned faults, saying:

Sectantem levia nervi
deficiunt animique; professus grandia turget;
serpit humi tutus nimium timidusque procelle.

Ubi enim dicit "sectantem levia nervi deficiunt animique,"
ostendit vicium fluctuans et dissolutum; ubi dicit "professus
grandia turget," ostendit vicium turgidum et inflatum; ubi
vero dicit "serpit humi tutus nimium timidusque procelle,"
ostendit vicium aridum et exangue.

11   Prodigialis variacio quintum vicium est. Ad cuius declara-
cionem sciendum est quod variare materiam causa tollendi
fastidium et idemptitatis fugiende "laus est et maxima virtus." "Idemptitas" enim "mater est sacietatis." Ad illam igitur removendam debet materia variari quibusdam ornatibus
novitatis. Unde dicit Esopus in *Apologis,* in principio sui libri:

Ut iuvet et prosit, conatur pagina presens:
   dulcius arrident seria picta iocis.

Similiter Oracius:

Aut prodesse volunt aut delectare poete.

Et postea:

Omne tulit punctum qui miscuit utile dulci.

Istud preceptum imitatur Oracius in quadam satira,
introducendo fabulam de mure urbano et rusticano ad

> Aiming at smoothness, I fail in force and fire. One,
> promising grandeur, is bombastic; another, overcau-
> tious and fearful of the gale, creeps along the ground.

For when he says "aiming at smoothness, I fail in force and
fire," he indicates the wavering and the loose fault; when he
says "one, promising grandeur, is bombastic," he indicates
the turgid and the inflated fault; but when he says "another,
overcautious and fearful of the gale, creeps along the
ground," he indicates the dry and the bloodless fault.

Excessive variation is the fifth fault. In explanation of 11
which you should know that varying the subject matter for
the purpose of removing tedium and avoiding monotony "is
a praiseworthy thing and a very great virtue." For "monotony is the mother of boredom." Therefore, in order to remove that, the subject matter should be varied with certain
ornaments of novelty. For this reason Aesop says in the *Fables,* at the beginning of his book:

> The present page strives to give pleasure and to be use-
> ful: serious matters smile more sweetly when adorned
> with jests.

Likewise Horace:

> Poets aim either to benefit, or to amuse.

And later:

> He has won every vote who has blended profit and
> pleasure.

Horace follows this precept in one of his satires, by insert-
ing the tale of the city mouse and the country mouse in

397

comparacionem vite urbane et vite ruralis. In gravi materia introducenda sunt gravia, sicut facit Lucanus, ubi narrat luctam Herculis et Anthei gigantis. Unde incidit quis in variacionem prodigialem quando introducit gravem materiam in iocoso tractatu vel iocosam in gravi. Et sic in uno et eodem opere contrarius quasi sibimet inveniatur.

12   Set notandum diligenter quod ubi fit mutacio realis eventus, non erit prodigialis variacio ex illa causa, ut per Oracium patet. Verbi gracia, Thelephus rex Mesorum pugnavit cum Achille redeunte per regnum suum a bello Troiano, et ab Achille graviter vulneratus, responsum accepit a diis quod non sanaretur nisi prius eadem manus et eadem lancea Achillis in vulnus suum reverteretur. Regalibus itaque vestibus exutus, sub vili veste in modum pauperis processit ad genua Achillis, ubi fusis precibus votum optinuit. Unde qui prius descripsit eum regem potentissimum, quando venit ad illum locum supplicandi, per mutacionem realis eventus, ex necessitate stilum mutavit et verbis dolentibus ipsius supplicacionem expressit, utens tenore humilis stili. Similiter Peleus pater Achillis, interfecto a se fratre suo, factus exul, regem suplex adiit et ut ab eo hospitaretur in regno suo suppliciter impetravit. Hic eciam realis eventus fuit causa mutacionis stili. Istud innuit Oracius, dicens:

order to compare urban life and rural life. In a serious subject matter serious things should be inserted, as Lucan does
when he recounts the wrestling match of Hercules and the
giant Antaeus. For this reason one falls into excessive variation when one inserts serious subject matter into a humorous treatment or humorous subject matter into a serious
treatment. And in this way, in one and the same work, the
writer would come across as self-contradictory.

But you should be careful to note that when there is a 12
change due to an actual event, variation that results from
that cause will not be excessive, as is clear from Horace. For
example, Telephus, the king of the Mysians, fought with
Achilles, who was returning from the Trojan War through
his kingdom, and, after he had been seriously wounded by
Achilles, he received a reply from the gods that he would
not be healed unless the very hand and the very spear of
Achilles should first be applied to his wound. Thus, having
taken off his royal garments, poorly dressed in the manner
of a pauper, he approached the knees of Achilles, where with
ample prayers he obtained his wish. So he who at first described Telephus as a most powerful king, upon coming to
the place in the narrative where he is pleading, because
there has been a change due to an actual event, of necessity
changed his style and expressed his plea in sorrowful words,
employing the register of the low style. Likewise, Peleus, the
father of Achilles, made an exile after having killed his
brother, came to a king as a suppliant and pleadingly obtained his request that he be treated as a guest by him in his
kingdom. Here, too, an actual event was the cause of a
change of style. Horace affirms this, saying:

Thelephus et Peleus, cum pauper et exul uterque
proicit ampullas et sesquipedalia verba.

13   Quintum vicium, scilicet prodigialem variacionem, ostendit Oracius hiis versibus:

Qui variare cupit rem prodigialiter unam,
delphinum silvis appingit, fluctibus aprum.
In vicium ducit culpe fuga, si caret arte.

Bene dicit Oracius "delphinum silvis appingit etc.," quasi
diceret: proprietates aquarum attribuit silvis et econtrario.

14   Inconveniens conclusio est quando quis materiam inceptam aut ex negligencia aut ex ignorancia debite non consum-
mat. Quomodo autem sumenda sit conclusio protinus
ostendemus. Hoc vicium dampnat Oracius per similitudinem a fusore inductam. Quidam fusor, nomine Imus, cum
funderet statuam Emilii gigantis, eo modo quo se habuit
dum ludere solebat, ungues et capillos et cetera usque ad
pedes satis artificialiter expressit, set in pedibus formandis
turpiter deliravit. Unde Oracius dicit quod, quia opus suum
nescivit artificialiter terminare, non magis vellet similis esse
illi in componendis poematibus quam habere pulcrum caput
et nigros oculos et decentes set nasum recurvum et defor-
mem, quasi diceret: adeo michi placeret quod faceret vicium
in principio sicut in fine. Istud vicium dampnat Oracius hiis
sex versibus:

Telephus and Peleus, when, in poverty and exile, either hero throws aside his bombast and foot-and-a-half-long words.

Horace indicates the fifth fault, namely, excessive varia- 13 tion, in these verses:

The man who tries to vary a single subject in monstrous fashion, is like a painter adding a dolphin to the woods, a boar to the waves. Shunning a fault may lead to error, if there be lack of art.

Horace aptly says "adding a dolphin to the woods etc.," as if he were to say: he assigns the proper characteristics of the waters to the woods and vice versa.

A discordant conclusion is when someone, either through 14 neglect or ignorance, does not properly end the subject matter he has begun. However, we will show straightaway how a conclusion should be composed. Horace condemns this fault by means of a comparison drawn from a sculptor. A certain sculptor, Imus by name, when he was casting a statue of the giant Aemilius posed as though he were at play, represented the nails and the hair and the rest up to the feet skillfully enough, but he went completely wrong by shaping the feet in a repulsive manner. For this reason Horace says that, because this man did not know how to finish his work skillfully, he would no more wish to be like him in composing his own poems than to have a beautiful head and attractive black eyes but a bent and misshapen nose, as if he were to say: it would please me just as much that he committed a fault at the beginning as at the end. Horace condemns this fault in these six verses:

Emilium circa ludum faber imus et ungues
exprimet et molles imitabitur ere capillos,
infelix operis summa, quia ponere totum
nesciet. Hunc ego me, si quid componere curem,
non magis esse velim quam naso vivere pravo,
spectandum nigris oculis nigrisque capillis.

15   Ita dictum sit de viciis.

Near the Aemilian school, at the bottom of the row, there is a craftsman who in bronze will mold nails and imitate waving locks, but is unhappy in the total result, because he cannot represent a whole figure. Now if I wanted to write something, I should no more wish to be like him, than to live with my nose turned askew, though admired for my black eyes and black hair.

And so we have discussed the faults.   15

Capitulum 15

De generibus sermonum et
varietatibus carminum

Sermonum tria sunt genera, que Greca appellacione vocantur: primum dragmaticum, secundum eremeneticum vel distinctum, tercium didascalicum. Dragmaticum est ubi auctor operis nichil loquitur set tantum persona introducta, ut in libris Terencii. Eremeneticum vel distinctum est ubi auctor totum loquitur, ut in *Georgicis* Virgilii. Didascalicum, id est doctrinale, ubi tam auctor quam persona introducta loquitur, persona querens et auctor respondens, ut in Boecio, *De consolacione* et in *Dialogis* Gregorii. Sub secundo genere cadit narracio, que seccionem recipit a Tullio, sic: Est enim quoddam genus narracionis alienum et remotum a causis civilibus et illud duplex est: unum quod in negociis positum est, aliud quod in personis. Quod positum est in negociis tres habet partes: fabulam, historiam et argumentum.

2   Fabula est que nec est vera, nec verisimilia continet, ut in Ovidii *Methamorphoseos* et in quolibet apologo. Unde si contingat narracionem esse fabulosam, debemus probabiliter

Chapter 15

On the kinds of discourses and the varieties of poetic compositions

There are three kinds of discourses, which are called by Greek names: the first is the dramatic, the second the hermeneutic or distinct, the third the didactic. The dramatic is when the author of the work says nothing but only a character who has been represented, as in the books of Terence. The hermeneutic or distinct is where the author says everything, as in the *Georgics* of Virgil. The didactic, that is, the one concerned with teaching, is when the author speaks as well as a character who has been represented, the character inquiring and the author responding, as in Boethius's *Consolation* and in the *Dialogues* of Gregory. Under the second kind falls narrative, which gets a paragraph from Cicero, as follows. For there is a certain type of narration that is separate from and not used in causes actually pleaded in court, and that type is twofold: one kind that is based on actions, the other on persons. The one that is based on actions has three subdivisions: fable, history, and argument.

Fable is that which neither is true nor contains likely events, as in the *Metamorphoses* of Ovid and in any kind of fabulous tale. So if a narrative should happen to be fabulous, 2

mentiri, ut scilicet narracio falsa narretur ut esset vera. Istud optime facit Ovidius, *Methamorphoseos,* loquens de reparacione hominis post diluvium. Fingit enim ibi lapides quos iecit Deucalion in viros mutari et quos Pirra uxor Deucalionis iecit mutari in feminas. Et quia aliqua pars lapidum succosa fuit et humida, finxit humorem lapidis in sanguinem mutari. Et "vena" lapidis "sub eodem nomine mansit."

Quod solidum est flectique nequit mutatur in ossa.

Istud docet Oracius, dicens:

Ficta voluptatis causa sint proxima veris.

3   Apologus est sermo sumptus de brutis animalibus ad instruccionem humane vite, ut patet in Esopo et Aviano, et interpretatur "sermo de longe sumptus." Longe enim sumitur sermo ille qui de brutis ducitur ad homines.

4   Historia est res gesta, ab etatis nostre memoria remota. Et dicitur ab "histeron" Grece, quod est "videre," siquidem apud veteres nemo historias scripserat nisi is qui intererat et scribenda viderat. Historie tres sunt partes: ephimeris, annalis et kalendaria. Epimeris vel diarium interpretatur "unius diei gestio." Mos enim veterum erat omnia ut acciderant pro meliori memoria singulis diebus scribere. Kalendaria est historia continens omnia gesta unius mensis, annalis

we ought to lie plausibly, that is, so that the false narrative is related as if it were true. Ovid does this exceptionally well in the *Metamorphoses,* when he speaks about the restoring of mankind after the flood. For there he pretends that the stones that Deucalion cast were changed into men and those that Deucalion's wife Pyrrha cast were changed into women. And because some portion of the stones was moist and damp, he pretended that the moisture of the stone was changed into blood. And "the veins" of the stone "remained under the same name."

But what was solid and incapable of bending became bone.

Horace makes the same point, saying:

Fictions meant to please should be close to the real.

The type of fable called *apologus* is a dialogue between 3 brutish animals whose purpose is teaching about human life, as exemplified by Aesop and Avianus. And *apologus* can be translated "speech taken from afar." For speech that is directed from brutes to men is taken from far away.

History is an account of exploits actually performed, but 4 far removed from recent memory. And it is derived from the Greek "histeron," which is "to see," inasmuch as among the ancients no one wrote histories except one who had been present and saw the things to be written about. There are three subdivisions of history: ephemera, annal, and calendar. Ephemera or diary is translated "the doings of a single day." For it was the custom of the ancients each day to write down everything as it happened, for the sake of better remembrance. A calendar is a history comprising all the deeds

que continet quid singulis eveniat annis. Et nota quod omnis historia "cronica" potest appellari a "cronos," quod est "tempus," quia singulorum temporum gesta declarat.

5   Sub historia multa sunt carmina, ut epithalamicum, id est carmen nupciale quale cecinerunt antiqui in honorem sponsi et sponse. Epichedium, id est nudum sine sepultura, quod fit de viventibus insepultis. Epithafium, id est carmen suprascriptum tumulis mortuorum. Apothesis, id est carmen de leticia deificacionis vel glorificacionis. Heroicum, id est carmen quod texitur de gestis heroum, id est virorum forcium, et hoc carmen maxime convenit versibus exametris. Elegiacum, id est carmen de miseria vel dolore, et convenit maxime versibus exametris et pentametris. Amabeum, quod proprietates amancium representat. Bucolicum, id est pastorale, quod ostendit de cultura boum et boum custodibus. Georgicum, quod agit de agricultura. Liricum, quod agit de communitate deorum et amore. Epodon, id est clausulare, quod agit de certamine equestri. Seculare vel hympnus, quod fit de laude deorum. Invectivum, quod agit de conviciis et verbis mordaciter reprehensivis. Satira, in quo reprehenditur vicium et inseritur virtus, cuius proprietates hiis versibus continentur:

Indignans satira deridet, nudat aperta,
voce salit, viciis fetet, agreste sapit.

Tres enim satirici inveniuntur: Oracius, Persius et Iuvenalis.

of a single month, an annal one that comprises what happens in individual years. And note that every history can be called a "chronicle" from "chronos," which is "time," because it makes known the deeds of particular times.

Under the heading of history fall many poetic compositions, such as the epithalamion, that is, the kind of marriage song that the ancients sang in honor of the bride and groom. The epicedion, that is, a plain song without a burial, which is made about the living who are unburied. The epitaph, that is, a song inscribed upon the tombs of the dead. The apotheosis, that is, a song about the joy of deification or glorification. The heroic, that is, a song that is composed about the deeds of heroes, that is, of strong men; and this type of song is most suited to hexameter verses. The elegy, that is, a song about affliction or sorrow; and it is most suited to hexameter and pentameter verses. The amabeic, which portrays the characteristics of lovers. The bucolic, that is, the pastoral, which depicts cattle tending and cowherds. The georgic, which deals with agriculture. The lyric, which deals with the company of the gods and with love. The epode, that is, the clausular, which deals with equestrian competition. The secular song or hymn, which is made in praise of the gods. The invective, which deals with reproofs and words that are sharply critical. Satire, in which vice is criticized and virtue is instilled, whose characteristics are comprised in these verses:

Indignant, satire laughs in scorn; it strips things bare;
it jumps in tone, it stinks with vices, it savors of the
rustic.

Three satirists are to be found: Horace, Persius, and Juvenal.

Tragedia carmen est in quo agitur de contemptu fortune, ostendens infortunia gravium personarum, et incipit a gaudio et finit in luctu. Et dicitur a "tragos," "hircus," quia antiquitus tragedo hircus dabatur in premium, ad fetorem materie designandum. Unde Oracius:

Carmine qui tragico vilem certavit ob hircum.

6   Argumentum tercium genus est, et est res ficta, non vera set verisimilis, ut in eglogis et comediis. Egloga est sermo contextus de gestis vilium personarum et interpretatur "sermo fetidus" vel "caprinus." Et est triplex: quedam enim fit in amaris reprehensionibus et sic est pars satire et tali utitur Oracius; quedam in colloquio vilium personarum, ut in *Bucolicis;* alia in colloquio honeste persone contra vilem, ut in *Theodolo,* ubi Pseustis, per quem intelligitur "falsitas," disputat contra Alathiam, per quam "veritas" denotatur. Comedia, large loquendo, est quodlibet carmen iocosum; proprie tamen et stricte loquendo, est cantus villanus de humilibus personis contextus, incipiens a tristicia et terminans in gaudio. Talis enim comedia quinque actus requirit, nec plures nec pauciores. Unde Oracius:

Neve minor neu sit quinto produccior actu
fabula, que posci vult et spectata reponi.

Talis autem comedia secessit ab usu nostro. Qui igitur

Tragedy is a song in which the contempt of fortune is treated, showing the misfortunes of important persons, and it begins in joy and ends in grief. And it is named from "tragos," "goat," because in ancient times a tragedian was given a goat as a prize, by way of signifying the unsavory nature of its subject matter. So Horace:

> The poet who in tragic song first competed for a paltry goat.

Argument is the third kind, and it is an invented matter, 6 not true but like the truth, as in eclogues and comedies. An eclogue is a speech composed of the deeds of lowborn persons, and it is translated as "stinky" or "goatish speech." And it is threefold: for one kind takes the form of bitter rebukes and thus is a subdivision of satire, and Horace employs that sort; one kind takes the form of a dialogue of lowborn persons, as in the *Bucolics;* and another takes the form of a dialogue of a decent person in opposition to a lowborn one, as in the *Theodolus,* where Pseustis, who represents "falsehood," debates against Alathia, by whom "truth" is designated. Comedy, broadly speaking, is any humorous song whatsoever, but, more properly and narrowly speaking, is a rustic song composed about lowly persons, beginning from sadness and ending in joy. Such a comedy requires five acts, neither more nor fewer. For this reason Horace says:

> Let no play be either shorter or longer than five acts, if when once seen it hopes to be called for and brought back to the stage.

This sort of comedy, however, has faded from our use. Therefore, whoever wishes to know the characteristics of

proprietates comedie scire voluerit, consulat *Poetriam* Oracii pro artificio et Terencium pro practica.

7   Set nos de iocosa materia qualiter tractanda sit doceamus. Si iocosam materiam pre manibus habeamus, per totum corpus materie utamur verbis et levibus et communibus et ad ipsas res vel personas de quibus est sermo proprie pertinentibus. Talia enim verba poscit talis materia, qualia sunt inter colloquentes et non alia nec magis difficilia. Oportet enim in omni dictamine sermones esse cognatos rebus de quibus est loquendum. Amplius, cum pervenerimus ad illum punctum materie ubi iocus reponitur, id est ad finem, quanto expressius poterimus sequamur unum idyoma per aliud, ut scilicet ita sedeat iocus in uno idiomate sicut et in alio. Huius doctrine exemplum habemus in "Libro versuum," ubi dicitur:

Tres sumus expense socii pueroque caremus etc.

Utendum est eciam in locis convenientibus ad iocum excitandum duobus coloribus, scilicet prescisione et occupacione, de quibus dictum est. Occupacione, sic: "Iste archidiabolus—archidiaconus dixissem"; "Isti iuris perditi—iuris periti dixissem"; "Iste qui legit indiscretis—in decretis dixissem." Prescisione, sic:

"Vade." "Mavisne vocem?" "Que michi cura? Voca."

comedy should consult the *Poetics* of Horace for the rules of the art and Terence for the practice.

But let us teach how humorous subject matter ought to 7 be treated. If we have a humorous subject matter to hand, let us employ throughout the body of the subject matter words that are both lighthearted and colloquial and that properly pertain to the things or persons this discourse is about. For such a subject matter demands such words as are current among those who are speaking to one another and not other words or more difficult ones. For in every composition the speech needs to be related to the things that are being spoken about. What is more, when we have arrived at that point in the material where the jest is placed, that is, at the end, let us follow one turn of phrase by means of another as clearly as we can, namely, in such a way that the jest sits in the one turn of phrase just as it does in the other. We have an example of this teaching in the "Book of Verses," where it says:

Three of us are sharing expenses and we have no servant etc.

Also, in topics designed to arouse mirth one should employ two colors, namely, aposiopesis and paralipsis, which already have been discussed. Paralipsis, thus: "This archdemon—I meant to say archdeacon"; "These law perverters—I meant to say law professors"; "This one who reads indiscreetly—I meant to say in decretals." Aposiopesis, thus:

"Go!" "Do you want me to call?" "What do I care? Call!"

Sunt eciam isti colores necessarii plerumque in materia indignacionis, sicut in primo *Eneidis,* ubi introducitur Neptu-
nus, id est deus maris, iratus et indignans, increpando ventos
quia sine licencia sua turbaverunt mare. Unde ita scribitur
ibidem:

Quos ego . . . !

(subintellige "puniam")

Set prestat motos impellere fluctus.

8   Ita dictum sit de iocosa materia.

These colors are often particularly indispensable in subject matter expressing indignation, as in the first book of the *Aeneid,* where Neptune, that is, the god of the sea, is introduced, angered and indignant, reproaching the winds because they have stirred up the sea without his permission. So, in that passage is written:

Whom I . . . !

(understand as unexpressed: "will punish")

But better is it to constrain the troubled waves.

And so we have discussed humorous subject matter. 8

Capitulum 16

De conclusione et quomodo sit sumenda

Conclusio est artificialis terminus oracionis vel aliter, conclusio est tenorem dictaminis complectens legitima terminacio. Tripliciter autem sumi potest conclusio, scilicet vel a corpore materie vel a proverbio vel ab exemplo.

2   A corpore materie, ut in Ovidio, *Epistolarum,* ubi singule epistole suam habent materiam. In prima siquidem epistola, quam mittit Penalope Ulixi propter longam moram quam ipse fecerat, quia per decem annos absens ab ea fuerat, finis epistole sumitur a corpore materie, sic:

> Ipsa ego, que quondam te discedente puella,
> protinus ut venias, facta videbor anus.

Similiter et in epistola quam scribit Phillis Demophonti, conquerens de fide lesa qua ipsam decepit, propter quod se

Chapter 16

On the conclusion and
how it should be fashioned

The conclusion is the end of the discourse, formed in accordance with the principles of the art or, alternatively, a conclusion is an appropriate ending of a composition that completes its overall design. A conclusion can be fashioned in three ways, namely, from the body of the subject matter or from a proverb or from an exemplum.

From the body of the subject matter, as in Ovid's *Epistles,*   2 where individual epistles each have their own subject matter. Accordingly, in the first epistle, which Penelope sends to Ulysses on account of his long delay, because he had been away from her for ten years, the end of the epistle is derived from the body of the subject matter, thus:

> As for myself, who once, when you left my side, was but a girl, though you should come straightaway, I surely shall seem grown an aged dame.

Likewise also in the letter that Phyllis writes to Demophon, complaining of the broken faith by which he deceived her,

ipsam interfecit, finis epistole sumitur a corpore materie, sic:

> Inscribere meo causa invidiosa sepulcro.
>   Aut hoc aut alio carmine notus eris:
> "Phillida Demophon leto dedit hospes amantem;
>   ille necis causam prebuit, illa necem."

Similiter et in materia de descripcione Troie, finis sumitur a corpore materie sub hac forma:

> Urbs abit in cineres, urbis cinis ultimus heres;
> qua steterant proceres militat arce ceres.

3   A proverbio sumitur finis quando, tota materia decursa, elicimus quandam sentenciam communem que pendet et sequitur ex premissis. Unde post predictos versus possumus hanc elicere sentenciam communem:

> Tolle bonas leges, licet ornat purpura reges, . . .

Quod idem est ac si diceretur: "Regni stabilitas a statu suo de facili subtrahitur nisi freno bonarum consuetudinum excessus hominum reprimatur." Quod satis manifestum est in predicta materia de Troia, quia si excessus Paridis repressus fuisset et ipse coactus ad restitucionem uxoris aliene, Grecia nequaquam machinata fuisset in destruccionem Troie.

4   Tercio modo sumitur conclusio ab exemplo quando ali-

on account of which she killed herself, the end of the letter is derived from the body of the subject matter, thus:

> On my tomb shall you be inscribed the hateful cause of my death. By this, or by some other verse, shall you be known: "Demophon—her guest—killed Phyllis, who loved him. He supplied her death's cause, she the death itself."

Likewise also in a subject matter concerning the description of Troy, the end is derived from the body of the subject matter in this form:

> The city is reduced to ashes, ash is the city's last heir; on the citadel where its leaders had stood, now only grain stands guard.

The end is fashioned from a proverb when, having traversed the entire subject matter, we draw forth some general maxim that hangs on and follows from what has gone before. Thus, after the verses above, we can extract this general maxim: 3

> Dispense with good laws, and though purple may adorn your kings, . . .

This is the same as if one were to say: "A kingdom's stability is easily removed from its place unless the transgressions of men are held in check by the rein of good customs." This is clear enough in the previous subject matter concerning Troy, because, if the transgression of Paris had been held in check and he had been compelled to restore the wife of another, Greece never would have plotted the destruction of Troy.

In a third way, a conclusion is fashioned from an exem- 4

quid in fine materie dicturi, non illud dicimus sed ex eo quoddam simile inducimus ex quo intelligimus illud quod intendimus, ut in fine *Poetrie* Oracii:

> Quem semel arripuit, tenet occiditque legendo,
> non missura cutem nisi plena cruoris hirudo.

Similiter et in *Epistolis* Oracii:

> Lusisti satis, edisti satis atque bibisti:
> tempus abire tibi, ne potum longius equo
> rideat et pulset lasciva decentius etas.

5   Fit eciam quandoque conclusio per licenciam, ut in *Bucolicis:*

> Ite domum sature, venit Hesperus, ite capelle.

Et Alanus:

> O michi continuo multum sudata labore
> pagina, cuius adhuc minuit detraccio famam etc.

Similiter et *Architrenius:*

> O longum studii gremio nutrita, togati etc.

6   Fit eciam conclusio per venie peticionem. Ovidius:

> Emendaturus, si licuisset, eram.

plum when we are about to say something at the end of the subject matter and we do not say that thing, but we adduce something similar to it, from which we understand the thing that we have in mind, as at the end of Horace's *Poetics:*

> If he once catches a man, he holds him fast and reads him to death—a leech that will not let go the skin, till gorged with blood.

Likewise also in the *Epistles* of Horace:

> You have played enough, have eaten and drunk enough. It is time to quit the feast, lest, when you have drunk too long, youth mock and jostle you, playing the wanton with better grace.

Also, a conclusion sometimes is made by granting per- 5 mission, as in the *Bucolics:*

> Go home, my full-fed goats—the Evening star comes, go home!

And Alan of Lille:

> O my book, born of ceaseless and exhausting toil, though even now detraction diminishes your fame etc.

Likewise also the *Architrenius:*

> O nursed so long at the breast of study, clothed etc.

A conclusion also can be made through a plea for indul- 6 gence. Ovid:

> I would have made corrections, had it been permitted me.

7   In epistolis autem plerumque fit conclusio per has dicciones: ut, ne, quia, prout et huiusmodi. Set semper com-
mendabilior conclusio in epistolis sumitur vel a proverbio
vel ab exemplo, ut habetur in secunda epistola superius posita, cuius finis est "Vere generose menti sufficit potencia
vindicandi."

8   Ita dictum sit de conclusione.

9   In hoc igitur libro continetur fere quicquid utilitatis habet Oracius in *Poetria*. Et habet capitula 16 que sequuntur
etc.

Primum capitulum est de principio naturali et artificiali
et de octo modis principii artificialis.

Secundum de prosecucione materie et quibus terminis
precedencia subsequentibus copulentur.

Tercium de octo modis prolongandi materiam et eam inveniendi et de artificio epistolas componendi.

Quartum de septem modis abbreviandi materiam et de
consideracione materie quibus ornatibus vestiatur.

Quintum de decem speciebus transumpcionis quibus ornata difficultas efficitur et scripturarum gravitas aperitur.

Sextum de hiis in quibus omnis ornatus attenditur et in
quibus diccionibus melior sit ornatus.

Septimum de ornata facilitate et de determinacione, que
est potissimum elocucionis condimentum, et de coloribus
verborum et sentenciarum.

In letters, however, the conclusion often is made by means ₇ of these words: so that, lest, because, just as, and the like. But always more praiseworthy is the conclusion in letters that is fashioned either from a proverb or an exemplum, as is the case in the second letter provided above, whose end is "To a mind truly noble the power of punishing suffices."

And so we have discussed the conclusion. ₈

In this book is contained virtually everything useful that ₉ Horace provides in his *Poetics*. And it contains the sixteen chapters that follow.

The first chapter is about the natural beginning and the artificial type and about the eight methods for artificial beginnings.

The second is about the development of the subject matter and the expressions with which what comes before is joined to what follows.

The third is about the eight ways of extending the subject matter and generating it and about the technique of composing letters.

The fourth is about the seven ways of shortening the subject matter and about considering with which ornaments the subject matter should be adorned.

The fifth is about the ten kinds of transumption by means of which ornamented difficulty is produced and the weightiness of writings is disclosed.

The sixth is about the things with which all ornament is concerned and in which words the best ornament consists.

The seventh is about ornamented facility and about determination, which is the principal seasoning of style, and about the colors of words and thoughts.

Octavum de officio omnium colorum et quomodo figure coloribus reducuntur.

Nonum de arte inveniendi ornata verba quibus omnis ruditas quibusdam novitatis flosculis exornetur.

Decimum de execucione materie illibate.

Undecimum de execucione materie communis.

Duodecimum de attributis persone et negocio, quorum artificio proprietates materie comparantur.

Terciumdecimum de stilis poeticis et modernis et eorum proprietatibus.

Quartumdecimum de sex viciis capitalibus in dictamine quolibet evitandis.

Quintumdecimum de generibus sermonum et varietatibus carminum.

Sextumdecimum et ultimum de conclusione et quomodo sit sumenda.

10   Explicit.

11   Hoc opus exegi. Sit celi gracia regi. Amen.

The eighth is about the function of all the colors and how the figures are related to the colors.

The ninth is about the art of generating ornamented words by means of which every uncouthness may be beautified with certain flowerlets of novelty.

The tenth is about developing original subject matter.

The eleventh is about developing common subject matter.

The twelfth is about the attributes of a person and an action, by means of which characteristics are fitted to the subject matter.

The thirteenth is about the poetic and the modern styles and their characteristics.

The fourteenth is about the six chief faults to be avoided in any kind of composition.

The fifteenth is about the kinds of discourses and the varieties of poetic compositions.

The sixteenth and last is about the conclusion and how it should be fashioned.

It ends. 10

I have completed this work. Thanks be to the King of 11 Heaven. Amen.

Note on the Text

The edition is based on a collation of all known manuscript witnesses: twelve complete copies of *Tria sunt (ABCpCsD FLNObOlOsW)*; a once-complete copy that has lost an entire gathering and a single leaf *(Ct)*; an incomplete copy that breaks off near the end of chapter 3 *(Od)*; and a one-leaf fragment that contains all of chapter 8 and parts of 7 and 9 *(Or)*. Most of these manuscripts are written in English hands characteristic of the first half of the fifteenth century. The latest copy *(A)*, from the mid-fifteenth century, is also the only one made outside England (Italy).

Widespread contamination, often visible in the surviving witnesses, has obscured the lines of filiation to the point where a reliable recension is not possible. Therefore, the manuscript copy that most consistently represents the consensus of the other witnesses has been chosen as base text *(W)*, and whenever possible that consensus has been used to correct faulty readings, restore text omitted due to eye skip, and eliminate occasional idiosyncrasies in the base text. Emendations generally are made when the other witnesses offer a reading that is clearly superior, especially when additional support is provided by a source that is being quoted or paraphrased. In a few cases where errors ap-

parently were introduced very early in the tradition, readings that are supported by the sources but not by any of the
surviving witnesses have been adopted. Where corrupt
readings of this sort have been allowed to stand, the variant
readings from all the witnesses and the reading of the source
are recorded in the Notes to the Text, and a comment on the
corruption is provided in the Notes to the Translation.

All emendations of the base text are recorded in the
Notes to the Text, along with the variant readings from the
other witnesses. When the emendation restores text omitted in *W* but present in all or nearly all other witnesses,
however, the notes record only witnesses that share precisely the same omission. The same procedure is followed
for corrections of readings that are unique to *W* or shared
by no more than three other witnesses.

Variant readings that merely indicate manuscript affini-
ties and are not cited to support emendation of the base
text generally are not recorded. In a very few cases, where
there are grounds for questioning whether an acceptable
reading that *W* shares with some of the other witnesses is
the original one (e.g., where an equally valid reading that is
attested by many witnesses is also that of the source), the
variant readings are provided in the notes, but the reading
of *W* is allowed to stand in the edited text.

At least two hands, one of them possibly that of the original scribe, have made corrections in *W.* These have not been
recorded in the notes when the correction either restores
what clearly is the best reading or when it introduces what
obviously is an inferior or erroneous reading. An example of
the latter occurs in 3.27, line 20 of the long quotation from

Alan of Lille: Ulmi *ABCpCsDFLNOdOl(Alan)*: Olim *Os*; Ul-
nis (*corrected from* ulmi?) *W.*

The scribe of the base text typically uses *v* in initial position and *u* everywhere else, whether the sound in question is
a consonant or a vowel; but in this edition *v* is used only to
represent consonants and *u* to represent vowels. Otherwise,
the orthography of *W* has been changed only when it is
likely to cause confusion, as in the case of certain proper
names and unusual terms. All such changes are recorded in
the Notes to the Text.

Like the scribes of the other witnesses, the scribe of *W*
employs some typically medieval spelling practices that de-
viate from classical norms. He consistently uses *e* in place of
classical *ae* and *oe,* for example. Since he would have pronounced *c* before *i* or *e* as a sibilant rather than a stop, he oc-
casionally uses *c* where the classical spelling would be *s* (7.21:
censato = sensato) and vice versa (9.6: *resiprocacio = reciproca-
tio*), and similar variation occurs with the spelling *sc* (3.26:
sintillant = scintillant; 7.63: *prescisio = praecisio*; 12.19: *ceptrum
= sceptrum*). For the same reason, *c* occurs regularly in place
of *t* before *i.* In certain words, the placement of *h* is always
different from the classical spelling (*rethorica = rhetorica*);
elsewhere an *h* may be added (3.2: *rethe = rete*) or omitted
(3.26: pulcra = pulchra). Among the other types of ortho-
graphic variation encountered are double letters where the
classical spelling has only one (9.15: *dupplici = duplici*) and
vice versa (12.30: *oportunitatem = opportunitatem*), and the in-
sertion of letters not found in the classical spelling, often to
facilitate pronunciation (9.14: *solempnius = solemnius*). The
facing English translation will help to resolve any confusion

the reader may experience as a result of these and other common medieval spellings in the Latin text.

A = Bologna, Biblioteca comunale dell'Archiginnasio A.163, fols. 75r–125v

B = Berlin, Staatsbibliothek, Stiftung preussischer Kulturbesitz, Lat. qu. 515, fols. 69r–132v

Cp = Cambridge, Pembroke College 287, fols. 105ra–64vb

Cs = Cambridge, Sidney Sussex College 56, pp. 1–148

Ct = Cambridge, Trinity College R.14.22, fols. 49r–91r

D = Douai, Bibliothèque municipale 764, fols. 1r–108r

F = Ferrara, Biblioteca comunale Ariostea, Classe II.206, fols. 94r–180r

L = London, BL, Cotton Cleopatra B.vi, fols. 33r–87v

N = Chicago, Newberry Library 55, fols. 1r–90v

Ob = Oxford, Balliol College 263, fols. 7vb–32rb

Od = Oxford, Bodleian Library, Douce 147, fols. 76ra–84va

Ol = Oxford, Bodleian Library, Laud misc. 707, fols. 36r–85r

Or = Oxford, Bodleian Library, Rawlinson D.893, fol. 55r–v

Os = Oxford, Bodleian Library, Selden Supra 65, fols. 1r–72v

W = Worcester Cathedral, Chapter Library Q.79, fols. 81r–158v (base text)

ed. = editor

om. = omitted

Notes to the Text

Chapter 1

1   inde: *om. FOlOsW*

2   Nisi de crine *ACpCsCtDOdOlOs(Geoffrey)*: Nisi nisi de crine *BF LObW*

     patris: *om. OlW*

Chapter 2

4   dolus *ACtDOl*: dolor *BCpCsFLNObOdOsW*

13   inventur per hanc primam partem: invenitur per hanc primam partem invenitur *FW*

Chapter 3

1   prolonga *ABCpCsCtDFLObOdOs*: prolongant *OlW*; prolongat *(corrected from* prolonga*) N*

4   cathenans: cathenas *FOlW*

5   umbram brume ... Proscribit: *om. CtOlW*

12   Thetis *ABCsCtFLNOdOl*: Tethis *CpDObOsW*

15   truculenta *ACsFNObOdOlOs*: triculenta *BCpLW*

16   quoque *D*: sic *A*; quo *BCpCsCtFLNObOsW*; quomodo? *Ol*

18   placet *(Marbod)*: scelus *ABCpCsCtFLNObOdOlOsW*; scillus *D*

     Volucrum *ALOd*: *om. BCpCsCtDFNObOlOsW*

20   in materia ... digredimur: *om. OlW*

21   venanti *ABCpCsLN*: venantis *CtD*; venenant *FOs*; venantur *Od*; venenat *OlW*

     serta *ACs(Geoffrey)*: certa *BCpCtDFLNObOdOlOsW*

431

22   primo . . . veris: *om. OlW*

23   lugerent: lugerunt *OlOsW*

      trutam *ACsLOd*: turtram *BCpCtDFNOlW*; turram *Ob*; tontan?
      Os; tructam *(Horace)*

24   meruere tue: merure tue *DW*

25   id est *BCpCsCtDFLNObOd*: et *AOlW*; in *Os*

      Huius *ABCpCsCtFLNOdOs*: Et huius *D*; Huiusmodi *Ob*; Hoc
      OlW

      deferat *ABCpCsCtFLNObOdOs*: differat *D*; deferret *OlW*

      quod *ABCpCtDFNOb*: *om. CsLOdOlOsW*

26   persone dicenda *CsDOb*: persone dicendi *ABCpCtFLNOdOl
      OsW*

27   inter quas . . . ponatur et *BCpCsDFLNObOdOs*: assignatas poni-
      tur enim *A*; assignatas in libro De planctu Nature hec *OlW*

      Reddidit *ACpCtD(Alan)*: Reddit *BFNOlOsW*; Reddit et *CsLOb
      Od*

      Quo noctem: Et noctem *OlW*

28   eloquentissimus modernorum: *Ct has lost a quire at this point; the
      text resumes early in chapter 4.*

      vos *ABCpCsNOl*: nobis *D*; nos *FLOdOsW*

31   Igitur *ACpDOb(Geoffrey)*: Ideo *BCsFLNOdOlOsW*

32   negociandum est: negociandum *W*

43   illius unici . . . sentencia: *om. OlOsW*

      in infinitum: infinitum *BCpLNW*

46   foras et: foras id est *FW*

      exuxit *BCpNOd*: exussit *A*; exigit *CsW*; excussit *D*; exuit *F*; ex-
      unxit *LOb*; exsugit *OlOs*

      rimabar *ACpCsDFObOlOs*: rimabor *BLNOdW*

      sciencia *ACpN?ObOl*: scienciam *BCsFLOdOsW*; sentenciam *D*

47   sentencia rudis *ACpCsLDObOd*: sciencia rudis *BFOlOsW*; rudis
      N

51   dulcia: dulce *OlW*

      sunto *ACpDNOb(Horace)*: sumpto *BFOdOlOs*; sumpta *CsW*;
      sumto *L*

      quocumque *ACpCsDOb(Horace)*: quodcumque *BFLOdOlOsW*

      tua me *ACsLNOdOlOs(Horace)*: tua mea *BCpDFObW*

53	que vero . . . extrinsecis: *om. OlW*
58	iusticia *(Matthew)*: In iusticia *ABCpCsDFLNObOdOlOsW*
	id est: id est est *FOdW*
59	aut sibi *CsLOdOs(Horace)*: vel *ACp*; aut *BDFNOlW*
60	generaliora *ABCpCsDFLOdOs*: generalia *NObOlW*
61	floridis colorum: *The text in Od ends at this point.*
63	invenitur ex: invenitur *W*

CHAPTER 4

3	Vos per clemenciam: *The text in Ct resumes at this point.*
10	in gerundivum *ACsCtN*: in verbum *BCpDFLObOlOsW*
14	volet: velut *W*
15	Ludentem: Eludentem *FW*
16	parcium materie: *The text in Ct breaks off at this point.*
17	inutiliter et: inutiliter *FW*
20	emblematis: emblametis *F*; emblamatis *W*
21	ornatibus vestiatur: *The text in Ct resumes at this point.*
	Inspuitur *(Gervase)*: Inspicitur *ABCpCsCtDFLNObOlOsW*
	Vindocinensis *ABCpCsCtLNOlOs*: Vindoniensis *DFObW*
	crebro: crebo *FOsW*
22	promissio *CsDNOb*: promisso *ABCpLOs*; permissio *CtFW*; prouisio *Ol*
	rutilant: ritulant *W*

CHAPTER 5

1	Recedimus: Recedemus *FW*
4	est: *om. BFW*
13	exprimitur nota *BCpCtDFLNObOs*: exprimitur *A*; exprimitur non *CsOl* (non *corrected from* nota *Ol*); exprimitur nomen *W*
	glacie temporali *ALOs*: glaciali tempore *BCpCsDFObOlW*; glacie yemali *Ct*; glaciali temporali *N*
	cristallum: glaciem *W*
14	Ut sol *CsOl*: sol *ABCpCtDFLNObOsW*
15	dabiturque *ABCpCsLNOl(Horace)*: dabitur *DFObOsW*
	raritas *ACpCsCtDLNObOl*: rarietas *BFOsW*

433

16   eciam *ACpCsCtDObOl*: enim *BFLNOsW*

17   novas et inauditas *CpCsCtDLNOl*: novas inauditas *A*; nova *BFOs*;
       novas et laudatas *Ob*; novas *W*

       callida iunctura *ABCpCsCtDNObOl*: talis iunctura *FLOsW*

18   in voce *ACsOb*: voce *BCpCtDFLNOlOsW*

       cinctutis *CsCtDFLObOs*: cuncticis *A*; cinctutus *B*; cinctitas *Cp*;
       cincturis *N*; cuncticos *Ol*; cuctutis *W*

19   tragodia *ACsN*: tragedia *BDOl*; tragodi *CpL*; trogodia *CtFW*;
       tragogi *Ob*

       quod est *ABCpCsDLNObOl*: id est *Ct*; id est quod *FOsW*

       Latine *BCpDLNObOlOs*: om. *ACsCtFW*

21   signatum *Ob(Horace)*: signo *ABCpCsDFLNOlOsW*; signatum no-
       men *Ct*

       Hoc *ABCtDFNObOlOs*: Hec *CpCsLW*

22   cuius: cui *OsW*

       Inter ... facultas *BCpDLNObOl*: om. *ACsCtFOsW*

       et cum: et quod *BFW*

23   ista verba *ACpCsCtDLNObOl*: ista *BFOsW*

25   admonet ut: admonet et *W*

26   appellativis *ACtN*: et appellativis *BCpCsDFLObOlOsW*

       significacionem *ACpCsDLNObOlOs*: significandum *BCtFW*

       si *ACpCsCtDLNObOl*: om. *BFOsW*

27   que quasi *ABCpCsCtDLNObOl*: quasi *FOs*; quando *(corrected)* *W*

       extraneo *ABCsCtDLNObOlOs*: extrane *Cp*; extranee *FW*

       quodam: quo *FW*

       Cresus *ACpCsCtDObOl*: Gresus *B*; Cresis *FOsW*; Crisus *L*; Cur-
       sus *N*

       Sinon *CtLOl*: Simon *ABCpCsDFNOsW*

       quoniam: quando *FOsW*

28   quando tota: tota *BFW*

32   omne *CpCsCtDLNObOl*: om. *ABFOsW*

       Tandem ... nutrimentum: om. *W*

       humiditas segetis *ACsDLOb?Os*: humiditas solis *BCpCtFNOl*

33   causam: casum *FOsW*

       subde: om. *FOsW*

36 ponitur pro contento *CpCsCtDNObOl*: pro contento *BFLOsW*

ut utens *ACpCsCtDLNObOl*: utens *BFOsW*

37 Libero *BCpDLObOs*: Lieo *ACsW (corrected W)*; libere *CtF*; Bacho *NOl (corrected N)*

39 aliquid: aliquod *FOsW*

Nunquam enim *ABCpCsCtDNObOl*: Nunquam *FLOsW*

40 Per hunc modum: Per hunc modum dicitur *CtW* (dicitur *added in margin by different hand W*)

42 id est . . . hasta: *om. BFW*

43 hec *ACpCsCtDLNObOl*: *om. BFOsW*

virum *Ct(Walter)*: viri *ABCpCsDFLNObOlOsW*

Ebur est color disgregativus: Ebur est color *ACtW*

45 manifestam *ALN?*: manifesta *BCpCsCtDFOlOsW*

48 eciam *ABCpCsDNOl*: enim *FLOsW*

Latrones id est *CpCsDLNObOl*: id est *ABCtFOsW*

49 ut si: Et si *W*

51 vel: et *W*

53 Fit . . . casuali: *om. W*

54 invitat: invitat et *DObW*

sub: et sub *BOsW*

57 autem eciam *BCpL*: eciam *ACsCtN*; autem et *D*; autem *FObOsW*; *om. Ol*

Alexandreide *CpCtDOlOs*: Alexandriade *A*; Alexandride *BFW*; Alexandrido *D*; Alexandridede *L*; Alexandrede *N*; Alaxandride *Ob*

sue *ACpCsCtDLNObOl*: *om. BFOsW*

prevertere *ABCpCsLN(Walter)*: pervertere *CtDFObOlOsW*

59 apposicio est: id est apposicio est *W*

CHAPTER 6

2 tali ornatu *DLObOlOs*: ut talis ornatus *A*; tali ornatu ornatur qui causatur et *B*; tali ornatu qui causatur *CpN*; tali scilicet ornatu *Cs*; talis ornatus *CtFW*

3 pleniorem *CpCsNObOl*: planiorem *ABCtFLOsW*; perlaniorem *D*

teste Oracio *ABCpCtDLNObOl*: Oracius *CsFW*; Oracio *Os*

4   famulare *ABCpCsFLNObOl*: famuliare *D*; familiare *OsW*

5   ornatum sive *ACpCsCtDLNObOl*; ornatum sue *BFOsW*

6   Squinancem *ACpCsCtLNOl*: Si qui nance *B*; Squinacem *DOb*; Squinancio *F*; Squinanciam *OsW*; synanchen *(Gellius)*

squinancem *ABCpCsCtFLNOl*: squinacem *DOb*; squinanciam *OsW*

arginancem *ABCpCsCtDFLNObOl*: arginanciam *OsW*; argyranchen *(Gellius)*

arginancem *ABCpCsCtDFLNObOl*: arginanciam *OsW*

7   vitalem *ACsCt(Matthew)*: vtilem *BCpDFLNObOlOsW*

materie et *(Matthew)*: materie *ABCpCsCtDFLNObOlOsW*

posicionem *ABCpCsCtDFLNObOl (corrected from* pocionem *Ob Ol)*: pocionem *OsW*

CHAPTER 7

1   36 *BCpCsCtLNObOs*: 3 *AD?Ol*; 30 *FW*

6   aliquid: aliquod *FOsW*

7   parantes currum *BCpCsCtLObOlOs*: preparantes currum *A*; parentes currum *DFN*; parentes cursum *W*

Milo *BCsCtDObOlOs*: nilo *A*; mili *Cp*; mulo *FW*; nullo *L*; milus *N*

11   racionalia *ABCsCtFNObOlOs(Geoffrey)*: racionabilia *CpDLW*

12   umbone: umbrone *FW*

13   respondet *BCpCsDNOl*: correspondet *Ct*; respondit *FLOsW*

Stacii: Oracii *W*

15   conformantur *BCpCtDLNOl*: conformiter *AFObOsW*; confirmantur *Cs*

16   triplex: *om. BFW*

Theodorici *ABCpFLNObOlOs*: Ceodorici *Cs*; Theorici *Ct*; Thodorici *DW*

et *(Vegetius)*: *om. ABCpCsDFLNObOlOsW*

17   posterius: *om. W*

intericitur *ABCpDLNObOl*: interponitur *CsCt*; intericietur *F OsW*

19 Per dativum: Per ablativum *FW* (ablativum *expunged W*)

Beata Virgine: Beate Virginis *CsW* (laude *added in margin by different hand W*)

20 obliquo: oliquo *W*

vel: et *FW*

23 aut determinatur: aut terminatur *BOsW*

arida: *om. FW*

determinatur verbum *ACpCsCtLNObOl*: determinatur *BDF OsW*

25 oracionem: *om. FW*

26 casum: accusativum *FOlW*

popularitate *BCpDLOl(Geoffrey)*: pluralitate *ACsFNObOsW*

27 sic scilicet *ACpCtDLNObOl*: sic *BFOsW*; scilicet *Cs*

adverbium: verbum *D*; adiectivum *FW*

determinaciones *ABCpCsCtNObOlOs*: terminaciones *DFLW*

iste *FOsW*: idem *ABCpCsCtDLNObOl*

30 ut et: ut *FOsW*

35 falsitatis ... pretendentes: *om. CsFW*

impossibilitatis apparenciam *(Gervase)*: impossibilitatem *ABCp CtDLNObOlOs*

in promisso *ABCpCsDNObOlOs*: promisso *CtFLW*

38 cum petit *(Marbod)*: competit *ABCpCtDFLNObOlW*; *om. CsOs*

39 que aut *ABCpCtDNObOl*: que erit *FLOs*; quid erit *W* (quid *corrected W*)

41 excipitur: explicatur *W*

43 spei *BCpFLOlOs(RadH)*: *spem ADObW (corrected W)*; in spe *Ct*

multum: multipliciter *FOsW*

47 dicit *ABCpCtNOl*: dixit *DFLObOsW*

voluit *ABCsDLObOs*: noluit *CpCtNOl*; *om. FW*

scilicet *AW (corrected from* set *W)*: set *BCpCtDFLNObOlOs*; *om. Cs*

puerili *ACtLNObOl*: pueri *B*; pueruli *Cp*; et peruili *D*; et puerili *FOsW*

48 homini cupido *BCtDLNObOlOs*: cupido *A*; *om. Cp*; homini *FW*

Ciceronis *ACpLNOlOs*: Citheronis *BCtDFOb*; Cithereonis *W*

52 epilogus: ypilogus *LW*

54 nolle: nichil nolle loqui *F*; nichil nolle *OsW*

60 Murmura: Murmur *FOsW*

61 ergo: igitur *ObW*

62 asintheton *ABCpOb*: asintheon *CtFOsW*; absyntheton *DOl*; asynthethon *L*; asintheethon *N*

63 Mavisne *B?CpCtFLN?OlOs*: magis ne *A*; *om. Cs*; via vis ne *DObW*

64 ergo *AFOl(Eberhard)*: *om. BCs*; igitur *CpCtDLNObOsW*
relinque *CpNObOl(Eberhard)*: relinquo *ACtDFLOsW*; *om. BCs*

67 quod causam: quod propter causam *W*
suscipiat quod nemo: *om. W*

68 Nimium *CsW(RadH) (corrected from* Nimirum *CsW)*: Nimirum *ABCpCtDFLNObOlOs*

69 me *W(RadH) (added above by a different hand W)*: *om. ABCpCs CtDFLNObOlOs*

77 alio usui *ACtDFLObW*: alii usui *BCpNOl*; aliorum usui *Cs*; alio ut in *Os*; adeo *(RadH)*

78 preditus *ABCsCtN(RadH)*: proditus *CpDFLOlOsW*

79 cum dicitur . . . subicitur: *om. W*

83 exercitum: exercicium *AOl*; exceritum *W*
excercitum: excerciter? *FW*

86 dignitatem si: dignitatem set *FW*; dignitatem scilicet *Os*

87 propositio *AOb(RadH)*: proprio *BCpCtDFLNOsW*; preposito *Cs*; proposito *Ol*

88 collacio *BCpCtDLNOlOs(RadH)*: collocacio *AFObW*
truci *B*: truce *ACtDFLNObOlOsW*; cruce *Cp*

90 natura *ABCpCtDNObOl(RadH)*: nota vel in finem *L*; nomen *F OsW*

93 furi vicinia: *The text of the fragment Or begins at this point.*

Chapter 8

2 Ad difficultatem . . . dictum est: *om. W*
permissio: *om. W*

3 Antithesis *CsCtDFLObOlOs*: Anthitesis *AW*; Antitesis *BCpOr*

5 Grece *BCpCtDLNObOs*: ergo *ACsF*; Greco *or* ergo (g°) *Ol*; Greci *or* igitur (g^i) *OrW*
paranomasia *CpCtDLNOb*: per anthonomasiam *A*; paranama-

438

siam *B*; paranomosia *CsFOsW*; per antimasiam *Ol*; antonomasia *Or*

CHAPTER 9

title	ornata verba quibus locucio rudis venustatur egregie: ornata verba quibus omnis ruditas etc. *F*; ornata verba *W*
3	ut Vindocinensis: *The text of the fragment Or ends at this point.*
	tanti: tanta *CpOlW*
	invitaret *ABCpCsCtFNObOl*: imitaret *DLOsW*
8	luce sua: *om. W*
10	torrente: de torrente *DLW* (de *inserted above, by original hand? W*)
11	competenciorem *CsCtFLOs*: competentem *AW*; convenienciorem *BCpNObOl*
	eligamus: elegamus *DW*
12	convertere: converte *W*
	Animi mei *BCpCsDLNOl*: Anime *ACtFW*; Animi *Ob*; Anime mee *Os*; Animi tui *(Geoffrey)*
13	aureum et argenteam *ed.*: aureum et argenteum *BCpCsCtNOb Ol(Geoffrey)*; auream et argenteam *FLOsW*
14	adiectivum splendidi: adiectivum *FOsW*
15	habeat *ABCpCsCtNObOl*: habet *DFLOsW*

CHAPTER 10

1	preter premissa *CsCtDLObOs*: pretermissa *ABCpFNOlW*
2	suo: *om. W*
	philosophum Architrenium *ACpDLNObOl*: Iohannem Architrenium *B*; philosophum *CsCtFOsW*
	exponat *BCpCsCtNObOlOs*: exponit *A*; expendit *D*; expona *F*; exponet *L*; exponeret *W*
3	imitacione Terencii *ACpDLNOl*: in imitacione Terencii *B*; imitaciones Terencii *CsFOsW*; ymitemur Tarensium *Ct*; imitacionem Terencii *Ob*
	sibi: ibi *CsFOsW*
4	ait: *om. CsFOsW*
	usus consuetudoque dicendi *ABCpDLNOl(RadH)*: dicendique consuetudo *CsFOsW*

439

CHAPTER 11

1   enim Oracius: enim *W*

       primus *BCpCtNObOl(Horace)*: primis *ACsDFLOsW*

5   Ennius *ACsCt*: Eminus *BCpNOl*; Ennimus *DL*; Enminus *F*; En-
       ninus *OsW*

6   modus est: modus *W*

       ab: in *W*

7   pertractare: observare pertractare *F*; observando pertractare *W*

       pudor *BCpCtDLNObOl(Horace)*: pudet *ACsFOsW*

       Cidicus *ACpCsCtFLNObOlOsW*: aditus *BD*; Cyclicus *(Horace)*

8   a Troia: *om. FLOsW*

       fumido *B?CtNOb (corrected N)*: fundo *ACp?Ol*; profundo *CsDF
       LOsW*

9   ac id est *ed.*: aut id est *ABCpCsCtDFLNObOlOsW*

       tractata: tracta *CsFW*

10   ducere id est *CtD*: deducere id est *ABCpCsFLNObOlOsW*

CHAPTER 12

1   eliciuntur *ABCpCsCtDNObOl*: conuiciuntur *FLOsW*

2   mutant *ABCpCtDFLNObOlW*: mutat *Cs?*; mutauit *Os*; nutant
       (Alan)

3   per significacionem *ABCpCsCtNObOl*: pro significacione *DFL
       OsW*

4   membrorum: membra et *W*

6   Pretermittit *ACsCtFObOlOs*: Pretermittet *BCpNW*; Pretermit-
       tat *D*

       Davusne *CsL*: Danosve *A*; spumas ne *B*; spuavusve *Cp*; Davusve
       CtFOsW; Damusne *D*; spunusve *N*; spiavusve *Ol*; divusne *(Hor-
       ace)*

9   pateris: patriis *ACsW*

11   gestit: gessit *Cs*; gestat *OsW*

       temere et *ABCpCsNOl*: temere *DFLObOsW*

       inservit: inserunt *OsW*

       inventis: iuventus *OsW*

       se: de *W*

12   Sillanum *BCpCsFLNOs(Matthew)*: Scillanum *AOb*; Solanum *Ct*;
       Siblanum *D?*; sillabam *Ol?*; Cillanum *W*; Sullanum *(Lucan)*
       Sille *L*: Scille *ABCpCtNObOlOs*; Cille *CsDFW*

13   pauperiem: pauperem *CsW*
       actu: acta *Cs*; actum *W*

15   mutacio: imitacio *W*

17   Brutus *ed.*: liricus *ACpCsCtDFLNObOlOsW*; bricus *B*

20   esse: *om. W*
       nullas *N(Lucan)*: nullos *ABCpCsCtDFLObOlOsW*

22   De hiis per ordinem doceamus *ABCpCsDFLNOb*: De hiis per
       ordinem est dicendum *Ct*; De his per ordinem dicamus *Ol*; De
       hiis tribus per ordinem doceamus *Os*; *om. W*

24   noto *BCpNOl(Horace)*: voto *ACsCtDFLObOsW*

26   eadem: edem *W*

30   Quantitas est: Quantitas *FLW*
       nequam *DL*: nunquam *ABCpCsCtFNOlOsW*; antequam *Ob*
       sola: solo *W*
       est *BCpCtNObOl(Statius)*: eius *AD*; ergo *CsF*; ego *LW*; igitur *Os*
       si aliquis: aliquis *FW*
       latenti: latente *W*
       malignis: malignus *FW*

31   cum *Ob(Cicero)*: cuius *ABCpCsDLNOlOs*; ut *Ct*; *om. F*; scilicet
       (corrected) W

33   agentis *ACt*: gentis *BCpCsDFLNObOlOsW*
       remiscet *ACpCsCtNObOl(Horace)*: remiset *B*; remittet *DFLOsW*
       impetus omnis habet *(Ovid; Matthew)*: *om. ACtNOl*; inspeciosa
       manus *B*; impetuosa manus *CpDFLObOsW*; impetusus manus
       Cs

34   fieri . . . potest: *om. (fieri expunged) W*

37   ostensum est: planius demonstratur *W*

CHAPTER 13

1   stilus: *om. W*
       Mediocris est qui *ACpCsCtDLNOlOs*: Mediocris est que *BFW*;
       Mediocris est quando *Ob*

constat *Ct(RadH)*: constat nec *AOb*; constat neque *BCpCsDFL NOlOsW*

pervulgatissima *ACpObOl(RadH)*: provulgatissimam *B*; promulgatissime *Cs*; promulgatissima *DFOsW*; provulgatissima *LN*

3   penultimam: antepenultimam *FW*

clausule *CsCtNObOlOs*: clause *ABCpDFLW*

periodus: pariodus *W*

6   stupescant *ABCpCtDNObOl*: stupescunt *CsFLOsW*

CHAPTER 14

1   Crimina: Carmina *W*

2   Fingentur: Finguntur *W*

cervicem equinam *CsLOs*: cesariem *A*; cesariem equi *BCpCt NObOl*; cesarem sequi *D*; cesariem equinam *FW (corrected from* cervicem equinam *W)*

finiat: sumat *B*; definiat *FW*

fingentur: finguntur *W*

3   faciat *BCpCsCtDFLOlOs*: facit *AObW*; faciant *N*

6   parte sentencie: parte sciencie *W*

et floridis *ACpCtDFLNObOl*: et floribus vel floridis *B*; et floribus *CsOsW*

7   turgidum in . . . sentencia: *om. W*

10   timidusque *ACsCtLOs(Horace)*: tutusque *BCpDFNObOlW*

levia: levi *BLNW*

timidusque *AL*: tutusque *BCpCsCtFNObOsW*

11   inveniatur *BCpCsCtDNObOlOs*: invenitur *AFLW*

14   ludere: ledere *W*

CHAPTER 15

1   distinctum *BNOl*: *om. ACs*; distictum *CpF*; disticum *CtDLOsW*

distinctum *BCpNObOl*: disticum *ACtDFLOsW*; *om. Cs*

et in Dialogis *CsObOs* (et in *added Ob*): Dialogis *ABCpCtDFLW*; et *(added)* Dialogis *N*; in Dialogis *Ol*

2   verisimilia: verisisimilia *W*

loquens: Ovidius loquens *FOsW*

flectique *BCpNObOl(Ovid)*: flecti quod *AW (corrected W)*; flecti
quia *CsDFLOs*

5   satirici *ACtDLOl*: satiri *BFCsObOsW (corrected from* satirici *Ob)*;
satura *Cp*; satiriciri *N*

6   est quodlibet . . . loquendo: *om. W*

7   isti: alii *W*

CHAPTER 16

2   Penalope *DLOs*: Penolope *ABCsObOl*; Penolpole *Cp*; Penolepe
Ct; Penapole *FW*; Pepenole *N*

3   repressus: *om. W*

4   Epistolis Oracii: Epistolis Oracius *FW*

6   venie: veniem *W*

7   prout: protinus *(corrected) W*

9   determinacione que *ACsDObOs*: determinacione quod *BCpCtF
LNOlW*

10   Explicit *CtFW*: Explicit hoc opus etc. *A*; *om. BCpNOl*; Explici-
unt tractatus de arte dictandi qui intitulatur tria sunt et capitula super eodem *Cs*; Explicit iste tractatus *D*; Explicit tractatus de dictamine *L*; Explicit tractatus qui dicitur Tria sunt *Ob*;
Explicit tractatus de arte dictandi qui intitulatur tria sunt *Os*

11   Hoc . . . Amen *BCpFNW* (Amen *om. BCpN*): *om. ADLObOl*; Deo
gracias. Amen *Cs*; Ihesu parce *Ct*; Amen. Pur charite *Os*

Notes to the Translation

Chapter 1

1–15   The principal source is Geoffrey of Vinsauf, *Documentum* Prol.–
1.17, with additional verse examples that are found in Geoffrey
of Vinsauf, *Summa de coloribus rhetoricis.*

2   *And except . . . everything*: This line is not from any work by Ovid,
but the transformations of Nisus and Scylla are depicted in
Metamorphoses 8.145–51. Geoffrey of Vinsauf also attributes the
line to Ovid in *Summa de coloribus rhetoricis* 19–20.

3   *according to Cicero's teaching . . . and clear*: See Cicero, *De inventione*
1.20.28; *Rhetorica ad Herennium* 1.9.14.

4   *Brilliant . . . his child*: Geoffrey of Vinsauf, *Summa de coloribus
rhetoricis* 23–24.

6   *The invidious virtue . . . his family*: Geoffrey of Vinsauf, *Summa de
coloribus rhetoricis* 29–30.

8   *A proverb . . . acquiesces*: Matthew of Vendôme, *Ars versificatoria*
1.16.

10   *Envy . . . them all*: Geoffrey of Vinsauf, *Summa de coloribus rhetoricis* 41–42.

11   *Virtue seldom . . . to sin*: Geoffrey of Vinsauf, *Summa de coloribus
rhetoricis* 44–45.

14   *Through the shrub's . . . languishes*: Geoffrey of Vinsauf, *Summa de
coloribus rhetoricis* 52–53.

Chapter 2

1–12   The principal source is Geoffrey of Vinsauf, *Documentum* 2.1.1–
12, with additional verse examples that are found in Geoffrey's
Summa de coloribus rhetoricis.

445

4   *Scylla, wounded by the beauty of Minos etc.*: The first of many instances where accurate citation of the opening words in the
English translation requires including some words (here,
"wounded by the beauty") that do not appear in the corresponding citation in the Latin text.

       avenge upon the head the crime of the limbs: That is, to punish the
ruler for a crime committed by his subjects.

       Whom the hope . . . father's means: Geoffrey of Vinsauf, *Summa de
coloribus rhetoricis* 90–91.

7   *Overthrown . . . as much*: Geoffrey of Vinsauf, *Summa de coloribus
rhetoricis* 100–101.

8   *Having worked . . . these things*: Geoffrey of Vinsauf, *Summa de coloribus rhetoricis* 103–4.

11   *With an equal . . . its pestilence*: Geoffrey of Vinsauf, *Summa de coloribus rhetoricis* 128–29.

12   *By a similar . . . sinful deed*: Geoffrey of Vinsauf, *Summa de coloribus
rhetoricis* 133–34.

15   Geoffrey of Vinsauf, *Documentum* 2.1.12–2.2.1.

CHAPTER 3

2   *Interpretation . . . entices them*: Geoffrey of Vinsauf, *Documentum*
2.2.29.

       Book of Verses: *Tria sunt* always uses this title to designate Geof-
frey of Vinsauf's *Poetria nova*.

       Although . . . raiment: Geoffrey of Vinsauf, *Poetria nova* 220–22.

       My laughter . . . to tears: Alan of Lille, *De planctu Naturae* 1.1–2.

       when we have only . . . love unites: Gervase of Melkley, *De arte ver-
sificatoria et modo dictandi*, p. 40, ll. 11–18, quoting "Consulte
teneros" 137–38.

3   Geoffrey of Vinsauf, *Documentum* 2.2.11, quoting Virgil, *Aeneid*
1.1–3.

4   *And you . . . previous example*: Geoffrey of Vinsauf, *Documentum*
2.2.12–13.

       father . . . of men: Virgil, *Aeneid* 1.65, 2.648, 10.2, 10.743.

       O child . . . face of the land: Alan of Lille, *De planctu Naturae* 7.1–4,
9–12, 5–8, 13–40.

5 *We can circumlocute . . . to the Fates*: Geoffrey of Vinsauf, *Documentum* 2.2.15.

 The sun's . . . of winter: Alan of Lille, *De planctu Naturae* 5.21.

6 *We circumlocute . . . to hanging*: Geoffrey of Vinsauf, *Documentum* 2.2.16.

 in a voice . . . fitting reply: Alan of Lille, *De planctu Naturae* 8.2.

7 *The wild boar . . . in touch*: Walther, *Proverbia,* no. 18,772a.

9 *Money has . . . stars*: "In terra summus rex est hoc tempore Nummus" (*Carmina Burana* 11) 18.

 The smooth . . . silvery glow: Alan of Lille, *De planctu Naturae* 2.2.

12 *Ships sail . . . of art*: John of Hauville, *Architrenius* 1.1–6.

 Alexander . . . husband etc.: "Magnus Alexander" 1–10. The poem's editor, Bruce Harbert, believes its author could be Gervase of Melkley: *A Thirteenth-Century Anthology*, p. 5.

 Alcides: That is, Hercules.

13 *the book . . . Phoebe etc.*: Alan of Lille, *Liber parabolarum*.

 As Peter . . . of Norwich: Peter of Blois, *Libellus de arte dictandi rhetorice*, ll. 574–83.

 Just as the stag . . . scriptures: Adapts Psalms 41(42):2.

14 *Apostrophe . . . other thing; Four kinds of embellishment . . . indecision*: Geoffrey of Vinsauf, *Documentum* 2.2.24.

 as is done . . . and England: Geoffrey of Vinsauf, *Poetria nova* 368–430 and 326–66.

15 *Exclamation . . . the gods?*: Geoffrey of Vinsauf, *Documentum* 2.2.25, quoting Marbod of Rennes, *De ornamentis verborum* 36–38.

 O sorrow . . . Would that etc.: Geoffrey of Vinsauf, *Poetria nova* 386–87.

16 *Reduplication . . . of anxiety*: Gervase of Melkley, *De arte versificatoria et modo dictandi*, p. 38, ll. 19–20. While the addition of "the same word" (*idem verbum;* not in Gervase) appears to make "the beginning" grammatically redundant, the intended sense is confirmed by the scribe's emendation of *principium* to *in principio* in manuscript *A*.

 Impelled by sorrow . . . my sister, etc.: Geoffrey of Vinsauf, *Documentum* 2.2.26, quoting Virgil, *Aeneid* 4.9, combined with Ovid, *Heroides* 7.191.

 Bernard Silvestris . . . sevenfold heavens: Gervase of Melkley, *De*

arte versificatoria et modo dictandi, pp. 38, l. 23–39, l. 6, quoting Bernard Silvestris, *Mathematicus* 381–86.

Impelled by love . . . stay! etc.: Geoffrey of Vinsauf, *Documentum* 2.2.26, quoting Ovid, *Metamorphoses* 1.504–5.

17   *Hypophora . . . your children*: Combines Geoffrey of Vinsauf, *Documentum* 2.2.27, with Gervase of Melkley, *De arte versificatoria et modo dictandi,* p. 27, ll. 7–20, both quoting Lawrence of Durham, *Hypognosticon* 93–100.

18   *Indecision . . . satisfies me*: Combines Geoffrey of Vinsauf, *Documentum* 2.2.28, with Gervase of Melkley, *De arte versificatoria et modo dictandi,* pp. 25, l. 18–26, l. 4. Geoffrey quotes Marbod of Rennes, *De ornamentis verborum* 126–29, while Gervase quotes only line 126.

What will . . . movements etc.: Geoffrey of Vinsauf, *Poetria nova* 348–49.

19   *Prosopopoeia . . . could speak*: Geoffrey of Vinsauf, *Documentum* 2.2.22.

I, the ravished . . . world etc.: Geoffrey of Vinsauf, *Poetria nova* 469 (and variants: Faral, p. 211).

I was once . . . blemish etc.: Geoffrey of Vinsauf, *Poetria nova* 509–11.

Similarly . . . in Claudian: Geoffrey of Vinsauf, *Documentum* 2.2.23 (without the quotation from Ovid).

If this is . . . perish etc.: Ovid, *Metamorphoses* 2.279–81.

Rome in Lucan: See Lucan, *Bellum civile* 1.185–92.

Africa in Claudian: See Claudian, *De bello Gildonico* 1.134–200.

20   *And note . . . poetic fiction*: Compare Gervase of Melkley, *De arte versificatoria et modo dictandi,* p. 65, ll. 14 and 8.

Moreover . . . extraneous to that subject matter: Geoffrey of Vinsauf, *Documentum* 2.2.17.

21   *We digress . . . restores him*: Geoffrey of Vinsauf, *Documentum* 2.2.18–19.

22   *Similarly . . . friends parted*: Geoffrey of Vinsauf, *Documentum* 2.2.20.

A single bond . . . other etc.: Geoffrey of Vinsauf, *Poetria nova* 538–39.

23   *We also . . . to the subject matter*: Geoffrey of Vinsauf, *Documentum* 2.2.21.

All things . . . a point: Gervase of Melkley, *De arte versificatoria et modo dictandi,* pp. 153, l. 18–154, l. 4, quoting "Magnus Alexander" 141–45.

Consider another . . . the hours: Geoffrey of Vinsauf, *Documentum* 2.2.21, quoting Horace, *Epistles* 1.1.20–23. The *Tria sunt* author-compiler completes line 23 and adds line 24 ("which defer . . . vigorously etc.").

Due to . . . endures unscathed: Gervase of Melkley, *De arte versificatoria et modo dictandi,* p. 152, ll. 17–18.

24   *Digression . . . guilty realm*: Gervase of Melkley, *De arte versificatoria et modo dictandi,* p. 65, ll. 8–13, quoting Statius, *Thebaid* 1.240–42.

But now by Jove's . . . heavens etc.: Statius, *Thebaid* 1.197.

25   *as Cicero says in his first* Rhetoric: Cicero, *De inventione* 1.19.27.

as Cicero does . . . to the hearer that Verres had committed adultery: No such passage is found in the Verres. The sources are the *accessus* to the "Materia" Commentary on Horace, *Ars poetica,* pp. 336–37, and Matthew of Vendôme, *Ars versificatoria* 1.110.

Now the trumpet . . . uncontrolled song etc.: Alan of Lille, *De planctu Naturae* 17.1–7.

Digression . . . the case: *Marii Victorini Explanationes in Ciceronis Rhetoricam,* p. 86, 1.19.33–36.

It is a happy . . . unwanted days: Boethius, *De consolatione philosophiae* 1.metrum1.13–20.

26   *So that when . . . unequal below*: Geoffrey of Vinsauf, *Documentum* 2.2.3.

27   *Zephyr . . . prologue to sleep*: Alan of Lille, *De planctu Naturae* 5.1–50.

28   *In amplified form, a woman's etc.*: Geoffrey of Vinsauf, *Poetria nova* 562–621.

either of Alan of Lille's books: That is, Alan of Lille's *De planctu Naturae* or *Anticlaudianus.*

Matthew of Vendôme . . . my garments: Matthew of Vendôme's *Ars versificatoria.*

Bernard Silvestris . . . Microcosmus: Bernard Silvestris's *Cosmographia.*

Wherefore . . . and other things: Geoffrey of Vinsauf, *Documentum* 2.2.10, referencing Sidonius, *Epistles* 1.2.

And you . . . of argument: Gervase of Melkley, *De arte versificatoria et modo dictandi,* p. 65, ll. 18–19.

29   *Collocation . . . that will follow*: Compare Geoffrey of Vinsauf, *Documentum* 2.3.101.

the artifice that will follow: Refers either to the technique illustrated in *Tria sunt* 3.46 or more broadly to the various techniques that constitute "artificial" style, treated in *Tria sunt* 5–9.

I do not speak; I am silent: The example does illustrate the collocation of opposites, but it expresses a sentiment that is the opposite of the one expected ("I am not silent; I speak").

30   *Not for us . . . reject us*: Unidentified.

We encounter . . . is reverence: Geoffrey of Vinsauf, *Documentum* 2.3.101, quoting Sidonius Apollinaris, *Epistles* 4.13.2 (with variants). See also *Tria sunt* 7.10.

Here the beauty . . . contains it: Alan of Lille, *Anticlaudianus* 1.64–73.

31–47   The principal source is Geoffrey of Vinsauf, *Documentum* 2.2.45–70.

32   *For Boethius . . . of things*: A variant of Ralph of Longchamp, *In Anticlaudianum Alani Commentum,* p. 62, ll. 6–7, whose editor believes the reference is to Boethius, *In Topica Ciceronis Commentaria,* PL 64:1145. However, the statement is quoted not from this or any other work by Boethius, but apparently from medieval canon law: *Animal est Substantia,* Causa 3 q.2 c.1.

37   *Read books*: Preface to *Distichs of Cato,* proverb no. 26.

45   *And thus much water . . . little*: Unidentified pentameter, perhaps from a version of Aesop's fable of the crow and the water jar (quoted by Geoffrey of Vinsauf, *Documentum* 2.2.63).

47   *subsequent chapters . . . is facile*: See *Tria sunt* 5–7.

48   *The topics . . . and actions*: See *Tria sunt* 12.

50   *write it on the back of the letter*: After a medieval letter had been folded up and sealed, it was "endorsed" with a greeting that was written on the outside, "on the back" *(in dorso).*

51   *Not enough . . . hurt me*: Horace, *Ars poetica* 99–103.

52   *But Cicero . . . and actions*: Cicero, *De inventione* 1.24.34.

we must speak . . . separate chapter: See *Tria sunt* 12.

If I fail . . . as poet?: Horace, *Ars poetica* 86–87.

53   *every poetic . . . and blame*: Aristotle/Averroes, *De arte poetica*, translated by Hermann the German (Averroes's Middle Commentary on Aristotle's *Poetics*), chap. 1.

    The characteristics . . . external circumstances: See *Rhetorica ad Herennium* 3.6.10.

    from race . . . from fatherland: The distinction is between ethnicity defined by language (*gens;* also called *nacio:* see *Tria sunt* 12.10) and place of birth or citizenship (*patria*).

54–56   The principal sources appear to be Matthew of Vendôme, *Ars versificatoria* 1.42–44, and a commentary on Horace's *Ars poetica*.

54   *Vast difference . . . at Argos*: Horace, *Ars poetica* 114–18.

    Davus: The stock character of the rascally slave, replacing Horace's *divus* (a rich man).

55   *You must note . . . their years*: Horace, *Ars poetica* 156–57.

    So, lest . . . the age: Horace, *Ars poetica* 176–78.

56   *Writer . . . Orestes sorrowful*: Horace, *Ars poetica* 120–21, 123–24.

57   Matthew of Vendôme, *Ars versificatoria* 1.63, quoting Ovid, *Remedia amoris* 420.

    a singular pearl that is hidden in many a marsh: This comparison does not make as much sense as the rose among thorns, but *pluribus . . . paludibus* (many marshes) comes from Matthew of Vendôme.

58   *Furthermore . . . his disadvantage*: Matthew of Vendôme, *Ars versificatoria* 1.64–66.

    to spare . . . the proud: Compare Virgil, *Aeneid* 6.853 (quoted correctly by Matthew of Vendôme, *Ars versificatoria* 1.65).

    Similarly . . . allotted it: Matthew of Vendôme, *Ars versificatoria* 1.70, quoting Horace, *Ars poetica* 92.

59   *the greatest . . . self-consistent*: Matthew of Vendôme, *Ars versificatoria* 1.73, quoting Horace, *Ars poetica* 119.

    In short . . . and uniform: Horace, *Ars poetica* 23.

60   *as was said before*: See *Tria sunt* 3.48–49.

    For invention . . . our case: Compare Cicero, *De inventione* 1.7.9; *Rhetorica ad Herennium* 1.2.3.

    an argument is a process . . . another: Quintilian, *Institutio oratoria* 5.10.11.

62   *By the same . . . very proclamation*: The dense and not easily trans-
      lated wordplay in these two sentences is meant to obfuscate a
      simple message: the more this boaster speaks, the more his
      words are contradicted by what everyone knows to be the case.
      The final part of the second sentence also could be translated,
      "the irony of common rumor mockingly proclaims in an offi-
      cial edict of its own promulgation"; but the rhetorical ques-
      tions in the next sentence follow more naturally if the procla-
      mation is characterized as both self-authored (*auctentico*) and
      ludicrous (*deridendo*: read as a gerundive, positioned at the end
      of the clause to produce a *cursus velox*).

      Let the deed overcome . . . renown: Geoffrey of Vinsauf, *Poetria nova*
      303.

63   *Not smoke . . . Cyclops*: Horace, *Ars poetica* 143–45.
      we will show . . . is embellished: See *Tria sunt* 5 and 7.

64   *A certain Arthur . . . same king*: Duke Arthur of Brittany was im-
      prisoned by his uncle King John of England in 1203. The letter
      itself is fictional.

65   The English translation of the letter duplicates the three varie-
      ties of rhythmical clause endings (*cursus planus, tardus, velox*)
      employed in the original Latin.

CHAPTER 4

1–14 The principal source is Geoffrey of Vinsauf, *Documentum* 2.2.30–
      45, but recast in a form that aligns the doctrine with *Poetria
      nova* 690–736.

1   Geoffrey of Vinsauf, *Documentum* 2.2.30.

2   *Emphasis, parataxis . . . same word*: Geoffrey of Vinsauf, *Poetria
      nova* 707–10.

3   *Emphasis . . . besides sin*: Geoffrey of Vinsauf, *Documentum* 2.2.32–
      34.
      Scipio's prudence destroyed Carthage: Compare *Rhetorica ad Heren-
      nium* 4.32.43.

4   *Parataxis . . . alone, unarmed*: Geoffrey of Vinsauf, *Documentum*
      2.2.35.

By your harshness . . . adversaries: *Rhetorica ad Herennium* 4.19.26.

5   *This way . . . adorns the subject matter*: Geoffrey of Vinsauf, *Documentum* 2.2.36, 35.

    And this method . . . famous city: Compare Gervase of Melkley, *De arte versificatoria et modo dictandi*, p. 35, ll. 9–12. The quotation is from Simon Aurea Capra, *Ylias* 1–2. Gervase quotes a similar couplet without naming its author.

6   *when we want . . . done, I came*: Geoffrey of Vinsauf, *Documentum* 2.2.38.

7   *The narrative . . . has been said*: Cicero, *De inventione* 1.20.28.

    so that once . . . before them: *Marii Victorini Explanationes in Ciceronis Rhetoricam*, p. 91, 1.20.91–92.

    As, when . . . repaid one hundred pounds: Compare Geoffrey of Vinsauf, *Documentum* 2.2.41.

    Whenever . . . from the harbor: Quintilian, *Institutio oratoria* 4.2.41.

8   *Asyndeton . . . previous example*: Geoffrey of Vinsauf, *Documentum* 2.2.36.

    Likewise also . . . garments of delight: Peter of Blois, *Libellus de arte dictandi rhetorice*, ll. 187–88.

    nothing . . . is said: Compare Quintilian, *Institutio oratoria* 4.2.41.

    One must . . . are brief: Cicero, *De inventione* 1.20.28.

10   *so that instead . . . the person coming*: Geoffrey of Vinsauf, *Documentum* 2.2.39–40.

11   *which Cicero enumerates in the first* Rhetoric: Cicero, *De inventione* 1.20.28.

    We will show . . . theme's intention: Compare Geoffrey of Vinsauf, *Documentum* 2.2.42–43.

12   *Her husband . . . by sun*: Geoffrey of Vinsauf, *Poetria nova* 713–17.

13   Compare Geoffrey of Vinsauf, *Documentum* 2.2.43.

    A husband . . . by sun: Geoffrey of Vinsauf, *Poetria nova* 733–34.

    Since his wife . . . by sun: Geoffrey of Vinsauf, *Poetria nova* 735–36.

14   *Now we . . . are two*: Geoffrey of Vinsauf, *Documentum* 2.2.44–45.

    one is . . . always please: Geoffrey of Vinsauf, *Documentum* 2.3.1–2, quoting Horace, *Ars poetica* 361–62, 365. The *Tria sunt* author-compiler also includes lines 363–64 ("This courts . . . the judge").

Lest ... pauper's rags: Geoffrey of Vinsauf, *Poetria nova* 755.

15   *Sad tones ... the grave*: Horace, *Ars poetica* 105–7.

16   *It is evident ... florid constructions*: Geoffrey of Vinsauf, *Documentum* 2.3.2; compare Horace, *Ars poetica* 47.

    For this reason Horace ... his shoulders: Horace, *Ars poetica* 38–41, quoted at the end of this section.

17   *that is, Pallas*: Pallas is an epithet of Athena, who is associated with the Roman goddess Minerva. Perhaps the author-compiler (or his source) confused Athena with Artemis, the Greek goddess associated with Diana.

18   *Perhaps, too ... wrecked vessel*: Horace, *Ars poetica* 19–20.

19   *Works ... a pitcher*: Horace, *Ars poetica* 14–22.

20   *Let rich ... pauper's rags*: Geoffrey of Vinsauf, *Poetria nova* 754–55.

    So just ... more elegant: Matthew of Vendôme, *Ars versificatoria* 2.11.

    The duty ... certain grace: Isidore, *Etymologiae* 8.7.10.

    Poets ... may emerge: Alan of Lille, *De planctu Naturae* 8.18.

21   *Badly spun ... course of time*: A Latin version of the popular proverb, "An ill-spun weft will out either now or eft."

    Often old ... new shame: Walther, *Proverbia*, no. 27,218.

    The phallus . . . the Fates: Bernard Silvestris, *Cosmographia* 2.14.165–66.

    This one ... blind pen: Gervase of Melkley, *De arte versificatoria et modo dictandi*, p. 135, ll. 4–9. Only the earliest copy of Gervase's work has what must be the correct reading *(Inspuitur)*, while the three later copies and all copies of *Tria sunt* share a simple misreading *(Inspicitur)* that changes the meaning of the final clause to "and whose favorite text is examined in a pink book by a blind pen."

    The hexameter's ... pounding: Matthew of Vendôme, *Ars versificatoria* 1.53.79–80. The male genitals are here metaphorized not only as battering ram but also as metrical unit, with the erect penis representing the single long syllable and the testicles the two short syllables that together constitute a dactyl.

    Grave apprehension ... exiled blushes: Matthew of Vendôme, *Ars versificatoria* 1.87.

22   *for just as . . . mutual favor*: Matthew of Vendôme, *Ars versificatoria* 3.49, quoting Ovid, *Remedia amoris* 420 ("things avail . . . are many").

23   *according to Cicero*: See *Rhetorica ad Herennium* 4.13.18.

CHAPTER 5

title   *transumption*: The translation employs this anglicized form of the Latin term *transumptio*—as opposed to the Greek term, *metalepsis*—in order to preserve the relationship between the noun that denotes the master trope and the verb (*transumere:* here translated "to transume") used to denote the process of transference that produces the trope's effects.

1–61   The chapter blends Geoffrey of Vinsauf, *Documentum,* especially 2.3.4–47, and *Poetria nova* 765–1093, with Gervase of Melkley, *De arte versificatoria et modo dictandi,* pp. 44–49, 69–73, 86, 91–97, 102, 108–16, 138; *Rhetorica ad Herennium* 4.31.42–34.46; and examples from a wide variety of sources.

1   *Ten things . . . second* Rhetoric: See *Rhetorica ad Herennium* 4.31.42.

2   The *Tria sunt* typically uses the term "colors" to designate the figures of speech and thought as treated in Book 4 of the *Rhetorica ad Herennium.* The English names of individual colors are frequently derived from their names in Greek. This complicates the task of translation when a particular "color" is compared to a corresponding "figure" whose name is derived from the same Greek word as the English name. In such cases, in this chapter and elsewhere (see esp. chaps. 7 and 8), the untranslated form of the color's Latin name and/or the clarifying modifier "color" is provided in the English translation.

4   Compare Isidore, *Etymologiae* 1.37.3.

5   *In its midst . . . murmurs*: Geoffrey of Vinsauf, *Documentum* 2.2.19, line 6.

    In its midst the earth weeps: Alan of Lille, *Anticlaudianus* 1.97.

6   *Flowering . . . in years*: Geoffrey of Vinsauf, *Poetria nova* 917.

    While he flourishes . . . declining age: Unidentified.

7   Geoffrey of Vinsauf, *Documentum* 2.3.9–11.

8   Geoffrey of Vinsauf, *Documentum* 2.3.12, 16.

       sweet taste . . . honeyed taste: The likely source of this curious detail is a series of adjectives that Geoffrey of Vinsauf applies metaphorically to "words": "we can say 'savory' words, 'seasoned' words, 'honeyed' words" (*verba 'sapida,' verba 'condita,' verba 'melliflua' dicamus; Documentum* 2.3.16).

9   *Her forehead . . . the lily*: Alan of Lille, *De planctu Naturae* 2.2.

       For the human . . . of Venus: Alan of Lille, *De planctu Naturae* 8.8.

10–15   The principal source is Gervase of Melkley, *De arte versificatoria et modo dictandi,* pp. 91, l. 8–97, l. 7.

10   *Master John of Hauville confirms*: Probably a reference to his oral teaching, as recorded by his former student Gervase of Melkley, *De arte versificatoria et modo dictandi,* p. 91, ll. 10–12.

       It has ever . . . the day: Horace, *Ars poetica* 58–59.

       And he explicates the above quotation of Horace: This attribution, based on Gervase of Melkley, *De arte versificatoria et modo dictandi,* p. 91, l. 14, is the only evidence that the commentary on the *Ars poetica* quoted at several points in the *Tria sunt* may have been written by John of Hauville.

       buba: Like "blictrix," a conventional nonsense word.

11   *In her face . . . the roses*: The lines are quoted by Gervase of Melkley, *De arte versificatoria et modo dictandi,* p. 92, ll. 6–7, but he does not identify their author. They are not from the *Architrenius*.

13   The difference between the two sentences is that the first says the changing of the water into ice is temporary ("seasonal") and the second says it is permanent ("perpetual").

15   *From afar . . . greening leaves*: *Eclogue of Theodulus* 83, quoted by Gervase of Melkley, *De arte versificatoria et modo dictandi,* p. 95, l. 13. Gervase also quotes the beginning of line 84, which is included in the translation to complete the thought.

       To illustrate . . . stone themselves: The source is Gervase of Melkley, *De arte versificatoria et modo dictandi,* p. 97, ll. 3–7, who may be quoting from John of Hauville's oral teaching or from a poem that has not survived. Gervase does not quote the line from Horace.

and license . . . with modesty: Horace, *Ars poetica* 51.

16 *"Megacosmus" and "Microcosmus"*: The two parts of the *Cosmographia* by Bernard Silvestris.

17 *Be tasteful . . . the day*: Horace, *Ars poetica* 46–59.

18 *as the Philosopher says*: Aristotle, *De interpretatione* 1.1.

21 *This person . . . bread of love*: Peter of Blois, *Libellus de arte dictandi rhetorice*, ll. 193–95.

22 The principal source is Gervase of Melkley, *De arte versificatoria et modo dictandi*, pp. 110, l. 1–111, l. 4, quoting "Parce continuis" 47–48 ("He lives . . . by Thisbe") and "Consulte teneros" 83–84 ("The knot . . . second Pyramus").

deprived of his own will: The meaning is more explicit in Gervase's *exclusus a voluntate* (p. 110, ll. 21–22) than in *Tria sunt*'s *a voluntate*.

Since "I" . . . to ego: Geoffrey of Vinsauf, *Summa de coloribus rhetoricis* 766–67.

It is licit to join amo *to* nos *and* amamus *to* ego: In their love they are simultaneously two persons and one person, so when declaring it they are allowed to break the rules of grammar by using the singular form of the verb "love" with a plural pronoun or vice versa.

23 Compare Geoffrey of Vinsauf, *Poetria nova* 908–18. In *Documentum* 2.2.19–22, Geoffrey distinguishes only the first two "respects" and provides completely different examples.

In the delightful . . . with flowers: Compare Geoffrey of Vinsauf, *Poetria nova* 897–901.

The preacher . . . entire mind: Compare Geoffrey of Vinsauf, *Poetria nova* 902–4.

25 *Onomatopoeia . . . quite appropriate*: *Rhetorica ad Herennium* 4.31.42.

The "quarreling" . . . the storm: Geoffrey of Vinsauf, *Poetria nova* 922.

the storm for its wrath: The translation corrects the sense of the Latin text ("the wrath for its storm").

The thundering . . . the city: Geoffrey of Vinsauf, *Poetria nova* 920.

26 The principal source is Gervase of Melkley, *De arte versificatoria et modo dictandi*, pp. 114, l. 13–115, l. 9, quoting John

of Hauville, *Architrenius* 1.42; "Francia dulcis, aue, regio bona, bella, salubris" 94 ("He is a dwarf . . . in mind"); and Geoffrey of Monmouth, *Historia regum Britanniae* 7.3 ("Next will come . . . wickedness").

27   *Antonomasia . . . proper name*: *Rhetorica ad Herennium* 4.31.42.

        Agenor was . . . Caesar: Gervase of Melkley, *De arte versificatoria et modo dictandi*, p. 111, ll. 19–20.

        Pelides: That is, Achilles.

        Davus was . . . in heart: Gervase of Melkley, *De arte versificatoria et modo dictandi*, p. 112, ll. 5–6.

28   *Allegory . . . their meaning*: *Rhetorica ad Herennium* 4.34.46.

        The captain . . . Automedon: Geoffrey of Vinsauf, *Poetria nova* 927–29.

        I shall . . . of Love: Ovid, *Ars amatoria* 1.8.

        Shepherds . . . sheep: Geoffrey of Vinsauf, *Poetria nova* 938.

        I plow . . . depraved man: Walther, *Proverbia*, no. 13,916; compare Geoffrey of Vinsauf, *Poetria nova* 943.

29   *The meadow . . . the leaves*: Peter of Blois, *Libellus de arte dictandi rhetorice*, ll. 185–86.

        This sort . . . or "tight": Peter of Blois uses these metaphors to characterize different kinds of metaphor (*Libellus de arte dictandi rhetorice*, ll. 165–67), so the sentence makes an observation about metaphor even as it provides examples of metaphors.

31   *Periphrasis . . . simple idea*: Compare *Rhetorica ad Herennium* 4.32.43.

        as when . . . "disgraceful": Compare Geoffrey of Vinsauf, *Documentum* 2.3.28.

        as is said . . . was discussed: See *Tria sunt* 4.3.

32   Gervase of Melkley, *De arte versificatoria et modo dictandi*, p. 71, ll. 1–13, with minor changes in wording.

33   *The wantonness . . . of the trees*: Geoffrey of Vinsauf, *Documentum* 2.2.19, l. 9.

35   *This sin . . . sudden terror*: Unidentified.

        The succession . . . our city: Unidentified.

36   *Metonymy . . . own name*: *Rhetorica ad Herennium* 4.32.43.

        bounded (finitis): In the *Rhetorica ad Herennium* the corresponding word is "associated" (*finitimis*).

37 *The inventor . . . Venus freezes*: Donatus, *Ars grammatica* 3.6, p. 668, ll. 16–17, quoting Terence, *Eunuchus* 732 ("Without Ceres . . . Venus freezes"); compare Isidore, *Etymologiae* 1.37.9.

In my drinking . . . than he: Hugh Primas, "In cratere meo," 1–2 (also quoted by Geoffrey of Vinsauf, *Summa de coloribus rhetoricis* 677–78).

38 *He is stupid . . . Bacchus*: Unidentified.

39 *The cause or the agent . . . causes sickness*: Geoffrey of Vinsauf, *Documentum* 2.3.26.

O happy sorrow in sad joy: Benedict of Peterborough, Office of St. Thomas of Canterbury, Vespers 1, Magnificat antiphon, ll. 5–6.

O happy . . . redeemer; O necessary . . . Adam: From the Exultet for the blessing of the Paschal candle; *Missale ad usum Sarum*, p. 340.

40 *Lest my pen . . . rust*: Alan of Lille, *Anticlaudianus*, verse prologue 3.

41 *The finger rejoices in gold*: Geoffrey of Vinsauf, *Poetria nova* 997.

Not yet . . . other lands: Ovid, *Metamorphoses* 1.94–95.

42 *Conversely . . . were made*: Compare Berentinus, *Colores rhetorici seriatim* 43 (viii).

43 *And the weak . . . great heart*: Walter of Châtillon, *Alexandreis* 1.57.

put on . . . your mind: Walter of Châtillon, *Alexandreis* 1.82.

murex: A shellfish from which purple dye is made.

Lilies . . . girl's face: Gervase of Melkley, *De arte versificatoria et modo dictandi*, p. 116, l. 13.

But you should . . . that is divisive etc.: Gervase of Melkley, *De arte versificatoria et modo dictandi*, p. 116, ll. 7–9.

divisive (disgregativus): In Gervase's example the corresponding word is "impoverished" *(degeneratus)*.

44 The principal source is Gervase of Melkley, *De arte versificatoria et modo dictandi*, p. 116, ll. 10–20, quoting "Consulte teneros" 39–40 ("In harmony . . . the teeth").

what is being conjoined (coniunccionis): In the earliest copy of Gervase's treatise, the corresponding word is "the construction" *(constructionis),* which makes better sense than the reading in *Tria sunt* and the later copies of Gervase's work.

For the word . . . "whiteness": In other words, the predicate of the sentence ("paint") must be applied to the word "face" to reveal

the meaning of the transumption in the subject of the sentence ("lilies"—white flowers—in place of the color "white"). The modifying *also* is "remote" in that "lilies" and "face" are not adjacent to one another but instead occupy the first and last positions in the line of verse.

45   *Hyperbole . . . diminishing praise*: *Rhetorica ad Herennium* 4.33.44.

Beside the maiden's face . . . is dull: "Consulte teneros" 41–42 (quoted by Gervase of Melkley, *De arte versificatoria et modo dictandi*, p. 86, ll. 12–13, who also supplies the sentence that follows: p. 86, l. 14).

Phoebus: That is, the sun.

You are more hydra . . . stone themselves: See note to *Tria sunt* 5.15.

And exaggeration . . . commend it: Geoffrey of Vinsauf, *Poetria nova* 1021.

You are neither . . . his own: Geoffrey of Vinsauf, *Poetria nova* 2068–71.

46   *Synecdoche . . . from the whole*: *Rhetorica ad Herennium* 4.33.44.

We recognize . . . four years; Likewise, this figure . . . great thing: Geoffrey of Vinsauf, *Documentum* 2.3.32.

The stern plows the sea: Peter Riga, *Floridus aspectus* 2.45, or Berentinus, *Colores rhetorici seriatim* 46 (i).

47   *We understand . . . of the sun*: Compare Berentinus, *Colores rhetorici seriatim* 46 (ii).

This year . . . cold winter: Geoffrey of Vinsauf, *Documentum* 2.3.33.

They carried . . . placed him: John 20:2.

as Bede says: Perhaps misattributing to Bede either Salonius, *In Parabolas Salomonis expositio mystica* (Migne, PL 53:976C), or Honorius Augustodunensis, *Quaestiones et ad easdem responsiones in duos Salomonis libros Proverbia et Ecclesiasten* (Migne, PL 172:318D).

It is done . . . of hair: Gervase of Melkley, *De arte versificatoria et modo dictandi*, p. 73, ll. 7–8, 11–12.

48   *Synecdoche . . . place of one*: The "others" are Berentinus, *Colores rhetorici seriatim* 46 and, to a lesser extent, Peter Riga, *Floridus aspectus* 2.47–48.

One in place of many . . . spoken about: Combines Berentinus, *Colo-*

res rhetorici seriatim 46 (iv), (iii), with Peter Riga, *Floridus aspectus* 2.48, 47.

And with . . . my face: Boethius, *De consolatione philosophiae* 1.metrum1.4.

The thieves . . . reproached him: Matthew 27:44.

as Bede explains: *In Lucae Evangelium expositio* 6.23.39, ll. 1660–76; *In Marci Evangelium expositio* 4.15.32, ll. 1468–83.

49   The principal source is *Rhetorica ad Herennium* 4.33.45.

50   *which is called . . . by Donatus*: See *Rhetorica ad Herennium* 4.32.44, and Donatus, *Ars grammatica* 3.6, pp. 670, l. 6–671, l. 11.

51   *Hyperbaton . . . and anastrophe*: *Rhetorica ad Herennium* 4.32.44.

Those whom . . . sins: The transposed elements in the examples have been marked with superscript letters to indicate normal word order. In the first example, hyperbaton allows the clauses to end with two of the standard cadences prescribed in letter-writing textbooks: *cursus tardus* (*impietatis calliditas*) and *cursus velox* (*gracia consolamen*). The model letters in *Tria sunt* (3.62 and 65) employ this system of rhythmical clause endings.

Often old . . . sins: Walther, *Proverbia,* no. 27,218.

has a narrower reference: Presumably meaning that every *transgressio* is also hyperbaton but not every hyperbaton is also *transgressio*.

52   The sentence as a whole illustrates the figure it defines, an effect that is possible in Latin but difficult to duplicate in English.

54   *the spirit of the listener*: Thus in *Tria sunt* (literally, "the breathing of the listener"); but the correct reading ("the ear of the listener") is found in the quotation that follows.

One should . . . the speaker: *Rhetorica ad Herennium* 4.12.18.

Hyperbaton does . . . is clear; A prolix . . . dainty details: Matthew of Vendôme, *Tobias* 2115–16, 2123–26.

when full of light (plena/Luce): Matthew of Vendôme's *plena/Lance* (on a full plate) makes better sense than the reading shared by all copies of *Tria sunt*.

Verse is . . . single thing: Matthew of Vendôme, *Ars versificatoria* 1.1.

55   *And it means . . . the lazy*: Compare Gervase of Melkley, *De arte versificatoria et modo dictandi,* pp. 44, l. 19, and 45, ll. 5–16.

56 *What makes ... joyous etc.*: Virgil, *Georgics* 1.1.

57 *Alas, how long ... swift galloping*: Walter of Châtillon, *Alexandreis* 1.33–36.

59 *Sleep ... Poverty*: John of Hauville, *Architrenius* 1.1.29–30.

  A tree ... the south wind: Unidentified. Found as a marginal verse with *ulmus* (elm) for *arbor* (tree) in a late thirteenth-century English manuscript: Cambridge, Gonville and Caius College 136/76, p. 26. Tony Hunt, *Teaching and Learning Latin in Thirteenth-century England,* 3 vols. (Woodbridge, Suffolk: D. S. Brewer, 1991), 1:166 (erroneously citing p. 25).

60 *And there is ... taken transumptively*: Gervase of Melkley, *De arte versificatoria et modo dictandi,* p. 138, ll. 4–5.

  And the lion ... his teeth: Walter of Châtillon, *Alexandreis* 1.54.

  Faith arms ... their bodies; Here the mind ... the tongue: Geoffrey of Vinsauf, *Poetria nova* 892, 595.

  The virgins ... shine equally: Gervase of Melkley, *De arte versificatoria et modo dictandi,* p. 138, ll. 6–8.

CHAPTER 6

1–2 *According to Cicero ... subject matter*: See *Rhetorica ad Herennium* 4.12.17–18.

2 *labdacism, metacism, and iotacism*: The excessive repetition of *l, m,* and *i,* respectively.

2–5 The principal source is Matthew of Vendôme, *Ars versificatoria* 2.10–38.

2 *are akin ... certain charm*: Matthew of Vendôme, *Ars versificatoria* 2.11.

3 *on the observance ... depends*: See Horace, *Ars poetica* 114–24, 156–78.

4 overfamiliar: The Latin *famulare* here seems to mean something like "servile," a meaning the translation attempts to capture while preserving the desired adjectival ending *-ar.*

6 *Moreover ... spoken already*: See *Tria sunt* 5.10–23.

  As Servius ... keeping silent: The ultimate source of the anecdote is Aulus Gellius, *Noctes Atticae* 11.9, but the immediate source

is almost certainly Gervase of Melkley, *De arte versificatoria et modo dictandi,* p. 104, ll. 7–12, who also cites Servius as his source.

7   The principal source is Matthew of Vendôme, *Ars versificatoria* 3.49–52.

Distinction . . . words and thoughts: Compare *Rhetorica ad Herennium* 4.13.18.

which are spoken about more fully later: See *Tria sunt* 7.29–96.

The constancy . . . native country: Benedict of Peterborough, Office of St. Thomas of Canterbury, Nocturn 1, Responsory 2, ll. 7–10 *(Versus)*.

<h2 style="text-align:center">Chapter 7</h2>

1–29   The principal source is Geoffrey of Vinsauf, *Documentum* 2.3.48–102.

3   *Cato's Marcia*: Lucan, *Bellum civile* 2.343–44 (quoted by Geoffrey of Vinsauf, *Documentum* 2.3.50).

4   *He was a Cicero . . . his youth*: Geoffrey of Vinsauf, *Documentum* 2.3.51; compare *Poetria nova* 1775–76.

5   *Let Medea . . . Orestes sorrowful*: Horace, *Ars poetica* 123–24 (partially quoted by Geoffrey of Vinsauf, *Documentum* 2.3.52).

Great Ovid: That is, the *Metamorphoses.*

The poplar-fringed . . . Oas: Ovid, *Metamorphoses* 1.579–80 (referred to but not quoted by Geoffrey of Vinsauf, *Documentum* 2.3.52).

in the place . . . a stag: See Ovid, *Metamorphoses* 3.206–24 (also referred to by Geoffrey of Vinsauf, *Documentum* 2.3.52).

In your presence . . . their flight: Geoffrey of Vinsauf, "Vexillum pacis," 15–16 (short version), or 31–32 (long version) (quoted in *Documentum* 2.3.52).

6   *That unconquered . . . received it*: Compare Geoffrey of Vinsauf, *Documentum* 2.3.53.

He unfolds . . . like Caesar: Sidonius Apollinaris, *Epistles* 4.3.6 (quoted by Geoffrey of Vinsauf, *Documentum* 2.3.53).

7   *The laurel . . . are rare*: Alan of Lille, *Anticlaudianus* 7.431, 436.

This sisterhood . . . Cicero himself: Alan of Lille, *Anticlaudianus* 2.343–44.

10   *His skin . . . not curved*: A variant of Sidonius Apollinaris, *Epistles* 4.13.2 (quoted by Geoffrey of Vinsauf, *Documentum* 2.3.57 and 2.3.101). See also *Tria sunt* 3.30.

The wind . . . the work: Geoffrey of Vinsauf, *Documentum* 2.3.57.

11   *Whence comes . . . abounds, lacks*: Lawrence of Durham, *Hypognosticon* 123–24 (quoted by Geoffrey of Vinsauf, *Documentum* 2.3.58).

12   *O thrice and four times blessed*: Compare Virgil, *Aeneid* 1.94 (quoted by Geoffrey of Vinsauf, *Documentum* 2.3.59).

Then shield . . . on lance: Statius, *Thebaid* 8.398–99 (quoted by Geoffrey of Vinsauf, *Documentum* 2.3.59, although *Tria sunt*'s wording is closer to the version in Matthew of Vendôme, *Ars versificatoria* 1.12).

Demophoon . . . death itself: Ovid, *Heroides* 2.147–48 (quoted by Geoffrey of Vinsauf, *Documentum* 2.3.59).

The sword . . . with carnage: Geoffrey of Vinsauf, *Documentum* 2.3.59 and 60.

13   The principal source is Matthew of Vendôme, *Ars versificatoria* 1.4–13.

As Isidore . . . three ways: Isidore, *Etymologiae* 1.36.3 (not named by Matthew of Vendôme).

adjunction; conjunction; disjunction: *Rhetorica ad Herennium* 4.27.38 (not cited by Matthew of Vendôme).

Cold things . . . weightless: Ovid, *Metamorphoses* 1.19–20 (quoted by Matthew of Vendôme, *Ars versificatoria* 1.6).

You my master . . . brother were: Ovid, *Heroides* 3.52 (quoted by Matthew of Vendôme, *Ars versificatoria* 1.11).

She yearns . . . her talons: Statius, *Thebaid* 2.130 (quoted by Matthew of Vendôme, *Ars versificatoria* 1.13).

Gracious conduct . . . enriches her: Matthew of Vendôme, *Ars versificatoria* 1.13.

15   *Sky, earth . . . grain, gulf*: The example appears to recast Ovid, *Ars amatoria* 2.467–72, using the device "each to each."

He hates . . . deceptions: Matthew of Vendôme, *Tobias* 89–90, 93–94.

16   *You can find . . . regal diligence*: Sidonius Apollinaris, *Epistles* 1.2.6
      (quoted by Geoffrey of Vinsauf, *Documentum* 2.3.62).

      Let the youth . . . firm sinews: Vegetius, *De re militari* 1.6.4 (quoted
      by Geoffrey of Vinsauf, *Documentum* 2.3.62).

      The feminine . . . merry fiddles: Geoffrey of Vinsauf, *Poetria nova*
      661–63 (first two words quoted in *Documentum* 2.3.62).

17   *The house . . . many ways*: Geoffrey of Vinsauf, *Documentum* 2.3.63.
      The puns in this distich are not easily translated but are not
      relevant to the technique being illustrated.

      which will be treated later: See *Tria sunt* 7.53.

      You seek . . . Solomon: Matthew of Vendôme, *Ars versificatoria* 3.9.

19   *She is . . . of chastity*: Alan of Lille, *Anticlaudianus* 5.487–89.

      Hope for the wretched . . . the weary: Alan of Lille, *Anticlaudianus*
      5.496–98.

      way (limes) *[for the blind]*: In the *Anticlaudianus* the correspond-
      ing word is "light" *(lumen)*.

      Woman . . . her innocence: Geoffrey of Vinsauf, *Documentum* 2.3.69.

20   *At her coming . . . after sorrow*: Alan of Lille, *Anticlaudianus* 5.505–
      7.

21   *Therefore . . . pious one*: Bernard Silvestris, *Mathematicus* 1.21–22
      (quoted by Geoffrey of Vinsauf, *Documentum* 2.3.73, who also
      attributes the lines to Bishop Hildebert of Le Mans).

      And you should note . . . proper usage: The accusative of respect, a
      usage borrowed from the Greek accusative, violates the nor-
      mal rules of Latin grammar but can be employed figuratively.
      Like the figure synecdoche, it can be understood to supply a
      part in place of the whole—the object of a preposition in place
      of the prepositional phrase that in "proper usage" would be
      necessary for a noun in the accusative case to "determine" an
      adjective, as in the examples that follow.

      Woman always . . . in fraud: Geoffrey of Vinsauf, *Documentum*
      2.3.77.

22   *He picks up . . . philosopher*: Sidonius Apollinaris, *Epistles* 1.2.7
      (quoted by Geoffrey of Vinsauf, *Documentum* 2.3.80).

23   *Your king . . . the pillar*: Geoffrey of Vinsauf, *Poetria nova* 330–31
      (in *Documentum* 2.3.82, a variant of *Poetria nova* 330–33 is quoted).

The mercy . . . his letters: The quotation and its attribution are from Geoffrey of Vinsauf, *Documentum* 2.3.85, but the source has not been identified.

I restore . . . been torn: Geoffrey of Vinsauf, *Documentum* 2.3.85.

Dry-eyed . . . noisy pleas: Geoffrey of Vinsauf, *Documentum* 2.3.86.

a color . . . parataxis: See *Tria sunt* 4.4–5.

Wicked not . . . with hand: Geoffrey of Vinsauf, *Documentum* 2.3.88.

25   *The beauty . . . her forehead*: Geoffrey of Vinsauf, *Documentum* 2.3.93.

27   *Here wild . . . each thing*: Geoffrey of Vinsauf, *Documentum* 2.3.95.

this method . . . all of them: Each of the variants in the manuscript copies of *Tria sunt—iste idem modus* (this/the same method)— loses the point of Geoffrey of Vinsauf, *Documentum* 2.3.96: *non in omni clausula variatur modus determinandi verbum, nec in omnibus est idem modus* (the method of determining is not varied in each clause, nor is it the same in all of them).

30–95   The principal source is *Rhetorica ad Herennium* 4.13.18–30.41, supplemented with examples from many other sources. Only direct quotations have been recorded in the notes.

30   *which have been treated sufficiently*: See *Tria sunt* 5.

the fine polish of the language itself: *Rhetorica ad Herennium* 4.13.18.

31   *You are the word . . . my right hand*: John of Hauville, *Architrenius* 1.6.200–201.

33   *Reject . . . the world*: William de Montibus, *Peniteas cito peccator* 10.

34   *You call . . . man's life*: *Rhetorica ad Herennium* 4.14.20.

If you . . . a rose: Frowin, *Antigameratus* 1.

35   *To friends . . . conciliatory*: *Rhetorica ad Herennium* 4.15.21.

However, the figure . . . give little: Gervase of Melkley, *De arte versificatoria et modo dictandi*, pp. 166, l. 15–167, l. 3.

Likewise, in the preceding . . . sad joy: See *Tria sunt* 5.39.

Gervase . . . fullest detail: See Gervase of Melkley, *De arte versificatoria et modo dictandi*, pp. 166, l. 14–181, l. 11.

36   *Exclamation . . . was discussed*: See *Tria sunt* 3.15.

O sorrow . . . you recall: Geoffrey of Vinsauf, *Poetria nova* 386–87.

37   *the color . . . delivered*: *Rhetorica ad Herennium* 4.15.22.

Don't you cast . . . found above: See *Tria sunt* 3.62.

38   *The covetous . . . be reduced*: Marbod of Rennes, *De ornamentis verborum* 44–45, possibly via Gervase of Melkley, *De arte versificatoria et modo dictandi*, p. 27, ll. 4–5, or Geoffrey of Vinsauf, *Summa de coloribus rhetoricis* 166–67.

39   *Maxim . . . in life*: *Rhetorica ad Herennium* 4.17.24.
      Often old sins cause new shame: Walther, *Proverbia*, no. 27,218.
      A man's . . . his face: *Miles gloriosus* 37 (Walther, *Proverbia*, no. 11,765).

40   *Reasoning by contraries . . . statements*: *Rhetorica ad Herennium* 4.18.25 (but the version in *Tria sunt* is missing key words).
      Who does . . . or you?: Marbod of Rennes, *De ornamentis verborum* 52, possibly via Gervase of Melkley, *De arte versificatoria et modo dictandi*, p. 158, l. 3, or Geoffrey of Vinsauf, *Summa de coloribus rhetoricis* 172.

41   *Colon . . . injuring yourself*: *Rhetorica ad Herennium* 4.19.26.

42   *Comma . . . subject matter*: See *Tria sunt* 4.4–5 (parataxis).
      Io was prompt . . . wealthy, noble: Gervase of Melkley, *De arte versificatoria et modo dictandi*, p. 45, ll. 14–15.

43   *Rhetorica ad Herennium* 4.19.27.

44   *A crowd . . . the eyes*: Peter Riga, *Floridus aspectus* 2.81.

45   *You praise . . . good fortune*: *Rhetorica ad Herennium* 4.20.28.
      For Troy . . . fate alone: "Pergama flere volo," 1.

46   *You dare . . . odiously*: *Rhetorica ad Herennium* 4.20.28.

47   *as was said . . . principle it is etc.*: The reference is to *Rhetorica ad Herennium* 4.20.28, but this example has not been quoted previously in *Tria sunt*.
      Cicero . . . sometimes mixed: See *Rhetorica ad Herennium* 4.20.28.
      Demophoon . . . death itself: Ovid, *Heroides* 2.147–48 (compare *Tria sunt* 7.12).
      And it should . . . treats paronomasia: *Rhetorica ad Herennium* 4.22–23.32.

48   *The plane . . . in valleys*: Bernard Silvestris, *Cosmographia* 1.3.265 (quoted by Gervase of Melkley, *De arte versificatoria et modo dictandi*, p. 11, ll. 5 and 12, and p. 12, l. 13).
      As is evident . . . many ways: See *Rhetorica ad Herennium* 4.21.29–23.32.

49   *Hypophora . . . under apostrophe*: See *Tria sunt* 3.17.

        O father . . . previously: Lawrence of Durham, *Hypognosticon* 1.93, the first of eight lines quoted in *Tria sunt* 3.17 (also quoted by Geoffrey of Vinsauf, *Summa de coloribus rhetoricis* 239–46 and *Documentum* 2.2.27, and by Gervase of Melkley, *De arte versificatoria et modo dictandi*, p. 27, ll. 10–17).

50   *Fame begets . . . finished work*: Matthew of Vendôme, *Tobias* 873–74, and *Ars versificatoria* 3.45. In the Latin, the repeated words alternate between the accusative and the nominative case.

        Moreover, anyone . . . agile versifier: Compare Matthew of Vendôme, *Ars versificatoria* 3.46.

        Sorrow me vexes . . . remedy: Unidentified.

51   *Rhetorica ad Herennium* 4.25.35.

52   A variant of *Rhetorica ad Herennium* 4.26.35.

53   *This man . . . at all*: Berentinus, *Colores rhetorici seriatim* 24.

54   *Paralipsis . . . are saying*: *Rhetorica ad Herennium* 4.27.37 (*occultatio*).

55   *that we touched upon . . . hypozeuxis*: See *Tria sunt* 7.13.

56   See *Tria sunt* 3.16.

57   See *Tria sunt* 3.2.

58   *Rhetorica ad Herennium* 4.28.39.

60   *Indecision . . . was treated*: See *Tria sunt* 3.18.

        Will your ear . . . (etc.): Geoffrey of Vinsauf, *Poetria nova* 348–49.

61   *Proof by elimination . . . are insisting*: *Rhetorica ad Herennium* 4.29.40.

        The one . . . of wisdom: A variant of Geoffrey of Vinsauf, *Poetria nova* 1186–92, 1196–97.

62   *The color . . . subject matter*: See *Tria sunt* 4.8.

63   *Aposiopesis . . . is left*: *Rhetorica ad Herennium* 4.30.41.

        Are you crying . . . That you love: Gervase of Melkley, *De arte versificatoria et modo dictandi*, pp. 28, l. 16–29, l. 17. The first example is also quoted by Geoffrey of Vinsauf, *Summa de coloribus rhetoricis* 741–42 and *Documentum* 2.3.168. The second example presumably comes from an otherwise unknown poem based on Ovid, *Metamorphoses* 9.454–665. Later in the same work (p. 83, ll. 22–25), Gervase quotes two lines from an "epistula Biblidis ad Caunum," perhaps from the same poem.

64   *Conclusion . . . done before*: Rhetorica ad Herennium 4.30.41.

The day . . . of death: Compare Eberhard the German, *Laborintus* 519–20, which concludes more logically: "therefore abandon the way of error" *(erroris ergo relinque viam)*.

66   *Nature weeps . . . noble station*: Alan of Lille, *De planctu Naturae* 1.13–14.

It pertains . . . try cases: Peter Riga, *Floridus aspectus* 2.62, or Berentinus, *Colores rhetorici seriatim* 49.

67   *as Cicero says*: See Rhetorica ad Herennium 4.36.48–37.49.

You wonder . . . wonder at it: Rhetorica ad Herennium 4.36.48.

68   *Fellow citizens . . . yourselves*: Rhetorica ad Herennium 4.37.49.

69   *I enjoyed . . . deprived me*: Rhetorica ad Herennium 4.37.49.

If heaven . . . God etc.: Geoffrey of Vinsauf, *Poetria nova* 412.

71   See *Tria sunt* 3.26–28.

72   *Division . . . subjoined*: Rhetorica ad Herennium 4.40.52.

Here beauty . . . your body: Peter Riga, *Floridus aspectus* 2.79.

73   *Rhetorica ad Herennium* 4.40.52.

74   *Rhetorica ad Herennium* 4.42.54 (with variants).

75   *We will vary . . . same thing*: Rhetorica ad Herennium 4.42.54 (with variants).

At the center . . . of water: Alan of Lille, *Anticlaudianus* 1.97–99.

77   *Rhetorica ad Herennium* 4.42–43.55 (with variants).

Dialogue . . . further on: See *Tria sunt* 7.91.

and for quite another use: In the *Rhetorica ad Herennium,* "and much more" *(adeo* in place of *alio usui).*

78   *Arousal . . . or terrible*: Rhetorica ad Herennium 4.43.55 (with variants).

Who . . . wit? etc.: Geoffrey of Vinsauf, *Poetria nova* 1325.

79   *"reasoning by contraries" . . . discussed previously*: See *Tria sunt* 7.40.

"conclusion" . . . discussed: See *Tria sunt* 7.64.

Very clear . . . Peter etc.: The line numbers for the examples from Geoffrey of Vinsauf's *Poetria nova* are (1) 1327–28, (2) 1331, (3) 1333–34, (4) 1335, (5) 1336, (6) 1340, (7) 1343.

80   *Dwelling on the point . . . cause rests*: Rhetorica ad Herennium 4.45.57.

81   *While you . . . the state*: Rhetorica ad Herennium 4.45.58.

82   *Comparison . . . different thing*: Rhetorica ad Herennium 4.45.59.

Consult with leaders . . . gentle again: Walter of Châtillon, *Alexandreis* 1.85–91.

by contrast . . . presentation: *Rhetorica ad Herennium* 4.45.59.

83–86   *Rhetorica ad Herennium* 4.46.59–47.60.

87   *Exemplification . . . a comparison*: *Rhetorica ad Herennium* 4.49.62.

Yet it . . . without fault: Geoffrey of Vinsauf, *Poetria nova* 1352–53.

88   *Simile . . . withstand*: *Rhetorica ad Herennium* 4.49.62 (with variants).

Every day . . . savage teeth: Eberhard the German, *Laborintus* 547–48, with variant readings in the second line.

89   *I mean . . . to memory*: *Rhetorica ad Herennium* 4.49.63.

90   *Character delineation . . . that character*: *Rhetorica ad Herennium* 4.50.63.

he attaches . . . his side: Compare Matthew of Vendôme, *Ars versificatoria* 1.51.9.

Do you . . . man? etc.: Geoffrey of Vinsauf, *Poetria nova* 1366.

91   *Dialogue . . . character*: *Rhetorica ad Herennium* 4.52.65.

92   See *Tria sunt* 3.19.

93   *Rhetorica ad Herennium* 4.53–54.67 (with variants and additional examples drawn from other sources).

Of the extensive . . . carry water: Peter Riga, *Floridus aspectus* 2.74, or Berentinus, *Colores rhetorici seriatim* 58.

I say . . . can conquer: A variant of Ennius, *Annales* 167 (179); compare Quintilian, *Institutio oratoria* 7.9.7.

This complexion . . . of that: Geoffrey of Vinsauf, *Poetria nova* 1559–60.

When Alexander the Great declared war etc.: Geoffrey of Vinsauf, *Poetria nova* 1567. The reference is to the fable at 1571–75.

When a woman . . . heat storm do?: Aesop, *Fabulae* 7.1–6.

94   *Conciseness . . . words*: *Rhetorica ad Herennium* 4.54.68.

Christ was conceived . . . was buried: From the Nicene Creed.

95   *Ocular demonstration . . . followed the event*: *Rhetorica ad Herennium* 4.55.68 (with additions).

We will speak . . . an action: See *Tria sunt* 12.27.

Flirting . . . virginity's loss: Matthew of Vendôme, *Ars versificatoria* 1.102.

CHAPTER 8

3   *Faults, figures . . . distinctions there*: Gervase of Melkley, *De arte versificatoria et modo dictandi,* pp. 7, l. 22–8, l. 8. The first example is from Donatus, *Ars grammatica* 2 (pp. 654, l. 1, and 663, l. 1).

    like "thee" in place of "they" . . . like "preyers" in place of "prayers": In the example of a "barbarism" or error, an archaic form of "they" *(olli)* is substituted for the current form *(illi)*. A literal translation of the example that illustrates the same process when employed to create a "color"—"like 'robbers' *(predones)* in place of 'heralds' *(precones)*"—lacks the pun and so misses the point.

5   *Scheme . . . ornamenting speech*: Compare Isidore, *Etymologiae* 1.36.1.

    For the method used in the translation to distinguish among the different names for the same figure, see the note to *Tria sunt* 5.2.

    Under scheme . . . similar cases: Compare Matthew of Vendôme, *Ars versificatoria* 3.45.

CHAPTER 9

1–4   The principal source is Matthew of Vendôme, *Ars versificatoria* 4.20–24.

2   *"synonymy" . . . permit it*: Isidore, *Etymologiae* 2.21.6. Isidore's examples are from Cicero, *In Catilinam* 1.8 and 1.10, respectively.

3   *The hexameter's . . . pounding*: Matthew of Vendôme, *Ars versificatoria* 1.53.79–80. See *Tria sunt* 4.21.

    For it . . . indignation: Alan of Lille, *De planctu Naturae* 8.26.

    And now . . . the earth: Virgil, *Aeneid* 4.584–85 (quoted by Matthew of Vendôme, *Ars versificatoria* 4.21).

    Practice . . . mastery: Matthew of Vendôme, *Ars versificatoria* 4.21, quoting *Tobias* 875–76.

5–14   The principal source is Geoffrey of Vinsauf, *Documentum* 2.3.105–31.

6   *The thundering . . . the city*: Geoffrey of Vinsauf, *Poetria nova* 920.

Love torments . . . by cunning: Matthew of Vendôme, *Ars versifica-toria* 4.22.

7   *A man's . . . face*: *Miles gloriosus* 37 (Walther, *Proverbia,* no. 11,765).

14   *And the noble . . . deep valleys*: Alan of Lille, *De planctu Naturae* 3.7–8.

15   *that we provided . . . "periphrasis"*: Probably *Tria sunt* 5.31–35, but see also 3.3–6 and 4.3.

The drunken earth . . . heedlessly: Unidentified. The expected epithet for "rain shower" is lacking in all manuscript copies of *Tria sunt*.

Chapter 10

1   *as Boethius says . . . to these*: See Boethius, *De topicis differentiis* 4.10.3–4 (PL 64:1212C–D).

Either follow . . . self-consistent: Horace, *Ars poetica* 119.

2   *diligent . . . expression*: Gervase of Melkley, *De arte versificatoria et modo dictandi,* p. 3, ll. 24–25.

3   *My aim . . . commonplace*: Horace, *Ars poetica* 240–43.

4   *imitation of brevity*: *imitacio brevitatis*—the reading in all copies of *Tria sunt*—may be a corruption of *imitacio veritatis* (imitation of the truth) or even of *vitacio brevitatis* (avoidance of brevity), a reading consistent with the supporting quotation from Horace.

Shunning . . . of art: Horace, *Ars poetica* 31.

By theory . . . experience in speaking: *Rhetorica ad Herennium* 1.2.3.

Three things . . . craftsmen: Geoffrey of Vinsauf, *Poetria nova* 1705–8.

Chapter 11

1–5 The principal source is Geoffrey of Vinsauf, *Documentum* 2.3.132–36.

1   *It is hard . . . unsung*: Horace, *Ars poetica* 128–30 (quoted by Geoffrey of Vinsauf, *Documentum* 2.3.132).

5   *Of Priam's fate . . . I'll sing*: Horace, *Ars poetica* 137 (quoted by Geoffrey of Vinsauf, *Documentum* 2.3.136). Neither Horace nor Geoffrey of Vinsauf identifies the poet as Ennius.

Here our modern . . . There etc.: Alan of Lille, *Anticlaudianus* 1.165–66.

6   Like sections 8 to 10, below, this material does not appear in the extant version of Geoffrey of Vinsauf's *Documentum*. Its ultimate source is a commentary on Horace's *Ars poetica* that is related but not identical to the anonymous twelfth-century "Materia" Commentary edited by Friis-Jensen (see Bibliography) and was either incorporated by Geoffrey of Vinsauf into a revised version of the *Documentum* or cited directly by the *Tria sunt*'s author-compiler.

Meleager begot: This is the reading in all manuscript copies of *Tria sunt.* Earlier in the sentence Tydeus is identified as the father of Diomedes.

7   The principal source is Geoffrey of Vinsauf, *Documentum* 2.3.137, quoting Horace, *Ars poetica* 131–37 ("In ground . . . I'll sing").

Cydic: Translates *Tria sunt*'s nonword *cidicus,* an obvious misreading of Horace's *ciclicus* (Cyclic).

What will . . . mouse!: Horace, *Ars poetica* 138–39.

nor Diomede's . . . death etc.: Horace, *Ars poetica* 146.

8   *Sing . . . men etc.*: Horace, *Ars poetica* 141–42.

How much . . . the Cyclops: Horace, *Ars poetica* 140–45.

9   *Nor does . . . with the middle*: Horace, *Ars poetica* 146–52.

10   *Another's life is a teacher for us*: *Distichs of Cato* 3.13.

I would advise . . . sonorous trifles: Horace, *Ars poetica* 317–22.

which Aesop tells in his fables: Aesop, *Fabulae,* 12.

fitly awaited: Here the commentator has mistaken Horace's adjective *morata* for the past participle of the verb *moror* (delayed, lingered).

He calls . . . that rhyme: Compare Matthew of Vendôme, *Ars versificatoria* 2.43.

Chapter 12

1–36   Although they are never cited by name, Thierry of Chartres's *Commentarius super Rhetoricam Ciceronis* and Ralph of Longchamp's *In Anticlaudianum Alani Commentum* are among the

principal sources for this chapter. They are cited in the notes only when they have been quoted verbatim or nearly verbatim.

1   *Two things . . . said or did*: Ralph of Longchamp, *In Anticlaudianum Alani Commentum,* p. 164, ll. 5–7.

A person . . . or did: Compare Boethius, *De topicis differentiis* 4.9.3 (PL 64:1212A).

For every . . . blame: Aristotle/Averroes, *De arte poetica,* translated by Hermann the German (Averroes's Middle Commentary on Aristotle's *Poetics*), chap. 1.

2   *Therefore . . . of a person*: Ralph of Longchamp, *In Anticlaudianum Alani Commentum,* p. 164, l. 16.

According to Cicero . . . achievement: See Cicero, *De inventione* 1.24.34.

How the attributes . . . of strength: Alan of Lille, *Anticlaudianus* 3.215–19.

change (mutant) *with the false appearance*: In the *Anticlaudianus,* "rely *(nutant)* on the false appearance."

3   *Slayer Caesar . . . his name*: Matthew of Vendôme, *Ars versificatoria* 1.78, and 1.51.31–32, deriving "Caesar" from *caesus,* the past participle of *caedere* (to cut, strike, kill).

4   *Nature . . . by nature*: A variant of Ralph of Longchamp, *In Anticlaudianum Alani Commentum,* p. 164, ll. 26–27.

For this attribute . . . from externals: See *Marii Victorini Explanationes in Ciceronis Rhetoricam,* p. 110, 1.24.162–64; compare Matthew of Vendôme, *Ars versificatoria* 1.79.

Statius drew . . . limbs etc.: A variant of Ralph of Longchamp, *In Anticlaudianum Alani Commentum,* p. 165, ll. 3–6.

Taller he . . . limbs etc.: Statius, *Thebaid* 1.414 (quoted by Matthew of Vendôme, *Ars versificatoria* 1.80).

5   *Yet was Tydeus . . . held sway*: Statius, *Thebaid* 1.415–17 (quoted by Matthew of Vendôme, *Ars versificatoria* 1.81).

A whole assembly . . . of honor: Matthew of Vendôme, *Ars versificatoria* 1.50.19–20.

6   *those five that we mentioned earlier*: Apparently a reference to *Tria sunt* 3.53–55. However, in chapter 3, not five but six external attributes are treated, three of them also listed here by the same names *(etas, sexus, patria)* and one by a different name *(gens,* in

place of *nacio*), and two that are here supposedly added to the earlier list *(condicio, officium)*. Kinship *(cognacio)* is not among the external attributes identified by name in chapter 3, but it is the basis of the argument of the second model letter in that chapter (3.65).

To these Horace ... civil rank: Horace, *Ars poetica* 114–18.

Vast difference ... speaks etc.: Horace, *Ars poetica* 114.

7   *Cadmus ... Mavortian Thebes*: Statius, *Thebaid* 1.680 (quoted by Matthew of Vendôme, *Ars versificatoria* 1.82).

8   *Ho! ... ever etc.*: Virgil, *Aeneid* 4.569–70 (quoted by Matthew of Vendôme, *Ars versificatoria* 1.82).

An extravagant ... judgment: A variant of Juvenal, *Satires* 6.362 (quoted by Matthew of Vendôme, *Ars versificatoria* 1.82).

9   *My race Mavortian Thebes*: Compare Statius, *Thebaid* 1.680 (quoted correctly by Matthew of Vendôme, *Ars versificatoria* 1.82).

Vendôme's tribe ... punch bowl: Matthew of Vendôme, *Ars versificatoria* 2.38.29.

10   *Scarce ... barbarian hand*: Ovid, *Heroides* 3.2.

11   *Is it ... and eager?*: Ovid, *Heroides* 5.129 (quoted by Matthew of Vendôme, *Ars versificatoria* 1.82).

The child ... every hour: Horace, *Ars poetica* 158–60.

The beardless youth ... his fancies: Horace, *Ars poetica* 161–65.

With altered aims ... to change: Horace, *Ars poetica* 166–68.

Many ills ... the young: Horace, *Ars poetica* 169–74.

So, lest ... age etc.: Horace, *Ars poetica* 176–77.

12   *Way ... upbringing*: Ralph of Longchamp, *In Anticlaudianum Alani Commentum*, p. 166, l. 7.

Cicero divides ... what tradition: See Cicero, *De inventione* 1.25.35; *Marii Victorini Explanationes in Ciceronis Rhetoricam*, p. 112, 1.25.15–16.

He once ... of Sulla: Lucan, *Bellum civile* 1.330 (quoted by Matthew of Vendôme, *Ars versificatoria* 1.83).

of Sulla: I have translated the reading *Sillanum*, shared by Matthew of Vendôme and many copies of *Tria sunt*, as if it were simply a variant spelling of Lucan's *Sullanum;* but the meaning of the term seems to have caused as much trouble as the spell-

ing. The spelling *Scille* that many copies of *Tria sunt* employ in the passage explaining Lucan's line suggests that readers may have understood Lucan as referring (metaphorically) to the monster Scylla.

Did you not . . . your chastity?: Sallust(?), *In M. Tullium Ciceronem Oratio* 1.2.

It is difficult . . . habitual evil: Matthew of Vendôme, *Ars versificatoria* 1.53.25–26, and 1.83 (in part).

13   *Virgil draws . . . son's love*: A variant of Ralph of Longchamp, *In Anticlaudianum Alani Commentum*, p. 166, ll. 18–20.

Fare forth . . . son's love: Virgil, *Aeneid* 3.480 (quoted by Ralph of Longchamp and by Victorinus, *Marii Victorini Explanationes in Ciceronis Rhetoricam*, p. 113, 1.25.56–57).

By his wickedness . . . creation: Matthew of Vendôme, *Ars versificatoria* 1.53.81–82. Matthew sharpens the satire by employing the theological term for the Creation (*opus condicionis*).

14   *Habit, according to Cicero . . . and application*: Compare Cicero, *De inventione* 1.25.36. The immediate source is probably a combination of Ralph of Longchamp, *In Anticlaudianum Alani Commentum*, p. 167, ll. 1–2, and Thierry of Chartres, *Commentarius super Rhetoricam Ciceronis*, p. 134, ll. 93–94.

To know something . . . way of life: Marii Victorini Explanationes in Ciceronis Rhetoricam, p. 113, 1.25.36–39.

Moreover . . . "application": Thierry of Chartres, *Commentarius super Rhetoricam Ciceronis*, p. 134, ll. 4–5.

Ulysses . . . eloquent: Ovid, *Ars amatoria* 2.123 (quoted by Matthew of Vendôme, *Ars versificatoria* 1.85).

15   *Feeling . . . be cheerful*: Thierry of Chartres, *Commentarius super Rhetoricam Ciceronis*, p. 134, ll. 7–9; but compare also Victorinus, *Explanationes in Rhetoricam M. Tullii Ciceronis*, p. 115, 1.25.114–15.

O how . . . the face: Ovid, *Metamorphoses* 2.447 (quoted by Matthew of Vendôme, *Ars versificatoria* 1.87).

A man's . . . face: Miles gloriosus 37 (Walther, *Proverbia*, no. 11,765).

16   *Interest is . . . or poetry*: Cicero, *De inventione* 1.25.36; *Marii Victorini Explanationes in Ciceronis Rhetoricam*, p. 115, 1.25.121–23.

If we want . . . way of life: *Marii Victorini Explanationes in Ciceronis Rhetoricam,* pp. 115–16, 1.25.127–32.

With altered aims . . . wealth etc.: Horace, *Ars poetica* 166–67.

17 *Counsel . . . something*: Cicero, *De inventione* 1.25.36.

"Plan" . . . truthfully discovered: Thierry of Chartres, *Commentarius super Rhetoricam Ciceronis,* p. 135, ll. 19–20.

Counsel . . . to choose: Matthew of Vendôme, *Ars versificatoria* 1.88.

Guide me . . . unwavering strength: Lucan, *Bellum civile* 2.244–45 (quoted by Matthew of Vendôme, *Ars versificatoria* 1.88).

And let . . . your mind: Claudian, *Panegyricus de quarto consulatu Honorii Augusti* 268 (quoted by Matthew of Vendôme, *Ars versificatoria* 1.88).

It is difficult . . . in counsel: Thierry of Chartres, *Commentarius super Rhetoricam Ciceronis,* p. 136, ll. 53–55.

18 *Accident . . . men's characters*: Matthew of Vendôme, *Ars versificatoria* 1.89.

Accident differs . . . been said: A variant of Ralph of Longchamp, *In Anticlaudianum Alani Commentum,* p. 167, ll. 31–33.

Anyone . . . stood firm: Boethius, *Philosophiae consolatio* 1.metrum1.22.

Only with . . . angry fortune: Matthew of Vendôme, *Ars versificatoria* 1.89.

accident is . . . greater effect: Matthew of Vendôme, *Ars versificatoria* 1.90.

19 *Speech is . . . a person*: Matthew of Vendôme, *Ars versificatoria* 1.92.

Every word . . . full mind: Horace, *Ars poetica* 337 (quoted by Matthew of Vendôme, *Ars versificatoria* 1.92).

The prayer . . . naked sword: Walther, *Proverbia,* no. 7758.

The pope . . . spiritual sway: Matthew of Vendôme, *Ars versificatoria* 1.50.13–14.

20 *Achievement . . . some person*: Matthew of Vendôme, *Ars versificatoria* 1.91.

whatever . . . practicing: Thierry of Chartres, *Commentarius super Rhetoricam Ciceronis,* p. 135, ll. 21–22.

Caesar . . . blood etc.: Lucan, *Bellum civile* 2.439–40 (quoted by Matthew of Vendôme, *Ars versificatoria* 1.91).

21   *There are . . . from the action*: Ralph of Longchamp, *In Anticlaudianum Alani Commentum*, p. 168, ll. 15–17.

             What comprise . . . normal procedure: Alan of Lille, *Anticlaudianus* 3.220–22.

22   *Coherent . . . from it*: Cicero, *De inventione* 1.26.37.

             There are . . . after the fact: Matthew of Vendôme, *Ars versificatoria* 1.112.

23   *a brief summary . . . of country*: Cicero, *De inventione* 1.26.37.

             And this . . . Victorinus says: Victorinus does not make this point in his commentary on the passage from Cicero: *Marii Victorini Explanationes in Ciceronis Rhetoricam*, p. 118, 1.26.61–67. The likely source is either Thierry of Chartres, *Commentarius super Rhetoricam Ciceronis*, p. 137, ll. 99–3, or, more likely, Ralph of Longchamp, *In Anticlaudianum Alani Commentum*, p. 168, ll. 20–22.

             O soldier . . . depends etc.: Lucan, *Bellum civile* 7.250–51 (l. 250 quoted by Matthew of Vendôme, *Ars versificatoria* 1.95).

             A roaming buffoon . . . the world: Matthew of Vendôme, *Ars versificatoria* 1.53.1–2, and 1.95.

24   *Cause is . . . impulsive*: A variant of Ralph of Longchamp, *In Anticlaudianum Alani Commentum*, p. 168, l. 26.

             Magnus . . . of strength: Lucan, *Bellum civile* 2.526–27 (quoted by Matthew of Vendôme, *Ars versificatoria* 1.98).

             My aim . . . success etc.: Horace, *Ars poetica* 240–41 (quoted by Matthew of Vendôme, *Ars versificatoria* 1.98).

             Lest haply . . . of manhood: Horace, *Ars poetica* 176–77 (quoted by Matthew of Vendôme, *Ars versificatoria* 1.98).

             So as . . . or gifts: Matthew of Vendôme, *Ars versificatoria* 1.98.

25   *A cause . . . commotion of the mind*: Matthew of Vendôme, *Ars versificatoria* 1.97.

             any cause . . . impulsive cause: *Marii Victorini Explanationes in Ciceronis Rhetoricam*, p. 119, 1.26.94–96.

             As in Ovid . . . willingly: Matthew of Vendôme, *Ars versificatoria* 1.97, quoting Ovid, *Metamorphoses* 4.96 ("Love made her bold") and Juvenal, *Satires* 3.78 ("Your hungry . . . he will").

             He gives . . . gave willingly: Compare Ovid, *Metamorphoses* 1.610–21.

26 *But perhaps . . . an action*: Matthew of Vendôme, *Ars versificatoria*
    1.99.

    *For if counsel . . . attributes of a person; If, on the other hand . . . from
    ratiocinative cause*: Compare Thierry of Chartres, *Commentarius
    super Rhetoricam Ciceronis,* p. 138, ll. 27–30.

    *In every statement . . . be seen: Marii Victorini Explanationes in Cic-
    eronis Rhetoricam,* p. 88, 1.19.84–86.

28 *after the fact . . . secluded place*: Compare Boethius, *De topicis dif-
    ferentiis* 4.10.7 (PL 64:1213A).

    Flirting . . . threefold etc.: Matthew of Vendôme, *Ars versificatoria*
    1.102. See *Tria sunt* 7.95.

30 *The quality . . . the like*: Compare Thierry of Chartres, *Commen-
    tarius super Rhetoricam Ciceronis,* p. 140, ll. 84–85.

    He makes . . . boulder etc.: Statius, *Thebaid* 2.554–59, 561.

    A nearer road . . . between etc.: Statius, *Thebaid* 2.496–99.

31 *is a part . . . or night's*: Cicero, *De inventione* 1.26.39.

    Now all things . . . its fairest: Matthew of Vendôme, *Ars versificato-
    ria* 1.106, a variant of Virgil, *Eclogues* 3.57.

32 *Occasion . . . of the time*: Thierry of Chartres, *Commentarius super
    Rhetoricam Ciceronis,* p. 141, ll. 20–21.

33 *And so skilfully . . . the middle*: Horace, *Ars poetica* 151–52 (quoted
    by Matthew of Vendôme, *Ars versificatoria* 1.105).

    Did I . . . its songs?: Virgil, *Eclogues* 3.21–22 (quoted by Matthew of
    Vendôme, *Ars versificatoria* 1.105).

    Quick credulity . . . flimsy effects: Matthew of Vendôme, *Piramus et
    Tisbe* 125–26, and *Ars versificatoria* 1.105.

    Impetuous force is always hard to face: Ovid, *Remedia amoris* 120. In
    Tria sunt, the last words of the previous example have been
    repeated by mistake: *Difficiles aditus impetuosa manus* (A quick
    hand is hard to face). The line from Ovid is quoted correctly by
    Matthew of Vendôme, *Ars versificatoria* 1.105.

34 *Means . . . more readily*: Thierry of Chartres, *Commentarius super
    Rhetoricam Ciceronis,* p. 142, ll. 76–77, and/or Ralph of Long-
    champ, *In Anticlaudianum Alani Commentum,* p. 169, ll. 21–22.

    To beguile . . . earned: Ovid, *Heroides* 2.63–64 (quoted by Matthew
    of Vendôme, *Ars versificatoria* 1.104).

    It is easy . . . misled: Matthew of Vendôme, *Ars versificatoria* 1.104.

36   Compare Boethius, *De topicis differentiis* 4.10.1–13 (PL 64:1212C–1213B).

     Who, what . . . how, when: Matthew of Vendôme, *Ars versificatoria* 1.116.

     The attributes . . . "to stand": Thierry of Chartres, *Commentarius super Rhetoricam Ciceronis,* pp. 128, l. 31–129, l. 33, and/or Ralph of Longchamp, *In Anticlaudianum Alani Commentum,* p. 164, ll. 13–15.

CHAPTER 13

1   *Some call . . . characters*: Thierry of Chartres, *Commentarius super Rhetoricam ad Herennium,* p. 324, ll. 71–72.

     The grand . . . standard speech: *Rhetorica ad Herennium* 4.8.11.

2–7   The source is either John of Garland, *Parisiana Poetria,* chap. 5, ll. 402–67, or its source—perhaps a revised version of Geoffrey of Vinsauf's *Documentum.* In an appendix to his edition of the *Parisiana Poetria* (pp. 328–30), Lawler prints these sections of *Tria sunt* (from manuscript *Ol,* with corrections from *Ob*). See also Lawler's commentary on pages 256–58.

4   *the first letter that we provided earlier*: See *Tria sunt* 3.62.

     Bernard Silvestris . . . in verse: Gervase of Melkley, *De arte versificatoria et modo dictandi,* p. 1, ll. 10–11.

6   *just as has been said . . . isocolon*: See *Tria sunt* 7.44.

CHAPTER 14

1–15 The ultimate source for much of this chapter is a commentary on Horace's *Ars poetica* that is related but not identical to the "Materia" Commentary edited by Friis-Jensen, who prints this chapter as an appendix to his edition (pp. 385–88; from manuscript *Ol,* with variants from *Os*). A second source is either John of Garland, *Parisiana Poetria,* chap. 5, ll. 1–111, or its source—perhaps a revised version of Geoffrey of Vinsauf's *Documentum,* which probably derives from the same Horace commentary. In an appendix to his edition of the *Parisiana Poetria* (pp. 330–31), Lawler prints the portions of *Tria sunt* 14 that most closely resemble portions of *Parisiana Poetria,* namely, the title and ex-

cerpts from sections 1, 2, 11, and 13 (from manuscript *Ol,* with corrections from *Ob*). The extant version of Geoffrey of Vinsauf's *Documentum* covers the same topics (2.3.146–62) but does not draw on the unknown Horace commentary. However, it does cite most of the same lines from Horace's *Ars poetica* that are cited in *Tria sunt* 14.

1   At several points, the mnemonic verses illustrate a vice in the process of naming it. Thus, *breve* is shorter but also more obscure in this context than *brevitas* would have been, and the "variation" in the way the fifth vice is named can be seen as "excessive" because it disrupts the syntactic parallelism.

2   *If a painter . . . lambs with tigers*: Horace, *Ars poetica* 1–13 (ll. 1–9 quoted by Geoffrey of Vinsauf, *Documentum* 2.3.155).

      "such pictures," that is, paintings: The Latin *tabule* refers literally to the material objects ("tablets, panels") that hold painted images *(picture)*.

      this is the figure tmesis: The commentator apparently reads Horace's *uni . . . formae (forme* in medieval spelling) as two parts of the single word *uniforme*.

      anthypophora: Along with "hypophora," the Latinized Greek term for the figure whose Latin name is *subiectio,* as in *Tria sunt* 3.17.

3   *as has been said earlier*: See *Tria sunt* 3.25.

      And, as we said . . . finish skillfully: See *Tria sunt* 4.17.

      which we provided earlier: See *Tria sunt* 4.19.

      Works with . . . wide etc.: Horace, *Ars poetica* 14–15 (ll. 14–18 quoted by Geoffrey of Vinsauf, *Documentum* 2.3.156).

4   *However, we have treated . . . quite thoroughly*: See *Tria sunt* 4.

      Most of us . . . obscure etc.: Horace, *Ars poetica* 24–26.

5   *concerning which we have spoken*: See *Tria sunt* 13.1.

10   *Aiming . . . the ground*: Horace, *Ars poetica* 26–28.

11   *is a praiseworthy . . . virtue*: The second half of an unidentified hexameter.

      monotony is the mother of boredom: A variant of Cicero, *De inventione* 1.41.76.

      The present page . . . with jests: Aesop, *Fabulae,* prol. 1–2.

      Poets aim . . . to amuse: Horace, *Ars poetica* 333.

He has won . . . and pleasure: Horace, *Ars poetica* 343.

Horace follows . . . rural life: See Horace, *Satires* 2.6.79–117.

as Lucan does . . . Antaeus: See Lucan, *Bellum civile* 4.593–660.

12   *Telephus and Peleus . . . words*: Horace, *Ars poetica* 96–97.

13   *The man . . . lack of art*: Horace, *Ars poetica* 29–31 (ll. 29–30 quoted by Geoffrey of Vinsauf, *Documentum* 2.3.161).

14   *However . . . should be composed*: See *Tria sunt* 16.1–8.

it would please . . . at the end: That is, neither would please me.

Near the Aemilian . . . black hair: Horace, *Ars poetica* 32–37. If (mis)translated to match the commentator's gloss, the first two lines would read as follows: "The craftsman Imus will depict Aemilius at play and in bronze will imitate nails and waving locks."

CHAPTER 15

1–6   The principal source is either John of Garland, *Parisiana Poetria*, chap. 5, ll. 303–72, or its source—perhaps a revised version of Geoffrey of Vinsauf's *Documentum*. In an appendix to his edition of the *Parisiana Poetria* (pp. 331–32), Lawler prints these sections of *Tria sunt* (from manuscript *Ol*, with corrections from *Ob*), omitting the portions that come from other sources. See also Lawler's commentary on pages 254–56.

1   *For there is . . . and argument*: Paraphrases Cicero, *De inventione* 1.19.27, or *Rhetorica ad Herennium* 1.8.12–13.

2   *Fable is . . . likely events*: Cicero, *De inventione* 1.19.27, or *Rhetorica ad Herennium* 1.8.13 (quoted by John of Garland, *Parisiana Poetria*, chap. 5, l. 317).

Ovid does this . . . the flood: See Ovid, *Metamorphoses* 1.395–415.

the veins . . . same name: Ovid, *Metamorphoses* 1.410.

But what . . . became bone: Ovid, *Metamorphoses* 1.409.

Fictions . . . the real: Horace, *Ars poetica* 338.

4   *History is . . . recent memory*: Cicero, *De inventione* 1.19.27, or *Rhetorica ad Herennium* 1.8.13 (quoted by John of Garland, *Parisiana Poetria*, chap. 5, ll. 321–22).

And it is derived . . . written about: Compare Isidore, *Etymologiae* 1.41.1.

5 *about the living* (viventibus): Not in John of Garland's definition
  of this type of "plain song" *(nudum . . . carmen),* which apparently is an epitaph delivered before the body was buried.

 hexameter and pentameter verses: Elegiac couplets, in which a hexameter line alternates with a pentameter line.

 Indignant . . . the rustic: These verses appear both in John of Garland's *Compendium grammaticae* (as hexameters) and in his *Pari-*
  siana Poetria, chap. 5, ll. 363–64 (an elegiac couplet, as in *Tria*
  sunt), as Lawler points out in the notes to his edition of the latter (pp. 255–56).

 The poet . . . paltry goat: Horace, *Ars poetica* 220.

6 *Let no play . . . the stage*: Horace, *Ars poetica* 189–90.

7 Compare Geoffrey of Vinsauf, *Documentum* 2.3.163–69.

 Three of us . . . servant etc.: Geoffrey of Vinsauf, *Poetria nova* 1888.

 which already have been discussed: See *Tria sunt* 7.63 and 7.54, respectively.

 Whom I . . . troubled waves: Virgil, *Aeneid* 1.135 (quoted by Geoffrey of Vinsauf, *Documentum* 2.3.169).

Chapter 16

1–4 The principal source is Geoffrey of Vinsauf, *Documentum* 3.1–6.

1 *The conclusion . . . the art*: A variant of *Rhetorica ad Herennium* 1.3.4.

 a conclusion . . . overall design: A variant of Matthew of Vendôme,
  Ars versificatoria 4.49.

2 *As for myself . . . aged dame*: Ovid, *Heroides* 1.115–16 (quoted by
  Geoffrey of Vinsauf, *Documentum* 3.3).

 On my tomb . . . death itself: Ovid, *Heroides* 2.145–48 (quoted by
  Geoffrey of Vinsauf, *Documentum* 3.4).

 The city . . . stands guard: "Mens erit huic operi Priamo duce digna
  timeri" 77–78.

3 *Dispense . . . your kings*: "Mens erit huic operi Priamo duce digna
  timeri" 79. Geoffrey of Vinsauf, *Documentum* 3.5, quotes this
  line as well as line 80, which completes the thought: "From this
  plague you will see how great its harvest would be" *(Ex hac peste*
  leges, quanta sit inde seges).

4 The source for this section, Geoffrey of Vinsauf, *Documentum*

3.6, perhaps in a revised version, is also the source for John of Garland, *Parisiana Poetria,* chap. 5, ll. 120–27. Geoffrey quotes Horace, *Ars poetica* 475–76 and *Epistles* 2.2.214–16.

5   *Also, a conclusion . . . go home*: Not in Geoffrey of Vinsauf's extant *Documentum* but may come from a revised version of that work, since it does appear in John of Garland, *Parisiana Poetria,* chap. 5, ll. 114–16, quoting Virgil, *Eclogues* 10.77.

      O my book . . . fame etc.: Alan of Lille, *Anticlaudianus* 9.410–11.

      O nursed . . . clothed etc.: John of Hauville, *Architrenius* 9.468.

6   Matthew of Vendôme, *Ars versificatoria* 4.50, quoting Ovid, *Tristia* 1.7.40.

7   *In letters . . . lest, because*: Compare John of Garland, *Parisiana Poetria,* chap. 5, ll. 128–29.

      But always more . . . suffices: See *Tria sunt* 3.65, and, for the doctrine, 3.49.

Glossary of Technical Terms

Most of the terms glossed below designate various means of ornamentation, which is a central concern in the *Tria sunt*. The names of the sixty-five "colors" are those used by Caplan in his Loeb translation of the principal source for the canonical list: Book 4 of the *Rhetorica ad Herennium*. However, the brief definitions supplied here are meant to capture the *Tria sunt*'s interpretation of those terms, which may not correspond exactly to other, better-known definitions of the same terms, including those in the *Rhetorica ad Herennium*. A term that is glossed in its own right is put within single quotation marks when it appears within the gloss of another term.

ablative absolute (ablativus absolutus): a Latin grammatical construction that is also a means of 'shortening,' 4.6.

accumulation: See colors of thoughts 6.

adjunction: See colors of words B.27.

allegory: See colors of words A.3.

ambiguity (ambiguum): a statement that can be understood in more than one sense but is framed in such a way that the desired sense is implied; a variety of the 'color of thoughts' called 'emphasis,' 7.93.

analogy (similitudo): juxtaposing two things whose resemblance is implied rather than stated; a variety of the 'color of thoughts' called 'emphasis,' 7.93. The term "analogy" is used to distinguish this technique from the related 'color of thoughts' [10] called 'comparison' *(similitudo),* which is not required to signify by implication.

485

anthypophora: See colors of words B.19.

antistrophe: See colors of words B.2.

antithesis: See colors of words B.5; colors of thoughts 9.

antonomasia: See colors of words A.2.

aposiopesis: See colors of words B.35.

apostrophe: a means of 'extending' by pausing to address a person or thing outside the text; its four varieties—'exclamation,' 'reduplication,' 'hypophora,' and 'indecision'—are all 'colors of words,' 3.14–18.

argument (argumentum): the subdivision of 'narrative' that recounts events that are not true but are verisimilar, as in an eclogue *(egloga)* or a comedy *(comedia),* 15.6.

arousal (exuscitacio): expressing one's own emotions in order to evoke the same emotion in another; one of the techniques employed to produce the 'color of thought' called 'refining,' 7.78.

asyndeton: See colors of words B.34.

attributes of an action (attributa negocio): important sources for developing probable arguments (only those coherent with the action—the gist of the action, the cause of the action, and the triple handling of the action—and those in the performance of the action—place, time, occasion, manner, and means—are relevant to writers and orators); correspond to six of the seven 'circumstances,' esp. 12.21–36.

attributes of a person (attributa persone): important sources for developing probable arguments (name, nature, way of life, fortune, habit, interest, feeling, counsel, accidents, speech, and achievement); correspond to the first of the seven 'circumstances,' esp. 3.53–58; 12.1–20, 36.

avoidance of repetition (repeticionis vitacio): a means of 'shortening,' 4.9.

barbarism (barbarismus): a word that is defective in form, especially one that mixes elements from two different languages. *See also* metaplasm.

catachresis: See colors of words A.9.

character delineation: See colors of thoughts 14.

circumlocution (circumlocucio): a means of 'extending' by expressing a simple sentiment in a roundabout way, 3.3–6. *Compare* periphrasis (colors of words A.5).

circumstances (circumstancie): represented as a set of seven questions, an alternative formulation of the 'attributes of a person' (who?) and the 'attributes of an action' (what? where? with what aids? why? how? when?), 10.1, esp. 12.35–36.

climax: See colors of words B.20.

collocation of opposites (locus oppositorum): a means of 'extending' by pairing a positive assertion with the negation of its opposite, or elaborating a sentiment by denying its opposite, 3.29–30.

colon: See colors of words B.11.

colors of thoughts (colores sentenciarum): the nineteen 'figures' or 'schemes' of thought, which produce 'ornamented facility,' esp. 7.65–95.

1. *distribution* (distribucio): a series of statements, in each of which a distinct action is assigned to a particular person or thing, 7.66.

2. *license* (licencia): expressing criticism in ways that mitigate the likelihood of giving offense, 7.67–69.

3. *understatement* (diminucio): expressing praise of oneself or another in ways that reduce the impression of arrogance; also called "litotes" *(liptote),* 7.70.

4. *vivid description* (descripcio): a means of 'extending' by introducing descriptions of persons, places, or things; also, a variety of 'digression,' 3.26–28, 7.71.

5. *division* (divisio): a statement in which several qualities are ascribed to a person or a thing, followed by an explanation of how each quality is applicable to that person or thing, 7.72.

6. *accumulation* (frequentacio): a concise and forceful reiteration of the chief accusations made previously, 7.73.

7. *refining* (expolicio): repeating the same point or speaking about the same topic while making each iteration seem new by varying the wording, the oral delivery, or the format, 7.74–79. Options include other colors and techniques such as 'dialogue,' 'arousal,' 'reasoning by contraries,' and 'conclusion.'

8. *dwelling on the point* (commoracio): returning to and elaborating on the strongest point in the case in order to emphasize it, 7.80.

9. *antithesis* (contencio): juxtaposition of clauses that express opposite meanings; differs from the 'color of words' [B.5] with the same name, in which words with opposite meanings are juxtaposed within the same clause, 7.81.

10. *comparison* (similitudo): brief or extended comparison of two things for the sake of ornament, proof, clarity, or vividness, 7.82–86.

11. *exemplification* (exemplum): citing past words or actions, along with the name(s) of the person(s) responsible, for the same purposes as those served by 'comparison,' 7.87.

12. *simile* (ymago): comparison of one person or thing to another for purposes of praise or blame; differs from 'comparison' in focusing on the interchangeability of the things compared, rather than on some particular feature that both share, 7.88.

13. *portrayal* (effeccio): description of a person's physical appearance, 7.89.

14. *character delineation* (notacio): description of a person's characteristic behavior as outward evidence of that person's inner qualities, 7.90.

15. *dialogue* (sermocinacio): imitation of a person's characteristic speech in order to reveal that person's inner qualities, 7.77, 7.91.

16. *personification* (conformacio): a means of 'extending' by intro-

ducing a speech delivered by something that is incapable of speaking; also called 'prosopopoeia,' 3.19, 7.92.

17. *emphasis* (significacio): implying more than what is actually stated, by means of 'hyperbole,' 'ambiguity,' 'logical consequence,' 'aposiopesis,' or 'analogy'; also, a means of 'shortening' (where it is called *emphasis*), 4.3, 7.93.

18. *conciseness* (brevitas): using only the minimum number of words needed to express a particular sentiment, 7.94.

19. *ocular demonstration* (demonstracio): description of an action in such a way that it appears to take place before the audience member's eyes, 7.95.

colors of words (colores verborum): the forty-six figures of speech, comprising (A) ten 'tropes' that produce 'ornamented difficulty' and (B) thirty-six 'figures' or 'schemes' that produce 'ornamented facility,' esp. 5.24–54, 7.30–64.

(A) Sources of 'ornamented difficulty' (varieties of 'transumption'; 'tropes')

Weightier kinds:

1. *onomatopoeia* (nominacio): using a word in a transferred sense either to imitate some aspect of what is designated or to designate something for which there is no precise name, 5.25–26.

2. *antonomasia* (pronominacio): employing epithets to highlight features of a person or a thing that are being praised or blamed, 5.27.

3. *allegory* (permutacio): making a statement whose intended meaning is different from (even ironically opposed to) its literal meaning, 5.28.

4. *metaphor* (translacio): using a word in a transferred sense by implying a comparison between the context in which it is being used transumptively and the context in which it signifies properly, 5.29.

Lighter kinds:

5. *periphrasis* (circuicio): elaborating a simple statement, especially by changing the grammatical category of keywords and supplying additional words and phrases that modify the words that have been transferred in this way, 5.31–35, 9.3. *Compare* circumlocution.

6. *metonymy* (denominacio): designating one thing by means of another thing that is related to it, 5.36–44. The 'color' *denominacio* has broader reference than the 'figure' *methonomia*, 8.5.

7. *hyperbole* (superlacio): exaggerating the truth, in order to praise or to blame; also, a variety of the 'color of thoughts' called 'emphasis' (where it is called *exuperancia*), 5.45, 7.93.

8. *synecdoche* (intelleccio): designating the whole by means of a part or a part by means of the whole, 5.46–48, 8.5.

9. *catachresis* (abusio): deliberately misusing a similar or related word to replace the proper word, 5.49.

10. *hyperbaton* (transgressio): deliberately disrupting the proper word order rather than the proper meaning of the words, 5.50–54.

(B) Sources of 'ornamented facility'

1. *epanaphora* (repeticio): a sequence of clauses, each of which begins with the same word or phrase, 7.31.

2. *antistrophe* (conversio): a sequence of clauses, each of which ends with the same word or phrase, 7.32.

3. *symploce* (complexio): a sequence of clauses, each of which begins with the same word or phrase and ends with the same word or phrase, 7.33.

4. *polyptoton* (traduccio): frequent repetition of the same word (including homonyms) within a brief passage of text, 7.34.

5. *antithesis* (contencio): juxtaposition of opposites within a single clause or sentence, 7.35.

6. *exclamation* (exclamacio): expressing strong emotion by crying out; a variety of 'apostrophe,' 3.15, 7.36.

7. *rhetorical question* (interrogacio): asking a series of questions, the answers to which are presumed to be obvious, 7.37.

8. *reasoning by question and answer* (raciocinacio): asking a series of questions and providing the answer after each of them, 7.38.

9. *maxim* (sentencia): citing a wise saying, such as a proverb, 7.39.

10. *reasoning by contraries* (contrarium): a compressed argument in which the logical relation between the premise and the conclusion depends on some kind of opposition, 7.40.

11. *colon* (membrum oracionis): a clause that expresses a complete thought and occurs together with at least one additional colon in the same sentence, 7.41.

12. *comma* (articulus): a clause that does not express a complete thought but must be combined with other clauses to form a complete sentence, 7.42.

13. *period* (continuacio): a sentence that combines several 'colons' and 'commas' to express a complete thought, 7.43.

14. *isocolon* (compar): a sequence of clauses, each of them containing approximately the same number of syllables, 7.44.

15. *homoeoptoton* (similiter cadens): rhyme in which the rhyming words share the same grammatical inflection, 7.45.

16. *homoeoteleuton* (similiter desinens): rhyme in which the rhyming words lack grammatical inflection, 7.46.

17. *mixture* (commixtum): a combination of the previous two types of rhyme, 7.47.

18. *paronomasia* (agnominacio): using several words whose sound is similar but whose meanings are different within a brief passage (punning), 7.48. The 'figure' *paranomasia* has broader reference than the 'color' *agnominacio*, 8.5

19. *hypophora* (subieccio): asking a question and immediately supplying the answer; a variety of 'apostrophe,' 3.17, 7.49. Also called 'anthypophora,' 14.2.

20. *climax* (gradacio): linking together a sequence of clauses by repeating or echoing the final word or phrase of each clause at the beginning of the clause that follows it, 7.50.

21. *definition* (diffinicio): a concise account of the characteristic properties of some thing, 7.51.

22. *transition* (transicio): briefly stating what has just been said and then briefly indicating what will be said next; also called "epilogue" *(epilogus)*, 7.52.

23. *correction* (correccio): retracting what has just been said and replacing it with a more accurate expression, 7.53.

24. *paralipsis* (occupacio): speaking about something while stating the intention not to speak about that thing, 7.54.

25. *disjunction* (disiunctum): a sequence of clauses, each of which has a different verb; a variety of 'hypozeuxis,' 7.13, 7.55.

26. *conjunction* (coniunctum): a sequence of at least three clauses linked by a shared verb that appears only in the middle clause but is understood in the clauses that precede and follow it; a variety of 'zeugma,' 7.13, 7.55.

27. *adjunction* (adiunctum): a sequence of clauses linked by a shared verb that appears only in the first or the last clause but is understood in the others; a variety of 'zeugma,' 7.13, 7.55.

28. *reduplication* (conduplicacio): expressing strong emotion by reiterating the same word or group of words; a variety of 'apostrophe,' 3.16, 7.56.

29. *interpretation* (interpretacio): a means of 'extending' by repeating the same sentiment in different words, 3.2, 7.57, 9.2.

30. *reciprocal change* (commutacio): a statement followed by a coun-

terstatement that employs the same keywords in a different order, 7.58.

31. *surrender* (permissio): yielding the matter at hand to the will of the person being addressed, 7.59.

32. *indecision* (dubitacio): proposing a series of alternatives and claiming difficulty in choosing among them; a variety of 'apostrophe,' 3.18, 7.60.

33. *proof by elimination* (expedicio): naming several options and then rejecting all but the one favored by the speaker, 7.61.

34. *asyndeton* (dissolutum, dissolucio): a means of 'shortening' by not using conjunctions to link together the constituent clauses of a sentence, 4.8, 7.62. *Compare* parataxis.

35. *aposiopesis* (prescisio): either cutting short what one has begun to say or a dialogue in which the alternating statements are extremely brief; also, a variety of the 'color of thoughts' called 'emphasis' (where it is called *abscisio*), 7.63, 7.93.

36. *conclusion* (conclusio): a concise statement of the consequences that follow from what has been said previously, 7.64.

comma: See colors of words B.12.

comparison or juxtaposition (comparacio or collacio): a means of 'extending' by drawing an explicit or implicit analogy between two things in order to emphasize certain characteristics of one of the things being juxtaposed; also, a variety of 'digression,' 3.7–13.

comparison (similitudo)*: See* colors of thoughts 10.

conciseness: See colors of thoughts 18.

conclusion: See colors of words B.36.

conjunction: See colors of words B.26.

conversion: See permutation.

correction: See colors of words B.23.

dactyl (dactilus): when used in connection with the prose cadences that define the Gregorian or the Hilarian 'style,' the final three syllables of a word whose penultimate syllable is unstressed or short, 13.3, 13.5.

definition: See colors of words B.21.

description: See colors of thoughts 4.

determination (determinacio): specifying and elaborating the meaning of a keyword by modifying that word with other words or phrases; a technique for producing 'ornamented facility,' esp. 7.1–28.

dialogue: See colors of thoughts 15.

didactic discourse: See kinds of discourses.

digression: a means of 'extending' by interrupting the linear progression of a text with a 'description,' an extended 'comparison,' or a 'poetic fiction' that is either extraneous to the main subject matter or anticipates a topic that is treated later in the progression of the text, 3.20–25.

discovery (invencio), *used mainly in the form of the verb* (invenire): in its technical meaning, the process of finding or selecting the contents and stylistic techniques most appropriate for the compositional task at hand and/or the process of generating new text by means of such techniques; derived from invention—first of the five canonical parts of classical rhetoric (the others are arrangement, style, memory, and delivery).

disjunction: See colors of words B.25.

dispondee: See spondee.

distribution: See colors of thoughts 1.

division: See colors of thoughts 5.

dramatic discourse: See kinds of discourses.

dwelling on the point: See colors of thoughts 8.

each to each (singula singulis): a variety of 'hypozeuxis' in which several

identically structured clauses are divided up so that the first words of all the clauses occur together sequentially, followed by the second words in the same sequence, and so on, 7.15.

emphasis: See colors of thoughts 17.

enthymeme (emptimema): a compressed argument, often drawing its conclusion from a proverb, an 'exemplum,' or a quotation from an authoritative source, 3.51.

epanaphora: See colors of words B.1.

exclamation: See colors of words B.6.

exemplification: See colors of thoughts 11.

exemplum: a brief statement of fact that, like a proverb, can be used as the basis for a compressed argument, 1.13–15; 2.9–12; 3.39–41, 48–50, 63; 7.79, 84; 16.4. *Compare* exemplification (colors of thoughts 11).

extending (prolongacio): together with 'shortening,' one of the two basic ways to develop a given subject matter; accomplished by eight means—'interpretation,' 'circumlocution,' 'comparison,' 'apostrophe,' 'prosopopoeia,' 'digression,' 'description,' and 'collocation of opposites'—and by converting each element of a simple statement into a longer statement, 3.

fable (fabula): the subdivision of 'narrative' that recounts events that are neither true nor verisimilar; when it takes the form of a dialogue among animals, it is also called *apologus,* 15.2–3.

figures (figure): an alternative term both for the 'colors' (encompassing 'metaplasm,' 'scheme,' and 'trope') and, more narrowly, for the 'schemes' as distinct from the 'tropes,' 8.3–6.

hermeneutic or distinct discourse: See kinds of discourses.

history (historia): the subdivision of 'narrative' that recounts true events from the past; also called "chronicle" *(cronica).* Its varieties include "ephemera" *(ephimeris),* "annal" *(annalis),* "calendar" *(kalendaria),* and many verse genres, 15.4–5.

homoeoptoton: See colors of words B.15.

homoeoteleuton: See colors of words B.16.

hyperbaton: See colors of words A.10.

hyperbole: See colors of words A.7.

hypophora: See colors of words B.19.

hypozeuxis: See colors of words B.25; each to each.

inculcation (inculcacio): increasing the ornamentation of a passage by juxtaposing in it several different figures and/or multiple examples of the same figure. Also used as a verb: 'inculcate' *(inculcare),* esp. 7.3, 7.28

indecision: See colors of words B.32.

interpretation: See colors of words B.29.

invention: See discovery.

isocolon: See colors of words B.14.

kinds of discourses (sermonum genera): a tripartite classification of texts according to the nature of the speaker(s)—"dramatic" *(dragmaticum),* in which only characters within the text speak; "hermeneutic or distinct" *(eremeneticum vel distinctum),* in which only the author speaks; and "didactic" *(didascalicum),* in which a character poses questions and the author responds, 15.1.

license: See colors of thoughts 2.

litotes: See colors of thoughts 3.

logical consequence (consequencia): stating something that implies but does not spell out certain consequences that follow from it; a variety of the 'color of thoughts' called 'emphasis,' 7.93.

maxim: See colors of words B.9.

meaning of many clauses contained in one (sentencia multarum clausularum in una): a means of 'shortening' by using a participle or a gerund to combine two clauses into one, 4.10.

metaphor: See colors of words A.4.

metaplasm (methaplasmus): a 'figure' in which an individual word is altered by the substitution, omission, or addition of a letter or a sound; overlaps with the fault called 'barbarism,' 8.3–4.

metonymy: See colors of words A.6.

mixture: See colors of words B.17.

narrative (narracio): a type of 'hermeneutic or distinct discourse'; the kind that is not concerned with cases in court and is based on actions rather than persons has three subdivisions—'history,' 'fable,' and 'argument,' 15.1–6.

ocular demonstration: See colors of thoughts 19.

onomatopoeia: See colors of words A.1.

ornamented difficulty (ornata difficultas): discourse that is ornamented by means of 'transumption,' which makes the sense more difficult to grasp, esp. 5.

ornamented facility (ornata facilitas): discourse that is ornamented by means of techniques that do not affect ease of comprehension, esp. 7, 9.

paralipsis: See colors of words B.24.

parataxis (articulus): a means of 'shortening' by avoiding conjunctions within a sequence of words, 4.4–5. The term 'parataxis' is used to distinguish this technique from the 'color of words' [B.12] called 'comma' *(articulus),* which does not require omission of conjunctions. Compare the means of 'shortening' and 'color of words' [B.34] called 'asyndeton,' in which conjunctions are omitted between clauses rather than individual words.

paronomasia: See colors of words B.18.

period: See colors of words B.13.

periphrasis: See colors of words A.5.

permutation (permutacio): replacing one expression with another that has an equivalent meaning, by changing the case of a keyword or substituting one part of speech for another; also called "conversion" *(conversio)*; partially overlaps 'colors' such as 'interpretation' and 'periphrasis,' 9.

personification: See colors of thoughts 16.

poetic fiction (poeticum figmentum): a fable that is introduced as a type of 'digression,' 3.24.

polyptoton: See colors of words B.4.

portrayal: See colors of thoughts 13.

proof by elimination: See colors of words B.33.

prosopopoeia: See colors of thoughts 16.

reasoning by contraries: See colors of words B.10.

reasoning by question and answer: See colors of words B.8.

reciprocal change: See colors of words B.30.

reduplication: See colors of words B.28.

refining: See colors of thoughts 7.

rhetorical question: See colors of words B.7.

scheme (scema): any 'color' that does not employ 'transumption,' 8.5.

semi-spondee: See spondee.

shortening (abbreviacio): together with 'extending,' one of the two basic ways to develop a given subject matter; accomplished by seven means—'emphasis,' 'parataxis,' 'ablative absolute,' 'understanding of one thing in another,' 'asyndeton,' 'avoidance of repetition,' and the 'meaning of many clauses contained in one,' 4.1–13.

simile: See colors of thoughts 12.

spondee (spondeus): when used in connection with the prose cadences that define the Gregorian or the Hilarian 'style,' a two-syllable unit—

either a bisyllabic word or part of a longer word. A "semi-spondee" (*semispondeus*) is a monosyllabic word, and a "dispondee" (*dispondeus*) is a tetrasyllabic word whose penultimate syllable is stressed or long, 13.3, 13.5.

style (stilus): either, one of three broad categories of discourse based on the level of diction and amount of ornamentation (grand or high, middle, low or simple) or, one of four more narrowly defined varieties employed by "modern"—i.e., medieval—writers (Ciceronian, Gregorian, Hilarian, Isidorian), 13. On the faults associated with each of the three broader categories, 14.5–10.

surrender: See colors of words B.31.

symploce: See colors of words B.3.

synecdoche: See colors of words A.8.

tmesis: separating the parts of a compound word by interposing one or more words between them, 14.2.

transition: See colors of words B.22.

transumption (transumpcio): shifting words from their ordinary meanings or their usual order in a sentence for the purpose of ornamentation; the technique that distinguishes the 'tropes' (the ten 'colors of words' that produce 'ornamented difficulty'). Also used as a verb, "transume" *(transumere)*, and as an adjective/adverb, "transumptive/ly" *(transumptivus/-ve),* esp. 5.1–23.

tropes (tropi): the ten 'colors of words' that employ 'transumption' to produce 'ornamented difficulty,' esp. 8.6.

understanding of one thing in another (intellectus unius in alio): a means of 'shortening' by naming an action that encompasses a number of other actions that are not named, 4.7.

understatement: See colors of thoughts 3.

vivid description: See colors of thoughts 4.

zeugma: See colors of words B.26, B.27.

Bibliography

PARTIAL EDITIONS OF *TRIA SUNT*

Camargo, Martin. "Toward a Comprehensive Art of Written Discourse: Geoffrey of Vinsauf and the *Ars dictaminis*." *Rhetorica* 6 (1988): 167–94. Edition of *Tria sunt,* chap. 3.48–67 (pp. 186–92).

———. "*Tria sunt* (after 1256, before 1400)." In *Medieval Grammar and Rhetoric: Language Arts and Literary Theory, AD 300–1475,* edited by Rita Copeland and Ineke Sluiter, 670–81. Oxford: Oxford University Press, 2009. Translation of *Tria sunt,* chap. 3.42–67.

Friis-Jensen, Karsten. "The *Ars Poetica* in Twelfth-Century France: The Horace of Matthew of Vendôme, Geoffrey of Vinsauf, and John of Garland." *Cahiers de l'Institut du Moyen-Age Grec et Latin* 60 (1990): 319–88. Edition of *Tria Sunt,* chap. 14 (pp. 385–88).

Lawler, Traugott. *The* Parisiana Poetria *of John of Garland.* New Haven: Yale University Press, 1974. Edition of selections from *Tria sunt,* chaps. 3.53–54; 13.2–7; 14.1–2, 11, 13; 15.1–6 (pp. 327–32).

PRIMARY SOURCES

Aesop ("Walter of England"). *Fabulae.* Edited by Kenneth McKenzie and William A. Oldfather, *Ysopet-Avionnet: The Latin and French Texts.* University of Illinois Studies in Language and Literature 5.4. Urbana: University of Illinois Press, 1919.

Alan of Lille. *Anticlaudianus.* Edited and translated by Wetherbee, *Literary Works,* 219–517.

———. *De planctu Naturae.* Edited and translated by Wetherbee, *Literary Works,* 21–217.

———. *Liber parabolarum.* PL 210:581–94.

Aristotle. *De interpretatione vel Periermenias.* Translated into Latin by Boethius. Edited by Lorenzo Minio-Paluello. Translated into Latin by William of Moerbeke. Edited by Gerard Verbeke; revised by Lorenzo Minio-Paluello. Aristoteles Latinus 2.1–2. Bruges and Paris: Desclée de Brouwer, 1965.

Aristotle/Averroes. *De arte poetica cum Averrois expositione.* Translated into Latin by Hermann the German (1256). Edited by Lorenzo Minio-Paluello. Corpus philosophorum medii aevi: Aristoteles Latinus 33. 2nd ed. Brussels, 1968.

Bede the Venerable. *In Lucae evangelium expositio; In Marci evangelium expositio.* Edited by D. Hurst, *Bedae Venerabilis opera,* pt. 2: *Opera exegetica,* 3. Corpus Christianorum, Series Latina 120. Turnhout: Brepols, 1960.

Benedict of Peterborough. Rhymed Office of St. Thomas of Canterbury. Edited by Guido Maria Dreves, *Analecta hymnica medii aevi* 13: 238–42. Leipzig: O. R. Reisland, 1892.

Berentinus. *Colores rhetorici seriatim* [treatise on the figures]. Edited by Martin Camargo, "Anonymous de Berentino, *Colores rhetorici seriatim:* A Twelfth-Century Treatise on the Figures in Two Parts." *Mittellateinisches Jahrbuch,* forthcoming.

Bernard Silvestris. *Cosmographia.* Edited by Peter Dronke. Leiden: Brill, 1978. Translated by Winthrop Wetherbee. New York: Columbia University Press, 1973.

——. *Mathematicus.* Edited and translated by Deirdre M. Stone, "Bernardus Silvestris, *Mathematicus:* Edition and Translation." *Archives d'histoire doctrinale et littéraire du moyen age* 63 (1996): 209–83.

Boethius. *De topicis differentiis.* Edited by Dimitrios Z. Nikitas. Corpus philosophorum medii aevi: Philosophi Byzantini 5. Athens: Akademia Athenon, 1990. Translated by Eleonore Stump. Ithaca: Cornell University Press, 1978.

——. *Philosophiae consolatio.* Edited by Ludwig Bieler. Corpus Christianorum, Series Latina 94. Turnhout: Brepols, 1957. Translated by S. J. Tester. Loeb Classical Library 74, 2nd ed. Cambridge, Mass.: Harvard University Press, 1973.

Camargo, Martin. *Medieval Rhetorics of Prose Composition: Five English Artes dictandi and Their Tradition.* Binghamton, N.Y.: Medieval and Renaissance Texts and Studies, 1995.

Cicero. *De inventione.* Translated by H. M. Hubbell. Loeb Classical Library 386. Cambridge, Mass.: Harvard University Press, 1949.

———. *In Catilinam.* Translated by C. Macdonald. Loeb Classical Library 324. Cambridge, Mass.: Harvard University Press, 1977.

[Cicero]. *Rhetorica ad Herennium.* Translated by Harry Caplan. Loeb Classical Library 403. Cambridge, Mass.: Harvard University Press, 1968.

Consulte teneros non claudit tutor amantes (inc.) [anonymous Pyramus and Thisbe poem]. Edited by Harbert, *A Thirteenth-Century Anthology,* 54–60.

Court of Sapience. Edited by E. Ruth Harvey. Toronto: University of Toronto Press, 1984.

Donatus. *Ars grammatica.* Edited by Louis Holtz, *Donat et la tradition de l'enseignement grammatical: Étude sur l'*Ars Donati *et sa diffusion (ive–ixe siècle) et édition critique,* 603–74. Paris: Centre National de la Recherche Scientifique, 1981.

Eberhard the German. *Laborintus.* Edited by Faral, *Les arts poétiques,* 336–77.

Educational Charters and Documents 598–1909. Edited and translated by A. F. Leach. Cambridge: Cambridge University Press, 1911.

Faral, Edmond. *Les arts poétiques du XIIe et du XIIIe siècle.* Paris: Champion, 1924.

Francia dulcis, aue, regio bona, bella, salubris (inc.) [anonymous panegyric]. Edited by Jan M. Ziolkowski and Bridget K. Balint, with Justin Lake, Laura Light, and Prydwyn Piper, *A Garland of Satire, Wisdom, and History: Latin Verse from Twelfth-Century France (Carmina Houghtoniensia),* 102–5. Cambridge, Mass.: Houghton Library, 2007.

Frowin, John. *Antigameratus.* Edited by Edwin Habel, "Der Antigameratus des Frowinus von Krakau." In *Studien zur lateinischen Dichtung des Mittelalters. Ehrengabe für Karl Strecker zum 4. September 1931,* edited by W. Stach and H. Walther, 60–77. Dresden: Wilhelm und Bertha v. Baensch Stiftung, 1931.

Geoffrey of Vinsauf. *Documentum de modo et arte dictandi et versificandi.* Edited by Faral, *Les arts poétiques,* 263–320.

———. *Poetria nova.* Edited by Faral, *Les arts poétiques,* 194–262. Translated by Margaret F. Nims. Toronto: Pontifical Institute of Mediaeval Studies, 1967; rev. ed., 2010.

———. *Summa de coloribus rhetoricis.* Edited by Carsten Wollin, "Die erste Poetik Galfrids von Vinsauf: Eine vorläufige Edition der 'Summa de coloribus rethoricis.'" *Mittellateinisches Jahrbuch* 49 (2014): 393–442.

———. Vexillum pacis, sera belli, purpura regum (inc.) [poems in praise of Henry II (short and long version)]. Edited and translated by Martin Camargo, "Geoffrey of Vinsauf's Memorial Verses." In *Inventing a Path: Studies in Medieval Rhetoric in Honour of Mary Carruthers,* edited by Laura Iseppi De Filippis, 90–95. *Nottingham Medieval Studies* 56 (2012).

Gervase of Melkley. *De arte versificatoria et modo dictandi.* Edited by Hans-Jürgen Gräbener, *Gervais von Melkley: Ars poetica.* Forschungen zur romanischen Philologie 17. Münster: Aschendorff, 1965. Translated by Catherine Yodice Giles, "Gervais of Melkley's Treatise on the Art of Versifying and the Method of Composing in Prose: Translation and Commentary." PhD diss., Rutgers University, 1973.

Harbert, Bruce. *A Thirteenth-Century Anthology of Rhetorical Poems: Glasgow MS Hunterian V.8.14.* Toronto: Pontifical Institute of Mediaeval Studies, 1975.

Horace. *Ars poetica.* Translated by H. Rushton Fairclough. Loeb Classical Library 194. Cambridge, Mass.: Harvard University Press, 1926; revised and reprinted, 1929.

In terra summus rex est hoc tempore Nummus (inc.) [anonymous poem about money]. Edited by Alfons Hilka and Otto Schumann, *Carmina Burana: Mit Benutzung der Vorarbeiten Wilhelm Meyers.* 2 vols., 1.1:15–16 (no. 11). Heidelberg: Carl Winter, 1930, 1941.

Isidore. *Etymologiae.* Edited by W. M. Lindsay. Oxford: Oxford University Press, 1911.

John of Garland. *Parisiana poetria.* Edited and translated by Traugott Lawler. New Haven: Yale University Press, 1974.

John of Hauville. *Architrenius.* Edited and translated by Winthrop Wetherbee. Cambridge: Cambridge University Press, 1994.

Juvenal. *Satires.* Translated by Susanna Morton Braund. Loeb Classical Library 91. Cambridge, Mass.: Harvard University Press, 2004.

Lawrence of Durham. *Hypognosticon.* Edited by Susanne Daub, *Gottes Heilsplan—verdichtet: Edition des Hypognosticon des Laurentius Dunelmensis.* Erlangen and Jena: Palm & Enke, 2002.

Lucan. *Bellum civile.* Translated by J. D. Duff. Loeb Classical Library 220. Cambridge, Mass.: Harvard University Press, 1928.

Magnus Alexander bellorum sepe procellas (inc.) [anonymous praise poem]. Edited by Harbert, *A Thirteenth-Century Anthology,* 47–52.

Marbod of Rennes. *De ornamentis verborum.* Edited and translated (Italian) by Rosario Leotta, *Marbodo di Rennes,* De ornamentis verborum; Liber decem capitulorum. *Retorica, mitologia e moralità di un vescovo poeta (secc. xi–xii),* 1–25. Florence: SISMEL-Edizioni del Galluzzo, 1998.

Marii Victorini Explanationes in Ciceronis Rhetoricam. Edited by A. Ippolito. Corpus Christianorum, Series Latina 132. Turnhout: Brepols, 2006.

'Materia' commentary on Horace, *Ars poetica.* Edited by Karsten Friis-Jensen, "The *Ars poetica* in Twelfth-Century France: The Horace of Matthew of Vendôme, Geoffrey of Vinsauf, and John of Garland." *Cahiers de l'Institut du Moyen-Age Grec et Latin* 60 (1980): 319–88.

Matthew of Vendôme. *Ars versificatoria.* Edited by Franco Munari, *Mathei Vindocinensis opera,* 3. Rome: Storia e Letteratura, 1988. Translated by Aubrey E. Galyon. Ames: Iowa State University Press, 1980.

———. *Tobias.* Edited by Franco Munari, *Mathei Vindocinensis Opera,* 2:161–255. Rome: Storia e Letteratura, 1982.

Mens erit huic operi Priamo duce digna timeri (inc.) [anonymous Troy poem]. Edited by J. Huemer, "Ein Trojanerlied aus dem Mittelalter." *Zeitschrift für die österreichischen Gymnasien* 38 (1887), pt. 1: Abhandlungen, 7–9.

Merke, Thomas. *Formula moderni et usitati dictaminis.* Edited by Camargo, *Medieval Rhetorics,* 105–47.

Miles gloriosus. Edited by Robert Baschet, *La "comédie" latine en France au XII siècle* 1: 179–210. Paris: Société d'édition "Les Belles-lettres," 1931.

Missale ad usum insignis et praeclarae ecclesiae Sarum. Edited by F. H. Dickinson. Oxford, 1861–1883.

Ovid. *Ars amatoria.* Translated by J. H. Mozley. Loeb Classical Library 232. Cambridge, Mass.: Harvard University Press, 1929; revised and reprinted, 1939.

———. *Metamorphoses.* Translated by Frank Justus Miller; revised by G. P. Goold. Loeb Classical Library 42 and 43. 3rd ed. Cambridge, Mass.: Harvard University Press, 1977.

Parce continuis (inc.) [anonymous poem]. Edited by Wilhelm Meyer. Reprinted in F. J. E. Raby, *A History of Secular Latin Poetry in the Middle Ages.* 2 vols. 2nd ed. 2:313–15. Oxford: Clarendon Press, 1957.

Patrologiae cursus completus [= PL]. Edited by J.-P. Migne. Series Latinus. 221 vols. Paris, 1844–1868.

Pergama flere volo, fato Danais data solo (inc.) [anonymous Troy poem]. Edited by Harbert, *A Thirteenth-Century Anthology,* 34–37.

Peter of Blois. *Libellus de arte dictandi rhetorice.* Edited by Camargo, *Medieval Rhetorics,* 37–87.

Primas, Hugh. In cratere meo Tetis est sociata Lieo (inc.) [drinking poem]. Edited and translated by Christopher J. McDonough, *The Arundel Lyrics; The Poems of Hugh Primas,* 180–81. Dumbarton Oaks Medieval Library 2. Cambridge, Mass.: Harvard University Press, 2010.

Quintilian. *Institutio oratoria.* Translated by H. E. Butler. Loeb Classical Library 124–27. Cambridge, Mass.: Harvard University Press, 1920–1922.

Ralph of Longchamp. *In Anticlaudianum Alani commentum.* Edited by Jan Sulowski. Wroclaw: Polska Akademia Nauk, 1972.

Riga, Peter. *Floridus aspectus* [redaction preserved in MS Saint-Omer 115 (O) and MS Egerton 2951 (E), Part 2: treatise on the figures]. Edited by Charles Fierville, "Notices et extraits des manuscrits de la bibliothèque de Saint-Omer, nos. 115 et 710." *Notices et extraits* 31.1 (1884): 99–112 [MS 115, item 31].

Sallust. *In M. Tullium Ciceronem oratio.* Translated by J. C. Rolfe. Loeb Classical Library 116. Cambridge, Mass.: Harvard University Press, 1921; revised and reprinted, 1931.

Sidonius. *Epistulae.* Translated by W. B. Anderson. Loeb Classical Library 296 and 420. Cambridge, Mass.: Harvard University Press, 1936.

Simon Aurea Capra. *Ylias.* "La version parisienne du poème de Simon Chèvre d'Or sur la guerre de Troie (Ms. Lat. 8430)." *Scriptorium* 1 (1946–47): 267–88. Republished in The Library of Latin Texts. Turnhout: Brepols, 2010.

Statius. *Thebaid.* Translated by J. H. Mozley. Loeb Classical Library 206 and 207. Cambridge, Mass.: Harvard University Press, 1928.

Statuta antiqua universitatis oxoniensis. Edited by Strickland Gibson. Oxford: Clarendon Press, 1931.

Thierry of Chartres. *Commentarius super Rhetoricam Ciceronis; Commentarius super Rhetoricam ad Herennium.* Edited by Karin M. Fredborg. Toronto: Pontifical Institute of Mediaeval Studies, 1988.

Virgil. *Aeneid; Georgics.* Translated by H. Rushton Fairclough. Loeb Classical Library 63 and 64. Cambridge, Mass.: Harvard University Press, 1916, 1918; rev. ed. 1935, 1934.

Walter of Châtillon. *Alexandreis.* Edited by Marvin L. Colker. Padua: Antenore, 1978.

Walther, Hans. *Proverbia sententiaeque latinitatis medii aevi: Lateinische Sprichwörter und Sentenzen des Mittelalters in alphabetischer Anordnung.* 6 vols. *Carmina medii aevi posterioris latina,* pt. 2. Göttingen: Vandenhoeck & Ruprecht, 1963–1967. New Series: Paul Gerhart Schmidt. 3 vols. Göttingen, 1982–1986.

Wetherbee, Winthrop. *Literary Works/Alan of Lille.* Dumbarton Oaks Medieval Library 22. Cambridge, Mass.: Harvard University Press, 2013.

William de Montibus. *Peniteas cito peccator.* Edited by Joseph Goering, *William de Montibus (c. 1140–1213): The Schools and the Literature of Pastoral Care,* 116–38. Toronto: Pontifical Institute of Mediaeval Studies, 1992.

Secondary Sources

Camargo, Martin. "Chaucer and the Oxford Renaissance of Anglo-Latin Rhetoric." *Studies in the Age of Chaucer* 34 (2012): 173–207.

———. "In Search of Geoffrey of Vinsauf's Lost 'Long *Documentum.*'" *Journal of Medieval Latin* 22 (2012): 149–83.

———. "The Late Fourteenth-Century Renaissance of Anglo-Latin Rhetoric." *Philosophy and Rhetoric* 45.2 (2012): 107–33.

———. "Rhetoricians in Black: Benedictine Monks and Rhetorical Revival in Medieval Oxford." In *New Chapters in the History of Rhetoric,* International Studies in the History of Rhetoric 1, edited by Laurent Pernot, 375–84. Leiden: Brill, 2009.

———. "*Tria sunt:* The Long and the Short of Geoffrey of Vinsauf's *Documentum de modo et arte dictandi et versificandi.*" *Speculum* 74 (1999): 935–55.

Denholm-Young, Noël. "The *Cursus* in England." In *Oxford Essays in Medieval History Presented to Herbert Edward Salter,* edited by F. M. Powicke,

68–103. Oxford: Clarendon Press, 1934. Reprinted with revisions in *Collected Papers of Noël Denholm-Young,* 42–73. Cardiff: University of Wales Press, 1969.

Friis-Jensen, Karsten. "Horace and the Early Writers of Arts of Poetry." In *Sprachtheorien in Spätantike und Mittelalter,* edited by Sten Ebbesen, 360–401. Tübingen: Narr, 1995.

Howlett, David. "Studies in the Works of John Whethamstede." D.Phil thesis, University of Oxford, 1975.

Hunt, Tony. *Teaching and Learning Latin in Thirteenth-Century England.* 3 vols. Woodbridge, Suffolk: D. S. Brewer, 1991.

Kelly, Douglas. *The Arts of Poetry and Prose.* Typologie des sources du moyen âge occidental 59. Turnhout: Brepols, 1991.

Nims, Margaret F. "*Translatio:* 'Difficult Statement' in Medieval Poetic Theory." *University of Toronto Quarterly* 43.3 (Spring 1974): 215–30.

Parkes, Malcolm Beckwith. "The Influence of the Concepts of *Ordinatio* and *Compilatio* on the Development of the Book." In *Medieval Learning and Literature: Essays presented to Richard William Hunt,* edited by J. J. G. Alexander and M. T. Gibson, 115–41. Oxford: Clarendon Press, 1976.

Index of Names